THE HIDDEN WISDOM IN THE HOLY BIBLE, Vol. II

THE HIDDEN WISDOM IN THE HOLY BIBLE

BY

GEOFFREY HODSON

VOLUME II

THE GOLDEN GRAIN OF WISDOM IN THE BOOK OF GENESIS

(*Genesis*—Chapters One to Twenty-five)

1972

THE THEOSOPHICAL PUBLISHING HOUSE

ADYAR,   MADRAS-20,   INDIA

Wheaton, Ill., 60187, U.S.A.   London, England

First Edition 1967

Second and Revised Edition 1972

SBN 0—7229—7057—9

ISBN 0—8356—7057—0

PRINTED IN INDIA

At Hoe & Co., 31, Stringers Street, Madras-1.

DEDICATION

This work is dedicated to Philo Judaeus,
the great Alexandrian Sage.

ACKNOWLEDGEMENTS

I acknowledge with gratitude the help in the production of this work received from my wife, Sandra, who at dictation wrote out all the original interpretations of Biblical passages, and is continuing to do so; my valued literary assistant, Myra G. Fraser; and my friend Nell K. Griffith, who for many years cared for my domestic needs and assisted in typing from the first draft of the manuscript. I also wish to express my heartfelt thanks to my valued friends, Roma and Brian Dunningham, for their unfailing support, their provision of stenographers, and their generous help throughout many years of collaboration.

All quotations and references in this work are taken from the King James version of the Holy Bible.

THE HIDDEN WISDOM AND WHY IT IS CONCEALED

THE greatest degree of power which occult science can bestow is to be derived from knowledge of the unity and interaction between the Macrocosm and the microcosm, the Universe and man. " The mystery of the earthly and mortal man is after the mystery of the supernal and immortal One ", wrote Eliphas Levi. Lao Tzu also expresses this truth in his words: " The Universe is a man on a large scale."

The whole Universe with all its parts, frcm the highest plane down to physical Nature, is regarded as being interlocked, interwoven to make a single whole—one body, one organism, one power, one life, one consciousness, all cyclically evolving under one law. The " organs " or parts of the Macrocosm, though apparently separated in space and plane of manifestation, are in fact harmoniously interrelated, intercommunicative and continually interactive.

According to this revelation of occult philosophy the Zodiac, the Galaxies and their component Systems, and the planets with their kingdoms and planes of Nature, elements, Orders of Beings, radiating forces, colours and notes, are not only parts of a co-ordinated whole and in " correspondence " or mutual resonance with each other, but also—which is of profound significance—have their representations within man himself. This system of correspondences is in operation throughout the whole of the microcosm, from the Monad to the mortal flesh, including the parts of the mechanism of consciousness, or vehicles and their *chakras*,[1] by means of which the Spirit of man is manifested throughout his whole nature, varying in degree according to the stage of evolutionary development. *The human being who discovers this truth could enter the power aspect of the Universe and tap any one of these forces. He would then become endowed with almost irresistible influence over both Nature and his fellow men.*

H. P. Blavatsky writes:[2]

" The danger was that such doctrines as the Planetary Chain, or the seven Races, at once give a clue to the seven-fold nature of man, for each principle is correlated to a plane, a planet, and a race, and the human

---

[1] Chakra (sk.)—A vortex or " wheel " in the etheric and superphysical bodies of man. q.v. *The Chakras*, C. W. Leadbeater, and Glossary to this Vol.

[2] q.v. *The Secret Doctrine*, Vol. I (Adyar Ed.), pp. 57–58, H. P. Blavatsky.

principles are, on every plane, correlated to seven-fold occult forces, those of the higher planes being of tremendous power. So that any septenary division at once gives a clue to tremendous occult powers, the abuse of which would cause incalculable evil to humanity; a clue which is, perhaps, no clue to the present generation—especially to Westerns, protected as they are by their very blindness and ignorant materialistic disbelief in the occult—but a clue which would, nevertheless, have been very real in the early centuries of the Christian era to people fully convinced of the reality of Occultism, and entering a cycle of degradation which made them rife for abuse of occult powers and sorcery of the worst description.

" The documents were concealed, it is true, but the knowledge itself and its actual existence was never made a secret of by the Hierophants of the Temples, wherein the MYSTERIES have ever been made a discipline and stimulus to virtue. This is very old news, and was repeatedly made known by the great Adepts, from Pythagoras and Plato down to the Neo-Platonists. It was the new religion of the Nazarenes that wrought a change—for the worse—in the policy of centuries."

In his *Yoga Aphorisms*, Patanjali writes:[1]

" The (successful) ascetic acquires complete control over the elements by concentrating his mind upon the five classes of properties in the mani-fested universe; as, first, those of gross or phenomenal character; second, those of form; third, those of subtle quality; fourth, those susceptible of distinction as to light, action, and inertia; fifth, those having influence in their various degrees for the production of fruits through their effects upon the mind.

" From the acquirement of such power over the elements there results to the ascetic various perfections, to wit, the power to project his inner-self into the smallest atom, to expand his inner-self to the size of the largest body, to render his material body light or heavy at will, to give indefinite extension to his astral body or its separate members, to exercise an irresis-tible will upon the minds of others, to obtain the highest excellence of the material body, and the ability to preserve such excellence when obtained.

" Excellence of the material body consists in colour, loveliness of form, strength, and density."

This knowledge of the relationship between Universe and man is also part of the secret wisdom of Kabbalism, which teaches that in the chain of being everything is magically contained within everything else. Where one stands, there stand all the worlds; what is below is above, what is inside is outside and, in addition, ceaselessly acts upon all that exists. Kabbalism thus stresses the inter-relationship of all worlds and levels of being according to exact, though unfathomable, laws. All things, moreover, possess their infinite depths which from every point may be contemplated.

[1] q.v. *Yoga Aphorisms of Patanjali*, Book III, slokas 45-47.

Such is a portion of the wisdom which is said to be implicit—and, indeed, revealed under the veil of allegory—in the *Torah*.[1] This sacred book is for Kabbalists a revelation of the laws of the Cosmos and the intimate and active relationship between the parts of the Cosmos, the Spirit of man, and the vehicles in which that Spirit is incarnate. The history of the Jews forms a foundation upon which the edifice of this secret knowledge is erected. Modern Christian theology would seem to have fallen into the grievous error of regarding the sub-structure of meta-phoricised history as a total and divinely inspired revelation of God's guidance to mankind.

The mission of the Jews and the purpose of the erudite and Initiated authors of the Bible was, I submit, to preserve, to enunciate and to deliver to humanity this wisdom of the Chaldeo-Hebrew Sanctuaries. It is for this and not for lordship over the Earth, I suggest, that the Jews were a chosen people, a nation or " kingdom of priests "[2] in very truth. May not their tribulations have partly arisen from their neglect of this mission, and may not their earthly wanderings and centuries of physical homelessness have followed upon and resulted from their departure from their true Sanctuary and the real purpose for which they were " chosen "? Happily the light still shines, however deeply veiled, in and through this marvellous record of the Scriptures of the Hebrew Race.

The task of unveiling the hidden truth demands some knowledge of Cosmogenesis, of the emanation of the Universe from the Absolute, the finite from the Infinite, and of the successive cycles, major and minor, of involution and evolution. In addition, both knowledge of the Symbolical Language, its purposes, methods and classical symbols, and the faculty of analysing and interpreting historical metaphors, are necessary to open the casket containing the treasures of concealed wisdom—the Holy Bible itself.

" Where the Word found that things done according to the history could be adapted to these mystical senses, he made use of them, concealing from the multitude the deeper meaning; but where in the narrative of the development of super-sensual things, there did not follow the performance of those certain events which were already indicated by the mystical meaning, the Scripture interwove in the history the account of some event that did not take place, sometimes what could not have happened; sometimes what could, but did not."

> *De Principiis*, Origen, Christian philosopher and Biblical scholar, famed for his teaching at Alexandria and Caesarea (C. 185—C. 254 A.D.).

[1] *Torah* (Heb.): " Law ". The *Pentateuch* or Law of Moses.
[2] *Ex.* 19: 16.

" What man of sense will agree with the statement that the first, second and third days in which the *evening* is named and the *morning*, were without sun, moon and stars, and the first day without a heaven? What man is found such an idiot as to suppose that God planted trees in Paradise, in Eden, like a husbandman, and planted therein the tree of life, perceptible to the eyes and senses, which gave life to the eater thereof; and another tree which gave to the eater thereof a knowledge of good and evil? I believe that every man must hold these things for images, under which the hidden sense lies concealed."

Origen: Huet., *Origeniana*, 167, Franck, p. 142.

" Every time that you find in our books a tale the reality of which seems impossible, a story which is repugnant to both reason and common sense, then be sure that the tale contains a profound allegory veiling a deeply mysterious truth; and the greater the absurdity of the letter, the deeper the wisdom of the spirit."

Moses Maimonedes, Jewish theologian, historian, Talmudist, philosopher and physician (1135–1205 A.D.).

" Woe . . . to the man who sees in the Thorah *i.e.*, Law, only simple recitals and ordinary words! Because, if in truth it only contained these, we would even today be able to compose a Thorah much more worthy of admiration. . . . The recitals of the Thorah are the vestments of the Thorah. Woe to him who takes this garment for the Thorah itself! . . . There are some foolish people who, seeing a man covered with a beautiful garment, carry their regard no further, and take the garment for the body, whilst there exists a still more precious thing, which is the soul. . . . The Wise, the servitors of the Supreme King, those who inhabit the heights of Sinai, are occupied only with the soul, which is the basis of all the rest, which is Thorah itself; and in the future time they will be prepared to contemplate the Soul of that soul (*i.e.*, the Deity) which breathes in the Thorah."

Zohar III, 152b. (Soncino Ed. Vol. V, p. 211).

" Rabbi Simeon said: ' If a man looks upon the Torah as merely a book presenting narratives and everyday matters, alas for him! Such a Torah, one treating with everyday concerns, and indeed a more excellent one, we too, even we, could compile. More than that, in the possession of the rulers of the world there are books of even greater merit, and these we could emulate if we wished to compile some such Torah. But the Torah, in all of its words, holds supernal truths and sublime secrets.' "

Zohar III, 152a.

" Like unto a beautiful woman hidden in the interior of a palace who, when her friend and beloved passes by, opens for a moment a secret window, and is only seen by him: then again retires and disappears for a long time; so the doctrine shows herself only to the elect, but also not even to these always in the same manner. In the beginning, deeply veiled, she only beckons to the one passing, with her hand; it simply depends (on himself) if in his understanding he perceives this gentle hint. Later she approaches him somewhat nearer, and whispers to him a few words, but her countenance is still hidden in the thick veil, which his glances cannot penetrate. Still later she converses with him, her countenance covered with a thinner veil. After he has accustomed himself to her society, she finally shows herself to him face to face, and entrusts him with the innermost secrets of her heart (Sod)."

Zohar II, 99a (Soncino Ed. Vol. III, p. 301).

THE TORAH

" Jewish mystics are at one in giving a mystical interpretation to the Torah; the Torah is to them a living organism animated by a secret life which streams and pulsates below the crust of its literal meaning; every one of the innumerable strata of this hidden region corresponds to a new and profound meaning of the Torah. The Torah, in other words, does not consist merely of chapters, phrases and words; rather is it to be regarded as the living incarnation of the divine wisdom which eternally sends out new rays of light. It is not merely the historical law of the Chosen People, although it is that too; it is rather the cosmic law of the Universe, as God's wisdom conceived it. Each configuration of letters in it, whether it makes sense in human speech or not, symbolizes some aspect of God's creative power which is active in the Universe."

Major Trends in Jewish Mysticism, Gershom G. Scholem.

A SYMBOL

" A symbol retains its original form and its original content. It does not become, so to speak, an empty shell into which another content is poured; in itself, through its own existence, it makes another reality transparent which cannot appear in any other form. A mystical symbol is an expressible representation of something which lies beyond the sphere of expression and communication, something which comes from a sphere whose face is, as it were, turned inward and away from us. A hidden and inexpressible reality finds its expression in the symbol. The symbol ' signifies ' nothing and communicates nothing, but makes something transparent which is beyond all expression. Where deeper insight into the structure of the allegory uncovers fresh layers of meaning, the symbol is intuitively understood all at once—or not at all. The symbol in which the life of the Creator and that of creation become one, is—to use Creuzer's words—' a beam of light which, from the dark and abysmal depths of existence and cognition, falls into our eye and penetrates our whole being.' It is a ' momentary totality ' which is perceived intuitively in a mystical *now*—the dimension of time proper to the symbol."

Major Trends in Jewish Mysticism, Gershom G. Scholem.

" The shell, the white, and the yolk form the perfect egg. The shell protects the white and the yolk, and the yolk feeds upon the white; and when the white has vanished, the yolk, in the form of the fledged bird, breaks through the shell and presently soars into the air. Thus does the static become the dynamic, the material the spiritual.

" If the shell is the exoteric principle and the yolk the esoteric, what then is the white ! The white is the food of the second, the accumulated wisdom of the world centring round the mystery of growth, which each single individual must absorb before he can break the shell. The transmutation of the white, by the yolk, into the fledgling is the secret of secrets of the entire Qabalistic philosophy."

The Secret Wisdom of the Qabalah, J. F. C. Fuller.

' Having taken the Upanishad as the bow, as the great weapon, let him place on it the arrow, sharpened by devotion ! Then having drawn it with a thought directed to that which is, hit the mark, O Friend, namely, that which is Indestructible ! Om [1] is the bow, the Self is the arrow, Brahman [2] is called the aim. It is to be hit by a man who is not thoughtless, and then as the arrow becomes one with the target, he will become one with Brahman."

Mundaka Upanishad, II.

" Know the Self as the Lord of the chariot and the body as, verily, the chariot; know the intellect as the charioteer and the mind as, verily, the reins.

" The senses, they say, are the horses; the objects of sense the paths (they range over); (the self) associated with the body, the senses and the mind—wise men declare—is the enjoyer.

[1] OM or AUM: The name of the triple Deity. A syllable of affirmation, invocation and divine benediction.
[2] Brahman (Sk.): The impersonal, supreme and incognisable Principle of the Universe, from the Essence of which all emanates and into which all returns.

" He who has no understanding, whose mind is always unrestrained, his senses are out of control, as wicked horses are for a charioteer.

" He, however, who has understanding, whose mind is always restrained, his senses are under control, as good horses are for a charioteer.

" He, however, who has no understanding, who has no control over his mind (and is) ever impure, reaches not that goal but comes back into mundane life.

" He however, who has understanding, who has control over his mind and (is) ever pure, reaches that goal from which he is not born again.

" He who has the understanding for the driver of the chariot and controls the rein of his mind, he reaches the end of the journey, that supreme abode of the all-pervading."

> The *Kathopanishad* 1-3-3- to 1-3-9, Dr. Radha-
> krishnan's translation from *The Principal Upanishads*.

" And the disciples came, and said unto him, Why speakest thou unto them in parables?

" He answered and said unto them, Because it is given unto you to know the mysteries of the kingdom of heaven, but to them it is not given. . . .

" But blessed are your eyes, for they see; and your ears, for they hear."

> *Matt.* 13: 10, 11 and 16.

" Whoso eateth my flesh, and drinketh my blood, hath eternal life; and I will raise him up at the last day.

" For my flesh is meat indeed, and my blood is drink indeed.

" He that eateth my flesh, and drinketh my blood, dwelleth in me, and I in him.

" As the living Father hath sent me, and I live by the Father: so he that eateth me, even he shall live by me."

> *Jn.* 6: 54–57.

" The early Genesis accounts of the creation, Adam and Eve and the Fall of man contain truths of a religious nature which do not depend for their validity upon historical or scientific confirmation.   Such accounts expressed truths of a timeless nature.   They were myths, teaching spiritual truths by allegories."

> From a Sermon by The Most Reverend Dr. Frank
> Woods, Anglican Archbishop of M lbourne, speak-
> ing at St. Paul's Cathedral on the 18th February,
> 1961.

The same may well be said of the narratives of the temptation of Christ in the wilderness, *Luke* 4: 1-13 and His agony in the Garden of

Gethsemane. These do not include references to the presence of a third person. Under normal circumstances, however, this would be necessary if record were to be made, preserved and introduced into the Gospel narrative.

Support for a symbolical reading of the Bible also is gained by comparison of the promises of perpetual prosperity and divine protection [1] made by God to Abram and his successors with the subsequent defeats by invaders, exile under their commands in Babylon and Egypt, and the destruction of the Temples of King Solomon and King David. To these misfortunes may be added the later fate of the Hebrew people, including their miseries and homelessness since the *Diaspora* and the holocaust of German Jews under Nazi rule. This marked divergence between divine assurances and promises on the one hand and what actually happened on the other provides strong grounds for a non-literal reading of the Scriptures.

The alternative of a total rejection of the *Pentateuch* as being, on the surface, unworthy of serious consideration would, I suggest, involve the loss of invaluable treasures of wisdom which are revealed when the veil of allegory and symbol is removed.

GEOFFREY HODSON.

---

[1] *Gen.* 17: 2, 5–8; 26: 2–5; 28: 13–16

AUTHOR'S PREFACE TO VOLUME TWO

In the first Volume of this series, certain relevant parts of which are reproduced in this one, the theory is advanced that many of the narratives recounted in both the Old and the New Testaments, as also in the inspired portions of the Scriptures and Mythologies of other ancient peoples, contain far more than is apparent on the surface. Undermeanings are said to have been deliberately introduced and are conveyed by the use of a system —widely recognised in ancient times—of so narrating actual events that they also reveal underlying laws governing the emanation, involution and evolution of both Universe and man. To this end the characters of the people in such stories are made to personify Intelligences, forces, procedures and stages of development in the unfolding Universe and the spiritual, intellectual, psychological and physical components of every human being.

Acceptance of this view gives to World Scriptures a far deeper significance than if they were regarded as narratives of physical events alone. This approach also helps to explain the inclusion of passages which either contradict known scientific and historical facts, or else repel because recording criminal, immoral or very cruel actions.

If I seem to apologise too much for condemning the literal meaning of certain passages and advancing possible hidden meanings—and I have been so charged by one reviewer of my first Volume—it is because I remember and do not wish to hurt or harm those to whom orthodox beliefs mean much in their religious life. Having suffered myself from atheistic iconoclasm, I wish to lead my readers along a more pleasant pathway to what I have come to regard as truth; preferring to win over and persuade to further examination than entirely to crush.

Many Biblical passages do indeed present grave difficulties, particularly when deeds are stated to have been performed either, as in the Old

Testament, at the instance of the Supreme Deity or, as in Mythology, even by deities themselves. Many such textual problems are resolved when the classical keys of interpretation are applied, and the successive Volumes of this work offer some of the results of study of the Scriptures and Mythologies of ancient peoples as if the Sages of old had recorded them in the Sacred Language of Allegory and Symbol.

GEOFFREY HODSON

Auckland,
New Zealand,
1966.

THE HOLY BIBLE

THE BIBLE OF TODAY

THE Old Testament is a collection of thirty-nine books containing poetry
and philosophy, ritual law and social legislation, history, symbolism and
metaphysics. Its oldest passages are thought to have been written in the
days of Moses (about 1200 B.C.), and its latest parts belong to 200 B.C.

Though now translated into over 1,000 different dialects and languages
its original was written in Hebrew, once again the language of a living
people dwelling in the State of Israel. More than a hundred authors
wrote it, including priests, prophets and social revolutionaries. Whilst
the Bible tells the early history of the Jewish people, then still known as
Israelites, it differs from all other historical records. First in importance
are the Five Books of Moses, known as the *Pentateuch* (Gr. " five books ")
or by the Hebrew term *Torah* (Heb. " law "). The *Torah* describes the
beginning of the world and the formative history of the Jewish people
from Abraham—the first Jew and the creator of the monotheistic Hebrew
religion—up to the death of Moses, and contains the Ten Command-
ments.

The Bible as a whole is not written systematically, however, but is
a collection of books of history, historical metaphor, biography, law and
poetry, all leading into one another without an apparent plan. The
Books of the Prophets include both historical narrative and an anthology
of Divine revelations. Those of Joshua, Judges, Samuel and Kings tell
the history of the Jewish people from Joshua's conquest of the Holy Land
to the destruction of the first temple by Nebuchadnezzar of Babylon
in 586 B.C.

These Hebrew prophets were the conscience of the people; for in
the face of powerful priests and raving multitudes they spoke up with
one chief purpose in mind—to teach man " to do justly, and to love mercy,

and to walk humbly with thy God." (*Micah* 6: 8). Isaiah writes with dignity and power, condemning social systems which forget the needs of the poor. Amos, a " herdman and a gatherer of sycomore fruit " (*Amos*, 7: 14), declared God's judgment upon the nations and upon Israel, also foretelling Israel's restoration. Jeremiah dedicated himself to God, but was despised and persecuted by the people. He called for peace when nations prepared for war, and demanded an inward religion of sincerity at a time when priests were enforcing their orthodox codes.

Altogether the Hebrew Bible contains the writings of three major and twelve minor prophets, so called because the volume of their writings was small compared to that of the major prophets—Isaiah, Jeremiah and Ezekiel. The third and last division of the Hebrew Bible is called *Hagiographa* ("sacred writings "). These include the *Psalms, Proverbs* and *The Book of Job*.

CONTENTS

PART THREE

ADAM, EVE, THE GARDEN OF EDEN AND THE "FALL" OF MAN

PART FOUR

CAIN, ABEL, NOAH, THE ARK, THE FLOOD, THE TOWER OF BABEL AND THE GENERATIONS OF SHEM

xxiii

PART ONE

"WHICH THINGS ARE AN ALLEGORY"

(Gal. IV : 24)

CHAPTER I

PROBLEMS ARISING FROM A LITERAL READING OF THE BIBLE, AND SOME SOLUTIONS

SINCE comprehension and appreciation of the esoteric teachings contained in the Bible depend upon a knowledge of the Sacred Language, a fuller and more detailed exposition of this particular category of literature must now be given. At the outset of this task it is recognised that to those who have hitherto regarded the Bible either as divinely inspired or solely as a record of historical events, the idea that it was written in allegory and symbol in order to transmit universal truths to mankind may seem strange and unacceptable.

As the subject is profound, impartial examination and progressive study are essential to its comprehension. Apart from the parables of Jesus, the language of analogy, dramatic allegory and symbol is for many people a little known art form. Vocabulary, grammar and composition must, in consequence, be mastered before the transmitted ideas can be perceived and wholly understood. Time, too, is always required in order to become accustomed to an unfamiliar method of presentation and hitherto unknown aspects of truth.

In the field of the Arts, for example, some training in appreciation is necessary in order to enjoy and understand a great picture and receive the artist's message. Preparation and experience are needed in order to open the eyes and prepare the mind. This is true also of music. With the exception of those passages—perhaps the slow Movements—which can be readily enjoyed, a Symphony can at first hearing be difficult to comprehend. As one begins to perceive its significance, however, the whole work takes on an added meaning and evokes a new delight. To a child a wonderful jewel is but a glittering toy. He will choose just as readily any shining thing, however tawdry and cheap. A connoisseur in precious stones, on the other hand, sees in them depths of beauty hidden from others, comprehends and appreciates both the stones themselves and, when they have been cut and set, the craftsmanship of the jeweller.

The Language of Allegory and Symbol may, in its turn, be regarded as an art form. One therefore similarly needs to acquire by practice the ability to appreciate the many and varied ways in which it is used and to discover the underlying meanings. Without such preparation allegories and symbols may be wrongly regarded as unnecessary obstructions and their interpretations as arbitrary, or at best far-fetched. Since profound truths are conveyed and spiritual experience, knowledge and power can be obtained by the successful unveiling of the symbolism of the Bible, the student's preparations must in their turn be not only intellectual, but to some extent spiritual as well. Indeed, such preparations almost assume the character of a vigil.[1]

THE VEIL OF ALLEGORY

Whilst many of the incidents in the Bible are doubtless founded upon fact, nevertheless great wisdom and light are also to be discovered within the Scriptural record of historical and pseudo-historical events. When, however, statements are made which could not possibly be true, three courses of action present themselves to the reader. He can accept such statements unthinkingly, in blind faith; he may discard them as unworthy of serious consideration; or he may study them carefully in search of possible under-meanings and revelations of hitherto hidden truths. Incidents such as the passage of three days and nights and the appearance on Earth of vegetation before creation of the sun,[2] and the action of Joshua in making the sun and moon stand still,[3] cannot possibly have occurred. Here, as in so many other places, the Bible piles the incredible upon the impossible. If, however, the intention was not to record supposed astronomical facts or historical events alone, but also to reveal abstract, universal and mystical truths and to give guidance in finding and treading " The way of holiness ",[4] and if night, sun and moon are but concrete symbols of abstract ideas, then the outwardly meaningless narrative may reveal inward truth and light. Before that truth and light can be perceived, the veil of allegory must be lifted and the symbols interpreted; for, as already stated, partly in order to render abstract ideas comprehensible by expressing them in concrete form and also to safeguard the truth and reveal it when the time should be ripe, the Teachers of ancient days deliberately concealed within allegory and symbol the deep, hidden wisdom of which they had become possessed.

TIME AS MIRROR OF ETERNITY

My own studies have led me to the conviction that the authors of the Scriptures saw eternal truths mirrored in events in time. For them, illumined as they were, every material happening was alight with spiritual

[1] *Vigil*—a devotional watching, as in the days of Chivalry for example.
[2] *Gen.* 1: 13–16.
[3] *Joshua* 10: 12–14. q.v. Vol. I of this work, Pt. I, Ch. V.
[4] *Is.* 35: 8.

significance. They knew the outer world for what it is—the shadow of a great reality. They could say with Elizabeth Browning: " Earth's crammed with heaven, and every common bush afire with God ", and with her would add " but only he who sees, takes off his shoes." [1] Their records of the history of the Universe and of the Earth—the Scriptures of the world—portray far more than events in time; they reveal in concrete and therefore more readily understandable form eternal truths, ultimate reality, universal occurrences. Sometimes the real was more visible to them than the shadow, whereupon history took second place. At other times the record of physical events predominated.

This concept of the purposes and the method of the ancient writers is advanced in this work as being the key to the mystical study of the Bible, the clue to the discovery of the inexhaustible treasures of wisdom and truth concealed within the casket of exoteric Scriptures. The spiritual Teachers of long ago, by using historical events as well as allegories and symbols, proved themselves able to overcome the limitations of time. They recorded history in such a way as to reveal to readers of their own and later times the deeper truths of life. Even thousands of years after their death such Teachers are able to give to mankind both guidance along the pathway of spiritual illumination and solutions of many human problems. Nevertheless a measure of concealment from the profane of truths which they desired to impart to the worthy, and to the worthy alone, was forced upon the ancient writers. The motive for such concealment, as earlier stated, was to safeguard both the individual and the race from the dangers of premature discovery and possible misuse of knowledge which could bestow theurgic and thaumaturgic powers. Thus, I believe, came into existence the inspired portions of the legends, Mythologies and Scriptures of the world, many of which are pregnant with spiritual and occult ideas, and therefore with power.

SOME DIFFICULTIES CREATED BY A DEAD-LETTER READING OF THE BIBLE

In addition to its value as a vehicle for hidden wisdom, the Sacred Language can prove helpful in solving otherwise insoluble Biblical problems. Whilst belief or faith in the possibility of super-natural intervention makes some Scriptural statements credible, nevertheless physical laws and astronomical facts cannot be changed. Indeed some " miracles "[2] do strain almost

---

[1] Poems of Elizabeth B. Browning, Bk. 7.

[2] *Miracle.* Occult science does not admit of the possibility of any action by any being, however lofty, which contravenes the laws of Nature. Whilst phenomena on the physical plane may appear to be miraculous, they are nevertheless the product of the action of the trained will applied according to the laws and processes of Nature appertaining to the superphysical as well as the physical worlds.

beyond reasonable limits one's power to believe in them. The hydrostatic pressure invisibly exerted in dividing and holding back on either side of a dry bed the waters of the Red Sea [1] and the river Jordan [2] would have involved the use of almost incalculable energy. Nevertheless, if direct theurgic action is presumed to have occurred then these " miracles " would not have been entirely impossible.

The heliocentric system, however, cannot be altered. The sun is at the centre of our Solar System, for which it is the source of light. Planets throughout their orbital motion round the sun revolve in their axes, and without that rotation there could be no alternation of day and night. In spite of this, in the First Chapter of *Genesis* it is plainly stated that, having brought light into existence and divided it from the darkness, ". . . God called the light Day, and the darkness he called Night. And the evening and the morning were the first day." [3] An even greater anomaly is added by the further statement that three days and three nights had passed before the sun, moon and stars were created.[4] Such events would have been astronomical impossibilities. Indeed, they could not have happened in the sequence affirmed in *Genesis*.

" AND IT REPENTED THE LORD THAT HE HAD MADE MAN ON THE EARTH " [1]

The story of Noah and his Ark also presents many grave stumbling blocks. One of these consists of the ideas implicit in verses five, six and seven of the Sixth Chapter of *Genesis*—namely that an all-loving Father in Heaven could conceive of an imperfect plan which failed, experience wrath at that failure, and with insensate cruelty decide to destroy " both man, and beast, and the creeping thing, and the fowls of the air. . . .[2] " In their literal reading these statements are an affront to reason. The assertion that God could be guilty of such actions and could later be moved to make the promises not to " again curse the ground any more for man's sake " [3] or " again smite any more every thing living ",[3] is either an erroneous ascription to the Deity of conduct of which even man would not be guilty or else a deliberately constructed blind for the concealment of an underlying truth.

The concept is inconceivable, surely, that there could be in existence a single, extra-cosmic, personal God Who could Himself fail as a Creator

[1] *Ex.* 14: 21–31.
[2] *Joshua* 3: 14–17.
[3] *Gen.* 1: 5.
[4] *Gen.* 1: 16.
[1] *Gen.* 6: 6.
[2] *Gen.* 6: 7.
[3] *Gen.* 8: 21.

of mankind and then be destructively wrathful at the wicked conduct of a human race which was solely and entirely the product of His own creation. Such a conclusion is strengthened by the divine proclamation that man was made in God's image.[4] It is similarly inconceivable that the conjoined *Elohim* [1] (wrongly translated as " God " in *Genesis*) could be capable either of imperfection in the planning and fulfilment of Their cosmic functions or of wrath at a failure which was solely attributable to Themselves. In the presence of such affronts to human reason, acceptance of the concept of the use of a special category of literature known as the Sacred Language is surely preferable to either blind faith or total unbelief in the Bible on account of the inconsistencies and errors which a literal reading of certain passages could bring about. Such rejection of the whole Bible with its inspiring message of the existence of a Supreme Being as the Directive Intelligence in Nature, on account of incredibilities and impossibilities found in certain passages, would indeed be a mistake. The great scientist, Dr. Albert Einstein, evidently felt himself to be under no necessity to make this rejection, for he wrote: " That deeply emotional conviction of the presence of a *superior reasoning power* (italics mine, G.H.) which is revealed in the incomprehensible Universe, forms my idea of God." Nevertheless, the actions attributed to the Deity in the Biblical verses under review certainly do not present Him in the guise of a " superior reasoning power ".

To return to the Biblical account of the Flood; if, as is indicated in several places, the Flood covered the whole of the Earth and if all the water in the atmosphere had thus been added to all the water in the oceans, the mixture would have been indistinguishable from sea water. In such case no animal that lived on Earth would have been able to drink it and survive, whilst in addition all land plants would have died. In consequence the inhabitants of the Ark would have had neither food nor water to sustain them after they landed.

---

[4] *Gen.* 1: 26, 27.

[1] *Elohim* (Heb.)—" Gods ". A sevenfold power of Godhead; the male-female Hierarchies of creative Intelligences or Potencies through which the Divine produces the manifested Universe; the unity of the powers, the attributes and the creative activities of the Supreme Being. " Elohim " is a plural name, the singular form of the word being " Eloha ", i.e. a " god ". " Elohim ", therefore, literally means " gods ", personifications of divine attributes or the forces at work in Nature. Admittedly the " Elohim " are also conceived as a Unity in the sense that They all work together as One, expressing One Will, One Purpose, One Harmony. Thus Their activities are regarded as the manifestation of the Eternal One, the Absolute. " Elohim " might therefore be explained as " the Unity of gods " or " the Activities of the Eternal One ", namely God omnipresent and revealing Himself outwardly in creative activity. (Partly paraphrased from *The Unknown God*, P. J. Mayers).

Furthermore, Noah would have found it extremely difficult, if not impossible, to collect animals and fowls from the four quarters of the Globe and persuade them to begin travelling towards the Middle East from many parts of the Earth—arctic, temperate, subtropical and tropical. In many cases this would have demanded the crossing of thousands of miles of ocean. Indeed, such incredibilities need hardly be mentioned save to underscore the absurdities into which a literal reading of the Bible can lead one, and to provide support for the approach advanced in this work. The sloth, for instance, which travels with extreme slowness— hence its name, perhaps—would have needed to begin its journey long before the onset of the Flood in order to reach the Ark in time. This would also apply to other animals travelling from great distances. In addition, the task of housing and feeding so large a number of animals throughout forty days and forty nights would have presented grave, if not insurmountable, difficulties.

The Scriptural account (A.V.) distinctly states that the animals and fowls were so collected together as to ensure that on arrival at the Ark in readiness to enter it they could be arranged in a certain numerical order. Their classification into categories, and the number of each class to be selected, is indicated thus: " Of every clean beast thou shalt take to thee by sevens, the male and his female: and of beasts that are not clean by two, the male and his female. Of fowls also of the air by sevens, the male and the female. . . ." [1]

The Revised Version, however, corrects the seeming anomalies by translating from the original as follows:

2. *Take with you seven pairs of all clean animals, the male and his mate; and a pair of the animals that are not clean, the male and his mate;*

3. *And seven pairs of the birds of the air also, male and female, to keep their kind alive upon the face of all the earth.* (R.V.)

The possible underlying significance of the story itself and of the numbers introduced into it will be considered at the appropriate place in the text.[2]

"THE LORD DID . . . . . CONFOUND THE LANGUAGE OF ALL THE EARTH " [3]

The story of the Tower of Babel—especially verses six, seven, eight and nine of the Eleventh Chapter of the *Book of Genesis*—would seem to imply that the Supreme Deity is deliberately and callously responsible for the major sufferings of mankind, rooted as they are in the human delusion of self-separated individuality and consequent egoism. According to verses

[1] *Gen.* 7: 2, 3.
[2] See Pts. II and IV of this Volume.
[3] *Gen.* 11:9.

six and seven many evil works by man upon man, including individual and organised crime and the waging of innumerable wars, arose and still arise from the two supposed actions of a personal Deity. The first of these was to confound human language so that men could no longer understand one another's speech, and the second to scatter humanity abroad upon the face of the Earth. Such supposed divine actions can, indeed, legitimately be regarded as having been major causes of those human errors which are born of individualism and self-separateness. The attribution to the Supreme Deity of motive and conduct so detrimental to humanity as to make difficult for long ages the attainment of harmonious human relationships between groups, nations and races of men upon earth, is totally unacceptable to the thoughtful and reverent mind. The study of the Bible less as literal history, and far more as a revelation of fundamental truths by means of historical metaphors and allegories, thus receives strong support from the passages concerning the building of the Tower of Babel.

" AND THEY (LOT'S DAUGHTERS) MADE THEIR FATHER DRINK WINE THAT NIGHT. . . " [1]

Incredibility apart, the obscenity—such as the drunkenness of Lot and the incest (admittedly unconscious on his part) with his two daughters[2] —and the attribution to the Supreme Deity of the human weakness of anger, jealousy and bloodthirstiness as evinced by " His " encouragement of the Israelites to attack and massacre the animals, men, women and children of other tribes [3]—these, with all the other Biblical incongruities, must in their turn be repellant to thoughtful and sensitive minds.

A great many other passages could be referred to, including verses seventeen and eighteen of the Nineteenth Chapter of *Revelation*, which read as follows:

17. *And I saw an angel standing in the sun; and he cried with a loud voice, saying to all the fowls that fly in the midst of heaven, Come and gather yourselves together unto the supper of the great God;*

18. *That ye may eat the flesh of kings, and the flesh of captains, and the flesh of mighty men, and the flesh of horses, and of them that sit on them, and the flesh of all men, both free and bond, both small and great.*

" SUN, STAND THOU STILL UPON GIBEON " [4]

Since the rotation of the Earth causes night and day and the sun does not move round the Earth, Joshua could not by any means have lengthened

---

[1] *Gen.* 19: 35.
[2] *Gen.* 19: 30–38.
[3] e.g. *Ex.* 23: 23–33, *De.* 9: 14; *Nu.* 31: 1–17; *Ezk.* 25: 16, 17 etc
[4] Joshua 10; 12–14. q.v. Vol I, Pt.1, Ch. V.

the day by making the sun and the moon stand still.   The prolongation of day or of night by the arrest of the motion of either sun or Earth (the moon would not be directly concerned in such a procedure) is a total impossibility; for if the Earth had suddenly stopped turning no human being would have lived to record the event.   Every movable object on Earth, including the oceans and the atmosphere, would have continued the normally rotating movement and thus travelled towards the East faster than the speed of sound.   Read literally, therefore, the narrative is totally unacceptable. '

' NOW THE LORD HAD PREPARED A GREAT FISH TO SWALLOW UP JONAH " [1]

If the Prophet Jonah—to take another example—had actually spent three days and three nights in the stomach of a large mammal like a whale, digestive secretions and processes would have rendered it most unlikely that he could have remained alive and unaffected throughout such a period.   This story in its literal reading must in its turn be regarded as extremely doubtful, if not totally false.   The possibility of the existence of a recondite meaning (as, for example, a description of the procedures of Initiation or spiritual regeneration as suggested by the symbol of the fish [4]) will be considered in a later Volume of this work.

Such verses as these are so obviously unacceptable in their literal reading that they scarcely call for comment.   The idea therefore receives support that, as already noted, the authors of certain passages in the Bible were spiritually instructed men writing for the following purposes, amongst others: to present abstract ideas in concrete and so more readily comprehensible form; to describe phases of human evolution and their associated psychological and mystical experiences; to evoke wonder and so initiate enquiry; to preserve for posterity profound spiritual, occult and potentially power-bestowing truths, to conceal from the profane knowledge which could be misused, even whilst revealing it to the trustworthy servant of humanity who possesses the keys of interpretation.

In the Sermon on the Mount Christ would seem to have given in allegorical form strict instructions that this last purpose more especially should be followed, for He is reported to have said:

> Give not that which is holy unto the dogs, neither cast ye your pearls before swine, lest they trample them under their feet, and turn again and rend you. [2]

In order to achieve these objectives—if further repetition be pardoned —the authors of the inspired portions of the world's Scriptures, allegories and myths used the methods of the Symbolical Language, which include

[1] *Jonah* 1: 17.
[2] *Matt.* 7: 6.

the occasional introduction of inconsistencies as part of the concealing veil.

BIOLOGY, NOMENCLATURE AND THE LIMITATIONS OF TIME

In the New Testament also, difficulties are met if a literal reading of certain passages be adopted. Two of the Evangelists affirm the immaculate conception of Jesus and consequently a virgin birth[1] —medically regarded as a virtual impossibility—whilst the others do not. The genealogies of Jesus as given in the Gospels of St. Matthew and St. Luke are totally different and could not apply to the same person. St. Matthew traces His descent through Joseph, which is meaningless in the case of a virgin birth, and St. Luke through Mary.

Furthermore, the events said to have occurred during the night before the Crucifixion of Jesus are too numerous to have happened within the prescribed time. Here is a list of them: the Last Supper (*Lu.* XXII: 15–20); the agony in the Garden (*Matt.* XXVI: 36–46); the betrayal by Judas (*Matt.* XXVI: 47–50); the questioning, firstly before Annas and Caiaphas (*Jn.* XVIII: 13–24), secondly before the Sanhedrin (*Matt.* XXVI: 59–66), thirdly before Pilate (*Matt.* XXVII: 11–14) and finally in the Hall of Judgment (*Jn.* XVIII: 28–38)—regardless of the fact that Courts to try malefactors did not usually sit in the middle of the night;[2] the visit to Herod (*Lk.* XXIII: 7–11), recorded only by St. Luke; the return to Pilate; Pilate's speeches and his washing of his hands (*Matt.* XXVII: 11–24); the scourging, the mocking and the arraying of Jesus in a purple robe (*Mk.* XV: 16–20); the long and painful bearing of the Cross to Golgotha, followed by the Crucifixion (*Jn.* XIX: 16–18) —all these events could not possibly have occurred in so short a time. According to estimated chronology the arrest of Jesus occurred at midnight on a Thursday, and the Crucifixion at 9-00 A.M. on Good Friday.[3] Biblical accounts of these and many other events present a completely insoluble problem, if only because of the unalterable demands and divisions of time itself; for time and space, or location are inflexible. This list is repeated and a solution of the problems is advanced in the Chapter entitled " Four Major Keys of Interpretation ".

SOME ECCLESIASTICAL ADMISSIONS

Although a number of Christian denominations proclaim the Bible to be the verbally inspired word of God, some churchmen frankly recognise the above-mentioned difficulties. Canon T. P. Stevens, Vicar of St. Paul's

---

[1] *Matt.* 1: 18; *Lk.* 1: 34, 35.

[2] The possibility that the urgency of the case could have made immediate action imperative has not been overlooked.

[3] q.v. *The Oxford Cyclopedic Concordance*, Oxford University Press.

Church, Wimbledon, when explaining his reasons for banning the teaching of certain Old Testament stories in his Sunday Schools, said:

"No matter how many say the Bible should be taught in full, I am not going to do it. Men like Bernard Shaw, Arnold Bennett and H. G. Wells all turned against the Church through wrongful teaching, when they could have been a powerful force to us. . . .

"It takes a man of considerable intelligence to understand the whole of the Bible. Some of the stories are helpful, interesting and lovely, but quite often they deal with rape, murder, lies and brutality, exaggerated nationalism and war. What purpose is to be served by teaching all these unpleasant stories to the young? If they are intelligent they will get the strangest ideas of God.

"I believe the Christian religion is in a state of decline partly because so many people cannot make head or tail of it. Unfortunately the whole (not entirely—G.H.) Christian Church is against me. I am the odd man out over this question."[1]

A new dark age was foreseen by Dean Inge, as reported in *The New Zealand Herald*, (8-6-'50): "Dean Inge, 'The Gloomy Dean', is aged 90 today (June 6th). . . . On the eve of his birthday, the Dean declared: 'We seem to be on the threshold of another dark age. . . . The first thing ought to be to get rid of a good deal of the Old Testament. We are living in an age different from the days when I had a fashionable West End Church, where ladies dripping with pearls and furs would sing the Magnificat with more fervour than a Communist ever sang the Red Flag".

The Most Reverend Dr. Frank Woods, Anglican Archbishop of Melbourne, speaking at St. Paul's Cathedral on the 18th February, 1961, on the early *Genesis* accounts of the creation, Adam and Eve and the Fall of man, said that Christians should not be dismayed if these were attacked on scientific or historical grounds. They contain truths of a religious nature, he stated, which do not depend for their validity upon historical or scientific confirmation. The *Genesis* accounts expressed truths of a timeless nature. They were myths, teaching spiritual truths by allegories.

In October, 1962, *The New Zealand Herald* published a statement by the Rev. Dr. Leslie Weatherhead, a former President of the Methodist Conference and Minister at the famous City Temple, London. In the course of an interview with the Press the Reverend Doctor, who is also the author of a booklet entitled *The Case for Reincarnation*, said "he would like to go through the Bible being very free with a blue pencil".

Still more recently *The Auckland Star* (23-3-'63) printed a news item concerning a recent book, *Honest to God*, written by the Bishop of Woolwich, Dr. John Robinson. In this article it is stated that the Bishop makes it

---

[1] q.v. *The New Zealand Herald*, 2-5-50.

clear in his book that, amongst other dogmas, he does not believe in God as a separate Being and that he is agnostic about the Virgin Birth.

A SOLUTION OF THE PROBLEM

Most, if not all, of these difficulties disappear when once it is assumed that the authors' intention was less to record history alone than also to present cosmogonical, solar, planetary and racial ideas and to describe mystical and psychological conditions and experiences of man.   An additional explanation of the otherwise inexplicable presence of these incongruities in the Bible as we know it today is that they were additions, and not part of the original writings.   Later interpreters, editors and translators are, by some Biblical scholars, held responsible.   My own studies have led me to the conclusion that deliberate interference with original texts, deletions, interpolations, or, successive editings and trans-lations and some deletions, have been partly responsible for the confusion, rendering the literal reading of many portions of the Old Testament entirely unacceptable.   Such offensive passages should, I think, be attri-buted to later writers, totally unillumined and still influenced by local superstitions and primitive moral standards.   These crude ideas and evidences of ignorance were, I feel sure, not included in the original inspired revelations.   Many of the resultant criticisms can successfully be met, however, and most of the problems solved once the existence of the Sacred Language is accepted and its symbolism applied to difficult passages of World Scriptures and Mythologies.

If this approach be regarded as both permissible and potentially valuable, then the choice of both subject-matter and language made by the *original* authors of the Scriptures suggests that a recondite meaning exists.   Amongst these indications are: the direct intervention *in propria persona* of the Supreme Deity; the occurrence of miracles, whether credible or incredible; and the appropriate use of classical symbols such as physical objects and features of the landscape including, for example, mountains, rivers, deserts, gardens, trees, animals and birds.[1]   Where these are included in the narrative in a manner and place which appear to suggest an allegorical intention on the part of the writer, then with due caution the method of interpretation herein described and employed may be helpfully applied, particularly to those portions of the Scriptures which are susceptible of such treatment.

As has heretofore been stated, impossibilities appearing in the Bible which bear the imprint of inspiration may, however, in conformity with the allegorical method of writing be part of a deliberately constructed cover or blind—a veil of incredibility, incongruity, absurdity, inconsequence,

[1] q.v. Vol. I of this work, Pt. III.

fantasy, and even horror.[1]   The previously quoted words of Moses Maimonedes, the Jewish theologian and historian, may perhaps usefully be here repeated: " Every time you find in our books a tale the reality of which seems impossible, a story which is repugnant to both reason and common sense, then be sure that the tale contains a profound allegory veiling a deeply mysterious truth; and the greater the absurdity of the letter, the deeper the wisdom of the spirit."

THE TESTIMONY OF EARLY AUTHORITIES [2]

Knowledge of the existence of a secret meaning contained within the Scriptures is openly confessed by Clement of Alexandria (A.D. 150–220 approximately) when he says that the Mysteries of the Faith are not to be divulged to all. " But ", he says, " since this tradition is not published alone for him who perceives the magnificence of the word; it is requisite, therefore, to hide in a Mystery the wisdom spoken, which the Son of God taught." [3]

Origen is no less explicit concerning the Bible and its symbolical fables. " If we hold to the letter ", he exclaims, " and must understand what stands written in the law after the manner of the Jews and common people, then I should blush to confess aloud that it is God who has given these laws; then the laws of men appear more excellent and reasonable." [4]

" What man of sense ", he writes, " will agree with the statement that the first, second and third days in which the *evening* is named and the *morning*, were without sun, moon, and stars, and the first day without a heaven? What man is found such an idiot as to suppose that God planted trees in Paradise, in Eden, like a husbandman, and planted therein the tree of life, perceptible to the eyes and senses, which gave life to the eater thereof; and another tree which gave to the eater thereof a knowledge of good and evil? I believe that every man must hold these things for images, under which the hidden sense lies concealed."[5]   St. Paul's unequivocal statements that the story of Abraham and his two sons is " an allegory " and that " Agar is Mount Sinai " [6] offer Biblical support for the acceptance of certain portions of the Bible as allegorical.

---

[1] Some of the reasons for such enveiling are also offered in Pt. I, Ch. I, of this Volume.

[2] Certain of the quotations which follow in this and other Chapters also appear at the beginning of this book.

[3] *Clement of Alexandria*, Vol. I, *Stromata*, Ch. XII, p. 388.

[4] See *Homilies* 7, in Levit., quoted in *The Source of Measures*, pp. 306–7, J. Ralston Skinner.

[5] Origen: Hurt, *Origeniana*, 167; Franck, p. 142.

[6] *Gal.* 4: 22–26.

H. P. Blavatsky writes:[1] " Rabbi Simeon Ben-'Jochai' (sic), the compiler of the *Zohar*,[2] never imparted the most important points of his doctrine otherwise than orally, and to a very limited number of disciples. Therefore, without the final initiation into the *Mercavah*,[3] the study of the *Kabbalah* will be ever incomplete, and the *Mercavah* can be taught only ' in darkness, in a deserted place, and after many and terrific trials.' (the preparation those days of Candidates for Initiation, G.H.).[4] Since the death of that great Jewish Initiate this hidden doctrine has remained, for the outside world, an inviolate secret.

" Among the venerable sect of the Tanaim, or rather the Tananim, the wise men, there were those who taught the secrets practically and initiated some disciples into the grand and final Mystery. But the *Mishna Hagiga*, 2nd Section, say that the table of contents of the Mercaba ' must only be delivered to wise old ones.' The *Gemara* is still more dogmatic. ' The more important secrets of the Mysteries[5] were not even revealed to all priests. Alone the initiates had them divulged.' And so we find the same great secrecy prevalent in every ancient religion.

" What says the *Kabbalah* itself? Its great Rabbis actually threaten him who accepts their sayings *verbatim*. We read in the *Zohar*: ' woe ... to the man who sees in the Thorah,[6] *i.e.*, Law, only simple recitals and ordinary words ! Because if in truth it only contained these, we would even to-day be able to compose a Thorah much more worthy of admiration. For if we find only the simple words, we would only have to address ourselves to the legislators of the earth, to those in whom we most frequently meet with the most grandeur. It would be sufficient to imitate them, and make a Thorah after their words and example. But it is not so; each word of the Thorah contains an elevated meaning and a sublime

---

[1] q.v. *The Secret Doctrine*, H. P. Blavatsky, Adyar Ed., Vol. V, pp. 67–68.

[2] *Zohar*. *The Book of Splendour*, the basic work of Jewish mysticism, the greatest exposition of the *Kabbalah*.

[3] *Mercavah* or *Mercaba* (Heb.)—A " chariot ". According to Kabbalists the Supreme Lord, after He had established the Ten Sephiroth, used Them as a chariot or throne of glory on which to descend upon the souls of men. Also a hidden doctrine delivered only as a mystery orally, " face to face and mouth to ear ". q.v., *Appendix, The Sephirothal Tree*.

[4] *Initiation*—see Glossary and Pt. VI of Vol. I of this work.

[5] *Muo* (Gr.)—" to close the mouth ", *Teletai* (Gr.)—" Celebrations of Initiation ". The Sacred Mysteries were enacted in the ancient Temples by the initiated Hierophants for the benefit and instruction of the Candidates. They formed a series of secret dramatic performances, in which the mysteries of cosmogony and Nature were personified by the priests and neophytes. These were explained in their hidden meaning to the Candidates for Initiation. q.v. *Eleusis and the Eleusinian Mysteries*, George E. Mylonas; *The Eleusinian and Bacchic Mysteries*, Thomas Taylor; *The Mysteries of Eleusis*, George Meautis, Prof. at the University of Neuchatel.

[6] *Thorah* (Heb.)—" The Law of Moses ". *Pentateuch* (Gr.)—*Penta*, " five " and *teukhos*, " book ". The first five books of the Old Testament.

mystery. . . . The recitals of the Thorah are the vestments of the Thorah. Woe to him who takes this garment for the Thorah itself. . . . The simple take notice only of the garments or recitals of the Thorah, they know no other thing, they see not that which is concealed under the vestment. The more instructed men do not pay attention to the vestment, but to the body which it envelops.' "

AN ILLUSTRATION

The story of the cursing of the fig tree [1] may here be taken as an example of an account of a somewhat unlikely event which, when interpreted as an allegory, becomes not only acceptable but also a source of illumination. It seems un-Christlike to curse the fig tree, and still more so since the act was performed in the early Spring before the Passover when, being out of season, the tree could not have had any figs upon it. Indeed, the story may rightly be regarded as self-contradictory, even absurd. In that very absurdity, however, is said to be both a clue to the meaning and an encouragement to look for the wisdom concealed within the supposed narrative of events.

The world's allegories are, in fact, less records of events in time and place than both descriptions of interior experiences and enunciations of universal laws. Simply put, the particular law here referred to is that if all living things and beings—including races, nations and men—do not share the fruits of their lives they will metaphorically, wither away and die. Applied to the individual, the person who seeks to have, to hold and to hoard for himself alone the fruits of his life—his material possessions and his discovered wisdom, truth and power—giving nothing to others, will inevitably find that his own life, outer and inner, stagnates and then atrophies.

SELFLESS GIVING BRINGS SPIRITUAL ENRICHMENT

Attention is thus drawn to a further mysterious law—it might be called " the law of flow "—under which he who wisely and unselfishly gives of himself gains a more abundant life. Obedience to this law brings not loss but gain, not death but everlasting life. Inversely, disobedience of this law brings not gain but loss, not life but death. This has been repeatedly demonstrated throughout the history of both nations and individuals. The same principle is allegorically presented in the story of Abraham's attempted sacrifice of his son Isaac. The act was supposedly to be performed as a sign of complete submission to the will of the Lord;

---

[1] *Matt.* 21: 19; *Mk.* 11: 14, 21.

yet even whilst Abraham's arm was raised to strike, an angel stayed his hand and later he found a substituted sacrifice in the form of a ram.[1] The incident allegorically portrays the truth that once complete readiness is shown wisely to surrender self and treasured personal possessions in pursuance of an ideal way of life, or in the service of the Lord, then the sacrifice is not demanded.

This principle is fundamental for it is the law by which the Universe subsists. The Logos Himself nourishes and sustains the Solar System by the perpetual outpouring, self-giving, " self-emptying " (kenosis, Gr.) of His own life. This kenosis (the self-emptying attitude of mind and mode of life) is a key-note in the Christian religion. It is applied to the life of the disciple by Our Lord in His words: " . . . he that hateth his life in this world shall keep it unto life eternal ",[2] and ". . . Except a corn of wheat fall into the ground and die, it abideth alone: but if it die, it bringeth forth much fruit." [3]   The neophyte must become " the wheat of Christ ", as a Christian mystic has said.

The poverty of the Nativity of Jesus, the surrender to Pilate, to the Jews and to Crucifixion, the exposure of the Sacred Heart, the endurance of open wounds and the piercing of the skin, are all symbols of this attitude of uttermost selflessness towards life. Such self-emptying, such entirely self-forgetting love and such figurative death are necessary, it is said, for the attainment of a more abundant life. To " die " to the sense of separated individuality, to outgrow egoism and possessiveness—this is to live unto life eternal. Mysterious, and even contradictory, though such a statement appears, it is nevertheless thought by mystics to be one of the greatest truths ever uttered.

Apparently we are in the presence of a strange law. In order to live the larger life in imitation of the Great Exemplar, the Lord of Love, we must die to self-desire, pour ourselves out in selfless sacrifice and service and surrender self for love's sake. Universal love is the only true way to eternal life, because it involves " self-emptying " of self. Self-forgetfulness is the basis of all spirituality. Every sincere esotericist is faced with this truth and with necessity, and the renunciation so often seems to be of that which we hold most dear.

Applied to the Logos, these words " self-emptying " and " dying " are not to be taken as wholly expressing the truth; for, of course, the Logos does not ever become empty, nor does " He " ever really die. Indeed, the Logos is ever Self-renewed from a higher dimension. Similarly the sun, which in occult philosophy is regarded as His physical " heart ", does not exhaust itself despite its immeasurable outpouring, for proportionate

[1] Gen. 22: 13.
[2] Jn. 12: 25.
[3] Jn. 12: 24.

2

inpouring or upwelling occurs. This is also true in every walk of life whether secular or spiritual.

REVELATION OF TRUTH BY MEANS OF ALLEGORY

In relating the incident of the withered fig tree, the author of the Gospel according to St. Matthew appears to have enunciated this principle in the form of an otherwise unacceptable story describing a supposed action of the Lord of Love which brought about the cessation of the life of a tree.[1] A profound spiritual truth of the greatest significance to every neophyte of every age who seeks to discover the " strait gate " and enter upon the narrow way [2] is thus portrayed by means of a miniature drama, an allegory concealing—to guard against unwise application of the law to necessary material possessions, for example—the all-important principle that life is not lost, but fulfilled, by renunciation. This interpretation is supported by the fact that after the incident Our Lord went on to refer to the nature and range of the tremendous powers attainable by those who enter upon the Path of Discipleship and Initiation, saying:

Jesus answered and said unto them, Verily I say unto you, If ye have faith, and doubt not, ye shall not only do this which is done to the fig tree, but also if ye shall say unto this mountain, Be thou removed, and be thou cast into the sea; it shall be done.

And all things, whatsoever ye shall ask in prayer, believing, ye shall receive.[3]

The entry of Jesus into Jerusalem and the acclamation by the crowd, commemorated by the Church as Palm Sunday, which immediately preceded the withering of the fig tree, indicated that a certain spiritual advance had been made, a triumph of Spirit over flesh, of the Christ power over mind, emotions, vitality and physical body—the lower quaternary (the docile ass)—and the multitude of habits, desires and appetites (the responsive crowd) inherent in the substance of the physical and superphysical bodies. Jerusalem is a symbol of the state of awareness of the Divine Self or Ego in the Causal Body, the universalised consciousness of an immortal, spiritual being. Entry into Jerusalem portrays realisation of the Self as divine, eternal, indestructible and universal. Absence, and especially exile, from a city may imply being temporarily or permanently cut off from a spiritual state of consciousness. The heavenly city, " the city of the living God ",[4] is thus a symbol of the *Augoeides*,[5]

---

[1] *Matt.* 21: 19.

[2] q.v. *The Hidden Wisdom in the Holy Bible*, Vol. I, Pt. VI, Geoffrey Hodson.

[3] *Matt.* 21: 21, 22.

[4] *Heb.* 12: 22.

[5] *Augoeides* (Gr.)—" The self-radiant divine fragment ", the Robe of Glory of the Gnostics and the *Kārana Sharīra*, " Causal Body ", of Hinduism.

the *Kārana Sharīra* (Sk.), the Robe of Glory of the Gnostics,[1] in which the self-radiant divine fragment, the Monad-Ego, abides and is self-manifest at the level of the spiritualised intelligence of man.

LITERAL OR SYMBOLICAL?

If it be objected—as would be very natural—that too much is being deduced from so simple and so briefly described an incident as the withering of the fig tree, firstly it can be repeated that a literal reading presents one with an unacceptable attribute in the character of the Christ, Who described Himself as a life-giver and not a death-dealer; for He said: " I am come that they might have life, and that they might have it more abundantly ".[2] Secondly, in its literal meaning the incident introduces a meaningless and somewhat repellent exercise of thaumaturgic power such as was and still is displayed, for example, by the medicine men of primitive peoples and by some, though by no means all, of the *Tohungas* of the Maoris [3] of New Zealand.

Whilst it is admitted that the fact that one idea is preferable to another is no proof of its verity, the cumulative evidence obtained by this and similar interpretations of a very great number of Bible stories is so strong as almost to amount to proof.   When to this is added the avowed intention of ancient writers, as evidenced by the quotations which appear at the front of this Volume, and the strongly worded command of the Christ to conceal from the profane, and yet reveal to the worthy, power-bestowing knowledge and " the mystery of the Kingdom of God "[4] (pearls[5]) which could be dangerous in the wrong hands (swine[5]), then the case for the existence and use of the Sacred Language would seem to be unassailable.

---

[1] All these titles are names for the same principle of man—the vehicle of the reincarnating Ego at the formless levels of the mental plane.

[2] *Jn.* 10: 10.

[3] q.v. *Lecture Notes of the School of the Wisdom*, Vol. II, Ch. IX, *The Sacred Science of Maori Tohunga*, Geoffrey Hodson.

[4] *Mk.* 4: 11.

[5] *Matt.* 7: 6.

CHAPTER II

SOME KEYS OF INTERPRETATION

WHILE the preceding chapter contains introductory examples of the use of the symbolical language and methods of interpretation, in this Chapter a fuller exposition is offered. This is very necessary, for those who would discover the truths concealed within the Scriptures of the world should first acquaint themselves with the various keys to the symbolical writings. Then, reading each story very carefully, giving special attention to the symbols employed, they should dwell in concentrated thought upon its various parts, meditatively seeking the reality behind the shadow, the eternal truth within the story in time; for successful interpretation is primarily an experience in consciousness.

Certain age-old symbols serve as signposts on the way, each with its meaning constant throughout all time, as the doctrine everywhere revealed is constant also. The Hierophants of Egypt, Chaldea, Assyria and Greece, the sages of the Eastern world and the inspired authors of the Bible all made use of these symbols as living, time-free ideographs which questing men of every age might comprehend. Nations, civilisations and religions rise and fall, but these earthly symbols of spiritual truths are ageless and unchanging. By their use an Egyptian Hierophant, a Jewish Prophet, an Essene monk, an Eastern sage, may speak direct from the remote past to the mind of modern man.

The authors who wrote in this allegorical manner wished to reveal Macrocosmic and microcosmic truths, to describe supersensuous conditions of consciousness. They used history only as weft and warp on which to weave a representation of everlasting verities, the esoteric wisdom of all ages, the deeply occult knowledge of the Initiates of the Mystery Schools of both ancient and more modern days. Time and the world of time were of far less importance to these inspired authors than eternity and the eternal truths of which they wrote.

When we open our Bible, then, we should remember that we are reading a special category of literature, foreign to us at first. In order to discover the intention of the authors we need to learn the meaning of the words, to understand the method of writing and to possess the keys of interpretation. We must, indeed, find a Rosetta stone. Then, as we learn to lift the veil of allegory, symbol, imagery, and even incongruity, the light of truth will illumine our minds.

FOUR KEYS OF INTERPRETATION

The foregoing enunciation of the principal theme of this work, namely that the inspired portions of World Scriptures and Myths are allegorical in character, may now be followed by a statement of four of the seven possible keys of interpretation and their Macrocosmic and microcosmic [1] applications to a number of such passages.

ALL HAPPENS WITHIN

The *first key* is that some narratives of supposedly historical events are also descriptive of subjective experiences of races, nations and individuals; in this sense, all happens within. When this key is " turned ", certain stories are found to have at least two possible underlying meanings. One of these refers to the experiences and attainments of those advancing by the normal evolutionary method, and the other to mystics who are treading the Way of Holiness or Path of Swift Unfoldment.

The need for the veiling of magical and occult knowledge in allegory and symbol is especially great in the latter of these two applications of the first key; for, quite early in the approach to and entry upon the Path, an enhancement of will-power and the mental and psychic faculties begins to be apparent. Premature awakening and development of these supernormal powers, and their employment for purely personal, and especially for destructive, purposes could prove extremely harmful both to those who misuse them and to their fellow men.

" CHRIST IN YOU, THE HOPE OF GLORY " [2]

The Apostle Paul would seem to have accepted this first key—the mystical interpretation. For him the Nativity of Christ, for example, is not only a particular event which occurred at a certain time in Bethlehem, but also refers to a universal human experience. The narratives of the Annunciation, the Immaculate Conception and the Nativity of Christ are so written as also to describe allegorically the gradual awakening of Christ-like

---

[1] Macrocosm and Microcosm. All allegories and symbols are susceptible of a threefold interpretation—Macrocosmic or applying to Logoi and Universes, microcosmic or applying to man, and Initiatory or applying to mystical experiences and stages of unfoldment passed through by those treading the part of discipleship and Initiation. (See Glossary and Pt. VI of Vol. I of this work).

[2] *Col.* 1: 27.

powers of perception within the Soul [1] of advanced man.   For St. Paul evidently, the birth and activities of the Lord Christ were descriptive of the interior awakening and perfecting of the inherent, redemptive Christ-power and nature *within* man.   Thus he wrote: ". . . I travail in birth again until Christ be formed in you " [2] and " To whom God would make known what is the riches of the glory of this mystery among the Gentiles; which is Christ in you, the hope of glory ".

As the student of the Bible reads the great narratives with this key in his hand, as it were, he may even himself share in the recorded experiences. He may ascend " the mount " with Abraham, Moses, Elijah and Jesus and, in however slight a measure at first, begin to participate in their exaltation.   With the two dejected disciples he may walk the road to Emmaus,[3] and hear the wise words of their temporarily unknown Companion.   At the description of the breaking of the bread he may then become illumined by that inner light which shone when ". . . their eyes were opened, and they knew him. . . .".   Such indeed, I suggest, is part of the intention of the inspired authors.   As one studies the Scriptures of the world, therefore, one must read intuitively, sensitively, with one's mind open and responsive to that vaster consciousness which so often seems waiting to burst through.   Thus, the first key is that some recorded events also occur interiorly.

PEOPLE PERSONIFY HUMAN QUALITIES

The *second key* is that each of the *dramatis personae* introduced into the stories represents a condition of consciousness and a quality of character. All the actors are personifications of aspects of human nature, of attributes, principles, powers, faculties, limitations, weaknesses and errors of man. When purely human beings are the heroes, the life of a person evolving normally is being described.   When the hero is semi-divine, however, the accent is upon the hastened progress of the spiritual Self of man, particularly after it has begun to assume preponderant power.   When the central figure is an *Avatār* [4] or " descent " of an Aspect of Deity, the account of His experiences also describes those passed through during the later phases of human evolution to the stature of perfected manhood. Such, I suggest, is the general purpose and such the method of the ancient writers of the world's immortal allegories, parables and myths.

---

[1] SOUL.   When spelt with a capital " S " this word refers to the unfolding, immortal, spiritual Self of man, the true individuality behind the bodily veil.   Whens spelt with a small " s " it is used for the *psyche* or mental, emotional and vital parts of the mortal man, Heb. *Nephesh chaiah,* " souls of life " or " living soul ".   *Gen.* 2: 7.

[2] *Gal.* 4: 19.

[3] *Lk.* 24: 13–31.

[4] *Avatār* (Sk.).   The doctrine of Divine incarnation or " descent ".   See Glossary.

The Deity or Father when introduced into a narrative generally refers to the highest spiritual Essence in man, the Divine Spark, the Monad,[1] as also to the Oversoul of the race. Those who are following the pathway of Initiation seek to hasten this realisation, first of their divine, immortal nature and thereafter of their unbroken unity with the Supreme Lord of All. This full recognition of man's unity with God, of the oneness of man-Spirit with God-Spirit, is the ultimate goal for all mankind. In Hinduism this state is called *Moksha* or Liberation; in Buddhism, *Nirvāna* or conscious absorption; in Christianity, Salvation, Ascension, Christhood.

In this method of Biblical study the characters—divine, semi-divine, patriarchal and human—are thus regarded as personifications of principles and powers of both Nature as the Macrocosm, and of man as the microcosm. Allowances must, however, be made for differing correspondences necessitated by the stories themselves. This reading is supported by St. Paul, who writes: ". . . all these things happened unto them for ensamples "[2] and ". . . it is written, that Abraham had two sons, the one by a bondmaid, the other by a freewoman . . . which things are an allegory. . . ."[3] It is not unreasonable to assume that such a theory may also be true of many other portions of the Bible. One may even go further than this and assert that the practice of studying the Scriptures of the world in their literal meaning, and as records of actual historical events alone, can lead to grave error and serious confusion of mind.

Other errors in modern Christianity urgently need to be corrected, I submit. Amongst these are: the already mentioned degradation of the concept of the Divine Emanator of the Universe to the level of a tribal god;[4] reliance upon an external (instead of an interior) redemptive power; and the erection of a vast though changing theological edifice founded upon dogmas, some of which are based upon a literal reading of the Scriptures.[5]

These difficulties are all avoided, and profound inspiration consistent with reason is gained, by the recognition of a mystical intent and meaning underlying many portions of the Scriptures and Mythologies of the peoples

[1] Monad. (Gr.)—" Alone". Other terms are the Immortal Germ, the Logos of the Soul, the Dweller in the Innermost. See Glossary.

[2] *I Cor.* 10: 11.

[3] *Gal.* 4: 22–24.

[4] Exoteric Hebraism, and a literal reading of certain Books of the Old Testament alone present this view of Jehovah. Kabbalism, the theosophy of the Hebrews, their esoteric wisdom, proclaims the unnamed Deity as the self-existent, impersonal Emanator of Cosmos and all that it contains. See Appendix, *The Sephirothal Tree.*

[5] Even as this work is in course of preparation, many of these dogmas are being subjected to critical re-examination by the clergy and laity of certain Christian denominations such as, for example, the Roman Catholic, notably at its Ecumenical Council of recent years.

of old. Thus the humility, the devotion and the selfless love of Mary, the Mother of Jesus; the human frailty and the inherent sainthood of a Magdalene and a Peter; the valuable busyness of Martha and, evidently in the eyes of Jesus, the even more valuable, spiritual, contemplative aspects of human nature and modes of life displayed by her sister Mary [1] —all these attributes form part of the character of every individual, the conditions of life drawing out now one and now another. On the surface the remark to Martha, which almost reads like a rebuke, might seem to be somewhat unfair. Apparently, however, Jesus was referring to the fact discovered and taught by every mystic that only in complete quietude of body and mind may the voice of the Master within be heard. Elijah appears to have made this discovery, for after the wind, the earthquake and the fire a silence fell upon him and in that silence he heard the " still small voice ".[2] The Psalmist in his turn received similar guidance from the Lord, Who said to him: " Be still, and know that I am God. . . ." [3]

Applying the second key, which is that the *dramatis personae of* many scriptural narratives represent human characteristics, the twelve disciples of Jesus are found to personify attributes and potentialities of man. For example, a twelvefold classification of them as microcosmic manifestations of the qualities given by astrologers to the Zodiacal Signs is discernible. Discipleship, or nearness to the divine Teacher, indicates that the evolution of the disciple has reached an advanced stage. Ultimately all powers of heart, mind and Spirit will be fully developed. Only as the twelve zodiacal qualities in man are " discipled "—or disciplined and refined—is he able to respond to his own inner spiritual will and to comprehend pure wisdom, both of which are personified by the Master. The Christ Presence and Power—whether asleep as in the ship on Galilee,[4] awakening or being " born " as in the mystical Nativity,[5] or fully grown to " the measure of the stature of the fulness of Christ " [6]—must, however, be added to all human attributes in order to present by means of personification a description of the fully " perfected " man.

The interaction between these various aspects of human nature, the effects they produce upon one another, the waxing or waning of one or more of them at different times and in different lives, and the gradual, triumphant emergence and predominance of the royal spiritual Self, the Immortal King within, personified by the Saviour and the hero of every saga—all this is allegorically portrayed by the Initiated authors of the

[1] *Lk.* 10: 38–42.
[2] *I Kings*, 19: 12.
[3] *Ps.* 46: 10.
[4] *Mk.* 4: 38.
[5] *Gal.* 4: 19.
[6] *Eph.* 4: 13.

inspired portions of the Scriptures of the world. The marriages in which many of these exploits culminate may be interpreted as symbolic references to the unification of the consciousness of the outer and the inner, the mortal and the immortal selves of men. In mystical literature they are not inaptly referred to as " heavenly marriages ". Thus the narratives themselves describe the experiences—particularly the tests, ordeals, defeats and victories—of one person, who is man himself. Successful exploits describe interior achievements, while partial and complete failures, defeats and surrenders are allegories of temporary victories of the purely human over the divine in man—conquests of matter over Spirit. Thus the second key is that each of the *dramatis personae* represents a condition of conscious-ness and a quality of character.

STORIES DRAMATISE PHASES OF HUMAN EVOLUTION

The *third key* is that each story may be regarded as a graphic descrip-tion of the experiences of the human Soul as it passes through the stages, and their intermediate phases, of its evolutionary journey to the Promised Land (cosmic consciousness)—the summit of human attainment. Inspired allegories are always distinguishable from mere novels and biographies by several characteristics, such as the intrusion of the supernatural and the inclusion in the story of angelic and divine beings, even of Deity itself. When these are found the existence of a hidden revelation may always be suspected. The reader possessed of and applying the keys may then penetrate the veil of symbolism and find that hidden wisdom which it had concealed.

In the main the manifold experiences of the immortal Self of each man on its pathway towards perfection are, as stated above, narrated as the adventures of numbers of persons in any one story. The twelve labours of Hercules, each susceptible of association with one of the twelve Signs of the Zodiac, the voyage of the Argonauts, the experiences of the Israelites, and the lives of the Lord Shri Krishna, the Lord Buddha and the Lord Christ, amongst many others, are all descriptive in the symbolic manner of the journey of the Soul and the psychological, intellectual and spiritual unfoldments which occur on that pilgrimage.

In this third method of interpretation, each story may be studied from at least two points of view. The first of these refers to normal evolutionary progress and the accompanying mental and emotional states, whilst the second reveals the allegories as more especially descriptive of the experiences of those who enter in at the strait gate and pursue the narrow way.[1]

---

[1] *Matt.* 7: 13–14.

In the Parable of the Sower [1] the different conditions of the ground —as the Christ explained privately to His disciples [2]—represent various evolutionary phases and states of spiritual receptiveness of the race and the individual, from complete unresponsiveness (wayside and rocky ground) to full perception and ratification (fertile ground). In the Parable of the Ten Virgins,[3] the foolish maidens may be regarded as those who are not as yet sufficiently evolved to be able to respond to impulses descending from their Higher Self (the bridegroom), and therefore not really to be blamed. The wise virgins, on the other hand, may be interpreted as personifying all those in whom the spiritual Self has attained to a considerable degree of evolutionary unfoldment. The outer, physical nature has then become sufficiently developed to be aware of this fact and to give expression in the conduct of daily life to higher idealism and the fruits of spiritual experiences. This state is, in its turn, followed by the progressive illumination of the mind-brain by the Ego (betrothal), leading to the fusion of the immortal and mortal natures (marriage).

The incidents of the marriage feast of Cana [4] may thus be taken to refer to this interior union achieved by those who have awakened the power of the Christ Presence which is within every man, allegorically indicated by the physical presence of the Master. After this attainment the coarser desires of the emotional nature (water) are transmuted into wisdom and spiritual intuitiveness (wine). Marriages of heroes and heroines in Mythologies and Scriptures, as we have seen, indicate that the all-essential blending of the mortal personality with the immortal Ego, and the further merging of the human individuality with the divine Self and life of the Universe as a whole, " the Mystic Identity " or cosmic consciousness, have both been attained.[5] The presence of the Christ in this story, as in all narratives in which He appears, including those which describe the " miracles ", implies that the phase of the evolutionary journey of the Soul has been entered at which spiritual wisdom, spiritual intuitiveness and a Christlike love and compassion are already well developed and active throughout the personal nature. The changing of water into wine at such ' marriages " is not a miracle, but rather a natural process which occurs when a steadfast aspirant finds and successfully treads the

[1] *Matt.* 13: 1-9.
[2] *Matt.* 13: 18-23.
[3] *Matt.* 25: 1-13.
[4] *Jn.* 2: 1-11.
[5] The numerous, and in the literal sense scandalous, *amours* of Zeus, the Father of the Gods, are all susceptible of similar interpretation, namely of unions between the Divine and the mortal in human nature. Indeed, each *amour* with its specific symbology (cloud, swan, shower of gold and bull, for example) may be interpreted as descriptive of a descent of the inner spiritual Self into union with the less Divine and also purely mortal levels of human consciousness.

narrow way. The grape and the wine also symbolise knowledge, wisdom and comprehension of the spirit of things. As fermentation gives a certain " strength " to wine, so the action of the intellect upon accumulated esoteric knowledge turns it into pure wisdom, implicit insight and deeply penetrative intuitiveness. Thus the third key is that many Scriptural stories allegorically describe phases of man's evolutionary journey and their accompanying mystical experiences.

THE SYMBOLISM OF LANGUAGE

The *fourth key* is that some physical objects, as also certain words, have each their own special symbolic meaning. In the cipher of the Bible such words are chiefly used to denote levels of human awareness. Those referring to earthly or physical objects are descriptive of states of consciousness and attributes of character pertaining to the waking state. Water and its associations refer Macrocosmically to universal Space and microcosmically to the emotions. With certain exceptions, air and fire refer to the intuition and the mind respectively. Fire, it should be added, also has reference to the manifested creative life-force of the Logos and that same force as the procreative power in man. This is referred to as the Serpent Fire or *Kundalini* [1] and frequently represented by dragons and serpents. Thus the fourth key is that some physical objects and certain words have each their own symbolic meaning.

SOME APPLICATIONS OF THE KEYS

The Sacred Language of the Initiates of the Mystery Schools of old is indeed formed of hierograms and symbols rather than of words alone, their interpretation being ever constant, as constant also is the doctrine which this Language everywhere reveals. Many such words might thus

---

[1] *Kundalini* (Sk.)—" The coiled up, universal Life Principle ". A sevenfold, occult power in Universe (*Maha Kundali*) and man (*Kundalini*), functioning in the latter in a spiral or coiling action, mainly in the spinal cord but also throughout the nervous systems. It is represented in Greek symbology by the Caduceus. When supernormally aroused, this fiery force ascends into the brain by a serpentine path, hence its other name—the " Serpent Fire ". Thus *Kundalini* is the power of life, one of the forces of Nature, and the seven-layered power in the base of the spine of man. In has three currents which flow along three canals in the spinal cord, named *Ida* (negative), *Pingala* (positive) and *Sushumna* (neutral). These names are sometimes also applied—erroneously—to the currents of force which flow in these canals. This occult electricity is intimately associated with Azoth of the Alchemists, the creative principle in Nature, and *Akasa* (Sk.), the subtle, supersensuous, spiritual essence which pervades all space. q.v. *The Hidden Wisdom in the Holy Bible*, Vol. I, Pt. III, Ch. I, under " Serpents " and *Lecture Notes of the School of the Wisdom*, Vol. II, Ch. I, Sec. III, Geoffrey Hodson; *The Serpent Power*, Arthur Avalon (Sir John Woodroffe).

be regarded as the locks into which the appropriate keys must be fitted. These keys consist of knowledge of the secret meanings given to the words by the Initiated writers of old.

The sacred wisdom consists of seven layers, and this fact is allegorically referred to on many occasions. The fiery furnace, for example, had to be heated " seven times more than it was wont to be heated " [1] before the three men—Shadrach, Meshach and Abednego—were joined by a fourth, who appeared " like the Son of God ".[2] Similarly, the walls of Jericho were circumambulated on the seventh day seven times before they fell down.[3]

The idea thus emerges that in order to discover the Sacred Wisdom of the Christian and other Scriptures we must divest ourselves of the notion that they were conceived and written entirely as chronologically and historically authentic accounts of actual events. Rather are they to be read as blends of history, metaphor and revelations of occult and mystic lore. The Gospel narrative, for example, in its Initiatory [4] interpretation describes the progress of an advanced and elevated Soul through the final ascending phases of evolution until the highest, the Ascension is attained. To be fully appreciated, the great drama must be transferred from purely material to psychological, intellectual and spiritual realms and levels of human experience. A commentary on the Gospel narrative from this point of view forms the subject-matter of Parts Five and Six of Volume I of this work.

The disciples are thus personifications of the noblest attributes of man (the second key). Though still imperfect, they are becoming increasingly spiritualised or brought into the presence of their Master, Who personates the Dweller in the Innermost, the God-Self of man, the Logos of the Soul. The disciples are not yet equal to the Christ, being younger in evolution and in consequence still under the delusion of self-separateness. This is shown by their question as to who will be greatest in the kingdom of heaven.[5] They are still tainted by grosser material attributes, hence the deeply symbolical washing of their feet by their Master.[6] A traitor (Judas, in one of several possible interpretations [7]

---

[1] *Dan.* 3: 19.

[2] *Dan.* 3: 25.

[3] *Joshua,* 6: 1–20 (Interpretations of these passages will be offered at the appropriate places in successive Volumes).

[4] q.v.   *The Hidden Wisdom in the Holy Bible,* Vol. I, Pt. VI, Geoffrey Hodson.

[5] *Matt.* 18: 1.

[6] *Jn.* 13: 3–17.

[7] Amongst these are that Judas created conditions in which he expected the Christ to display His divinity and escape His attackers, whilst another expectation was that the Lord would free Himself from the Cross and thus demonstrate before all men the truth of His affirmation—also proclaimed at the Baptism—that He was indeed the Son of God. The hope is also supposed to have been held by Judas that, in thus manifesting His divinity, the Lord would at the same time justify the disciples in their belief in Him as being one with the Father.

personifying cupidity and treachery) still lurks in their midst. He must be self-revealed and self-slain before the great Ascension can occur. The Master admonishes, rebukes and warns them, indicating the spiritualising activity of the divine Presence within.

By the exercise of theurgic powers many of the recorded—and mis-called—miracles could have been performed by an Adept, or even by an Initiate of lesser degree. In possible mystical interpretations they also illustrate the processes of arousing into activity the faculty of responsiveness to spiritual vision (restoring sight) and to the still, small voice within (restoring hearing), the free exercise of the intellect liberated from rigid orthodoxy (curing those paralysed), and an awakening to full spiritual awareness and knowledge (raising from the dead). This approach will be used in those later Volumes of this work in which the life of Christ as related in the New Testament will be considered.

If this view be accepted, then the Gospel Story, and indeed all the inspired portions of the Bible, are addressed less to the reasoning mind than to the intuition, which can perceive in them references to the evolution of the spiritual Soul of both Universe and man; for, as we have seen, the processes of the development and active use of latent deific powers are portrayed in World Scriptures by means of symbols and dramatic allegories. This mystical view, it may be repeated, does not totally deny the presence of history. The kernel of tradition within the stories can still be a record of real events, however much the illumined authors may have lifted them out of time and space by the use of the Sacred Language.

INCONGRUITIES AS CLUES TO DEEPER MEANINGS

The student of the allegorical language is nearly always given a hint or clue—one, moreover, which at first sight might seem to be rather strange. This clue consists of an additional veil, cover or blind which tends to increase confusion and so to repel those who regard as purely literal those portions of Scripture in which potentially dangerous, because power-bestowing, knowledge is both revealed and concealed. Those who seek the hidden wisdom should guard carefully against this repulsion, whether it is aroused by statements which are incredible or impossible, or by stories which offend logic and one's sense of justice, decency and morality. Unfortunately many people *are* turned away from the Scriptures, and even from religion itself, by the discovery of these characteristics. The study and exposition of the Sacred Language are for this reason I submit, of very great importance.

SOME INCREDIBILITIES AND THEIR POSSIBLE ELUCIDATION

An apparent digression is here made, therefore, briefly to examine certain incongruities in the Bible and to suggest solutions of the problems which they admittedly present. The statements concerning them given in Volume One of this work, Part One, Chapter Three, and in Part One, Chapter Two of this Volume, are here repeated in a somewhat revised form. They will also be further and more fully examined—together with many others—in their appropriate places in this and succeeding Volumes. These repetitions arise from a conviction of the great importance of the elucidation of the many incredible and incongruous accounts of supposed facts which occur in the Bible.

Certain admittedly difficult Bibilical passages are:

(*a*) Three days and nights of creation pass before the sun is created.[1] Here universal creative epochs of activity and quiescence,[2] rather than alterations of day and night on a single planet, are implied.

(*b*) Deity enjoins massacre and extermination.[3]

In the Sacred Language enemies sometimes personify attributes which are hostile to the happiness and spiritual unfoldment of the individual or nation whose story is being told. If the enemies of the Israelites are so regarded, then Divine commands to massacre them lose their offensiveness, since extermination of undesirable characteristics is being enjoined. Whilst the normal history of an immigrant nation confronted by local adversaries has a rightful place in the national story, whenever the Lord God is introduced into a narrative and made responsible for events described, the authors may be presumed to be deliberately drawing attention to a mystical revelation. In such a reading the Lord God personifies the inner spiritual Self of the individual, the Monad, which is bringing its purifying and directive influences to bear upon the moral man.

(*c*) Noah collects pairs of every living creature from all parts of the Earth—arctic, temperate and tropical—and keeps them alive in the Ark for forty days.[4]

According to a universal principle, also operative throughout physical Nature, the seeds of all living things are preserved during the quiescence ("Night" and "Flood") which intervenes between one period of activity or creative epoch and its successor. The fruits of each human rebirth are, for example, preserved between successive lives, the Ark being the symbol of the conserving vehicle—cosmic or human.

(*d*) The Lord declares Himself to be "a jealous God, visiting the iniquity of the fathers upon the children unto the third and fourth generation of them that hate me."[5]

[1] *Gen.* 1: 1–19.
[2] See Glossary—Brahmā's Day and Brahmā's night.
[3] *Gen.* 7: 4 and 23; 19: 13, 24, 25; *Ex.* 22: 20; *Joshua* 6: 21.
[4] *Gen.* 7: 2–4.
[5] *Ex.* 20: 5.

In the succession of reincarnations each human life is as the "father" of those which follow, they being referred to as its children. Read literally, the above quoted declaration makes of God a self-proclaimed monster of cruelty and injustice. Even a human father would not be guilty of such conduct. A more acceptable reading of this passage—depending upon the doctrine that the human Soul evolves to Christhood by means of successive lives on Earth—is that character developments are transferred from one life (the father) to its successors (the children), whilst the effects of actions may either be received in the same life in which such actions are performed or else precipitated in succeeding incarnations.

(e) Jericho is brought down by the sound of trumpets, horns and shouting.[1]

The Logos Doctrine [2] of the formation and the dissolution of Universes by the occult potencies of sound, and their use in chanting to break down limitations of consciousness (walls) and to purify its vehicles, may well be implied. Archaeologists have concluded that the destruction of the walls of Jericho was caused by an earthquake.[3]

(f) Joshua makes the sun and moon stand still to prolong the day.[4]

By the practice of contemplation the divine Will in man, his source of spiritual power and light (symbolically the sun), is brought to its maximum power (the midst of the heavens), enabling the mortal man to overcome the enemies of the Soul (Gibeonites) and attain serenity (victory and peace).

(g) The defeat of Samson by cutting off his hair, and his destruction of the temple by leaning his weight upon two of its pillars.[5]

Hair is the symbol of the effective relationship between the spiritual Soul and the mind-brain. When, symbolically, this contact is severed the power and the guidance of the inner Self are lost to the outer man, who becomes a slave to matter and the senses (Delilah). The spiritual relationship being restored, man attains to equilibrium between the pairs of opposites (the pillars), limitations (the walls of the temple) upon consciousness are dissipated and undesired qualities (the Philistines) are destroyed.

(h) Elijah goes to heaven in a chariot of fire.[6]

The sublimation of the fiery, creative force in man enables him to ascend to spiritual states of consciousness (heaven).

(i) Jonah enters the belly of a great fish and remains unharmed for three days and three nights.[7]

[1] *Joshua* 6: 1–20.

[2] q.v. *Lecture Notes of the School of the Wisdom*, Vol II, Pt. II, Ch. II, Sec. 2 ,Geoffrey Hodson.

[3] q.v. *The Bible as History*, pp. 156–157, Werner Keller.

[4] *Joshua* 10: 12–14.

[5] *Judges* 16: 17–30.

[6] *2 Kings* 2: 11.

[7] *Jonah* 1: 17.

At Initiation the Candidate is withdrawn from his body (the ship), enters the Underworld (the sea), and is then elevated into full spiritual awareness or attains to Christ-consciousness (the fish).[1] After the passage of sufficient time (generally three days and three nights), he returns to his body (is delivered to dry land).

(j) Tribute money is found inside a particular fish.[2]
All the necessities (the tribute money) for spiritual, intellectual—and sometimes even physical—living are to be found in the divine aspects of human nature (the fish). Man is encouraged to discover (catch) and draw upon the Christ power within him.

(k) A fig tree is withered for not bearing fruit in the early spring.[3]
Unless a man gives freely of the fruits of his life, they will wither away and be lost. The text may be regarded as the enunciation of a law as well as the description of an act. A fuller interpretation of this incident appears in Volume One, Part One, Chapter Three of this work.

(l) Lazarus is raised after being dead for four days.[4]
Death symbolises the total absence of spiritual awareness. Miraculous restoration to life implies its attainment or recovery by virtue of the action of the interior divine Power and Presence (the Christ). The period of death refers to the time during which the body of the Candidate is unconscious (figurative death) while Initiation is being conferred. In the Ancient Mysteries death metaphorically described the condition of the uninitiated, whilst resurrection referred to passage through the Sacred Rite of Initiation.[5]

(m) The flesh of Christ is described as " meat " and the blood of Christ as " drink ", their consumption being declared essential to life.[6]
Our Lord insists that salvation depends upon partaking of His flesh and blood. The " flesh " of a divine Being is a symbol for spiritual truth and law. Eating such flesh implies intellectual absorption and full comprehension of eternal verities. Blood symbolises the ever-outpoured divine life by which the Universe and man are spiritually sustained. Drinking such blood refers to conscious coalescence with the one life of the Universe and realization of unity with its Source. When read literally the passage is not only repellant and offensive to reason, but also closes the mind to the profound mystical import of the Lord's utterance. Furthermore, being confronted with its total incredibility if so read, the pronouncement might

---

[1] q.v. *Lecture Notes of the School of the Wisdom*, Vol. II, Pt. I, Ch. I, Sec. 1, Geoffrey Hodson.

[2] *Matt.* 17: 27.

[3] *Matt.* 21: 19.

[4] *Jn.* 11: 39–44.

[5] q.v. *The Mysteries of Eleusis*, p. 47, Prof. Georges Meautis.

[6] *Jn.* 6: 47–58.

even prevent or delay an endeavour to attain by contemplation to the state of illumination metaphorically described. Hence the great importance of mystical interpretation of such difficult passages.

(n) The events of the night before the Crucifixion are too numerous for all of them to have occurred in the period allotted to them.[1] Amongst these are:

The Last Supper.

The agony in the Garden.

The betrayal by Judas.

Appearance before Annas and then Caiaphas, and the questionings.

Appearance before the Sanhedrin and the questioning.

Appearance before Pilate and the trial in the Hall of Judgment. (Courts to try malefactors did not normally sit in the middle of the night).

The visit to Herod, told of by St. Luke.

The return to Pilate.

Pilate's speeches and the washing of his hands, recorded by St. Matthew only.

The scourging, mocking and arraying of Jesus in purple robes.

The long and painful journey to Golgotha, followed by the nailing to the Cross.

The difficulty disappears, however, if the whole experience is regarded as being descriptive of changes of consciousness as the state of human perfection is approached.[2]

A significant reference to this interpretation is found in the Apocryphal *Acts of John.* This is the earliest of five books which were formed into a corpus by the Manichaeans and substituted by them for the canonical *Acts.* The book contains the following passages, which describe actions of the Lord immediately before and during the Crucifixion. These include both singing an antiphonal hymn and ceremonial dancing, after which the Lord said to John, who found himself on a mountain beside Him: " ' John, unto the multitude below in Jerusalem I am being crucified and pierced with lances and reeds, and gall and vinegar is given me to drink. But unto thee I speak, and what I speak hear thou. I put it into thy mind to come up into this mountain, that thou mightest hear those things which it behoveth a disciple to learn from his teacher and a man from his God.'

" And having thus spoken, he showed me a cross of light fixed (set up) and about the cross a great multitude. . . . And the Lord himself I beheld above the cross, not having any shape, but only a voice: and a voice not

---

[1] *Lk.* 22 and 23.

[2] *Eph.* 4: 13. See also *The Hidden Wisdom in the Holy Bible,* Vol. I, Pt. VI, Ch. II, Geoffrey Hodson.

3

such as was familiar to us, but one sweet and kind and truly of God, saying unto me: ' John, it is needful that one should hear these things from me, for I have need of one that will hear. . . . But this is not the cross of wood which thou wilt see when thou goest down hence: neither am I he that is on the cross, whom now thou seest not, but only hearest his (or a) voice . . . for know thou that I am wholly with the Father, and the Father, with me.   Nothing, therefore, of the things which they will say of me have I suffered: nay, that suffering also which I showed unto thee and the rest in the dance I will that it be called a mystery.' " *et seq.*[1]

Whilst interpretations of these and a great many other incongruous statements in the Bible will be offered in their due place in this and later Volumes, fuller explanations of two or three of the more perplexing texts may, perhaps, usefully be added here.

With regard to (*a*), applying the fourth key—that some physical objects, as also certain words, have each their own special Macrocosmic meaning—the days and nights of creation refer to alternation of creative activity or " day " and quiescence or " night ".   These are referred to in the text of this work by their Sanskrit names of *Manvantara* [2] and *Pralaya* [2] respectively.

With reference to (*f*), Joshua personifies the Initiate who has brought his Monadic Will, symbolised by the sun, to its position of maximum power (the midst of the heavens or zenith).   In consequence, he prevents the oncoming of night (in a microcosmic interpretation, mental darkness) and maintains his personal nature (the battlefield of Gibeon) in that condition of prolonged illumination (day) which ensures victory in the interior battle between Spirit (the Israelites) and matter (their enemies). This wonderful allegory has been more fully considered in Volume I, Part One, Chapter V of this work.   Even from this brief interpretation, however, the element of impossibility may be regarded as both a hint or clue and an indication of a profound occult idea for which the reader is encouraged to search.

With regard to (*m*), quite clearly Our Lord was not exhorting mankind to consume human flesh and blood when He said: " Whoso eateth my flesh, and drinketh my blood, hath eternal life; and I will raise him up at the last day.   For my flesh is meat indeed, and my blood is drink indeed. He that eateth my flesh, and drinketh my blood, dwelleth in me, and I in him.   As the living Father hath sent me, and I live by the Father: so he that eateth me, even he shall live by me."[3]   The words " flesh ", " blood ", " eateth " and " drinketh " are not to be read in the usual

---

[1] *The Apocryphal New Testament*, newly translated by Montague Rhodes James, Litt. D., F.B.A., F.S.A., Oxford University Press, pp. 254-255.

[2] See Glossary—Chain.

[3] *Jn.* 6: 54-57.

sense. They are symbolical and metaphorical, and are so used in order to convey a hidden meaning.

What, then, could those four words—" flesh ", " blood ", " eateth " and " drinketh "—mean? The flesh of Christ may be interpreted as divine truths, spiritual laws, or that in which He as Logos is clothed, by which He is covered and through which He is made manifest. The time comes —and is hastened as " The way of holiness "[1] is entered upon—when the human intellect absorbs divine knowledge, becomes illumined and inspired by the interior discovery and revelation of spiritual truths. This experience in consciousness is symbolised as eating the flesh of Christ. Bread is also used to describe knowledge of divine laws, processes and purposes. Eating consecrated breads is an allegory for the reception, absorption and application to life of that knowledge, *gnosis*, *sophia*, esoteric wisdom. Bread is also a symbol of the cyclic regeneration of life after each return to the seed state.

The blood of Christ is the ever-outpoured divine life by which the Universe is sustained and without which it could not live. The life-force does, indeed, perform a function for the Universe and all it contains which closely resembles the office which human blood performs for the physical body. Normally man is unaware either of the omnipresence of this divine outpouring or of the fact that it is the spiritually sustaining power within him.

At a certain stage of the evolution of the human intellect this fact is intuitively perceived. Such realisation by the neophyte can be hastened by means of certain spiritual practices, by meditation and prayer, and by the aid of his Master, of the Hierophant and of other Officiants in the Sacred Initiatory Rites of the Temples of the Greater Mysteries. Ultimately full knowledge may be gained of the outpouring of the Christ-life into the Universe and man, and also of man's identity with that life and its divine Source. This attainment is described symbolically as drinking Christ's blood. Our Lord may be assumed to have been referring to a state of consciousness of unity with the Cosmic Christ and His outpoured vital energy rather than to an act of physical nutrition.

Once this symbolical eating and drinking, this spiritual *agape*, has occurred, then the process can be initiated in others who in their turn, starving for truth, can be fed in vast multitudes. As the incident of feeding the five thousand [2] allegorically tells, in such ministration there is not, neither can there be, any loss. On the contrary there is more of spiritual wisdom, knowledge and upwelling vitality afterwards than before—even unto " twelve baskets full ".

[1] *Is.* 35: 8.
[2] *Matt.* 14: 15–21.

Thus, in the fourth interpretation, all objects, as also many words, have each their own special meaning. The symbols employed of the Sacred Language are associated with one or more of the four elements of earth, water, air or fire.

PART TWO

INTERPRETATION OF FIVE EPISODES FROM THE BOOK OF GENESIS

Acknowledgements are made to the Journal of the Theosophical Society, *The Theosophist*, in which the subject-matter of this Part—here somewhat revised—appeared as Articles in 1964–65.

All Biblical quotations and references in this work are from the King James Version of the Holy Bible.

INTRODUCTION

THE following five interpretations of portions of the *Book of Genesis*, abridged from the fuller expositions which follow later, are here offered in advance in the hope that they may serve as a preparation for those more detailed studies.

My statements concerning the laws and processes behind the formation and physical manifestation of Universes and the evolutionary procedures throughout Nature, physical and super-physical, have as their main sources the literature, both ancient and modern, of the Ageless Wisdom. The Neo-Platonists named the fundamental truths which underlie all creeds *Theosophia*,[1] a title which has continued to be applied to the body of ideas which form the substratum and basis of all world religions and philosophies. Throughout this work the ancient knowledge, esoteric (Secret Doctrine) and exoteric (revealed teachings), is also referred to as occult science and occult philosophy.[2] Theosophy must not, however, be regarded as a completed system to be accepted as such. On the contrary, as must be true of everything both organic and spiritual, it cannot have a fixed geometrical outline the whole of which can, as it were, be traced on paper by rule and compass. The concepts of the oneness of all life and of the existence of the Eternal Selves of Universe and man refuse to be objectively defined; for this would be setting a limit to both truth itself and man's capacity to discover it.

Some fifty years' study of Theosophy, comparative religion and philosophy, and attempted personal investigation of the basic truths presented under the veil of allegory in the Scriptures and Mythologies of earlier races, have inevitably influenced both the trend of my thinking and the gradual unfoldment of the ideas here presented for the consideration of readers of this work. Whilst writing it I have several times repeated —too often it may be thought by some—my main theme. My chief reason for doing this has been that the idea that the Holy Bible is not the inspired word of God from beginning to end may appear somewhat strange and

---

[1] *Theosophia* (Gr.)—" *Divine Wisdom* "—later named Theosophy.

[2] Occult science and occult philosophy. The words " according to my limited understanding and interpretation of their teachings " are to be regarded as implicit in all references to these two aspects of the Secret Doctrine wherever they occur. See Glossary under Occult Science. For a fuller exposition see Vol. I, Pt. I, Ch. VI of this work.

new, even disturbing, to those who are unacquainted with the work of the Analogeticists and Symbologists. Other reasons were: to recall to the mind of the reader certain basic principles governing the allegorical method of writing and its interpretation; to meet the possibility that certain Chapters or parts in the book may be read without reference to the whole work; and to offer such assistance as would be helpful to those readers who may wish to apply these principles to the interpretation of the Scriptures and Mythologies of other ancient peoples.

As I now proceed to offer commentaries upon Biblical passages, briefly here and later more fully, I feel it necessary to warn my readers —particularly those hitherto unacquainted with occult philosophy, upon which I am drawing—that the subject is unavoidably somewhat abstruse. I have become personally convinced, however, that whatever mental effort is involved will be richly rewarding. Knowledge and comprehension of the general plan of human life on Earth are amongst the prizes to be won by those who are willing to delve into the mysterious secrets of Nature hidden beneath many of the apparently historical narratives of which the Bible partly consists.

CHAPTER I

EDEN, EVE AND THE "FALL" OF MAN

THE first of the five passages selected for abridged interpretation is taken from the Second Chapter of the *Book of Genesis*, in which the Lord God is said to have taken one of the ribs of Adam while he slept and made from it a woman—Eve.[1] Since the reasoning mind, familiar with modern anthropology, is unable to accept this statement literally, it must be either discarded out of hand or subjected to a close analysis. What, then, has occult philosophy to say concerning the first appearance on Earth of single-sexed man and woman?

The original human form typified by Adam, it is taught, was dual-sexed [2] and unconsciously self-reproductive. The play of the creative force within the cells of Adam's body did not directly affect either nerves or brain, no sex impulse being experienced. Self-fructified, he reproduced his kind much as plants or trees give of their seed-bearing flowers and fruit. As the evolutionary cycle progressed in which the physical body was developed and the dual-natured, masculine-feminine, human spiritual Soul [3] entered into closer association with it, a change began to occur. The single-sexed man and woman of today gradually developed out of the original, dual-sexed, single organism. Adam alone in the Garden of Eden typified the first androgynous, sexually innocent humanity, whilst Adam and Eve exemplify the first completely separate men and women. The production of Eve from a rib of Adam whilst he slept may therefore be regarded as an allegorical description of this natural process, the Lord God here personifying the evolutionary impulse and the effects which, through long ages, it eventually produces. A reference may also be discerned to the teaching of occult philosophy that the race which is personified by Adam had bones, whilst that which preceded it was boneless.

[1] *Gen.* 2: 21, 22.

[2] Dual-sexed. "All the invertebrate ancestors of man", writes Ernest Haeckel, "from the Gastraeda up to the Chordonia, must have been hermaphrodite. So, probably, were the earliest skulled animals. One extremely weighty piece of evidence of this is afforded by the remarkable fact that even in Vertebrates, in Man as well as other Vertebrates, the original rudiment of the sexual organ is hermaphrodite." *The Evolution of Man*, Ernst Haeckel.

[3] Soul—q.v. Glossary.

The Second Chapter of *Genesis* thus tells of both the bodily development of primitive man and also the psychological condition arising from it.   As stated above, androgynous, he was unconscious of sex; instinctually reproductive, he was innocent of passion.   This condition of human passionlessness, symbolised by Adam in the Garden of Eden, is itself descriptive of the state of the embodied soul before the awakening and activity of consciously exercised procreative power.   Eden thus emblematically represents both the period from birth to puberty, in the life of each human being, and also the childhood of the human race.

THE ANGEL WITH THE FLAMING SWORD [1]

The expulsion from Eden may, in its turn, be interpreted as an allegory describing the growing up process or the passage of the child from the state of innocence, through adolescence into adult life.   The procedure being perfectly natural, however, involves no sin of either soul or body, whether for the individual or the race.   Applied to consciousness, the story describes the pre-creative (Eden) and the pro-creative (" Fall " and expulsion) stages of human development.   In terms of bodily growth the account refers to the change which occurred in the first human bodies during evolution from the androgynous to the single-sexed state, with the consequent experience of sex desire and the present method of procreation. The Eden state is then outgrown, childhood having been *naturally* followed by adolescence.   Allegorically, Adam and Eve are " expelled " from Eden, not directly by the decree of a Divine Emanator (*Gen.* III: 23, 24), but by the action of the emitted, irresistible, propellant power of which evolution (growing up) is the result.

In the story of the making of Eve by the Creator out of a rib taken from Adam, his deep sleep refers to the condition of both the nascent mentality and the unawakened, inactive procreative power.   Adam alone thus aptly represents the human race at the first period of the encasement of the Monad [2] in an androgynous, mentally torpid, human form.[3]   Newly enclosed in physical matter, first man was of the earth, earthy.   His task

---

[1] *Gen.* 3: 24.

[2] The evolution of the Monad (Gr.)—" Alone ", " the number one ", " a unit "· The divine Spirit in man, the " Dweller in the Innermost ", which is said to evolve by means of the projection of its Ray (not an actual descent) through the sub-human kingdom, of Nature into the human, and thence to the stature of the Adept, beyond which extend unlimited evolutionary heights.   The description of the destiny of man given by the Lord Christ supports this concept; for He said: " Be ye (Ye shall be—R.V.) therefore perfects even as your Father which is in heaven is perfect."   (*Matt.* 5: 48—A.V.).

[3] Attention is here drawn to the Heb. text of *Gen.* 2: 21 and to the translations of key words as given on p. 161.

was to accustom himself to imprisonment within relatively inert physical substance and gradually to overcome its resistance.

The earliest human bodies were gigantic [1] and somewhat insensitive, with the minimum of nervous organisation and activity. They moved sluggishly and clumsily through tropical vegetation, impelled largely by the desire for food and the instinct for self-preservation. Apparently this was during the Miocene Period.[2] Reproduction was unconscious and passed through both exudatory or "sweat-born" and oviporous stages.[3] This mentally inactive condition is, as stated, typified by Adam in a deep

[1] The following evidence offers partial, but not entirely conclusive, support for the teaching of occult philosophy, concerning the existence of giants:

1. *Gigantopithecus Blacki* is a type of fossil hominoid also known as the Chinese Giant, Ape. Three large molar teeth were found in an apothecary's shop in Hong Kong in 1935. Van Koenigswald maintains that the teeth are non-human and Weidenreich has said they are human. (*Dictionary of Anthropology*, New York Philosophical Library, 1956, p. 232, Charles Winick).

2. *Gigantanthropus*. Professor Ashley Montagu has written: "These are the teeth of an early giant form of extinct man." Professor Franz Weidenreich has said that the teeth are those not of a giant ape but of "a giant man and should, therefore, have been named *Gigantanthropus* and not *Gigantopithecus*." (*Apes, Giants and Man*, Chicago, pp. 29–31 and p. 59, F. Weidenreich).

3. *Meganthropus Palæojavanicus*. At Sangiran, Java, in 1940–41 von Koenigswald found the remains of two jaw fragments that he named *Meganthropus Palæojavanicus*, "giant man from old Java". Weidenreich has ventured to guess that the ancient Javanese giant was bigger than any living gorilla. (*The Science of Man*, New York. Holt, Rinehart and Winstone, 1961, p. 91, Mischa Titiev).

I must add, however, that doubts of the conclusions of Weidenreich are at present based both upon his reliance alone upon the discovery of large molar teeth and jaws, and on the fact that bones of early man found up to now are no larger than those of men of today.

[2] q.v. *The Earth and Its Cycles*, Ch. VIII, E. W. Preston, M.Sc.

[3] Admittedly the latest discoveries by such palaeontologists as Dr. J. Robinson of the Transvaal Museum, Pretoria, and Dr. L. S. B. Leakey, Curator of the Coryndon Museum, Nairobi, Kenya, and Mrs. Leakey, have not revealed evidence supporting the statement of occult philosophy concerning the earliest men on Earth. Presumably the indication would appear in the soft-tissues, and so not be apparent in the fossilised remains. Such discoveries are, however, quite local and reveal nothing concerning beings who may have lived in other parts of the globe. q.v. *The Secret Doctrine* (especially Vol. III), H. P. Blavatsky, and *The Earth and Its Cycles* (especially Chs. 8 and 9), E. W. Preston, M.Sc., where we read: Professor Wood Jones in *Hallmarks of Mankind*, 1948, writes "We must avoid the snare . . . of regarding the more primitive apes as being on the road towards becoming men, since all evidence would seem to show that they are merely apes that fall short in some respects of attaining all the specialisations of their modern representatives. It is true that they have probably arisen nearer to that early parting of the ways in the Primate stem at which the human stock branched off; but they are definitely ape on the branch that leads to the modern Anthropoids and not on that which leads to Homo. . . ." (*Hallmarks of Mankind*, p. 85, F. Wood Jones, 1948).

sleep in the Garden of Eden. The creative life-force was present and active within him, however, even though he knew it not.

Very gradually changes, both physical and psychological, occurred. Physically, one sex attribute began to predominate over the other. Psychologically, awareness of opposite polarity was experienced, depending upon whether the positive or the negative current in the life-force was predominant. These two processes culminated at the end of the androgynous era in the establishment upon this planet of separate male and female forms. Since this first human pair, Adam and Eve, evolved out of a single racial progenitor—Adam by himself, whose body contained the attributes of both sexes—the description of the formation of Eve from the rib of Adam is allegorically appropriate.

Such, in outline, are some teachings of occult philosophy as applied to the story of the Garden of Eden.

THE DIVINE LIFE AS THE PRODIGAL SON

THE MACROCOSMIC CYCLE

The Parable of the Prodigal Son describes the process of the forthgoing of the outpoured, conscious life of the Logos, which bears with it into the field of evolution the Rays or radiations of the Monads of all beings (the " journey into a far country ").

At the beginning of each new manifestation these Monads are at varying stages of development and awareness, according to the degree of unfoldment reached in preceding cycles. At the farthest point of the path of forthgoing, represented in the Earth Scheme of our Solar System by the mineral kingdom of the physical plane, the power, the life and the consciousness of the Monad are most deeply encased in matter. In the parable this phase is portrayed by the deepest degradation of the prodigal son, who fain would have eaten " the husks that the swine did eat ".

The parable also describes in allegory the pathway of return, or evolution, at the close of which all the seed powers of the Monads have become developed to the highest degree possible in any particular cycle. The bliss and the enrichment of the spiritual Soul are symbolised by the welcome, the gifts and the feasting provided for the prodigal son on his return. This major cycle of involution and evolution is repeated in innumerable component sub-cycles of gradually diminishing degree and dimension. Man as Ego repeats it, for example, in each cycle of birth and death. Throughout this book the period of activity is called *Manvantara*, and the quiescence which always follows is termed *Pralaya*.

THE DIVINE LIFE AS THE PRODIGAL SON

THE MACROCOSMIC CYCLE

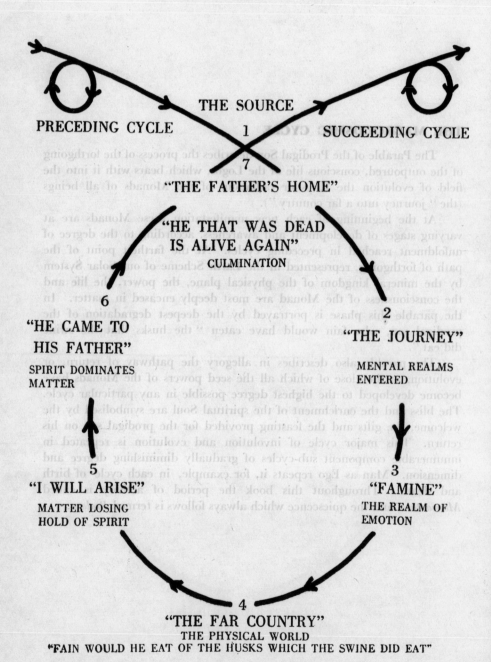

THE SOURCE
1

PRECEDING CYCLE   SUCCEEDING CYCLE

7

"THE FATHER'S HOME"

"HE THAT WAS DEAD
IS ALIVE AGAIN"
CULMINATION

6

"HE CAME TO
HIS FATHER"

SPIRIT DOMINATES
MATTER

2

"THE JOURNEY"

MENTAL REALMS
ENTERED

5

"I WILL ARISE"

MATTER LOSING
HOLD OF SPIRIT

3

"FAMINE"

THE REALM OF
EMOTION

4

"THE FAR COUNTRY"
THE PHYSICAL WORLD
"FAIN WOULD HE EAT OF THE HUSKS WHICH THE SWINE DID EAT"

THE HUMAN SPIRIT AS THE PRODIGAL SON

THE MICROCOSMIC CYCLE

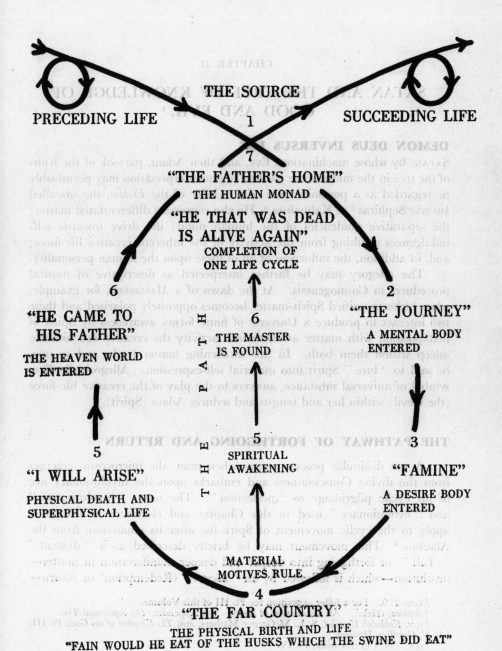

PRECEDING LIFE

THE SOURCE
1

SUCCEEDING LIFE

7

"THE FATHER'S HOME"
THE HUMAN MONAD

**"HE THAT WAS DEAD
IS ALIVE AGAIN"**
COMPLETION OF
ONE LIFE CYCLE

6

6

"THE JOURNEY"
A MENTAL BODY
ENTERED

**"HE CAME TO
HIS FATHER"**

THE HEAVEN WORLD
IS ENTERED

THE MASTER
IS FOUND

THE PATH

5

5
SPIRITUAL
AWAKENING

3

"I WILL ARISE"

PHYSICAL DEATH AND
SUPERPHYSICAL LIFE

"FAMINE"

A DESIRE BODY
ENTERED

4
MATERIAL
MOTIVES RULE.

"THE FAR COUNTRY"
THE PHYSICAL BIRTH AND LIFE
"FAIN WOULD HE EAT OF THE HUSKS WHICH THE SWINE DID EAT"

CHAPTER II

SATAN AND THE TREE OF KNOWLEDGE OF GOOD AND EVIL [1]

DEMON DEUS INVERSUS EST

SATAN, by whose machinations Eve, and then Adam, partook of the fruits of the tree in the midst of the garden, in one interpretation may permissibly be regarded as a personification of an Order of the *Elohim*, the so-called Inverse Sephiras [2] of Kabbalism. [3] He also represents differentiated matter; the separative tendencies of the human mind; the drive towards self-indulgences resulting from the activity of the inherent creative life-force; and, in addition, the influences of all of these upon the human personality.

The allegory may be further interpreted as descriptive of natural procedures in Cosmogenesis. At the dawn of a *Manvantara*, for example, when hitherto unified Spirit-matter becomes oppositely polarised and these two interact to produce a Universe of finite forms, awareness by Spirit of juxtaposition with matter awakens into activity the creative fire hitherto asleep within them both. In this awakening matter leads, and so may be said to " lure " Spirit into material self-expression. Allegorically Eve, symbol of universal substance, answers to the play of the creative life-force (the Devil) within her and tempts and seduces Adam (Spirit).

THE PATHWAY OF FORTHGOING AND RETURN

A not dissimilar process occurs when man, the microcosm, emerges from the divine Consciousness and embarks upon the involutionary arc of his cyclic pilgrimage to " perfection ". The terms " involutionary " and " evolutionary " used in this Chapter and elsewhere in this book apply to the cyclic movement of Spirit-life after its emanation from the Absolute. [4] This movement may be briefly described as a " descent " (" Fall ") or forthgoing into deeper and deeper manifestation in matter— involution—which is followed by an " ascent " (Redemption) or return—

---

[1] *Gen.* 2: 9. For a fuller exposition see Pt. III of this Volume.
[2] *Sephira*, (Heb.). An Emanation of Deity. See Appendix, *The Sephirothal Tree.*
[3] q.v. *Kabbalah Unveiled*, S. L. McGregor Mathers, and *The Kingdom of the Gods*, Pt. III, Ch. V, Geoffrey Hodson.
[4] q.v. Vol. I of this work, Pt. IV.

evolution—to the purely spiritual state from which the cyclic journey begins. The pure spiritual Essence of the human Monad must, in order to develop innate powers, be " lured " or tempted into intimate association with the matter of the worlds of mind, emotion and physical substance. This " descent " or " Fall " is, as stated above, assisted by the Order of Intelligences referred to in esoteric Kabbalism as the Inverse Sephiras (Satan). This Order includes Intelligences who fashioned the mental, emotional and etheric-physical bodies of the first three races of men to inhabit this Earth in the present world period. These *Pitris*,[1] as they are called in Hinduism, also fulfilled the office previously described of " including " or " luring " the Monad-Egos [2] of those races into the bodies which had been constructed for them. Since this materialising function associated with the involutionary phase appears evil from the point of view of the following evolutionary arc which tends towards spiritualisation, these Intelligences are sometimes also referred to as the Satanic Hierarchies.

In Chapter Five of Part Three of my book, *The Kingdom of the Gods*, and more particularly in the descriptive material associated with Plates 29 and 30, I state that when investigating the descent of human Egos into birth I received evidence that a corresponding function is also performed for all human beings by members of the Angelic Hosts. During the pre-natal or downward arc of the cycle of each successive birth, the reincarnating Ego projects a ray of its power, life and consciousness from the realm of Spiritual Intelligence in which it abides. Throughout the gestatory period members of one Order of the Angelic Hosts assist in building the mental, emotional, etheric and physical bodies, in assuring their mutual adjustment, and in inducting into them the reincarnating spiritual Self. A partial record of the research referred to above is to be found in my book *The Miracle of Birth*.

Thus the work of an Order of the so-called Satanic Hierarchy is to install the human Monad-Ego in vehicles of thought, emotion, and physical

[1] *Pitris* (Sk.)—" Forefathers ", " progenitors ". Highly evolved, incorporeal, spiritual beings, products of preceding evolutionary epochs, who build for the Monad the mental, emotional, etheric and physical vehicles whereby it is brought into touch with the external worlds at those levels and is enabled to act and evolve in them. Three of the ten main classes of *pitris* referred to in Hindu philosophy (*Vishnu purāna*) are the *Asuras* who build the mental bodies, the *Agnishvāttas* who build the emotional bodies and the *Barhishads* who build the etheric and physical bodies. Other classes are named *Kumāras* and *Mānasaputras*. The *Pitris* are also referred to as the Fathers who set the types for mankind at the beginning of the various great periods of solar and planetary evolution.

[2] Ego. The threefold, immortal, unfolding spiritual Self of man in its vesture of light, the " Robe of Glory " of the Gnostics and the *Kārana Sharīra* or Causal Body of Hindu philosophy. This higher Triad evolves to Adeptship by virtue of successive lives on Earth, all linked together because they are reincarnations of the same spiritual Self. Thus the Ego is an individualised manifestation of the Monad, which is the eternal Self of man, the Dweller in the innermost, a unit of the Spirit-Essence of the Universe. The term is used throughout this work to denote the spiritual Self of man in which the attribute of individuality inheres. The adjective " Egoic " refers to the Ego in this sense.

4

awareness and activity. The process of descent thereafter culminates in incarnation in physical, dust-formed [1] bodies through which the creative impulse can achieve self-conscious expression. The universal, creative life-force, the " Fire of Creation ", then finds individual manifestation as human love, desire and procreative activity. In addition, the Hierarchy of Intelligences associated with the process of reincarnation and, as we have seen, man's self-conscious sex-life, are personified by Satan. The strange, scriptural figure of the Devil is thus seen as a composite symbol of matter and its resistance to Spirit, of an Order of Intelligences, of natural processes and impulses, and of certain other forces and experiences acting upon and within mankind. Since the separative and prideful tendencies of the human mind and their deliberate expression, the surges of strong desire and the de-spiritualising effects of sexual excesses are all temporarily harmful to man, Satan has come to be regarded as an evil Being, an enemy of mankind. He has also been described as " the shadow of himself which a man sees when he turns his back to the light."

This profound occult knowledge of the completely impersonal Inverse Sephiras, their functions in Nature and the methods whereby their co-operation may be used for evil purposes, is dangerous. Hence, doubtless, its heavy enveiling in World Scriptures and allegories.

The Irish poet, James Stephens, intuited and expressed this profoundly occult teaching in his poem, *The Fullness of Time*: [2]

" On a rusty iron throne,
Past furthest star of space,
I saw Satan sit alone,
Old and haggard was his face;
For his work was done, and he
Rested in eternity.

" And to him from out the sun
Came his father and his friend,
Saying,—Now the work is done
Enmity is at an end—
And He guided Satan to
Paradises that He knew.

" Gabriel, without a frown;
Uriel, without a spear;
Raphael, came singing down,
Welcoming their ancient peer;
And they seated him beside,
One who had been crucified."

---

[1] *Gen.* 2: 7.

[2] *Collected Poems.* James Stephens, MacMillan & Co. Ltd., London, 1931.

THE SERPENT IN EDEN

The symbol of the serpent as tempter of Eve is also appropriate, since the characteristic superphysical mode of manifestation (*tattva* [1]) and manner of expression of the creative power in both Nature and man—the Serpent Fire or *kundalini*—is wave-like or serpentine. The supposed temptation of Eve by the serpent in Eden is an allegory of the allurement of the Spirit of man from primal innocence to self-conscious sex experience. The undulatory movement by which the creative life-force naturally manifests is aptly indicated by its personification as a serpent. Man's physical expression of this power in the natural procreative act constitutes the wrongly named " Fall " of Eve and Adam in the Garden of Eden, as a result of which the whole human race is dogmatically—erroneously according to occult philosophy—affirmed by Christian orthodoxy to have been born in " original sin ".[2] Man's generative power can indeed cause him to become either Godlike or a degraded demon of lust. When transmuted to spiritual and intellectual productivity it makes of man an inspired genius, and later an occult Sage endowed with superhuman capacities. When, however, it is expressed in excessive self-indulgence it can deeply degrade him; for undue sexual expression bedulls, takes the keen edge from, the mind-brain.

" THE TREE OF KNOWLEDGE OF GOOD AND EVIL "[3]

In one possible and somewhat limited interpretation the tree itself in the midst of the Garden of Eden typifies the active life-force, when in a state of balance or equipoise, in both Nature and man. As observed, the serpent associated therewith represents the twin currents of *kundalini*,[4] positive and negative, with the tree trunk as the neutral third. The fruit of the tree represents the faculties and powers accruing from the activity of the life-force within both Universe and man, especially when sublimated by the latter into mental and spiritual creativeness. Such,

[1] *Tattva* (Sk.)—" The abstract principle of substance ", physical and superphysical. Literally translated, " thatness " or " quiddity ". The subtle elements—five exoterically, seven in occult philosophy—which are correlative to the five (actually seven, two being latent as yet) senses of man. The essential nature of things. *Mahā-tattva*, the first differentiation of pre-cosmic space.

[2] Original Sin. q.v. *The Book of Common Prayer*, Church of England, Article IX of the Articles of Religion. According to the Roman Catholic Church this is " the sin by which the human race, rebellious against God through Adam's disobedience, was deprived of grace and Paradise, and made subject to ignorance, evil, death, and all other miseries." *Webster's International Dictionary*, 2nd Ed.

[3] *Gen.* 2 :9.

[4] q.v. *The Hidden Wisdom in the Holy Bible*, Vol. I, pp. 124–131, and *Lecture Notes of the School of the Wisdom*, Vol. II, Pt. I, Ch. I, Sec. 3, Geoffrey Hodson. See also Glossary.

indeed, is the harvest of the great Monadic pilgrimage of forthgoing and return.[1]

Since the subject-matter of this Chapter is admittedly somewhat abstruse, a brief recapitulation now follows. Adam by himself personifies early mankind as a race of androgyne beings. Adam and Eve as distinct entities represent the later stage of human evolution in which the Monad-Egos of men incarnated in single-sexed physical bodies. They are emblematic of the human race after separation into men and women endowed with male and female organisms and other characteristics. Before Adam and Eve are thus separated complete innocence (partheno-genesis) or unconscious reproduction exists, whilst afterwards conscious sex activity occurs. Knowledge of this latter and experience of its expression in procreation are thus gradually gained. Thereafter childlike innocence is naturally forfeited. Allegorically, Adam and Eve are expelled from Eden, Paradise is lost.

" YE SHALL BE AS GODS "[2]

Evolution and experience—to continue the recapitulation—bring to fruition in man knowledge of the Promethean[3] fire, ultimately making of him in his turn a Deity, a divine Emanator of Universes, The serpent therefore temptingly, albeit truthfully, said: " For God doth know that in the day ye eat thereof, then your eyes shall be opened, and ye shall be as gods. . . ." The price to be paid for the development of this deific power to " create " is heavy indeed. The Soul of man is encased in matter wherein, Prometheus-like, he becomes a prey to over-emphasized sex and sexual indulgence. Self-degraded as a result, his condition is scripturally described as being cursed by God. Nevertheless divine Intelligence—in the form of Cherubim[4]—ever watches over the human Monad, the Ego and the interior creative life-force, and guards man throughout the long pilgrimage through matter until, by virtue of the presence and activity of the Divinity within,[5] self-redemption, salvation or Adeptship is attained. Prometheus is unbound and Paradise regained.

---

[1] q.v. Vol. I of this work, Pt. IV, *The Cyclic Pathway of Forthgoing and Return.*

[2] *Gen.* 3: 5.

[3] In Greek Mythology Prometheus was chained to a rock on Mt. Caucasus, where in the daytime an eagle consumed his liver, which was restored during each succeeding night. He was thus exposed to perpetual torture, but Hercules (Redeemer) with the consent of Zeus killed the eagle and delivered the sufferer. His crime had been that he stole fire from Heaven *in a hollow tube* (the creative fire or *kundalini* sheathed within the spinal cord of man).

[4] *Gen.* 3: 24.

[5] *Ph.* 2: 13; *Col.* 1: 27.

A MICROCOSMIC INTERPRETATION

CHAPTER III

NOAH AND THE ARK [1]

A MACROCOSMIC INTERPRETATION

IN Chapter Six of the *Book of Genesis*, the blending of the cosmogonical
with the historical becomes marked. The account of the Flood is
allegorically merged with the engulfing of Universes and their several
components within the " waters of space " at the end of *Manvantaras*,[2]
major and minor. As a permutation of Jehovah, Noah represents the
masculine creative potency. His presence within the Ark—the feminine
aspect—represents a union from which arises the emanation of all created
things at the appointed time.

Noah is also a personification of one of the ten Sephiroth, together
with its associated Hierarchy of Archangelic and Angelic Hosts. As the
so-called Satanic Hierarchy (see second abridged interpretation) is associated with the outward pouring of Spirit into matter, and the induction
of conscious beings into forms, so the Order of the *Elohim* represented by
Noah is concerned with their return to the Source during the closing
phases of a period of manifestation. The Head of this Hierarchy, Noah-
like, has the task of gathering up and at the end sublimating into the
highest spiritual essence all the fruits of the major *Manvantara*. The essential
cosmic power, life and consciousness, as well as the Monads—symbolised
by the presence of pairs of all created things and by the family of Noah—
are preserved within the aura (the Ark) of this Representative of the
appropriate Order of the *Elohim* (Noah).

This process of the preservation throughout *Pralaya*[3] of the seeds of
living things within the aura of an exalted Member of the Inner
Government of the Solar System is repeated for all its components, as
also for a Solar System as a whole. The Ancient Wisdom teaches that

---

[1] For a fuller exposition see Pt. IV of this Volume.

[2] *Manvantara* (Sk.)—" Period between Manus ". Epoch of creative activity. See
footnote 1 on following page and Glossary.

[3] *Pralaya* (Sk.)—" Epoch of quiescence "—of creative activity. See footnote 1 on
following page and Glossary.

in the case of Planetary Chains, Rounds, and single Globes,[1] the preserving Official, known as a Seed *Manu*,[2] may be a member of the human kingdom of Nature who has attained to lofty superhuman stature.

A MICROCOSMIC INTERPRETATION

All Monads, with their potentialities and developed powers and faculties, are also thus preserved in a sublimated state during *Pralaya*. In this period forms disintegrate and their substance, losing its individualised vibratory frequencies, returns to the quiescent, pre-creative state symbolised by the waters of the Flood. *Pralaya* ended, either the Head of the *Elohistic* Hierarchy or the Seed *Manu* delivers his charges over to the corresponding Official of the new cycle. Then the great pilgrimage of involution and evolution (from unity through diversity and back to unity again) is repeated on a higher round of the spiral—the Ark comes to rest on Mt. Ararat—and so on and on throughout all eternity; for the Ageless Wisdom teaches that this cycle of evolutionary progression has neither conceivable beginning nor imaginable end.[3]

---

[1] *Chain.* In occult philosophy a Solar System is said to consist of ten Planetary Schemes. Each Scheme, generally named according to its physically visible representative, consists of seven Chains of Globes. In terms of time a Chain consists of the passage of the life-wave seven times around its seven Globes. Each such passage is called a Round, the completion of the seventh ending the life of the Chain. The Globes of a Round are both superphysical and physical and are arranged in a cyclic pattern, three being on a descending arc, three on an ascending arc and the middle, the fourth Globe, being the densest of all and the turning point. The active period of each of these units, from Solar System to Globe, called *Manvantara*, is succeeded by a passive period of equal duration, called *Pralaya*. The completion of the activity of the seventh Globe of the seventh Round of the seventh Chain brings to an end the activity of a Planetary Scheme. Our Earth's Scheme is now in its fourth Round of the fourth Chain, and the life-wave is half-way through its period of activity on the fourth Globe, the physical Earth. Thus the densest possible condition of substance is now occupied by Spirit, and so by the Monads or Spirits of men. The resistance of matter is at its greatest in this epoch, and this offers an explanation of the difficulties of human life at this period. The occupation of a physical planet by man consists of seven racial epochs and phases of evolutionary development. Throughout this work these are referred to as Root Races. q.v. *The Solar System*, A. E. Powell: *Lecture Notes of the School of the Wisdom*, Vol. I (Rev. Ed.), Ch. XIV, Geoffrey Hodson; also Glossary.

[2] *Manu* (Sk.). A generic term applied to Creators, Preservers and Fashioners. *Manvantara* means, literally, the period presided over by a Manu. According to their function and Office they are called Race *Manus*, Round *Manus* and Chain *Manus*, and so on up to the Solar Logos Himself. *Pralaya*, on the other hand, is a period of observation or repose, whether planetary or universal—the opposite of *Manvantara*—and is symbolised in *Genesis* and in all flood legends by their deluges.

[3] *The Secret Doctrine*, Vol. I (Adyar Ed.), p. 115, H. P. Blavatsky.

In one sense the covenant with the Lord and the appearance of the rainbow [1] symbolise the function of the *Elohim* in bridging the two epochs or cycles of manifestation. The return from simplicity to multiplicity, from the white light to the spectrum, from the one to the many, is also implied.

In the Planetary interpretation Noah represents the *Manu* of a single Root Race, an Official in the Hierarchy of the Adepts, who is responsible for the evolution of a complete Race with its seven sub-races. At a certain phase in its evolution this Official receives from his predecessor of the preceding Race such of its more advanced and successful members as are to be employed as future physical progenitors.

The Flood was a racial, historical fact—indeed a series of facts according to occult philosophy. In four great Floods the continent of Atlantis [2] and millions of the bodies of its inhabitants, human and sub-human, were drowned.[3] Symbolism apart, the one recorded in *Genesis*, taken as historical, was the fourth and culminating cataclysm. The Souls, psychical and spiritual, of the people thus destroyed were thereby saved from the deeper degradation into which, as sorcerers and black magicians, they might otherwise have sunk. Very large numbers of the Atlanteans did, however, fall into the error of sorcery and black magic of a deeply degrading character. This, also according to occult philosophy, is the sin referred to as provoking the wrath of the Lord.[4] In the strictly historical sense the Biblical statement that a Flood occurred is correct except for the fact that it was a purely local inundation, not one involving the whole of the planet.[5] Completely erroneous, however, is the implication that the Solar Logos, the *Elohim*, or any of the Members of the Occult Hierarchy of Adepts on Earth are capable of wrath. Only danger to the evolving Souls of men would have necessitated any occult intervention which may have occurred. The great war between the law-abiding Atlantean Emperor and his forces, and the vast armies of the sorcerers, is indirectly and partly referred to in the allegory of the War in Heaven.[6]

---

[1] *Gen.* 9: 9–17.

[2] For evidences of the existence of this continent see *Lecture Notes of the School of the Wisdom*, Vol. I (Rev. Ed.), Ch. XIV, Sec. 3, Geoffrey Hodson.

[3] q.v. *The Secret Doctrine*, Vols. II, III and IV, H. P. Blavatsky; *The Solar System*, A. E. Powell; *The Earth and Its Cycles*, pp. 90–94, E. W. Preston, M.Sc.; *Lecture Notes of the School of the Wisdom*, Vol. I (Rev. Ed.), Ch. XIV, Geoffrey Hodson.

[4] *Gen.* 6: 5–7.

[5] q.v. *The Bible as History*, Pt. I, Ch. III, Werner Keller (Wm. Morrow & Co., New York). *Abraham, Recent Discoveries and Hebrew Origins* (1936), Sir Charles Leonard Woolley.

[6] q.v. *The Secret Doctrine*, Vol. III, p. 225 and other parts of this great work, H. P. Blavatsky.

THE ARK

In terms of the seven bodies [1] of man and the successive reincarnations of the human Ego,[2] the Ark may be interpreted as the Auric Envelope, and more especially the Soul's vesture of light which is called the Causal Body.[3] This vehicle both contains, and preserves between reincarnations, the fruits harvested from each life-cycle. It is also an Ark in that it serves as a vehicle for the threefold spiritual Self, the divine Will, Wisdom and Intelligence which constitute the essential, unfolding spiritual Soul of man.

In this interpretation the inhabitants, human and sub-human, of Noah's Ark typify all these contents, the animals representing man's animal-like propensities. The three storeys refer to the three more spiritual levels of consciousness, those of will, wisdom and intelligence, at which the Immortal Self of man exists. In the succession of lives on Earth, at the death of the body, Egoic consciousness is withdrawn from the physical world and through the emotional and mental states [4] into its own realm.

To sum up: the arks and ships of the allegorical language employed by the Initiates of the Mystery Schools of early civilisations generally refer to containing vehicles of consciousness of whatever dimensions and at whatever level. The symbol is, however, susceptible of numerous other interpretations. In general it is any vehicle of consciousness, whether of Cosmos, Solar System, sun, planet, race or individual. Additional meanings include the substance and the ensouling and directing Intelligences of Cosmic and Solar Systems; the spiritual or Causal Body of man, the *Augoeides*; the animal and human wombs; the enclosing membrane of a cell and the " wall " of an atom. The universal principle of the conservation of attributes and developed qualities is exemplified by the symbol of the ark or boat.

FLOOD MYTHS IN WORLD SCRIPTURES

Modern archæology apart, the universality of the Flood legend supports the belief that a major—if not total—inundation did, in fact,

---

[1] The vehicles or vestures of the human Monad constructed of matter of seven successive degrees of density, from the most spiritual (Atmic) to the physical. Beginning with the most dense these are generally referred to as the physical body, the etheric double, the emotional or astral body, the " lower " mental body of concrete thought, the " higher " mental of abstract thought (the *Augoeides*), and the vehicles of intuition and spiritual will. q.v. *Man and His Bodies*, A. Besant.

[2] q.v. *Reincarnation, Fact or Fallacy*, Geoffrey Hodson.

[3] Causal Body. The immortal body of the reincarnating Ego of man, built of matter of the " higher " levels of the mental world. It is called Causal because it gathers up within it the results of all experiences, and these act as causes moulding future lives and influencing future conduct.

[4] q.v. *Through the Gateway of Death*, Geoffrey Hodson.

occur. Examples are found in the literature of other ancient peoples. Some of these, here recounted, are repeated at the appropriate place in the main text. The Chaldeo-Babylonian tablets state, for instance, that:

" Six days and nights the wind, deluge and storms over-whelmed. On the seventh day in the course (*sic*) was calmed the storm and all the deluge which had destroyed like an earthquake quieted. The sea he caused to dry, and the wind and deluge ended." . . . .

In the Hindu version, found in the *Mahābhārata*, the *Purānas* and the *Brāhmanas*, *Manu* Vaivasvata, the Hindu Noah, saves a little fish which wants to be an *Avatār* (descent or manifestation on Earth) of Vishnu, the Second Aspect of the *Trimūrti*. The fish warns the *Manu* that the world and all its inhabitants are about to be submerged, and orders him to construct a vessel in which he shall embark with all his family. When the ship is ready and Vaivasvata has taken aboard his family, the seeds of plants and pairs of all animals, the rain begins to fall. The fish, now gigantic and armed with a horn, places itself at the head of the " Ark " which it guides through the raging elements. When the storm subsided, the " Ark " settled on a peak of the Himalayas.

In Greek mythology, when Zeus had resolved to destroy the whole degenerate race of men Deucalion, the Greek Noah, and his wife Pyrrha, on account of their piety were the only mortals to be saved. Deucalion built a ship in which he and his wife floated to safety during the nine days of the Flood, which destroyed all the other inhabitants of Hellas. At last the ship rested on Mount Parnassus in Phocis. Thereafter, by very strange magical actions, the human race was restored.

The ancient manuscript known as the *Troana MS.*, which appears to have been written about 2,500 years ago by the Mayans of Yucatan and has been translated by Le Plongeon, gives the following description of the submergence of an Atlantic continent, presumably the Poseidonis referred to by Plato:

" In the year of 6 Kan, on the 11th Muluc in the Zac, there occurred terrible earthquakes, which continued without interruption until the 13th Chuen. The country of the hills was covered by mud, the land of Mu was sacrificed; being twice upheaved it suddenly disappeared during the night, the basin being continually shaken by volcanic forces. Being confined, these caused the land to sink and to rise several times and in various places. At last the surface gave way and ten countries were torn asunder and scattered. Unable to stand the force of the convulsions, they sank with 64,000,000 of their inhabitants, 8,060 years before the writing of this book."

Another ancient Mayan MS. known as the *Book of Chilam Balam*, later found by A. M. Bolic, states: ". . . and then in one watery blow, came the waters . . . the sky fell down and the dry land sank."

Thus both the Biblical account and the occult teaching concerning the Flood find some scientific and literary support. One difference between the Biblical and all other accounts is, as we have seen, that the former suggests that the Flood was universal, whilst the others describe it as being distinctly local. The misstatement in the Bible might be regarded by allegoricists as an indication that the story is so written as to possess a symbolical, and so cosmic, significance.

CHAPTER IV

THE TOWER OF BABEL [1]

A LITERAL reading of the story of the Tower of Babel suggests that the Lord God deliberately cast mankind into confusion by breaking up the unity of the early races of men and destroying their common language.[2] Since a great many of the subsequent sorrows of mankind arose from this supposed action on the part of the Supreme Deity, such a reading becomes unthinkable. The student of the Sacred Language, however, sees in Scriptural incongruities a possible indication of the presence of a hidden wisdom for which he is encouraged to seek.

In what way, then, may the story be interpreted? If regarded as an allegory descriptive of normal processes of evolution, then the term " the Lord " should be understood as referring to the creative and evolutionary impulses in Nature and in man, and to the laws under which they are objectively expressed. Babel thus marks an epoch in the history of man both as an individual and a race, whilst the allegory is also susceptible of a corresponding cosmic interpretation.

Primitive pre-Babel man was tribal and relatively mindless. Instinct guided his every action and that instinct was of the herd. The development of mind commenced with post-Babel man and when mentality entered in, replacing instinct with reason, individuality was born. Primeval unity then began to be destroyed. The Tower of Babel may thus be seen as a symbol of man's evolutionary ascent from the first purely physical race, through instinctual and emotional states, into a capacity for personal choice based upon individual thought. Natural evolutionary progression, and not the Lord of the Universe, brought about the disunified condition of mankind, which unfortunately to this day continues to be a basic cause of human suffering. Signs are not wanting—the growing acceptance of the idea of the brotherhood of man, as exemplified by the founding of the League of Nations, the International Red Cross, and later the United Nations with its many auxiliary international Agencies—that a further development is now occurring in which the mind of man is, however

---

[1] *Gen.* 11: 4–9.   For a fuller exposition see Pt. IV, Ch. IX of this Volume.
[2] *Gen.* 11: 5–8.

slowly, becoming intuitively illumined by a conscious recognition of the unity of all life, and so of all men.

THE SYMBOL OF THE TOWER

The building was unfinished because human evolution on this planet was then incomplete, and still is so. The emblematic Tower *will* be completed, however, by Seventh Race man, who allegorically will erect its pinnacle. Based upon the power of pure reason and rising through the faculty of controlled intuition to empowerment by the spiritual will, this symbolic completion of the metaphorical structure represents the highest development possible to humanity on this Earth in this World Period;[1] for the builders said: ". . . let us build us a city and a tower, whose top may reach into heaven. . . ."[2] The Tower of Babel is thus both an emblem and a chart of the evolution of man's consciousness. Its foundations are rooted deep in the earth and represent the Adam-Race, the first truly physical and androgynous humanity which existed on Earth and evolved physically and emotionally whilst still in a mental torpor (Adam's sleep).

The Tower symbol is susceptible of further and more detailed interpretation. The clay of which the bricks were made, for example, represents primordial substance. The sun which dried, hardened and baked them symbolises the supreme creative, spiritual Power presiding over the journey of forthgoing, during which archetypal ideas are projected into matter. The slime which was used for mortar represents mingled emotional and mental self-awareness in the physical body of man. The liquid state symbolises macro-cosmically the indwelling divine life, the cohesive principle, throughout Nature and microcosmically human emotion. Slowly the great edifice arose as sub-race followed sub-race, the Third and Fourth Root Races carrying these developments further and further, or higher and higher towards heaven (spiritual awareness). Since this progress occurred in man and was the result of his experience and effort, the authors of the allegory correctly affirm that the Tower of Babel was built by man.

The story, however, goes no further than the stage at which the development of the analytical reasoning faculty began. This was achieved by the masses about the middle of the Fourth Root Race, and when it happened the seeds of disunity, divided activity and competition came into the world. They germinated quickly, developed and began to produce their first fruit—the acute sense of separated individuality. The

---

[1] q.v. *The Earth and Its Cycles*, pp. 5, 6, 7 and 38, E. W. Preston, M.Sc.; *The Solar System*, A. E. Powell.

[2] *Gen.* 11: 4.

unifying, cohesive influence of the herd instinct, limited as it was to families, tribes and nations, then began to lose its hold.

Great expansion of consciousness also occurred and this led individuals and groups to explore the Earth and gradually to move from the great racial centres of civilisation to outlying districts, and thence by land and sea to other continents. Through vast ages, as the new power of intellection developed, so differences of language and custom expressed the diversity which accompanied that development. The change from unity to self-separateness was thus inevitable, and not in the least—as a literal reading would indicate—the result of harmful action by a Deity hostile to mankind. It was quite natural and, in fact, completely necessary to human evolution. Despite its grievous results, destined to endure far on into the Fifth Root Race—the present time—it is an essential phase of the process of the unfoldment of life and consciousness. Indeed, Nature may be said to have demanded it as the price of the triumph to follow and the crown to be won. That triumph is a conscious, self-chosen return to unification, and that crown is the vision and realisation of the unity of the life within all the diverse forms of Nature. Since the interval of disunity, with its adverse results, was the unavoidable concomitant of evolution, a dead-letter reading quite erroneously attributes to " the LORD " [1] the " confounding " of the original common tongue. The story of the Tower of Babel may thus be regarded as an allegorical account of the evolution of human consciousness out of unified tribal instinct into, and later through, the inevitable diversity produced by the development of the mind, with its attributes of individualism and egoism.

This knowledge—for reasons doubtless considered by the ancient Sages to be adequate—was in those days preserved among the many secrets to be revealed only to Initiates of the Greater Mysteries; hence, I suggest, its presentation in allegorical form.

THE HERESY OF SEPARATENESS

To sum up: since the accentuated sense of self-separateness, manifesting as extreme nationalism and individualism, is the primary cause of all unwarranted injury by man to man, any being who produces this state of mind must be held responsible for all the subsequent effects. Yet the literal reading of the Biblical text, and especially of verses six, seven, eight and nine of the Seventh Chapter of *Genesis*, indicates that the Supreme Deity deliberately and callously made Itself responsible for the major self-produced sufferings of mankind. Indeed, if this reasoning be applied, then all evil, including individual and organised crime and the

[1] q.v. *Gen.* 11: 7–8.

waging of innumerable wars, arose and still arises from two actions attributed on Biblical authority to the Lord God. Each of these—confounding human language and scattering mankind abroad—brought about the division of humanity into separate nations speaking different languages. Consequently the then existing unity of the human race was broken.

Such conduct, deliberately conceived and put into effect by the Deity during the early phases of post-diluvian human life on Earth, is quite unthinkable; for its attribution to the divine Parent of humanity affronts every ideal concept of such an exalted Being, and is therefore unacceptable to the thoughtful and reverent mind. The sense of outrage is deepened by the statement in the first verse of Chapter Eleven of *Genesis*, which says that ". . . the whole earth was of one language, and of one speech." Verse six also reports the Lord as saying: ". . . Behold, the people is one, and they have all one language . . .", whilst verses seven and eight record Him as giving the order: " Go to, let us go down, and there confound their language, that they may not understand one another's speech. So the LORD scattered them abroad from thence upon the face of all the earth. . . ."

The affront disappears, however, if the story be read not literally, but as an allegorical revelation of knowledge which at that time was reserved to the Initiates of the Mystery Schools—namely the methods and phases of human evolution and their effects upon human consciousness and life. The study and acceptance of the Bible less as literal history and far more as a revelation of fundamental truths by means of allegories, thus receives support from the story of the Tower of Babel.

THE ONE BECOMES THE MANY

Macrocosmically the incarnation of the one life into many forms, the expression of the one creative Idea through its innumerable objective manifestations in Nature, and the material appearance of the Primordial Archetype in myriads of different types on the physical plane—all these are, I suggest, allegorised by the supposed action of the creative Deity in scattering humanity abroad upon the face of the Earth. Such disruption of unity is bound to occur as soon as the pathway of forthgoing, or *involution*, is entered upon. Although the text affirms this to be a deliberate action by the Lord God, according to occult philosophy it is but the inevitable result of the emanation of the finite from the Infinite. No-one, therefore, is in the least blameworthy, since unavoidable natural procedures are alone being described. Whoever the authors may have been—inspired Kabbalists, according to the Zohar—one might be forgiven for regretting their concealment of these great fundamental verities under a veil which presents the Deity in such an undesirable light. They were, however, but following a universal custom, for in those days these teachings concerning racial involution and evolution according to an Archetype were restricted to members of the Mystery Schools, and under vows of secrecy only mentioned to the profane in allegorical form.

The actual procedure of building the Tower symbolises entry on the pathway of return from matter to Spirit, from Earth to Heaven, from diversity back to unity—or *evolution*. The unfinished state indicates a continuing process as yet incomplete, whilst the limitless regions of the sky above suggest an infinity of potential attainment. The Tower may thus be regarded as entirely symbolic, its undermeaning being one of the many jewels of wisdom scattered in prodigal abundance throughout the pages of the Bible.

A reference may also be perceived to the Sacred Language of the Mystery Schools, which was and still is a unity, one tongue, the same for all peoples throughout all time. The Ageless Wisdom was once known universally, but was gradually denied to subsequent generations who, because of the development of individualism, became temporarily unworthy to receive it directly. Thus both the primeval Wisdom Religion and its hierogrammatic Scriptures were forgotten by the many, as humanity gradually became restricted to the several tongues of the different nations of the world.[1]

---

[1] q.v. *The Secret Doctrine* (Adyar Ed.), Vol. V, p. 185, H. P. Blavatsky.

CHAPTER V

REBEKAH AT THE WELL

THE story of the discovery of Rebekah as the future wife of Isaac, in fulfilment of the prophetic vision of his father Abraham, takes its place with the great mystical romances of all time. There are, however, elements in the story which may indicate a deeper intention on the part of the authors of the *Pentateuch*. They themselves, for example, open this great work with an account of Cosmogenesis, and follow it with a highly allegorical description of the creation of man (Adam) and later, from his side, woman (Eve). Since a literal reading of this passage of Scripture cannot reasonably be accepted, the student of the Language of Allegory and Symbol may prefer to regard accounts of such generative procedures as also being capable of interpretation in the larger sense as allegories of macrocosmic and microcosmic " creations ".

This approach would seem to be encouraged by the inclusion of many symbols of formative, cyclic, numerically governed procedures in Nature. Readers interested in this view may find acceptable the proffered interpretations of parts of this symbology in the commentaries on the later days and years of Abraham's life which are included in Part Six of this Volume. Others may see in them a tendency to add unnecessary complexity to a simple and straight forward history of a mighty people. Those holding to this latter view may, if they desire—despite numerous affronts to both reason and morality—read the great stories of the Abrahamic cycle and its successors as Hebrew history alone. If, however, these portions of Scripture are approached as revelations of profound wisdom under a veil of allegory and symbol, then the three interpretations used throughout this work—macrocosmic, microcosmic and Initiatory—may usefully be applied, particularly as the above-mentioned affronts then disappear. In support of this approach, one may note the Presence of the Supreme Deity as Abraham's Counsellor, a completely fulfilled prophetic vision of that which was about to occur a great distance away, and an exceedingly strange form of oath taken by a servant. All these lift the narrative out of the purely historical and bestow upon it a distinctly mystical character.

Abraham sought a wife for his son Isaac, not from the land of Canaan but from the original country from which he had come. He was granted a vision in which he occultly saw Isaac's future wife, Rebekah, and the manner in which she would respond to an invitation delivered by his servant. This vision proved to be accurate in every respect. The servant journeyed to Nahor as instructed, met Rebekah at the well there, and on his request received from her water and an offer of hospitality. She and her family agreed to the union. She journeyed with the servant, met Isaac at Lahai-roi, and they were married.

This story, as we have seen, is susceptible of interpretation from two main points of view:[1] the macrocosmic or universal, and the microcosmic or human, which includes the Initiatory, descriptive of experiences on the Way of Holiness.

In the *Pentateuch*, and indeed throughout World Scriptures, characters in the stories are frequently used to personify both divine Beings and creative procedures. Abraham, for example, represents universal Spirit, whilst water is emblematical of universal Space. A well containing water typifies a circumscribed area of differentiated matter from within which a Universe is to be emanated. Rebekah also personifies substance both before and after impregnation by creative Spirit, she being a virgin before she married Isaac. Isaac becomes the Lord of the new Universe, having evolved out of universal Spirit (Abraham, his father, who also stands for the Logos of the preceding Universe).

These principles of cosmic Creation, impersonal and abstract as they are, would be completely incomprehensible to the uninstructed. Since, however, knowledge concerning Cosmogenesis is of importance to the race, the formative processes are skilfully described as actions and experiences of Deities and human personalities, together with their mutual relationships. Pre-cosmic and cosmic procedures are thus brought to the attention of mankind by means of symbolical dramas, in which the characters are designed to personify Intelligences and forces involved in the emanation, fashioning and evolution of Universes and their components.

The events of these Scriptural and mythological narratives are not always entirely natural. Divine interventions, the exercise of miraculous powers and the occurrence of occult happenings are introduced into them. These prompt the reader who is seeking both for solutions of the problems arising from a literal reading, and for knowledge possibly concealed beneath otherwise unacceptable statements, to look below the surface in search of hidden truths. In the story of Rebekah, for example, Abraham

---

[1] q.v. *Lecture Notes of the School of the Wisdom*, Vol. II, Ch. VII, Sec. III, Geoffrey Hodson.

is spiritually guided. He exercises remarkable clairvoyant vision, which reveals to him the existence of particular people dwelling at a distance. The power of pre-cognition, included within the faculty of clairvoyance, enables Abraham to foretell the future with remarkable exactness, for all took place precisely as he had prophesied.

A MACROCOSMIC INTERPRETATION

Cosmogenesis begins with an event in time: ". . . the Spirit of God moved upon the face of the waters."[1] Otherwise stated, the negative substance of undifferentiated, unparticled Space is first fructified and atomised from within itself by the action of a positive, creative power. Feminine and masculine potencies interact creatively and new Universes appear or, more correctly, preceding Universes reappear. Solar Systems within the vast sea of Space then begin to be formed, Isaac in the second part of the allegory personifying a presiding Deity, a Solar Logos. Thereafter the processes of the emanation of worlds and their inhabitants (offspring) and of involution and evolution follow according to eternal Law.

The narrative is clearly descriptive of two distinct procedures in Nature. In the first of these Abraham represents the masculine, generative power, or Spirit, whilst the element of water stands for the feminine, creative potency, or matter. These two are brought into mutual association by means of a verbal message or the utterance of the " Word ". Rebekah responds and the potentialities of creative procedure in time have come into existence. Thereafter, when marriage has occurred, the succeeding phase is described, in which the part of the male creator is taken by Isaac and the female by Rebekah. These two revelations by allegory need to be kept distinct, one being cosmic and revealing general principles, the other being local and referring to the succession of Solar Systems.

If the episode under consideration be thus interpreted macrocosmically as an allegory of Creation then, as we have seen, the second act in the great drama portrays the entry upon the stage of the succeeding masculine generator—Isaac, the husband-to-be. In this second phase Isaac in his turn personifies Spirit, and the element of water with which Rebekah was associated corresponds to undifferentiated matter. The water collected within the well represents matter which is no longer spread universally throughout the infinitudes of Space, but is now circumscribed and available for the production and preservation of living beings and things—human, animal and plant. In the story these three are represented respectively by people, camels and fodder. Rebekah personifies the consciousness of

---

[1] *Gen.* 1: 2.

substance or Space both before impregnation by Spirit (before she is married) and afterwards when she becomes wife and mother.

Isaac's servant who conveys the marriage proposal (like the Angel of the Annunciation [1]) represents the forth-shining Ray of creative power which meets virginal Space. Although completely unprepared Rebekah at once responds, a circumstance in itself so unusual, and even unlikely, as also to suggest the possibility of an under-meaning. Indeed, one is here reminded of the manner in which the Virgin Mary received, and with humility accepted, the announcement of her forthcoming mother-hood.[2] Whilst extremely personal, and susceptible of interpretation microcosmically,[3] the two stories may justly be thought of as allegories also descriptive of cosmogenetic procedures.

TWO MICROCOSMIC INTERPRETATIONS

At this point two possible human applications of this story of Rebekah at the well may be advanced. One of these refers to the relationship existing between the Monad of man and his spiritual Soul or Ego, and the other to that between the Ego and his physical personality.

In order to understand the first of these, it must be realised that on emerging from the divine Consciousness for the purpose of evolution (the setting forth of heroes or their representatives upon journeys) the Monad (Abraham) projects a Ray (the eldest servant) of its Spirit-Essence or Monadic power. As earlier stated, this Ray is generally portrayed as the voice of a messenger or an Angel of Annunciation. When the human kingdom is entered in the course of Monadic evolution, the Monad is connected by its Ray with the immortal spiritual Soul of the human being in its vesture of light or Causal Body (Rebekah).

Kabbalism expresses this idea as follows:

" Come and see when the soul reaches that place which is called the Treasury of Life, she enjoys a bright and luminous mirror, which receives its light from the highest heaven. The soul could not bear this light but for the luminous mantle which she puts on. For just as the soul, when sent to this earth, puts on an earthly garment to preserve herself here, so she receives above a shining garment, in order to be able to look without injury into the mirror whose light proceeds from the Lord of Light. Moses too could not approach to look into that higher light which he saw, without putting on such an ethereal garment; as it is written—' And Moses went into the midst of the cloud ' (Exod. xxiv, 18), which is to be translated by means of the

[1] Lu. 1: 26–38.
[2] Lu. 1: 38.
[3] q.v. The Hidden Wisdom in the Holy Bible, Vol. I, Pt. V, Ch. I, Geoffrey Hodson.

cloud wherewith he wrapped himself as if dressed in a garment. At that time Moses almost discarded the whole of his earthly nature; as it is written,—' And Moses was on the mountain forty days and forty nights' (ibid.); and he thus approached that dark cloud where God is enthroned. In this wise the departed spirits of the righteous dress themselves in the upper regions in luminous garments, to be able to endure that light which streams from the Lord of Light." (*Sohar, i, 56b, 66a* [1]).

A female character nearly always personifies this vehicle of the Monad, which is the instrument of consciousness through which the powers of the abstract intelligence—the spiritual and prophetic mentality of man —naturally function.   This Principle of man, the Causal Body,[2] is both receptive of the powers of spiritual will and intuitiveness and is also the conserver of powers developed through successive Earth lives.   It is therefore to be regarded as feminine, and even maternal, in character and is frequently symbolised by a ship, an ark or a womb.   In Kabbalism this vesture of light is also said to be symbolised by the Tree of Life in the Garden of Eden.   Christian D. Ginsburg, LL.D., writes: [3] ". . . the soul possesses two kinds of powers and two sorts of feelings.   It has the faculty for that extraordinary prophetical knowledge, which was vouchsafed to Moses in an exceptional manner, called *the Luminous Mirror*, and the ordinary knowledge termed *the Non-Luminous Mirror*, respectively represented in the earthly Paradise by the Tree of Life and the Tree of Knowledge of good and evil; . . . ." The symbol of the Ark is very apt, for the spiritual Soul of man contains throughout the whole period of human evolution both the potencies of the Monad and the products of the evolutionary procedure, which it preserves and makes available to the individual in succeeding reincarnations.

The story of Isaac and Rebekah, as already observed, includes elements which lift it above the usual association of courtship and marriage.   The symbols of water, the well, a servant and jewels, together with divine direction and the applied powers of obtaining knowledge of distant and future events, all combine to lift the story out of the purely human into the domain of the magical and the occult.   The student of symbology sees in these elements instruction given by the authors to regard the narrative as an allegory concealing profound truths.   The courtship, marriage and parenthood of Isaac and Rebekah are, I submit, more than

---

[1] *The Kabbalah, Its Doctrines, Development and Literature*, p. 120, Christian D. Ginsburg, LL.D.

[2] q.v. Glossary.

[3] q.v. *The Kabbalah, Its Doctrines, Development and Literature*, p. 119, Christian D. Ginsburg, LL.D.

romantic incidents in a beautiful love story; for they portray macrocosmic and microcosmic truths.

AN INITIATORY INTERPRETATION

If the story of Isaac and Rebekah be regarded as an allegory of Initiation, then Isaac personifies the Candidate who has learnt of the existence of the Mysteries, their sublime purposes and the wisdom which they enshrine (Rebekah). He is the son of a great patriarch who arranges the marriage by occult means. Abraham is thus the Initiator and Isaac a neophyte duly prepared to attain expansions of consciousness produced by passage through successive Rites. Such aspirations are always given due consideration by the occult Authorities on this planet.[1] On acceptance, arrangements are made to bring the aspirant into the presence of a member of the Temple, who will in due course present him before the Hierophant.[2] This secret procedure is indicated by Abraham's pre-vision concerning Rebekah and his very peculiar instructions to his messenger, who successfully accomplished his mission.

As a Hierophant, and therefore possessed of supernormal faculties, Abraham would have detected the place where Rebekah was to be found and foreseen her acquiescence, as also that of her family. Interpreted, this implies an occult knowledge that the Candidate was sufficiently evolved to justify his admission to the Greater Mysteries.

In this reading Rebekah as a member of a well-to-do family, and discovered by the servant at a well, in one meaning represents pure Wisdom, a word which in Kabbalism is used in a special sense. " It is the Principle of all the Principles, the mysterious Wisdom, the crown of all that which there is of the most High." [3] Many passages of the Old Testament also stress the value of spiritual discernment (*Buddhi*, Sk.). *The Book of Proverbs* (IV: 7) states, for example: " Wisdom is the principal thing; therefore get wisdom: and with all thy getting get understanding." In *Proverbs* XVI: 16 we read: " How much better is it to get wisdom than gold ! . . ." In *Daniel* XII: 3 it is written: " And they that be wise shall shine as the brightness of the firmament; and they that turn many to righteousness as the stars for ever and ever." The Candidate must make this treasure of pure wisdom (Rebekah) his very own. Metaphorically, a marriage must occur.

---

[1] q.v. *The Hidden Wisdom in the Holy Bible*, Vol. I, pp. 269 *et seq.*, Geoffrey Hodson.

[2] Hierophant (Gr.)—" One who explains sacred things ". The discloser of sacred learning and the Chief of the Initiates. A title belonging to the highest Adepts in the temples of antiquity, who were both teachers and expounders of the Mysteries and Initiator into the final Greater Mysteries. q.v. *The Theosophical Glossary*, H. P. Blavatsky.

[3] q. v. *Zohar* iii, folio 288.

Rebekah also personifies the Mysteries themselves, and the well of water their content of supernal knowledge; for the Mysteries, the most beneficent and enduring of all earthly Institutions, both possess and, as did Rebekah, purvey the " waters " of eternal Truth. Each successful neophyte receives that measure which his temperament and development permit him to assimilate. Rebekah at the well, drawing water for the servant and his camels, thus aptly symbolises the Greater Mysteries in their functions of preserving throughout the ages and delivering to the worthy the very " waters " of living Truth.

The fact that the incident occurred at Nahor in Mesopotamia, near Ur of the Chaldees, the original home of the family of Abraham, supports this view. Abraham's servant was very specially instructed to obtain for Isaac a wife, not from the land of Canaan but from the family's original home in Chaldea, at that time a Centre of the Ancient Mysteries.[1]   Here may be seen a statement of the necessity of going to the original source (Chaldea) for pure wisdom, and of avoiding colourations and encrustations inseparable from later human interpretations and expositions (other lands).

The Candidate's aspiring thoughts are turned in search of those aspects of the eternal wisdom which he can assimilate, and of that Temple of the Mysteries where that wisdom is to be found. The beautiful story indicates, it may here be repeated, that no worthy aspirant is ever refused admission to the Sanctuary, for this is a law both of life itself and of the Mysteries, under which law no-one ever selflessly cries for light in vain. The sincere search for truth, understanding and knowledge, sought for their own sake and solely with altruistic motives, must always be assisted by the Guardians of those treasures and granted in the fullest measures to the neophyte according to his *karma* and interior development. Thus Rebekah readily responds to the servant's request for water, food and hospitality for man and beast. Her family similarly receive with favour the plea that Rebekah should return with him to Isaac in order that they might be married. Their immediate response, despite lack of information concerning Isaac's family, is most unusual and may also be taken to indicate the presence of an undermeaning.

The subsequent meeting, mutual love and marriage of Rebekah and Isaac portray both the neophyte's assimilation of spiritual and occult knowledge, and his admission to the Temple and to membership of the Great White Brotherhood of the Adepts and Initiates of the planet, possibly referring to the high priests " for ever after the order of Melchisedec ", to which order Jesus was said to be admitted.[2]

---

[1] Founded partly upon worship of the Moon God.
[2] *Heb.* 6: 20.

Occult tradition suggests that St. Paul was an Initiate of the Greater Mysteries, an idea which is supported by his use of certain terms from Mystery Rituals in his Epistles. Amongst these are:

. . . as a wise masterbuilder, I have laid the foundation. . . ." (I *Cor.* III: 10).

Know ye not that ye are the temple of God, and that the Spirit of God dwelleth in you. (I *Cor.* III: 16).

Let a man so account of us, as of the ministers of Christ, and stewards of the mysteries of God. (I *Cor.* IV: 1).

Howbeit we speak wisdom among them that are perfect: yet not the wisdom of this world, nor of the princes of this world, that come to nought. (I *Cor.* II: 6).

How that by revelation he made known unto me the mystery. . . . (Eph. III: 3).

I know a man in Christ above fourteen years ago (whether in the body, I cannot tell; or whether out of the body, I cannot tell: God knoweth); such an one caught up to the third heaven.
And I knew such a man, (whether in the body, or out of the body, I cannot tell: God knoweth;).
How that he was caught up into paradise, and heard unspeakable words, which it is not lawful for a man to utter (the Initiate's solemn vow of silence). (II *Cor.* XII: 2–4).

H. P. Blavatsky writes: *Another proof that Paul belonged to the circle of the ' Initiates ' lies in the following fact. The Apostle had his head shorn at Cenchrea (Acts XVIII: 18) where Lucius (Apuleius) was initiated, because ' he had a vow.' The Nazars—or set apart—as we see in the Jewish Scriptures, had to cut their hair, which they wore long, and which ' no razor touched ' at any other time, and sacrifice it on the alter of initiation. And the Nazars were a class of Chaldean theurgists or Initiates."* (*The Secret Doctrine,* Vol. V, p. 137).

Verses eighteen and nineteen of the Sixth Chapter of *Hebrews* would appear to refer to the changeless wisdom as man's ultimate refuge and hope " as an anchor of the soul " and to its concealment " within the veil ". The text reads as follows:

18. *That by two immutable things, in which it was impossible for God to lie, we might have a strong consolation, who have fled for refuge to lay hold upon the hope set before us.*

19. *Which hope we have as an anchor of the soul, both sure and steadfast, and which entereth into that within the veil.*

The passage relating to Melchisedec is highly suggestive of the existence of a mystical Order of dedicated Beings to which Abraham made an offering, whilst Melchisedec himself can be no earthly man for he is said by St. Paul, himself an Initiate, to be " Without father, without mother, without descent, having neither beginning of days, nor end of life; but made like unto the Son of God; abideth a priest continually." (*Heb.* VII: 3).

A fuller interpretation of the story of Rebekah at the well is offered in the appropriate place in the text.

PART THREE

ADAM, EVE, THE GARDEN OF EDEN
AND THE " FALL " OF MAN

INTRODUCTION

THE reader will notice that in the early Chapters of Part Three of this Volume two forms of certain verses of the *Book of Genesis* are given. The first of these is taken from the King James Version, whilst in the second the Hebrew forms of certain words and their literal translations have been added. This procedure is followed partly to provide the original text and partly to indicate the basis for some of the proffered interpretations, all of which are founded upon that Ageless Wisdom to which the Greeks gave the title *Theosophia*, derived from the two Greek words *Theo* and *sophia*—Divine Wisdom.

The first known literary use of this Greek word is found in the writings of the Neo-Platonists in the Second Century of the Christian era, who employed it to connote the truths revealed to man by his evolutionary Elders at the dawn of human life on this planet. These truths have been added to, checked and re-checked down to the present day by an unbroken succession of Adept investigators. This term, Adept, refers to an Initiate of the Fifth Degree in the Greater Mysteries, a Master in the science of esoteric philosophy, a perfected man, an exalted Being who has attained complete mastery over his purely human nature and possesses knowledge and power commensurate with lofty evolutionary stature. Such fulfilment of human destiny is thus described by St. Paul: " Till we all come in the unity of the faith, and of the knowledge of the Son of God, unto a perfect man, unto the measure of the stature of the fulness of Christ." [1] Certain Adepts remain on Earth in physical bodies in order to assist humanity, and are presumably referred to by St. Paul as " just men made perfect ".[2] The Lord Christ referred to a far more lofty destiny for man, saying: " Ye therefore shall be perfect, as your heavenly Father is perfect." [3]

The full fruits of the processes of Adept research and revelation have been preserved by the still-living Hierophants and Initiates of the Greater Mysteries. In their doctrinal aspect these Mysteries consist of a vast body of teaching which embraces every conceivable subject to which the mind of man can be turned. The fundamental principles of religion, philosophy,

[1] *Eph.* 4: 13.
[2] *Heb.* 12: 23.
[3] *Matt.* 5: 48 (R.V.).

art, science and politics are all contained within this Wisdom of the Ages. From the time of the closing of the Neo-Platonic and Gnostic Schools to the last quarter of the Nineteenth Century, save for the few Alchemists, Kabbalists, Rosicrucians, occultly instructed Masons and the Christian mystics, Theosophy was little known in the Western world. Before then it was studied in various forms by the Platonists, the Pythagoreans, the Egyptians and the Chaldeans, whilst in India and China it has been preserved down the ages in unbroken continuity. It is the wisdom of the *Upanishads* and the *Vedas*,[1] the very heart of Hinduism, Buddhism, Taoism and Islam. By means of allegory and symbol it is revealed in the Christian Scriptures, the dead-letter reading of which has blinded Christians to their deeper significance.

The study of comparative religion does, in fact, reveal the existence of certain doctrines which are common to all World Faiths. Although differently presented in each, when collected and blended into a whole these teachings constitute a basic body of revealed Truth which can be studied independently of all religious systems. Each world religion reveals an arc of the circle of Eternal Wisdom. Theosophy, although as yet but partially revealed to man, is the full circle of Truth. Age by age, at the direction of Those who are the Guardians of knowledge and its accompanying power, aspects of this all-inclusive body of ideas are revealed to man through world religions and philosophies. The theme of this book is that certain power-bestowing aspects of *Theosophia* have always been partially concealed under a veil of allegory and symbol. This is because such knowledge can bestow theurgic, hypnotic and other powers susceptible of misuse. Rightly used, however, it can be of great value to mankind and since the present is an age when many are searching deeply for a philosophy of life which will support them when in danger, stress and need, the time has now arrived, I believe, when the outer layers of this veil may usefully, if but partially, be drawn aside. The interpretations of the Scriptures which now begin are based upon these convictions. Here, then, is an attempt to lift the mysterious veil of the Temple which one day for all men, we may hope, will be " rent in twain from the top to the bottom ".[2]

COSMOGENESIS

Since some of the concepts of the cosmogony of occult philosophy are included in the interpretations of the *Book of Genesis* which now follow,

---

[1] Since these most ancient Scriptures were written in the Sanskrit language, as explained elsewhere certain Sanskrit words are used throughout this work.

[2] *Matt.* 27; 51.

a brief statement of them may prove helpful, especially to those contacting these ideas for the first time.

The first five verses of the *Book of Genesis* describe the opening phases of the process of creation [1] as follows:

1. *In the beginning God created the heaven and the earth.*
2. *And the earth was without form, and void; and darkness was upon the face of the deep. And the Spirit of God moved upon the face of the waters.*
3. *And God said, Let there be light: and there was light.*
4. *And God saw the light, that it was good: and God divided the light from the darkness.*
5. *And God called the light Day, and the darkness He called Night. And the evening and the morning were the first day.*

Thus originally there existed duality in unity, namely the Spirit of God (the masculine creative potency) on the one hand and the face of the deep (the feminine creative potency) on the other. Primarily there was a dual Principle, a positive and a negative, Spirit-Matter. During the long creative " Night ", which in Sanskrit is called *Pralaya* [2] (rest), there was darkness upon the face of the deep. The whole of boundless Space was dark and quiescent. Then, it is stated, a change occurred. The Spirit of God, having emerged from Absolute Existence, moved upon the face of the waters. The " Great Breath " breathed upon the " Great Deep ", whereupon emanation began to occur and ordered manifestation (*Manvantara*) was initiated.

Thus, behind and beyond and within all is the Eternal and Infinite Parent from within which the temporary and the finite emerge, or are born. That Boundless Self-Existence is variously referred to as the Absolute, the Changeless, the Eternal ALL, the Causeless Cause, the Rootless Root. This is Non-Being, Negative Existence, No-Thing, *Ain* (as the Kabbalist says [3]), an impersonal Unity without attributes conceivable by man.

In occult philosophy the term " God " in its highest meaning refers to a Supreme, Eternal and Indefinable Reality. This Absolute is incon-

---

[1] *Creation.* The emergence and subsequent development of a Universe and its contents is regarded in occult philosophy as being less the result of a single act of creation, followed by natural evolution, than a process of emanation guided by intelligent Forces under immutable Law. The creation or emergence of Universes from nothing is not an acceptable concept, the Cosmos being regarded as emanating from an all-containing, sourceless Source, the Absolute.

[2] See footnote pp. 53 and 54 and Glossary.

[3] q.v. Appendix to this Volume.

ceivable, ineffable and unknowable. Its revealed existence is postulated in three terms: an absolute Existence, an absolute Consciousness and an absolute Bliss. Infinite Consciousness is regarded as inherent in the Supreme Being as a dynamic Force that manifests the potentialities held in its own infinitude, and calls into being forms out of its own formless depths. From *that*, the Absolute, emerged an active, Creative Power and Intelligence to become the formative Deity, the *Demiurgos*,[1] of the Universe-to-be. The illumined Sages thus taught that the Eternal One which is potentially twofold (Spirit-Matter), is subject to cyclic, rhythmic Motion, a primordial Third which is also eternal. Under certain conditions the relationship of the conjoined Spirit-Matter changes from passive unity into active duality—distinct positive and negative potencies.

Thus, when " interior " Motion causes hitherto unified, quiescent Spirit-Matter to become oppositely polarized or creatively active, then there is activity, light, " Day "; for these two (Universal Spirit and Universal Matter) produce a third, a " Son ", which becomes the presiding Deity, the Logos, the Architect, of the resultant Universe. A finite Principle has now emerged from the Infinite. Universal Spirit-Matter-Motion have become focussed into a " Being " Who is beyond normal human comprehension. This is the One Alone, the " only-begotten Son " [2] (when correctly translated, " alone begotten " or emanated from a unified, single Source), being of " one substance with the Father ", which in this case is the Absolute, the Uncreate. By this " Son ", the Cosmic Christ, all worlds are fashioned, " He " being the Emanator, Architect, Sustainer and Regenerator of Universes and all that they will ever contain.

This formative Logos is the first objective Emanation of the Absolute. It is the Principle of divine Thought, now to be made manifest in an individual sense, firstly as the Logos of the whole Cosmos, secondly as the Solar Deity of a single Solar System, and thirdly as the Logos of the Soul of every human being—the Dweller in the Innermost. These Three are One, indivisible, identical, an integral part of each other, a whole. In the beginning, when newly formed, the First, the One Alone, is purely spiritual and intellectual. Ultimately, as we have seen, It becomes manifested as both the presiding Power, Life and Intelligence transcendent beyond all that objectively exists and the indwelling and transforming divine Life immanent within all Nature, all beings and all things.

---

[1] *Demiurgos* (Gr.)—The Demiurge or Artificer, the Supernal Power which built the Universe. Freemasons derive from this word their phrase " Supreme Architect ". With the occultist it is the third manifested Logos, or Plato's second God, the second Logos being represented by him as the " Father ", the only Deity that he, as an Initiate of the Mysteries, dare mention. The demiurgic Mind is the same as the Universal Mind, named *Mahat* (Sk.), the first " product " of Brahmā.

[2] From *The Gloria in Excelsis*, a translation of an early Greek hymn.

Such, in outline,[1] are some of the cosmogonical ideas to be found in occult philosophy. Further expositions of them will be found in the interpretations of the *Book of Genesis* which follow.

A MISTRANSLATED WORD

As I embark upon the task of offering interpretations of the Bible and begin with its very first Book, the *Book of Genesis*, I wish to draw attention to a single important word which appears in the original Hebrew text. This word is *tho* and translated from the Hebrew means "symbolic". The reader is asked, therefore, especially to note the following three commentaries upon the presence of this word in the Hebrew text, and also the way in which it is translated in both the Authorised and Revised Versions of the Bible (Author).

On this subject, F. J. Mayers in his book *The Unknown God* writes as follows:

> Gen. II: 4. " *These are the generations of the heaven and the earth when they were created. In the day that the Lord God made earth and heaven. . . ."* (*R.V.*)[2]

" The first thing we notice when we compare the above version with the original Hebrew Text, is that the latter contains a word which is not translated at all in the English. It was also ignored in the Latin translation. The translators apparently did not know what to do with it. The Hebrew Text reads: ' aelleh **tho**-ledoth'. The little word ' tho', which the translators have passed over, denotes ' symbolic'. It may be applied to a **book,** a fable, a hieroglyph, a **discourse,** or anything else which is of a ' symbolic' nature. The translators of the ' Septuagint' did not ignore the word, but they ' by-passed' its real meaning . . . and translated it merely by the word ' book'; that avoided raising awkward questions. What the whole phrase really stated quite clearly was, that the ' generations' or ' productions' of the heavens and the earth . . . would be described in **symbolic** language. It is particularly illuminating that the writer of Genesis should himself tell us this in advance. He takes the ground from under the feet of those who are continually seeking to ' literalise' and ' de-spiritualise' the Bible. . . ."

(*The Unknown God*, Chap. Sixteen.)

[1] For a fuller description and other Scriptural accounts of these and succeeding phases of Cosmogenesis, see following pages and also *Occult Powers in Nature and in Man* and *Lecture Notes of the School of the Wisdom*, Vol. II, Pt. II, Geoffrey Hodson, T.P.H., Adyar, Madras, India.

[2] Although the learned author thus quotes the Revised Version, the Authorised Version reads as follows: " These are the generations of the heavens and of the earth when they were created, in the day that the LORD God made the earth and the heavens ".

Fabre d'Olivet states:

" The root ' tho ' contains every idea of sign, of symbol, of hieroglyphic character. . . ."

(*The Hebraic Tongue Restored*).

In his Foreword, the translator of *The Hebraic Tongue Restored* writes:

". . . . He (Fabre d'Olivet) asserts plainly and fearlessly that the Genesis of Moses was symbolically expressed and ought not to be taken in a purely literal sense. Saint Augustine recognized this, and Origen avers that ' if one takes the history of the creation in the literal sense, it is absurd and contradictory.'. . . .

"According to the Essenian tradition, every word in this *Sepher of Moses* contains three meanings—the positive or simple, the comparative or figurative, the superlative or hieratic. When one has penetrated to this last meaning, all things are disclosed through a radiant illumination and the soul of that one attains to heights which those bound to the narrow limits of the positive meaning and satisfied with the letter which killeth never know.

" The learned Maimonides says ' Employ you (sic) reason, and you will be able to discern what is said allegorically, figuratively and hyperbolically, and what is meant literally.' "

(From translator's Foreword to *The Hebraic Tongue Restored*, Fabre d'Olivet, by Nayán Louise Redfield, translator from original French).

CHAPTER I

" IN THE BEGINNING GOD CREATED THE HEAVEN AND THE EARTH "

For the guidance of readers I would here mention that many verses of the first three Chapters of Genesis are treated in the following manner: Verses from the King James Version are quoted. Then follows an analysis based upon the Hebrew words employed, their literal translations and the application of the results to an elucidation of the subject matter. Brackets are used to enclose the Hebrew words and their translations.

The following proffered commentary on the cosmogony of the *Book of Genesis* is largely founded upon occult philosophy or theosophic Cosmogenesis. I have, in consequence, used some of the Sanskrit words generally employed in this system such as *Pralaya*, which simply means " period of quiescence between Universes ", and *Manvantara* which means " period of activity ". These terms are fully explained in footnotes and in the Glossary, and I trust that their use will not render even more difficult the study of an admittedly abstruse, but profoundly interesting, subject. For those to whom this approach is new the interpretations may possibly seem somewhat complex, particularly compared with the comparative simplicity of the Biblical language.

Gen. I: 1. *In the beginning God created the heaven and the earth.*

2. *And the earth was without form, and void; and darkness was upon the face of the deep. And the Spirit of God moved upon the face of the waters.*

1. **In the beginning** (*b'resheth*,[1] Heb., " in principal, primarily, wisdom ") **God** (*Elohim*, Heb., " gods, the Unity of gods, powers, qualities, activities of the Supreme Being expressing one will, one purpose, one harmony ") **created** (*bara*, Heb., " an internal movement of Spirit originated,

---

[1] The Hebrew words and their translations are taken from *The Unknown God*, F. J. Mayers, Thomas's Publications Ltd., Severn St., Birmingham, England. This work is in its turn partly based upon *The Hebrew Tongue Restored* (Fabre d'Olivet) and a great many other works. The help derived from these two books especially is gratefully acknowledged.

He created ", and *shith*, Heb., " a hexad or complete relationship, cycle or work ") **the heaven** (*shamaim*, Heb., " exalted waters, the divine spiritual, positive pole of creation ") **and the earth** (*aretz*, Heb., " the primal element in its final, most material state, the lowest, most material negative pole ").

2. **And the earth was without form, and void** (*thohou wa bohou*, Heb., " a contingent and potential existence "); **and darkness** (*hosheck*, Heb., " that which closes in and brings a feeling of helpless ignorance, of being lost ") **was upon the face of the deep** (*tho-hom*, Heb., " all the potentialities of things to be universally ").

The Bible thus opens with the affirmation that an intelligent, self-knowing group of formative agencies of cosmic evolutionary stature (*Elohim*) [1] was responsible for the direction of the form-producing impulse which arose in pre-cosmic Space. Wherever the term " God " is used in *Genesis* the word in the original text is *Elohim*, meaning not a single Being, but an Order of creative Intelligences, as stated above. The terms " the heaven " and " the earth " refer to the separation of primordial substance (heavens) from the manifested Universe (the earth). J. Ralston Skinner writes: " It is made to be read ' B'rashith bārā Elohim ' etc., ' In the beginning God created the heavens and the earth; ' wherein *Elohim* is a plural nominative to a verb in the third person singular. Nachmanides called attention to the fact that the text might suffer the reading, ' B'rash ithbârā Elohim ', etc., ' In the head (source or beginning) created itself (or developed) *Gods, the heavens and the earth*,' really a more grammatical rendering." [2]

THE NAME " GOD "

The term " God " as used in these verses is thus not singular but plural in its implications. Although the original directive Intelligence—the Precursor and Source of Universal Mind—arose in a unitary state from its root in pre-cosmic Space, immediately that agency became outward-turned the rule of number obtained. One alone cannot manifest; three are essential to the production of any result. This is as true of cosmic manifestation as of microcosmic or human creation, whether intellectual or physical. No germ is a unit, each at its simplest being a triplicity of potentials, namely the positive, the negative and their

[1] q.v. *The Kingdom of the Gods* and *Occult Powers in Nature and in Man*, Geoffrey Hodson. See also Glossary.

[2] q.v. *The Cabbalah Masonic Review*, Sept. 1885, quoted from *H. P. Blavatsky Collected Writings*, Vol. 7, p. 261.

productive interaction. So also the germ of a Cosmos which, though a unit in *Pralaya*,[1] displays a number at the outset of *Manvantara*.[2] The term God, therefore, as used in these verses is to be understood, as in Kabbalism,[3] to refer to the group of intelligent, productive agencies inherent in and emanated from pre-cosmic Space, the *Elohim*.[4] The first Chapter of *Genesis* is, in consequence, called the Elohistic and the second the Jehovistic.

The question is sometimes asked, even by children: "If God made all things, who made God?" Occult philosophy answers "No-one"; for the *Demiurgos* or active Logos is an Emanation from the immutable Infinite, the Boundless, the Absolute, which cannot will, think or act until it has "become" partially manifest as finite. This it does by the projection of a Ray which penetrates into Infinite space, there to become the Architect of the resultant Universe. Kabbalism expresses this as follows: "There was a time when Heaven and Earth did not exist, but only an unlimited Space in which reigned absolute immobility. All the visible things and all that which possesses existence were born in that Space from a powerful principle, which existed by Itself, and from Itself developed Itself, and which made the heavens revolve and preserved the universal life; a principle as to which philosophy declares we know not the name. . . ."[5]

GOD, THE TOTALITY OF EXISTENCE

The term "God", therefore, carries a number of implications. It includes physical Nature; the evolutionary impulse imparted to it; the

---

[1] As stated in the Author's Preface to Volume I and elsewhere, Sanskrit words are used throughout this work, largely for the sake of brevity but also because such words traditionally and very aptly signify the ideas denoted by them. *Pralaya* (Sk.)—"Epoch of quiescence". A period of obscuration or repose, whether planetary or universal. There are said to be four kinds of *Pralayas* or such states of changelessness: cosmic *Pralaya*, when the totality of manifested Universes is dissolved; partial *Pralaya*, referring to any component which is dissolved during *Mahā-Manvantara*; human *Pralaya*, when man has identified himself with the One Absolute or entered *Nirvāna*, and physical *Pralaya*, as in state of profound and dreamless sleep. *Pralaya*, then, refers to the period when the life of a Globe, Round, Chain or Solar System is partially or completely indrawn, activity or manifestation ceasing in part or in whole. A *Pralaya* of a single Planet—corresponding somewhat to Winter—is a minor *Pralaya*, that of a Solar System a *Mahā-Pralaya*, and a general dissolution of the whole Cosmic System a *Prākritika-Pralaya*. During a minor *Pralaya* "the Planets remain intact, though dead, just as a huge animal, caught and embedded in polar ice, remains the same for ages." (*The Secret Doctrine*, p. 146, Original Ed.).

[2] *Manvantara* (Sk.)—"Period between Manus". A condition of manifestation, as opposed to *Pralaya*. See also Glossary under Chain.

[3] Readers who wish to compare the cosmogony of *Genesis* with that of the Theosophy of the Hebrews known as the Kabbalah, are referred to the Appendix to this Volume, which consists of a brief exposition of that subject.

[4] q.v. Glossary.

[5] q.v. *The Secret Wisdom of the Qabalah*, p. 52, J. F. C. Fuller.

irresistible formative force which bestows the attribute of self-reproduction and the capacity to express it; the creative Intelligences—the *Elohim*— which direct the manifestations and the operations of that force; the divine thought or ideation of the whole Cosmos from its beginning to its end; and the sound of the creative " Voice " (Logos) by which that ideation is impressed upon pre-cosmic substance. These, together with all seeds, beings, forces and laws, including those of expansion, alternation, cyclic progression and harmonious equipoise, constitute that totality of existence to which alone may be given with any measure of fitness the majestic and awe-inspiring title " God ".

If so vast a synthesis may be designated a Being, then that Being is so complex, so all-inclusive, as to be beyond the comprehension of the human mind and the possibility of restriction to any single form. The idea of God also includes everlasting Law, everlasting Will, everlasting Life and everlasting Mind.

In non-manifestation God is quiescent, in manifestation objectively active. Behind both quiescence and activity exists THAT which is eternal and unchanging, the Absolute, Self-Existent ALL. The divine Creator referred to by various names in the world's cosmogonies is the active expression of that eternal, incomprehensible One Alone.

EMANATION, NOT CREATION

Similarly, the word " create " has its particular significance. The production of something previously non-existent in any state is not to be understood or implied by this word. To emanate or make manifest more truly describe the process; for Cosmos is inherent in Chaos,[1] the difference being not of substance but of condition. Formlessness and darkness describe Chaos. Form and light describe Cosmos. Both conditions are inherent in pre-cosmic *substans*. The verses should therefore be translated as follows: " At the dawn of the return of *Manvantara*, the group of creative Intelligences[2] resumed activity, with the result that the germ of Cosmos

---

[1] The term " Chaos " is used in its more philosophic meaning throughout this work to connote, not utter confusion but the following various significations: the " Abyss ", the " Great Deep ", the primordial, pre-atomic condition in which matter existed before the first atoms and planes of Nature were " created "; primordial space; an infinite, formless void; the root of matter in its first remove from the unknown Absolute; the impenetrable veil between what can be seen by the cognisable eye and the invisible actuality of the first active Logos; the primeval " waters " of life; the Virgin Mother of Cosmos; the divine substance which alone exists throughout all eternity, boundless and absolute. q.v *The Theosophical Glossary*, H. P. Blavatsky.

[2] Creative Intelligences—The *Elohim*, the first and the succeeding Emanations or Essences; the male-female Creative Hierarchies of Beings who bring a Universe into objective existence. See Appendix and Glossary under *Elohim*.

inherent in Chaos commenced to unfold according to natural law." This process is continuous throughout the period of manifestation, for the Universe is a perpetual becoming, not a static condition of being. This applies equally to the primordial " elements ", to the substances derived from them, to the forms of Nature and to their ensouling life. All grows or expands from less to more from the dawn of the first " day " of emanation to the evening of the last or seventh " day ".

> *Gen.* 1: 2 (last sentence). And the Spirit (*ruach*, Heb., " breath, spirit, wind, expansion, spiritualisation ") of God moved (*mera-chepheth*, Heb., " breathes life into ") upon the face of the waters.

Herein is presented the primordial trinity, namely Spirit,[1] space (waters) and motion. The essential triplicity of the creative agencies is here perfectly described. " The Spirit of God " is the masculine potency within the germ of Cosmos pre-existent in Chaos. " The waters " and " the deep " are symbols or hierograms for the feminine potency, and the movement of the former upon or within the latter is the third potency essential to manifestation. In terms of electricity, it is the current which passes between positive and negative poles. Thus in the first two verses of *Genesis* the creative necessities are symbolically introduced and creative activity is allegorically described.

> *Gen.* 1: 3. *And God said, Let there be light: and there was light.*

> 3. **And God said** (*amor*, Heb., " enlightened, brought to light, made manifest "), **Let there be** (*ye-he*, Heb., " there shall be ") **light** (*aor*, Heb., " intelligence; God willed light and the Divine Intelligence flashed into active being "): **and there was light.**

Again a threefold agency is described but, be it observed, an agency differing from the first. Whereas the original triplicity is integral, comprising the whole of existence, its successor is productive only and is completed by a product. This latter trinity of *Genesis* consists first of ideation—the thought of light;[2] second of active productive power—speech; and third of the product—Universal Mind, here called light.

---

[1] Spirit—Not an entity but that which belongs directly to Universal Consciousness. The most tenuous, formless and immaterial spiritual substance.

[2] Light—To be regarded as the divine intelligence, the first Emanation of the Supreme, that light which, according to the Gospel of St. John, is the life of men. Not to be confused with the light of the sun, which is a focus or lens by which the rays of the primordial light become materialized and concentrated upon our Solar System and produce all the correlations of forces. The criticism that light appeared three days before the sun is thus disposed of.

Progression from the germinal to the active state is thus indicated. The manifesting process has not only been initiated, but has also become effective. Light is described as the first product of the generative act and this light is " born " of ideation and power, or thought and speech, the true " parents" of Cosmos. Yet these three are not separate existences, but one; for speech is thought expressed in sound and the product, light, was inherent in divine thought.

In almost all cosmogonies emanating from the world's Sanctuaries, sound is made the creative agency. Since words express thought, so behind the " Word " is divine thought or archetypal ideation, of which the Logos is an expression in Time, Space and Motion—the everlasting Trinity in unity. The energy which in an appropriate medium (air) produces the effect of sound is released and expressed in every physical sound. Vocal self-expression is the mark of man, and did he but realise that fact he would be infinitely careful of his speech. The rituals of the Sanctuaries of old, and the words uttered in such ceremonial Rites as have their origin therein, are all based upon recognition of the power in the human voice. When a man discovers the mystery of the soniferous Ākāsa he becomes an Adept, a Theurgist, a Magician—hence the practice of enveilment. All Nature obeys the " Voice " of the Divine, whether as Logos or illumined man. The ancient Sages knew this and revealed it solely by allegory in the form of the creative utterances which their cosmogonies relate.

In Kabbalism, the theosophy or hidden wisdom of Hebraism, creative procedures are indicated by means of a diagram known as *The Sephirothal Tree of Life*.[1] The ten Sephiroth of which this diagram consists are regarded as ten spheres of divine manifestation in which God emerges from His hidden abode in order to produce the Universe. This is accomplished with the aid of ten Hierarchies of spiritual Intelligences, or Archangels and angels. The action and development of the mysterious force which is the " seed " of all " Creation " is speech-force expressive of archetypal thought. The human faculty of speech is said to have been anticipated in God; for according to the *Zohar* the successive phases of the emanation of the Universe include the primeval Will, formative thought, the inner and inaudible " Word ", audible voice and ultimately man's utterance of words. Malkuth (the Kingdom) occupies the lowest point in the diagram and represents the " sounding-board " of physical Nature. Kether (the Crown) at the top of the Tree is regarded as the Source of the creative sound. The Sephiroth are but chords in the creative " Word ", component characteristics of the One Sound or " Song Divine ". Thus the Lord challenged Job concerning the time when He laid the foundations

---

[1] q.v. Appendix.

of the Earth, asking him ". . . who laid the corner stone thereof; When the morning stars sang together, and all the sons of God shouted for joy ?"[1]

To reiterate, these masculine and feminine creative potencies, together with motion, pre-existed within the germ. The first activity to occur within that germ is ideation, or the arising of the concept of the eternal design. This process is followed by the expression of that Archetype in terms of power or energy, the product being divine Intelligence symbolised as light. Thus six agencies are introduced in the first three verses. Two stages are also described, the pre-cosmic and the primary cosmic, the pre-existent and the first manifested existence.

LIGHT, AN EXPRESSION OF THE FIRST ACTIVE LOGOS

The first-born light contains the potencies of its parents and grand-parents, namely power, thought (the parents), and feminine and masculine potency endowed with motion (the grandparents). The first light, there-fore, is itself a complete creative power, a synthesis of the total essentials for manifestation, the Cosmic Christos or Son by Whom " all things were made ".[2] By light, self-existing as a unitary synthesis, the sevenfold creative agency is completed. The *Adonai* [3] is made manifest as *Elohim.*

The first light may therefore be defined as the active *Verbum* or *Logos,*[4] the potent, creative agency whose arising from latency in the cosmic germ is the mark, the sign and the demonstration that *Pralaya* has given place to *Manvantara.* This first light is the highest manifested Deity and, as observed, to it alone with all its implications may justly and truly be applied the term " God ".

No personalisation of THAT, which becomes " Creator " or Mani-festor according to law, is either philosophically sound or spiritually reverent. Though the producer of life-imbued form, it is itself essentially formless as its symbol—" light "—accurately portrays. Even in action as a manifesting agency its symbol is speech, or the potency and activity of thought-sound, which again is formless.

A further definition of God as presented in these verses of *Genesis* might be that it is a single, a threefold and a sevenfold directive Agency, originally inherent in pre-cosmic *substans* and now active throughout the whole field of creative activity. This activity is infallibly guided by

[1] *Job* 38: 6, 7.
[2] *Jn.* 1: 3.
[3] *Adonai* (Heb.)—Substitute for Lord or Jehovah. JHWH.
[4] *Logos* (Gr.)—" The Word ", " a divine spiritual Entity ". The manifested Deity, the outward expression or effect of the ever-concealed Cause. Thus speech is the *Logos* of thought, and *Logos* is correctly translated into Latin as *Verbum* and into English as " Word " in the metaphysical sense. q.v. Glossary under *Vach.*

numerical necessity. God as the first light is therefore not almighty, being subject to mathematical law, which is the absolute if abstract Monarch of the Cosmos. The dual title " Logos-Law " best depicts the true parental Deity of which the present Cosmos is the product or " Son ".

Gen. 1: 4. *And God saw the light, that it was good: and God divided the light from the darkness.*

External awareness is here postulated as an essential of cosmic formative procedure. The primordial Parent, having awakened from *pralayic* sleep, first becomes active in terms of light; for light and darkness respectively are symbols of spiritual activity and quiescence. In one interpretation, light in the allegorical language is descriptive of a condition of consciousness, a state of being in which Spirit predominates over matter. Darkness, on the other hand, symbolises the dominance of matter over Spirit. The first sentence of this verse is therefore repetitive, and says that pre-cosmic " night " or *Pralaya* had given place to cosmic " day " [1] or *Manvantara*, but adds that the newly-awakened creative Agency was now aware of that change and henceforth entered consciously upon its official activity.

The subsequent division of light from darkness described in the second sentence of the verse is the first Biblical reference to alternation. The primary pair consists of pre-Cosmos and Cosmos, allegorically called night and day, darkness and light, respectively. During the darkness no activity save absolute, and therefore incognisable, activity exists and only darkness —to the finite mind—obtains, alternation being confined to Cosmos, for once Cosmos appears alternation is inseparable from it. This is because a contrasting pair—quiescence and activity or absolute and finite existence —has come into being. These two constitute the darkness and the light which are automatically divided from each other when Cosmos appears.

The term " God ", therefore, here also refers to essential, inescapable law under which duality must obtain whenever there is finiteness. From

---

[1] Brahma's Day. " A period of 2,160,000,000 (Earth) years during which Brahmā having emerged out of his golden egg (*Hiranyagarbha*), creates and fashions the material world (being simply the fertilizing and creative force in Nature). After this period, the worlds being destroyed in turn by fire and water, he vanishes with objective nature, and then comes Brahmā's Night." Brahmā's Night. " A period of equal duration, during which Brahma is said to be asleep. Upon awakening he recommences the process, and this goes on for an AGE of Brahmā composed of alternate Days and Nights, and lasting 100 years (of 2,160,000,000 [Earth] years each). It requires fifteen figures to express the duration of such an age; after the expiration of which the *Mahāpralaya* or the Great Dissolution sets in, and lasts in its turn for the same space of fifteen figures," q.v. *The Theosophical Glossary*, H. P. Blavatsky.

these first "parents" all successive and subordinate dualities arise, and continue in a descending scale down to the smallest living things. Thus alternation may truly be stated to be both the law of existence and the essential condition of awareness. The moment light exists, darkness is known as its inseparable opposite.

Gen. 1: 5. *And God called the light Day, and the darkness he called Night. And the evening and the morning were the first day.*

> 5. **And God called the light Day** (*iom*, Heb., " a manifestation of light universally, or not limited to any mundane period ") **and the darkness he called Night** (chaos in which God was unmanifested). **And the evening** (*ereb*, Heb., " something which is over, finished, passed; the darkness which passes away "), **and the morning** (*boker*, Heb., " something which arises; the arising of the divine light or flashing into existence of divine intelligence ") **were the first day.**

This verse repeats the above-mentioned law of alternation and affirms divine awareness of its operation; for naming and name in the allegorical language describe conscious, *demiurgic* activity by mind and will, thought and power, to produce individuality out of that which hitherto was universal. A name is definite and separative. Once anything is named it has individuality and is therefore separated from other individualities.

By naming the new Cosmos, or area therein, the Logos limits the universal, marks out an area in which creative activity is to be confined. This insulation also is achieved, or automatically occurs, by the combined operation of consciousness and sound. In this verse, therefore, the external limits of the Universe-to-be are defined and marked out. Within those limits the precisely ordained frequencies of oscillation of the creative power must eventually rule.

As the genesis and fecundation of the universal " egg "—symbol of all new " creations " whether cosmic, universal or solar—these frequencies are apportioned by numerical law. They are affirmed by Universal Mind as expressive of both the underlying character and the potential attainment of the new Universe. The first sentence of the verse, therefore, describes these two processes.

The second sentence, referring to evening and morning, reintroduces the property of time, mentioned in the opening words of the Chapter. Subdivisions of time are thus affirmed as being inseparable from the change from Chaos to Cosmos. The words " in the beginning " (*b'resheth*, at first, in principle) actually mean the beginning, or rather the re-emergence, of all things. Evening and morning of the first day refer to the opening and the close of the first creative epoch or " day ".

The use of the word " first " suggests a succession, thus introducing the subject of Numbers. As indicated in Volume One of this work, numbers in the symbolical language carry significations beyond numerical figurations alone. Each number has its own metaphysical meanings, one of which includes the living Intelligence which it also represents.

Every creative " d.y ", for example, has its Deity or number; for numbers in this connection are, as stated, living Intelligences emanated from the " One ", meaning the finite but universal Intelligence which is the active, but not absolute, Parent of all. In terms of formative Intelligences, when the First of the Seven has completed its day of activity, has produced its inevitable effects, it withdraws to give place to its brother, who is the second in the succession.

> *Gen.* 1: 6. *And God said, Let there be a firmament in the midst of the waters, and let it divide the waters from the waters.*

> 6. **And God said, Let there be a firmament** (*rakia*, Heb., " an expanse stretching out, linked with both the spiritual and the material; the foundation of the heavens ") **in the midst of the waters, and let it divide the waters from the waters.**

In this verse the defining and insulating process is carried out in primordial substance, symbolised by waters, as earlier it has been carried out in primordial thought. The waters which were under the firmament, which represents the manifested visible Universe, were divided from the waters which were above the firmament, meaning the invisible, super-physical planes of Nature.

The term " firmament " (literally a rarifying) here refers to the enveloping " shell " or " membrane " in which the foetal, physical Universe is enclosed, and which separates substance without from substance within.

> *Gen.* 1: 7. *And God made the firmament, and divided the waters which were under the firmament from the waters which were above the firmament: and it was so.*

This verse allegorically describes the establishment of the membrane by the action of creative thought and will expressed as sound.

> *Gen.* 1: 8. *And God called the firmament Heaven. And the evening and the morning were the second day.*

The further establishment (by means of naming) of the limits of the selected creative area is here partly described. This may be likened to the natural process of the hardening into a shell or skin of the outer layer of an enclosing foetal membrane. In universal creative processes this shell is descriptively referred to as a " Ring-pass-not ",[1] and the verse shows that this is part of the activity of the Second Number or creative Intelligence, whilst its completion marks the successful fulfilment of that Second Number's work or " day ".

Numbered days and nights have therefore a dual significance. They refer both to the existence and activity of the creative Intelligence connoted by the number, and also to the condition of substance resulting from its completed work throughout the second " day " or creative epoch.

[1] *Ring-pass-not.* The outermost edge or limits marked out by the Logos within which His System is to appear. Also frontiers to which awareness is limited. See Glossary.

CHAPTER II

WATER, DRY LAND, FISHES AND BEASTS OF THE EARTH

Gen. 1: 9. *And God said, Let the waters under the heaven be gathered together unto one place and let the dry land appear: and it was so.*

9. **And God said, Let the waters under the heaven be gathered together** (*ikkavoo*, Heb., " to have a strong tendency towards some place, state or purpose ") **unto one place, and let the dry land appear: and it was so.**

In this opening description of the third cycle or " day " of creative activity, the first of many errors—if I may presume to say so—appears in the *Book of Genesis*. This consists of the erroneous merging into one cycle of two distinct processes which are in reality separated from each other by a vast period of time. Actually, each process occupies its own complete cycle from morning to evening of a creative " day ". As explained, so-called creative " days " are separated from each other by so-called " nights ".

The original authors, being Initiates of the Mysteries of Chaldea, must have known this truth. The error, therefore, must either be deliberate in order to conceal from full revelation the then secret knowledge of septenary cycles and sub-cycles, or else be a mistake made by less well-informed or uninitiated authors or translators. Whatever the explanation, a miscomputation was made and must be corrected for and by every student of cosmogony.

This division of intra-universal water, or primordial substance, into two states—liquid and solid—and the establishment in the demiurgic Mind of the thought of the mineral kingdom, followed by the slow process of the embodiment of that formative thought in appropriately densified substance, occupies a complete cycle or " day " and " night ".

The intermediate mineral stage between the division of the waters and the fashioning of the plant kingdom is omitted. Furthermore, fire is not introduced until the appearance of the sun. This creative act is placed in the fourth " day ", mineral and plant having erroneously and impossibly proceeded it. The account, therefore, is sadly muddled. The emergence of the plant kingdom should rightly be placed in the cycle which would have followed the establishment of the mineral kingdom.

> *Gen.* 1: 10. *And God called the dry land Earth*; *and the gathering together of the waters called he Seas*: *and God saw that it was good.*

>   10. **And God called the dry land** (*iabasha*, Heb., " the dryness, the stopping point of materialisation ") **Earth**; **and the gathering together of the waters called he Seas** (*iamin*, Heb., " manifested or visible waters "): **and God saw that it was good.**

The earth period or cycle occupied a whole " day ", and was the work of one of the seven creative Intelligences. Occult Cosmogenesis states that the Universe within the divine Thought became manifest as spiritual fire. Condensation and densification eventually produced the element rather than the solid substance of earth, the noumenon [2] of the mineral kingdom. Earth and water, meaning the solid and liquid states, then existed at the same time though separated one from the other, and it is to this co-existence that the verse refers. The naming of the two elements signifies their objective manifestation, each at its own individual level. The phrase " and God saw that it was good " refers to the end of the cycle, when the designated work had been brought to its highest pitch for that period.

> *Gen.* 1: 11. *And God said, Let the earth bring forth grass, the herb yielding seed, and the fruit tree yielding fruit after his kind, whose seed is in itself, upon the earth: and it was so.*

>   11. **And God said, Let the earth bring forth** (*thadeshae*, Heb., " to cause to vegetate or bring forth the more prolific and universal forms of green growth ") **grass, the herb yielding seed, and the fruit tree yielding fruit after his kind** (*mazeriah Zerah*, Heb., " seed seeding plants which have seed within them "), **whose seed is in itself, upon the earth: and it was so.**

This verse refers to the Plant *Manvantara* or Chain of the Planetary Scheme. As the germ of the whole Universe existed in pre-cosmic

---

[1] Noumenon. The unchanging essence from which the phenomenon arises; antithesis to phenomenon (Kant).

substance (*Mūlaprakriti*), so also do the seeds of all living beings and their natural forms ever potentially exist within the matter of the Universe (*Prakriti*).   As this becomes densified through all the stages on the descending arc down to the physical, the living divine seeds are densified also.

According to occult philosophy when the element of earth, however tenuous, ultimately comes into objective existence at its atomic level, amongst its atoms are master atoms which comprise the noumena of the physical seeds. When at last the dense, solid condition is reached, the master atoms constitute those seeds from which the first organic growth occurs. The plant kingdom then becomes manifest, occupies a whole cycle and continues its development in those which follow.

Just as the seed is in the fruit, so all seeds are present within the mother-substance from which everything is born. The statement that each plant yields fruit after its own kind simply refers to the divine " order " under which manifestation occurs. This order might be described as numerical law, abstract and everlasting, omnipotent and omnipresent, the supreme deific Power or creative Agency.

Under this governing law the *Elohim* carry out their work of making manifest through the seven planes or divisions of matter the primary creative Idea or Archetype, which is the " germ " from which the whole Universe is evolved. The constantly used term " God " is a mistranslation and a misnomer for the collective *Elohim*, which are imbued with and are embodiments of the primary divine Idea.[1]

These Intelligences make manifest the Archetype or thought-germ under the absolute rule of numerical law, as we have seen. Though the whole Order of the *Elohim* plays its part in all cycles and in all manifestation, one component Order is predominant in each cycle according to its office and function. There are seven in all, and by the authors of *Genesis*, they are indirectly designated by their numbers and their " days ".

> *Gen.* I: 14. *And God said, Let there be lights in the firmament of the heaven to divide the day from the night; and let them be for signs, and for seasons, and for days, and years:*
>
> 15. *And let them be for lights in the firmament of the heaven to give light upon the earth: and it was so.*
>
> 16. *And God made two great lights; the greater light to rule the day, and the lesser light to rule the night: he made the stars also.*

[1] q.v. *The Kingdom of the Gods*, Ch. III, Geoffrey Hodson.

17. *And God set them in the firmament of the heaven to give light upon the earth,*

18. *And to rule over the day and over the night, and to divide the light from the darkness: and God saw that it was good.*

19. *And the evening and the morning were the fourth day.*

14. **And God said, Let there be lights** (*maoroth*, Heb., The text here says not *shemesh*, Heb., " Suns ", or *iarech*, Heb., " Moon ", but " light givers, foci, sources of enlightenment, twin centres of one light or intelligence ") **in the firmament of the heaven to divide the day from the night; and let them be for signs** (*othoth*, Heb., or *aoth-oth*, Heb., " symbolic signs of the future, as if in reference to their astrological significance. The sun would then refer to the Spiritual Self and the moon to the mortal personality "), **and for seasons** (*moadim*, Heb., " limits or divisions of time, periods, intervals, determined or appointed times "), **and for days, and years** (*shanah*, Heb., " regular recurrent period "):

15. **And let them be for lights in the firmament of the heaven to give light upon the earth; and it was so.**

16. **And God made two great lights; the greater light to rule** (*memesheleth*, Heb., " symbolic representations of things to be; also to preside, to be a model, a representative, a symbol ") **the day, and the lesser light to rule the night: he made the stars** (*cocabbim*, Heb., " physical planets which are rolled or rotate and the forces, virtues or intelligences of the planets, their spiritual influences according to ancient astrology ") **also.**

17–19. **And God set them in the firmament of the heaven to give light upon the earth, and to rule over the day and over the night, and to divide the light from the darkness: and God saw that it was good. And the evening and the morning were the fourth day.**

The making of the first lights—sun, moon and stars—after the passage of three days and three nights and the creation of the plant kingdom (if such was the original statement) is, I repeat, clearly a chronological error. In the earliest available Hebrew original text, the words *shemesh* (Heb.) "sun", and *iarech* (Heb.), "moon", are not used. The abstract expression *maoroth* (Heb.), " sources of enlightenment " is the word employed. This suggests not only sources of physical light, but of mental and spiritual enlightenment also.

The five opening verses of the *Book of Genesis* describe the production and appearance of the first cycle, that of light. This refers to the emergence of the finite from the Absolute, of Cosmos from Chaos. The second creation of light referred to in verses 14–18 alludes to the appearance of suns in individual systems within the Cosmos. Actually Schemes, Chains, Solar and even Rounds[1], are inextricably mixed up in this exoterically imperfect but nevertheless, I suggest, deeply esoteric cosmogony.

The appearance of the physical sun should come first in the account of the manifestation of a single Solar System. The suggestion of a moon to rule the night as the sun rules the day, and the later creation of the stars, is a relic and an adaptation from Chaldean astro-metaphysical esotericism. Indeed, this whole account of creation in *Genesis* is borrowed from Chaldea, where it was taught that sun, moon and stars were the physical bodies of great creative Intelligences of varying evolutionary stature in the Occult Hierarchy of the Universe—the *Dhyān Chohans* [2] of Hinduism.

ELOHIM—CREATIVE INTELLIGENCES

Thus intimately associated with the physical sun, moon and stars were and are great Archangels, in the *Zend-Avesta*, the sacred books of the Parsees, referred to as *Amshashpends*,[3] who are none other than types of the Sephiroth or *Elohim*. These are the true creative Agents who take up their " stations " and carry out their functions in an ordered succession as the process of the production of the Universe continues. It is these Beings who as directive Intelligences preside over *Manvantaras* or " days ".

The verses under consideration describe that Synthesis of the Elohistic Hosts Who is the Solar Logos, the spiritual Sun behind the physical orb.

[1] q.v. Glossary—Chain.

[2] *Dhyan Chohans* (Sk.). The " Lords of Contemplation ", the divine Intelligences charged with the supervision of Cosmos.

[3] *Amshashpends* (Pers.). The Seven Planetary *Logoi*, as well as the Creative Hosts who carry out their will. The six Angels or divine Forces, personified as gods, who attend upon *Ahūra Mazda* (the personified Deity, the Principle of Universal Divine Light of the Parsees), of which He is the synthesis and the seventh.

At the dawn of Creation He with His physical heart, which is the visible sun, assumes His stations, superphysical and physical, at the centre of the new Solar System and through the *Elohim* rules over all *Manvantaras*, major and minor. *Pralayas* alternate with these *Manvantaras*, and throughout the periods of non-activity members of a special Order of the *Elohim* are said to contain and preserve within themselves all the seeds of life. Then, in the new cycle, these seeds are delivered to the Solar Logos and the *Elohim* for further evolution. This constitutes part of the deeply esoteric mystery teaching allegorically revealed in the story of Noah and the Ark, and similar Flood legends.

The reference to the stars takes thought beyond a single Solar System, and may perhaps be regarded as indicating that similar processes are occurring universally during *Mahā-Manvantara*.[1] The whole of the cosmogony of *Genesis*, like all esoteric cosmogonies, refers primarily to the noumena or essential nature of Universes, Solar Systems, suns and planets, as also to the planes and kingdoms of Nature. These, as we have already seen, include their ensouling Principles, which are made objectively manifest by great creative Intelligences, members of the Hosts of the Logos, the Numbers, the Lords of the Divine Face, the Embodiments of formative Powers, Principles and Orders—the *Elohim* in the fullest meaning of the term.

The physical manifestation or outer appearance of Nature in all her kingdoms refers to the material "clothing" or densified auras of these Mighty Ones. In esoteric cosmogony the true fashioners of Universes according to the divine Idea are these Beings, "the Fiery Lives",[2] major and minor. Their emergence, assumption of office and embarkation upon appropriate activity and function, are of the most profound significance. They should be thought of not only as Beings with bodies and auras, but also as centres of Power, Life, Consciousness and Law. They, their radiance and their spheres of influence and activity, constitute the ensouling Principle of every Order of Creation, whether it be a Universe, a Solar System, a planet, a plane or a kingdom of Nature.

In the *Elohim*, who constitute a vast Hierarchy of spiritual Beings—Planetary and Solar Spirits or *Dhyān Chohans*—the illusion of self-separated

---

[1] *Mahā-Manvantara* (Sk.)—"Great interlude between the *Manus* or Creative *Logoi*." The major, total period of universal activity which includes numberless inner cycles, finite and conditioned, or minor periods called *Manvantaras*. A day of Brahmā lasts 100 "years," each of which occupies a period of 2,160,000,000 (Earth) years, according to Hindu cosmogonical chronology. It requires fifteen figures to express the duration of such an age. q.v. *The Theosophical Glossary*, H. P. Blavatsky.

[2] The Fiery Lives. The seventh and highest subdivision of the plane of matter, corresponding in the individual with the One Life of the Universe, though only on that plane of matter. q.v. *The Secret Doctrine*, Vol. I, p. 306 and Vol. III, p. 125, H. P. Blavatsky (Adyar Ed.).

7

existence as experienced by pre-Initiate [1] man has entirely disappeared. They know themselves for what they truly are—component centres of the Power, Life and Consciousness of the one Synthesis of all Beings, the supreme directive Intelligence in Nature, the Solar Logos. Thus, although referred to as the Hosts of the Logos, we have seen that the *Elohim* may also be described as a unity, a summation and a synthesis embracing and including all divine Intelligences charged with the supervision of Cosmos.

This essential oneness of all spiritual Beings is the heart of esoteric philosophy and the key to all Cosmogonies. Universes are the bodies and the auras of resplendent Beings. Man is one such in-the-becoming, the Universe being the field of his evolution. Cosmoi are designed for him in order that from them he may learn to know both his current environment and his future activities therein. These will be to conceive, build and perfect Universes with their sun, planets, planes and kingdoms of Nature; for this is the destiny of man who is a pilgrim God.

Gen. 1 : 20. *And God said, Let the waters bring forth abundantly the moving creature that hath life, and fowl that may fly above the earth in the open firmament of heaven.*

21. *And God created great whales, and every living creature that moveth, which the waters brought forth abundantly, after their kind, and every winged fowl after his kind: and God saw that it was good.*

22. *And God blessed them, saying, Be fruitful, and multiply, and fill the waters in the seas, and let fowl multiply in the earth.*

23. *And the evening and the morning were the fifth day.*

20. **And God** (*Elohim*) **said, Let the waters bring forth** (*ishertzou sheretz,* Heb., "emit or swarm swarms") **abundantly the moving creature that hath life** (*nephesh chaiah,* Heb., "souls of life or living soul ") **and fowl that may fly above the earth in the open firmament of heaven.**

21. **And God created great whales** (*tanninim,* Heb., " God created the living souls of extensive groups or species of beings which could multiply after their own kind "),

---

[1] *Pre-Initiate.* The psycho-spiritual transformation known as Initiation, at which realisation of the oneness of all life is attained, is accompanied by ceremonial admission to the Greater Mysteries and marks a definite evolutionary stage. The term " pre-Initiate man " used throughout this work designates those who have not yet reached that stature.

**and every living creature that moveth, which the
waters brought forth abundantly, after their kind,
and every winged fowl after his kind: and God
saw that it was good.**

22. **And God blessed** (*barech*. Heb., "not so much blessed
as the bestowal of generative power ") **them, saying,
Be fruitful, and multiply, and fill the waters in
the seas, and let fowl multiply in the earth.**

23. **And the evening and the morning were the fifth
day.**

If restored to a correct chronological position, the emergence of fish,
reptiles and, far later, birds from primeval slime would follow the
production by Nature of her plant kingdom. These verses record this
process and, reducing description to an ascetic minimum, affirm the
presence of procreative and self-productive powers.

NATURE—LIVING PRODUCT OF AN INFINITE CREATIVE POTENCY

The instruction to be fruitful and multiply is of profound occult, as
well as natural, significance. Nature is here shown to be what she really
is, a self-perpetuating, living, conscious product of an infinite Power now
made finite. Both universal Spirit and universal substance noumenally
and phenomenally possess and contain the fiery energy by which all things
are made. This is the true, Immanent Logos, omnipresent, all-pervading,
inherent in both the Soul and the substance of the Universe. When to
the Order of created things are added beings with the power of free motion,
procreation becomes a consciously exercised power. The inherent reproductive capacity attains to conscious self-expression in the first creatures
endowed with the power of motion, for movement is an attribute of the
life-force. Locked up and held fast in the mineral, it is active there only
against immense resistance. The production of molecular and chemical
combinations, and therefore substances, within and from the one substance
is its sole activity in the mineral kingdom of Nature.

In the plant kingdom much freer motion occurs, and therefore far
fuller activity. Sentiency as possessed by animals has, however, not yet
been attained by the life-force in this mineral phase of its active
manifestation. No allegorical command to create is therefore given to
the plant kingdom, for no power of conscious response has yet been
developed. The first animal forms do possess the power consciously to

procreate, and may rightly be thus described in the text as receiving from the creative " Word " a verbal command to exercise it.

Gen. 1: 24. *And God said, Let the earth bring forth the living creature after his kind, cattle, and creeping thing, and beast of the earth after his kind: and it was so.*

25. *And God made the beast of the earth after his kind, and cattle after their kind, and every thing that creepeth upon the earth after his kind: and God saw that it was good.*

24. **And God said, Let the earth bring forth the living creature after his kind, cattle** (*behemah*, Heb., singular of *behemoth*, Heb. The meaning of the word is doubtful —possibly a huge beast, such as a hippopotamus. The root *hm* together with the letters *bh* do not indicate the name of any animal, but rather animation, life in general and, particularly, earth life, the universal, progressive life movement of physical nature. *Job* XL, 15 refers to *behemoth* as " the chief of the ways of God "), **and creeping thing, and beast of the earth after his kind: and it was so.**

25. **And God made the beast of the earth after his kind, and cattle after their kind, and every thing that creepeth** (*cal-remesh*, Heb., " all upward movement or progress ") **upon the earth** (*ha-adamah*, Heb., " not a synonym of earth or soil but something which is being contrasted with earth; a spiritual rather than a physical conception. All that moveth ' manwards ' ") **after his kind: and God saw that it was good.**

The land reptiles, and later the mammalia, followed the first denizens of water and air. Ultimately, as described in the verses which follow, the most significant event—the appearance of mankind—occurs. Nature reaches her highest achievement in the production of man.

CHAPTER III

MAN CREATED IN THE IMAGE OF GOD

Gen. 1: 26. *And God said, Let us make man in our image. after our likeness:*
and let them have dominion over the fish of the sea, and over
the fowl of the air, and over the cattle, and over all the
earth, and over every creeping thing that creepeth upon the
earth.

26. **And God said, Let us make man** (*Adam*, Heb., "the
kingdom of man") **in our image** (*tzelem*, Heb.,
"shadow, everything outside of Deity as Universal Light
being by contrast reflection, image, shadow"), **after our**
likeness: and let them have dominion over (the
text does not use this word, but distinctly says "in",
which appears to place man at the head of the four
kingdoms of Nature—his natural position) **the fish of**
the sea, and over the fowl of the air, and over the
cattle, and over all the earth, and over every creep-
ing thing that creepeth upon the earth.

In this verse three statements are made. First, God decides to make
man and announces that decision. Second, man is to be made in the
likeness of God, the plural pronoun "our" suggesting that plurality is
used by the Deity (*Elohim*) [1] in reference to Itself, the totality of
Intelligences. Third, man (also referred to as "them") is to have
dominion over all preceding orders of creation. Clearly, as stated, the
pronoun "our" refers to *Elohim*, a plural name which in English
translation erroneously tends to be regarded as singular and to be used
with a singular verb. Immediately after the words "our image" in
verse twenty-six, the statement is made in verse twenty-seven that *Elohim*
created Adam in "His" own image, which suggests *Elohim* as a unity.
Whilst this may seem to be contradictory, it is not so in reality; for all
divine attributes, powers and formative Intelligences are summed up in

[1] Glossary—*Elohim.*

Elohim, which makes of the active, manifesting God a united whole. From this point of view, at least, both plural and singular attributions are admissible.

Throughout this Cosmogony the mental decision of Deity and its verbal expression are continually posited as essentials of the process of the emanation and fashioning of a Universe. God first conceives in His mind and then expresses by His voice the name of whatever He is about to produce.[1] This is both an allegorisation of the process of creation by sound, or the " Word ", and a personification as one Being of the various formative Agencies, the *Elohim*. Always it must be remembered that the " Creator " is no single Being alone, and the importance of this fact justifies its many repetitions in this Volume, for which indulgence is nevertheless sought. Although a totality in unity, " He " should rather be described as the collective, natural agencies, forces and Intelligences which arise from within and emanate from the Absolute at the dawn of *Manvantara*. The use of the plural pronouns " us " and " our " in this verse is therefore highly suggestive, and indeed exact.

MAN—MODEL OF THE TOTALITY OF NATURE

The decision attributed to the Deity to make mankind in His own image introduces a profound and fundamental truth concerning man, namely that in his spiritual, intellectual, psychical and physical nature he is a miniature replica of the whole Order of created beings and things. Man, according to occult philosophy, is a model of the totality of Nature, containing within himself the collective aggregate of all that ever has existed, that does at any time exist, and that ever will exist throughout the eternity of eternities. This concept is also to be found in Kabbalism, where it is formulated somewhat as follows: Man may be regarded as a symbolic transparency through which the secrets of the Cosmos may be discerned.

Man may also be looked upon as the waist of an hour-glass through which passes the sand (creative power) from the upper receptacle—the past—into the lower which represents the future. All must pass through the human kingdom; for potentially all exists within man, however great the degree of latency may be in this present epoch and however germinal as yet the possibility of the emanation and formation of future Universes and Cosmoi. Man is a microcosm, a miniature reproduction of the Macrocosm, and is therefore rightly said to be made in the image of his

---

[1] *Occult Powers in Nature and in Man*, Ch. IV, Geoffrey Hodson, where this subject is considered in some detail.

Creator. The Chinese philosopher, Lao Tzu, expressed this in his famous phrase: " The universe is a man on a large scale." [1]

In *Genesis* man, as Nature's highest product up to that time, is also stated to have dominion over all earlier creations. At this point it is important to make clear the fact that man, said to be conceived and formed in the likeness of God, is not a new and separate production. As Monad [2] he pre-existed and as an individual intelligence in human form he is the product of the slow processes of the involution and evolution of the radiated Ray or " thread " [3] of Monadic life through elemental,[4] plant and animal kingdoms. In them, however, the deific potencies locked up and latent in the Monad experienced but diffuse and diverse manifestation as part of a Group Soul [5] embodied in many forms.

Nature's greatest miracle takes place when the summit—mental, psychical and physical—of animal development is reached. The Monadic Ray is then singly focussed—rather like the sun's rays when brought to a point of light beneath a burning glass—into one intellectual principle to constitute a new-formed spiritual Soul, a new-born Higher Self of man. It is this Monad-Ego,[6] and not the temporary physical personality, which is made in the likeness of its Creator; for it contains within itself the potentialities of the collective agencies and forces—the *Elohim*—as well as of all from which they emanate and could ever produce.

Such is the immortal, imperishable and eternal man, made in the image of his Creator. Embodied in vehicles of flesh, emotion and mind, he is made manifest in the three grossest densities of substance. As a totality, a unit, a consciousness with infinite potentialities, man is indeed greater than all preceding products of Nature and in *this* sense (only, I submit—G.H.) may be said to have dominion over them.

---

[1] q.v. *The Kingdom of the Gods*, Pt. I, Ch. IV and *Lecture Notes of the School of the Wisdom*, Vol. I (Rev. Ed.), Ch. XIII, Geoffrey Hodson.

[2] q.v. Glossary.

[3] Thread or *Sūtrātmā* (thread-self). A current of spiritual life-force, a golden thread of continuous life upon which the seed atoms or nuclei of the seven bodies of man are " strung ". q.v. *A Study in Consciousness*, A. Besant.

[4] Elemental kingdoms. Three pre-mineral kingdoms are passed through on the involutionary or descending arc, which is followed by the radiated Monadic Ray. Arrival at the mineral kingdom marks the stage of deepest descent into matter. Thereafter the upward or evolutionary arc is entered upon, the plant kingdom being the next embodiment of the ascending Monadic life. This phase is in due course followed by entry into and passage through the animal, human and superhuman kingdoms.

[5] Group Soul. The pre-individualised manifestation of the human Monads when evolving through the mineral, the plant and the animal kingdoms of Nature.

[6] q.v. Glossary.

Gen. 1 : 27. " *So God created man in his own image, in the image of God created he him; male and female created he them.*"

In this verse the most fundamental fact concerning man is first reiterated, demonstrating its importance in the minds of those inspired Sages who discovered and gave to man the truths upon which the *Book of Genesis* is founded.[1] This Ageless Wisdom teaches that man as Monad is an infinite manifestation of the deific Power, which in him is as yet largely germinal, although becoming increasingly active. The means whereby these latent potentialities in man become active powers are then indicated. These means partly consist of successive incarnations in male and female bodies on Earth, in and through which the necessary masculine and feminine experience is gained and the dual evolution attained; for the human Monad develops from within itself the attributes of the first divine, creative Pair, the positive and negative potencies, as the result of the interaction of which the Universe appears. Separate modes of manifestation—in the opposite sexes—are essential to the development of this threefold capacity inherent in the spiritual Soul of man. Nature, if her purpose is to be fulfilled, must produce two separate physical organisms with the distinct experiences and functions of man and of woman; for only thus may the twofold expression and development be gained and human evolutionary progress be achieved.

Gen. 1 : 28. *And God blessed them, and God said into them, Be fruitful, and multiply, and replenish the earth, and subdue it: and have dominion over the fish of the sea, and over the fowl of the air, and over every living thing that moveth upon the earth.*

AN INITIATORY INTERPRETATION

Whilst the more general significance of this verse is plainly apparent it is also susceptible of interpretation as guidance to those who are passing through advanced phases of evolution. Admittedly no such instruction may been intended, nevertheless the verse may possibly be thus interpreted in conformity with the method used by the writers of the Sacred Language of Allegory and Symbol.

As observed elsewhere in this work, there are two phases of unfoldment of very great importance in the evolution of the human Monad. One of these is its attainment of individual self-existence as the spiritual Soul of a human being, the Immortal Self in its vesture of light. The second development occurs much later in human evolution. After a considerable

---

[1] q.v.   Introduction to Pt, III of this Volume.

number of incarnations in successive civilisations and nations,[1] realisation of spiritual identity with the Logos, and through Him with all that lives, begins to be attained. This profoundly affects the outlook of the physical personality. Love for the life in all beings, service to that life in sentient forms, and a reduction of the sense of separated selfhood, eventually to vanishing point, find expression in the illumined man. When this phase becomes sufficiently established in both the inner and the outer individualities, a spiritual Teacher guides the neophyte's further development and eventually presents him as a Candidate for Initiation into the still existing Greater Mysteries, and for admission to the Great White Brotherhood of Initiates and Adepts which exists from eternity to eternity.[2]

One of the several possible interpretations of the Scriptures and Mythologies of ancient peoples—as previously mentioned—reveals the guidance and training thus received. Since, when applied, these bestow great mental and thaumaturgical powers, they are concealed from the profane by the use of the Symbolical Language. As the resultant knowledge could be of the greatest value in both the worldly and the spiritual life, in order to include it in these Volumes digressions from the main textual theme are, as now, occasionally made.

Reference to Chapter Three of Part One of this Volume will show that in the cypher of the Bible physical objects, inanimate and animate, and certain key words have a special significance. Amongst these the earth itself and the members of the sub-human kingdoms of Nature are used to symbolise man's more earthy and animal characteristics.

Thus interpreted, this verse may usefully be regarded as direction to the Candidate for Initiation to subdue his lower nature. In this sense the references to the earth, the sea and its denizens, the air and the birds and to " every living thing that moveth upon the earth " are to the undesirable aspects (earthy and animal-like) of his purely human characteristics, which it is man's task and destiny wholly to transmute into their corresponding higher attributes. This is especially important to the aspirant to the spiritual life who is hastening beyond the normal speed the evolution of the spiritual Self to the stature of the perfect man.

The next verse, as will be seen, is more readily susceptible of interpretation in a purely physical sense.

Gen. 1: 29. *And God said, Behold I have given you every herb bearing seed, which is upon the face of all the earth, and every tree, in the which is the fruit of a tree yielding seed; to you it shall be for meat.*

---

[1] q.v. *Reincarnation, Fact or Fallacy*, Geoffrey Hodson. (T.P.H., Adyar).
[2] q.v. Vol. I of this work, Pt. VI.

29. **And God said, Behold, I have given you every herb bearing seed, which is upon the face of all the earth, and every tree, in the which is the fruit of a tree yielding seed ; to you it shall be for meat** (*achelah*, Heb., "sustenance", also "consuming and consummating ").

A statement is here made of the ideal food for man's physical body —Nature's plan for the nutriment of mankind. Plants are said to be the source of that food, and from this it may be assumed that divergence from the divine plan is fraught with peril to both the Soul and the body of man. Presumably the danger partly arises from the inevitable infliction of unnecessary pain and the act of killing sentient beings, the animals; for such actions must constitute crimes against that perfect harmony which is a fundamental law of Nature. The discord generated by cruelty reacts upon man as suffering. When, furthermore, he disobeys the command given in the verse to use as food selected products of the plant kingdom, the severity of the reaction is thereby increased. One form which this may take is to produce in the human body susceptibility to and suffering from disease.

Thus divine and natural ordinances are given for the well-being of man's physical body and the purity and stainlessness of his Soul. Departure from these spiritual and physical rules of life may be assumed in large measure to contribute to the sufferings of man. To have dominion over the animals does not mean to exploit and oppress them. Rather does the verse state the relative positions on the ladder of evolution of man and the members of the kingdoms below him.

Gen. 1: 30. *And to every beast of the earth, and to every fowl of the air, and to every thing that creepeth upon the earth, wherein there is life, I have given every green herb for meat: and it was so.*

31. *And God saw every thing that he had made, and, behold, it was very good. And the evening and the morning were the sixth day.*

The first of these two verses further indicates that not only man, but also all creatures, were originally intended to be plant feeders. Departure by man from this ordinance may have its place amongst the factors which changed so radically the face of Nature from the original harmony and harmlessness of the Garden of Eden, the primeval world, to the tragic discordance of the post-Eden period. Indeed, it might almost be permissible to see in the increase, in more modern times, of meat-eating and of cruelty to animals, primal causes of the steadily mounting human suffering from disease and war.

The completion of the whole work of Creation in six days, is a chronological error. According to occult philosophy the total number of major *Manvantaras* and *Pralayas*, or successive periods of evolutionary activity and of rest, called " days " and " nights " in *Genesis*, should be seven. This point is further discussed in the commentary on verse two of the Second Chapter of *Genesis*.

CHAPTER IV

THE SEVENTH DAY

Gen. 2: 1. *Thus the heavens and the earth were finished, and all the host of them.*

2. *And on the seventh day God ended his work which he had made; and he rested on the seventh day from all his work which he had made.*

1. **Thus** (*vav*, Heb., " thus rather than and, as in the English R.V.") **the heavens** (*shamaim*, Heb., ' heavens, plural indicating gradations or degrees of density of matter and expansion of consciousness—many mansions ") **and the earth were finished, and all the host** (*chol-tzebaam*, Heb., "the ordered hosts or army of the Lord") **of them.**

2. **And on the seventh** (*ha-shebihi*, Heb., " seventh, completion, return to a starting point." No mention is made of a morning and an evening of the seventh day, suggesting that it is less a period than a condition and state of fulfilment, completion, final adjustment and harmonising of discords) **day God ended his work which he had made; and he rested** (*isheboth*, Heb., " rested, re-established, going back to a former state ") **on the seventh day from all his work which he had made.**

The following proffered commentaries on this Chapter of the " Book of Genesis ", which are largely based upon translations of the original Hebrew words and the cosmogony of occult philosophy, are to be regarded as additional to those presented in Part Two, Chapters I and II—" Eden, Eve and the ' Fall ' of Man " and " Satan and the Tree of Knowledge of Good and Evil ".

In occult cosmogony the completion of the process of objective manifestation or " creation " is achieved only at the end of the seventh cycle (in *Genesis* called "day"), whether major or minor. The seventh day, the end of the cycle of manifestation, is therefore by no means a day of rest throughout the Cosmos. Rather is it the day of culmination, of highest activity, in which all that was initiated on the first day is brought to its greatest possible development, expression and function within the major time-period, or at the end of the seventh day. The full period occupies seven cycles, not six.

The "day" on which God rested refers to the culmination or exhaustion in the dynamic sense, the completed outworking, of the original creative impulse. The perfect manifestation of original ideation within a given period has by then been achieved. Thereafter the whole impulse to produce dies down, having fulfilled itself, and this dying down and reduction of activity to a minimum, followed by its complete cessation, is thus the true meaning of the words "God rested".

At the end of the seventh day all Nature sleeps—as in the depth of winter—to awaken no more within the duration of the Major Cycle. Cosmos fades gradually back into Chaos.[1] Substances or elements return to their primordial Source, which is the One Maternal Root Substance, the Eternal Mother from whom all are "born". Evening descends upon the vast cosmic field, to be followed by that final "night" into which the whole Creation descends. Finiteness disappears. Infinity once more obtains.

The end of the First Chapter of *Genesis* might more correctly be regarded as descriptive of this close of the sevenfold period of activity, which begins with the first dawn of the first "day" and ends with the close of the seventh and the oncoming of "night". All is then withdrawn into a latent, germinal condition, there to rest in quiescence until the opening of the succeeding epoch or new "day". Thereafter the whole process will be repeated but with a greater fullness, since the condition at the beginning of the new cycle will be that which obtained at the end of the preceding one.

THE PATHWAYS OF FORTHGOING AND RETURN

As, when once begun, the swing of a pendulum continues, so the succession of cycles and sub-cycles, once initiated by an impulse arising from within the One Alone, continues according to law as long as that impulse is maintained. When this is no longer given, the swing continues through a decreasing arc until at last the pendulum returns to its preceding motionless state. So, also, does the cycle-governed Cosmos emerge from and return to quiescence, to Chaos, which means root-substance in an

[1] Chaos—q.v. Glossary.

equi-polarised state, unchanged and therefore at rest. This is the Abyss, the Great Deep upon which, at the dawn of *Manvantara*, the Great Breath is again breathed forth to initiate a new period of creative activity.

> *Gen.* 2: 3. *And God blessed the seventh day, and sanctified it: because that in it he had rested from all his work which God created and made.*

3. **And God blessed** (*ikaddesh*, Heb., " hallowed, consecrated, set apart, dedicated to God ") **the seventh day, and sanctified it: because that in it he had rested from all his work which God created and made** (*l'asoth*, Heb., " for the purpose of making ").

The third verse may be more literally, if less clearly, translated: " And *Elohim* [1] blessed the seventh day and hallowed it, because in it He returned from all His work, which He, the *Elohim*, had created in order to make." The word " Sabbath " means literally " the returning ", and the " seventh day " means the " day of full realisation ". Thus *Genesis* states that *Elohim* came forth from the unknown Eternal One in order to make Him manifest, knowable, through the process of Creation. Having finished His creative work, *Elohim* returned to the divine unity, the universal Sabbath.

> *Gen.* 2: 4. *These are the generations of the heavens and of the earth when they were created, in the day that the LORD God made the earth and the heavens.*

> 5. *And every plant of the field before it was in the earth, and every herb of the field before it grew: for the LORD God had not caused it to rain upon the earth, and there was not a man to till the ground.*

> 6. *But there went up a mist from the earth, and watered the whole face of the ground.*

4. **These are the generations** (*aelleh tho-ledoth*, Heb., " generations to be later described in symbolic language ") **of the heavens and of the earth when they were created, in the day that the LORD God made the earth and the heavens.**

[1] q.v. Glossary.

The Hebrew word *tho*, as I have said, is ignored by the translators. It denotes "symbolic" and is of first importance in discovering the true significance of certain verses, Chapters and Books of the Bible.

5. **And every plant of the field before it was in the earth, and every herb of the field before it grew: for the LORD God had not caused it to rain upon the earth, and there was not a man** (*Adam ain*, Heb., "Adam was not, except as a spiritual potentiality") **to till the ground.**

6. **But there went up a mist** (*iahleh-ad*, Heb., "ascended an emanation". In the context mist is impossible since the earth was dry) **from the earth, and watered the whole face of the ground.**

The Second Chapter of *Genesis* recapitulates the description of certain of the processes of Creation. The First Chapter, as I have said, describes the emergence of Cosmos from Chaos, form from the eternal Formless, and reveals creative principles which apply not only to the Earth and its Solar System, but to all Cosmoi; for the basic laws of manifestation and the ordered emergence and development of the successive phases and their evolutionary products do not change. Even though those products ascend to ever higher, more spiritual and more powerful manifestations, the underlying laws are the same. The Second Chapter, however, deals with a single unit such as a Solar System, a Planetary Scheme, a Chain, a Round or a Globe within the larger Universe.

In the main, though not entirely, the processes of condensation, solidification to the mineral level, and the successive emergence of plant, animal and man upon this planet, are described. The presence of the seeds of living things in a latent condition is indicated in the fifth verse, and this may be taken to refer to their primary existence in both divine thought and universal pre-cosmic substance.

Gen. 2: 7. *Ana the LORD God formed man of the dust of the ground, and breathed into his nostrils the breath of life; and man became a living soul.*

7. **And the LORD God formed** (*iitzer*, Heb., "formed", not *bara*, Heb., "created". "Gave permanent and homogeneous form to Adam as an individual spiritual entity") **man** (*Adam*, Heb., "the spiritual One

becoming the material Many, the human principle, the essence of humanity." The first letter of the word *Adam*, *a*, denotes anything primal, the first Cause, potential power, Deity. The following letter *d*, is the sign of multiplication, abundance and the final *m*, is one of unlimited plurality) **of the dust** (*aphar*, Heb., " a verb, present participle—in the act of refining, etherealising, elevating, spiritualising. Dust may be regarded as the refinement of matter, light, airy, easily blown into the air ") **of the ground, and breathed** (*iaphah*, Heb., "He breathed ") **into his nostrils** (*aphio*, Heb., "inspired the inspirational faculty or living soul ") **the breath of life; and man became a living soul** (*nishemath*, Heb., " to elevate, to ennoble, being raised to a higher state, becoming an individual human soul ").

Verse seven in its literal reading is deceptive; for it suggests somewhat the theory of special creation, which runs counter to that of the cyclic emanation, involution and evolution of all beings and all things, both material and spiritual. Esoterically, however, the order of evolution is not incorrect. The First Chapter of *Genesis* gives the history of the first three Rounds [1] of the present Fourth Chain of Globes, and of the first three races on Earth in the Fourth Round, when man had already attained to conscious life. In the First Chapter—which deals with the earlier Rounds—animals, fishes and birds are correctly placed before man, whilst in the Second Chapter, which continues the story, man rightly is introduced first.

Since evolution is a fact this verse, in both its exoteric and esoteric readings, may be taken to describe the passage of the human Monad through the mineral (dust), the plant and the animal kingdoms (life), to the attainment of self-conscious individuality or " Soulship " (man). The word " dust " as shown above is somewhat misleading, since the original *aphar*, (Heb.) is the present participle of a verb meaning " the process of refining ". The threefold nature of man—material, psychical and spiritual—is thus described, and especially the fact of his distinguishing characteristic of self-conscious individuality. The breath of life breathed into Adam, the man of dust, is the nascent, reasoning soul which in the animal is instinctual only.

Gen. 2: 8. *And the LORD God planted a garden eastward in Eden; and there he put the man whom he had formed.*

[1] q.v. Glossary—Chain.

9. *And out of the ground made the LORD God to grow every tree that is pleasant to the sight, and good for food; the tree of life also in the midst of the garden, and the tree of knowledge of good and evil.*

8. **And the LORD God** (*Elohim*, Heb.) **planted** (*itta*, Heb., " to set out, to appoint, to give a relatively permanent material form ") **a garden** (*gan*, Heb., " enclosure, a marked out sphere of activity in time and space "). It would seem permissible to assume the intention to state that Adam as a spiritual being is placed here by involution in order that he will assume a body of flesh and blood and by evolution become a redeemed man) **eastward** (*m'kedem*, Heb., [mistranslated] " from before in time ") **in Eden; and there he put the man whom he had formed.**

9. **And out of the ground** (*adamah*, Heb., " a spiritual term, unfortunately confused with *aretz*, Heb., physical earth ") **made the LORD God to grow every tree** (*whetz*, Heb., " In addition to tree or wood, substance, counsel, tree perhaps in the garden of divine and human consciousness ") **that is pleasant to the sight, and good for food; the tree of life also in the midst of the garden, and the tree of knowledge** (*d-ath*, Heb., " knowledge obtained by first hand, personal experience ") **of good** (*tob*, Heb., " inner integrity, healthiness, fruitfulness, resisting corruption ") **and evil** (*rah*, Heb.—here first used in the Bible—" that which moves away from the spiritual to the material.   Physical or moral, malignity, vice, perversity, disorder ").

The two trees planted in Eden can hardly have been material objects growing in material earth.   Rather do the words refer to spiritual trees with spiritual qualities—a tree of life and a tree of knowledge of good and evil.   More properly they are to be regarded as Archetypes [1] or models according to which the material Universe emanated and is evolving.

Gen. 2: 10. *And a river went out of Eden to water the garden; and from thence it was parted, and became into four heads.*

[1] q.v.   Glossary.

8

> 10. **And a river** (*nahar*, Heb., "a stream-like movement or current of the life force") **went out of Eden to water** (*hishekah*, Heb., "to make fertile, productive and capable of sustaining life") **the garden; and from thence it was parted, and became into four heads.**

The original, outflowing life-force is divided into four individual streams, each with its own characteristics. These are less branches or tributaries than starting points for creative activity occurring in their quarter or region of the Universe. In verse eight the garden is made to be not the garden *of* Eden, but *in* Eden—apparently a contradiction. Eden, however, is less a location in the physical world than a sphere of activity, an enclosed state of existence within the realm of universal time and space. In this sense, therefore, no contradiction occurs.

> Gen. 2: 11. *The name of the first is Pison: that is it which compasseth the whole land of Havilah, where there is gold;*

> 12. *And the gold of that land is good: there is bdellium and the onyx stone.*

> 11. **The name of the first is Pison** (*pishon*, Heb., "a symbolic name for the all-pervading creative life-force by which the physical universe and its contents come into being and evolve"): **that is it which compasseth** (*sobab*, Heb., "comprises") **the whole land of Havilah** (*havilah*, Heb., "the conditions and means of activity in the physical world including the efforts of man"), **where there is gold** (*sham-ha-tzahab*, Heb., "there was gold, the gold was in the work accomplished");

> 12. **And the gold of that land is good: there is bdellium and the onyx stone.**

The style and the language of verse twelve differ from those of the rest of the original text, and this has given rise to some doubts as to whether it is an interpolated commentary.

> Gen. 2: 13. *And the name of the second river is Gihon: the same is it that compasseth the whole land of Ethiopia.*

> 14. *And the name of the third river is Hiddekel: that is it which goeth toward the east of Assyria. And the fourth river is Euphrates.*

15. *And the LORD God took the man, and put him into the garden of Eden to dress it and to keep it.*

16. *And the LORD God commanded the man, saying, Of every tree of the garden thou mayest freely eat:*

17. *But of the tree of the knowledge of good and evil, thou shalt not eat of it: for in the day that thou eatest thereof thou shalt surely die.*

18. *And the LORD God said, It is not good that the man should be alone; I will make him an help meet for him.*

19. *And out of the ground the LORD God formed every beast of the field, and every fowl of the air; and brought them unto Adam to see what he would call them; and whatsoever Adam called every living creature, that was the name thereof.*

20. *And Adam gave names to all cattle, and to the fowl of the air, and to every beast of the field; but for Adam there was not found an help meet for him.*

21. *And the LORD God caused a deep sleep to fall upon Adam, and he slept: and he took one of his ribs, and closed up the flesh instead thereof;*

22. *And the rib, which the LORD God had taken from man, made he a woman, and brought her unto the man.*

23. *And Adam said, This is now bone of my bones, and flesh of my flesh: she shall be called Woman, because she was taken out of Man.*

13. **And the name of the second river is Gihon** (*gichon*, Heb., " force of a chemical instinctive nature "): **the same is it that compasseth the whole land of Ethiopia** (*Cush*, Heb., not Ethiopia but " the whole sphere of human, fiery, impulsive, forceful effort. Ethiopia was sometimes called Cush ").

14. **And the name of the third river is Hiddekel** (*Hiddekel*, Heb., " the force produced by human will, thought, desire "): **that is it which goeth toward**

the east of Assyria.   And the fourth river is
Euphrates (*houa phrath*, Heb., not Euphrates but " the
power to propagate, generate, be fruitful "). The author
is careful to omit the statement that Euphrates is the
name of the fourth river whilst having included it in
reference to the first three.

15. **And the LORD God took** [*la-kach*, Heb., " gave (to the
spiritual man, Adam) an inclination, tendency or desire
towards activity in the realm of time and space "] **the
man, and put** (*innach*, Heb., " the feeling of being at
home after a period of unsettlement has passed, repose
after completion ") **him into the garden of Eden to
dress it and to keep it.**

16. **And the LORD God commanded** (*itzaw*, Heb.,
" advised, forewarned, rather than ordered. Not a
threat ") **the man, Of every** (*chol*, Heb., " all, entirely,
whole, essence ") **tree** (*etz*, Heb., " the material or
spiritual substance of any object ") **of the garden thou
mayest freely eat** (*achol*, Heb., " consume, assimilate,
absorb, physically, mentally or spiritually ") :

17. **But of the tree of the knowledge of good and evil,
thou shalt not eat of it: for in the day that thou
eatest thereof thou shalt surely die** (*moth tamoth*, Heb.,
not physical death as Adam was still a spiritual unity
not physically incarnated but " passing into an alternative,
complementary or corresponding state ").

18. **And the LORD God said, It is not good that the
man should be alone;** (*l'baddo*, Heb., " in spiritual
unity with all powers latent, non-individualised ") ; **I will
make him an help** (*ezer*, Heb., " auxiliary force, support,
development of latent faculties, such as an evolutionary
impulse towards, the division of the spiritual unity which
included male and female into the physical development
of separate sexes, male and female." Spiritually and
physically androgyne, Adam, the first physical race on
earth, becomes single sexed and capable of reproduction)
meet (*be-negid-o* Heb., " suitable, a reflection of Adam's
being, a means by which his wishes can be realised and
made fruitful, an auxiliary faculty by which the spiritual

unity of Adam divides into two complementaries, masculine and feminine ") **for him.**

19. **And out of the ground the LORD God formed every beast of the field and every fowl of the air; and brought** (*iahbeh*, Heb., "caused to progress by a graduated advance from state to state") **them unto Adam to see what he would call them; and whatsoever Adam called** (*ikra*, Heb., "same root as English word scream; to hail, to cry out, to designate, to evoke, to bestow distinguishing, individualistic qualities and particularities, to individualise as if by naming ") **every living creature, that was the name thereof.**

20. **And Adam gave names to all cattle, and to the fowl of the air, and to every beast of the field; but for Adam there was not found an help meet for him.**

21. **And the LORD God caused a deep sleep** (*thareddemah*, Heb., "deep trance, torpor, even loss of self-hood ") **to fall upon Adam, and he slept: and he took one of his ribs** (*achath metz-alothaio*, Heb., ,, rib, root, meaning that which envelops, covers, protects "), **and closed up** (*issegor*, Heb., "not filling up a gap where the rib had been, but enclosed, built into a complete human form and given life ") **the flesh** (*bashar*, Heb., "visible substance, dormant duality becomes actively single sexed ") **instead thereof;**

22. **And the rib, which the LORD God had taken from man, made he a woman, and brought her unto the man.**

23. **And Adam said, This is now** (*ha phaam*, Heb., "actually, really ") **bone** (*etzem*, Heb., "substance in general, spiritual, physical, organic ", as if Adam said of the woman "this is of the very spiritual substance of my whole being ") **of my bones, and flesh of my flesh: she** (*zoth*, Heb., not *hoa*, Heb., "she, not in reference to a bodily woman but an impersonal pronoun ") **shall be called Woman** (*aisha*, Heb., spelt *a-sh-h*, "the faculty of willing, or freedom to exert individual will power without which the likeness of

God or the evolutionary goal of perfection could not be attained "), **because she was taken out of Man** (*aish*, Heb., "activity expressing one's individuality, selfhood; the elemental germ of will is built into an active force ").[1]

For the convenience of the reader the abridged interpretation given in Part Two, Chapter I, entitled " Eden, Eve and the 'Fall' of Man" is largely repeated here.

The *Book of Genesis* now proceeds to describe the formation and the evolution of man, the Second Chapter being partly concerned with the change produced in his physical body by evolutionary processes. As stated earlier the first human form, typified by Adam, was dual-sexed and unconsciously self-reproductive. Throughout that period play of the creative fire within the cells of his body left his nerves and his brain unaffected. Self-fructified, he gave of his kind much as the plant or the tree gives of its fruit.

"MALE AND FEMALE CREATED HE THEM "[2]

Gradually, however, as the cycle progressed in which the human form was developed and the masculine-feminine spiritual Soul entered into closer association with that form, a change began to occur. Out of the hitherto androgyne organism the single-sexed, separate man and woman of today developed. Adam (" man ") alone in the Garden of Eden personifies the first sexually innocent humanity, whilst Adam and Eve together typify the first separated men and women. The production of Eve from the side and out of a rib of Adam whilst he slept is an allegorical description of this process.[3]

Chapter Two of the *Book of Genesis* continues the description of both the psychical condition and the bodily development of primitive man. Androgynous, he was pure. Unconscious of sex, because instinctually self-reproductive, he was innocent of passion. This condition of human purity and this innocence are symbolised by the Garden of Eden itself, the state of the soul before the awakening and activity of consciously exercised procreative power. Eden therefore describes the childhood

---

[1] Cf. *shakti* (Sk.). Power, energy, creative or generative power. The female energy of Brahmā, Vishnu, Shiva, or other deity, personified as the wife of the god, any power or energy proceeding from a higher centre to a lower one. See also Glossary.

[2] *Gen.* 1: 24.

[3] An allegorical reference may also be intended to the fact that the human body had by this time (the separation of the sexes) become quite solid, or built of flesh and bone.

of the race, and also of every human being up to the stage of puberty.

Expulsion from Eden is an allegory of the passage of every human being through adolescence into adult life.   The process, being perfectly natural, involves no sin of either soul or body, whether for the race or for the individual.   In terms of consciousness the story describes the pre-creative and the procreative stages of human development.   Related to bodily growth the account refers to the evolutionary change from the androgynous to the single-sexed method of reproduction, with the consequent experience of sex desire and the expression of procreative power.

The ideas presented on this subject are chiefly drawn from The Secret Doctrine *by H. P. Blavatsky, which in its turn consists largely of commentaries on an ancient book entitled* The Stanzas of Dzyan. *Other works of a similar character have also been consulted, and an attempt is here made to offer the resultant concepts.   Since these will inevitably be strange and new to many Western readers, and are in themselves rather abstruse, pains have been taken to present them from several points of view.   Some repetition has, in consequence, been unavoidable and the indulgence of readers is requested should such repetition be found by them to be excessive.*

THE DOCTRINE OF ORIGINAL SIN

The orthodox doctrine of the " Fall " of man as a result of the so-called sinning of Adam and Eve in the Garden of Eden (eating of the fruit of the tree of knowledge of good and evil) is not in accord with the teachings of the Ageless Wisdom.   The " Fall " simply refers to the descent of human Monads into physical bodies and the consequent exercise of the *natural* procreative power in those bodies.   As will be more fully expounded later, in principle no slightest sin was committed by early man—nor has it ever been since then—when the process designed by Nature for the preservation and development of the human species was exercised. Admittedly, the abuse of the function can lead to degradation and disease, but this error cannot justly be attributed to the first men on Earth nor can it be charged against Nature's processes, which are neither pure nor impure, but impersonal and natural.   According to his use of it, man's procreative power can indeed make him either Godlike or a degraded demon of lust.   When transmuted to spiritual and intellectual creativity it makes of him an inspired genius, and later an occult Sage endowed with superhuman capacities.   When, however, it is expressed in sexual excesses, it can de-spiritualise and degrade him.   In all cases undue sexual expression bedulls and takes the keen edge from the mind-brain of man.

EVE PRODUCED FROM ADAM'S RIB

If the repetition be pardoned, the subject being of such great importance, the formation of Eve from a rib of Adam whilst he slept in the Garden is also entirely allegorical, as earlier references to the original Hebrew indicate. The deep sleep refers to both the nascent mentality and the unawakened, inactive procreative power. Supine and unconscious upon the ground, Adam aptly represents the human race at the first period of the encasement of the Monad in human form. Newly enclosed in dense matter, first man was " of the earth, earthy ". His task was to accustom himself to imprisonment within relatively inert physical substance and gradually to overcome its resistance. These first human bodies were gigantic,[1] with a minimum of nervous organization and activity. Sluggishly and clumsily they moved through tropical vegetation, impelled only by the desire for food and the instinct for self-preservation. Reproduction was unconscious and passed through both sweat-born and oviporous stages. This condition, and the mental torpor of primitive man, are typified by Adam in deep sleep in the Garden of Eden.[2]

The life-force was present, however, and active within the first physical race of men, even though unrecognised. Very gradually a change, which was both physical and psychical, began to occur. Physically, one sex attribute began to predominate over the other. Psychically, awareness of opposite polarity was experienced, as either the positive or the negative currents in the life-force became predominant in individuals. These two processes brought to an end the androgynous era and culminated in the establishment upon this planet of separate male and female forms. Since these evolved out of racial progenitors who hitherto had contained the attributes of both sexes, the description of the formation of Eve from the side (rib) of Adam is appropriate as an allegory. Hermaphroditism and the presence in the bodies of both sexes of the vestigial remains of the opposite sex support this theory of human evolution.

The reference to the rib of Adam has also been interpreted as an indication that the procedure of the " descent " of the Monadic Ray into denser and denser forms had culminated in incarnation in solid material bodies, or "coats of skin ".[3] This involved the production by Nature of a supporting bony structure, of which the rib of Adam may be taken as a representation. In occult anthropology this is said to have occurred in the third sub-race of the Third Root Race (the Lemurian) of the Seven Root Races of man.[4]

---

[1] Gen. 6: 4, supported by both occult tradition and anthropology. See Pt. II, Ch. 1 of this Volume.

[2] Gen. 2: 21.

[3] Gen. 3 :21.

[4] q.v. The Secret Doctrine, H. P. Blavatsky, and Lecture Notes of the School of the Wisdom, Vol. I (Rev. Ed.), Geoffrey Hodson.

The reference to Adam's rib as the basic substance from which Eve was formed is deeply esoteric. One possible interpretation, tentatively advanced, is that the spinal column and a projecting rib together form a right angle or square. This, as also the equal-armed cross, has ever been the symbol of the union of descending, positive, fructifying Spirit (the vertical) entering negative, receptive, gestatory and all-producing matter (the horizontal). All creation occurs as a result of this penetration in the above sense of the horizontal by the vertical and the process is symbolised by both the cross and the square. In the human skeleton the spinal column and each rib form a right angle. Eve, being feminine, is appropriately formed out of the horizontal arm of this " cross ".

Thus interpreted the allegory reveals that, as a result of universal processes, the hitherto combined dual polarity of the life-force was separated into two distinct manifestations. These produced in both the psychical and physical worlds oppositely polarised man and woman. God, as the triune Craftsman by Whom both Adam and Eve were formed, may therefore be regarded as universal Law and Life acting under the direction of universal Intelligence. As we have seen, this last becomes manifest as—and active in—the Hosts of Intelligences, the *Elohim*, ceaselessly at work throughout the whole of Cosmos as builders of forms, directors of consciousness into them, and quickeners of evolutionary development. These builders and their function of inducting the Monads of men into mortal, material bodies are also personified by the " old serpent ",[1] the Devil in the Garden of Eden. In occult philosophy[2] they are referred to as " the Satanic Hierarchy ".[3] Satan's co-partnership with God is suggested by the fact that he, the Devil, is—apart from the Lord God Himself— the only recorded visitant to the Garden of Eden before the " Fall ".

THE TREE OF KNOWLEDGE OF GOOD AND EVIL

The Devil in Eden, by whose machinations Eve and then Adam partook of the fruit of the tree of knowledge of good and evil, plays so significant a role in the great human drama which the Bible unfolds that a digression from the main theme of this Chapter of the *Book of Genesis* may usefully be made here.

Who and what, then, is meant by the Devil? In occult philosophy Satan is regarded as a personification of a synthesis of a number of formative forces, processes and Intelligences. The Devil is also a personification of differentiated matter, its inherent life-force, and their combined influence

---

[1] *Rev.* 12: 9 and 20: 2.

[2] q.v. Glossary—Occult Science.

[3] q.v. Glossary and *The Kingdom of the Gods*, Geoffrey Hodson, Pt. III, Ch. V, for a fuller exposition of this subject. See also Pt. II, Ch. II of this Volume.

upon human personality.   If Spirit and matter be regarded as the positive and negative poles respectively of one energy imbued with intelligence, then their mutual approach will tend to generate electro-magnetic attraction, thus awakening into activity the creative fire in both.   Matter leads in this awakening and so may be said to lure Spirit into material self-expression.   Allegorically, Eve, symbol of universal substance, both answers to the play of the life-force within her substance (the Devil) and tempts and seduces Adam (Spirit).

THE MONAD "DESCENDS" INTO MATTER

In the case of human Monads, although they are imbued with the formative fire and impulse, the process of the entry of Spirit into matter is far from being purely automatic.   Since they are primarily pure, stainless, spiritual beings existing within the life of the Logos, incarnation in matter inevitably involves severe limitations and a loss of complete purity.   A deeply esoteric teaching states that Monads shrink from the resultant self-limitation, since from the Monadic point of view the "descent" involves enslavement and degradation.   The adoption of individual mentality, incarnation in a physical body with cerebro-spinal system, and the dual experience of the delusion of self-separateness and the influences of repeated sexual impulses, are repellant to the Monad in so far as it is able to conceive of them.   For these and doubtless other reasons, Monads are said to hesitate on the threshold of individuality which, with its concomitant illusion of separateness together with the bedulling and clouding effect of incarnation in physical bodies, would most adversely affect purely spiritual beings whose innate consciousness is entirely universalised.   Admittedly these are all intellectual and purely human reactions which could hardly be expected to reach Dwellers in the Innermost, Sparks within the One Flame.   Nevertheless the suggestion is made that in some highly sublimated form the Monads embarking on the pathway of forthgoing are aware of such implications inseparable from that procedure.   At the same time, however, Monadic life is drawn towards matter by the operation of the law of polarity, or attraction and repulsion.

The Ageless Wisdom, source of these concepts, also advances the teaching that certain of the hosts of human Monads, thus hesitating to embark upon the great pilgrimage through matter, attempted to resist the universal creative and expansive impulse.   This shrinking and this resistance together are said to constitute one of the esoteric and spiritually historical realities behind the allegory of the War in Heaven.[1]   It may also be regarded in more general terms as the conflict between Spirit and

[1] *Rev.* 12: 7.

matter, whether cosmic or microcosmic, universal or human. In man, this struggle only ends when the outer terrestrial nature has been brought into complete conformity with the Spirit within. Every Candidate for the higher Initiations must win—and so end—this war by "slaying" every unspiritual attribute still remaining in the lower nature. Thus St. George—as did so many other heroes of world Mythologies—slew the dragon whilst the labours of Hercules doubtless possess the same mystical significance.

To sum up, the rebellious angels were none other than the Monads of men who hesitated to surrender their universality and their unstained ascetic purity in obedience to the cosmic evolutionary impulse, process and purpose. Eventually the "rebels" were obliged by that impulse to "descend" into generation. Kārmic disability is said to have followed, influencing some of them to become Lords of the Dark Face, rebels against society and scourges of the rest of mankind on this Earth in its Fourth Round.[1] Furthermore, an actual war was waged on Earth in the days of Atlantis when the Lords of the Dark Face, the black magicians and sorcerers, attacked the Adept Guardians of that race.[2]

Whilst all human Monads felt aversion, all did not rebel. Assistance was required, however, in embarking upon the path of forthgoing[3] and in accomplishing descent into the deeper densities of matter. To repeat, the necessary "allurement" or "temptation" to participate in the vast involutionary and evolutionary activity initiated at creative "dawn" is described in allegory in the account of the temptation of Eve by Satan. Members of the *Elohim*, full-formed because evolved from preceding cycles of manifestation, undertook[4] this work of induction into mental, emotional and physical bodies. The Devil is a personification of this Order of Intelligences, as also of their functions.

THE SATANIC HIERARCHY[5]

On the completion of its involutionary and evolutionary passage through the sub-human kingdoms the Monad attains one of its primary objectives, which is to become a member of the human kingdom of Nature. This process is referred to in occult philosophy as "individualisation", and results in the incarnation of a Ray of the Monad within a vesture constructed of matter of that realm of Nature and level of consciousness

---

[1] q.v. Glossary.

[2] q.v. *Lecture Notes of the School of the Wisdom*, Vol. I (Rev. Ed.), Ch. XIV, p. 354, Geoffrey Hodson.

[3] q.v. Vol. I of this work, Pt. 4, Ch. II.

[4] The procedure may still be taking place, if not in this then in other Solar Systems.

[5] q.v. Glossary—*Pitris*.

at which man is able to conceive of abstractions and to comprehend underlying principles and laws.   This new-formed individuality is referred to as the human Ego.   Such Egohood implies the development of the faculty of self-conscious thought, and self-realisation as a separate entity. As this phase is entered upon, the function of the *Elohim* consists of the encasement of the Monad in a mental body.   As has been observed earlier in this Volume, the resultant acutely separative sense of individuality, or I-am-ness, with its inevitable concomitants of acquisitiveness, pride, egoism and selfishness, is also personified by the Devil.

The work of another Order of the so-called Satanic Hierarchy is to induct the human Monad-Ego[1] into a vehicle of emotion in which sexual desire can be experienced.   The process of descent thereafter culminates in incarnation in physical, " dust-formed "[2] bodies through which the sex impulse can achieve self-conscious expression.   The universal life-force, the fire of creation, then finds individual manifestation as human love, desire and procreative activity.   Satan is thus seen as a composite personification of matter and its resistance to Spirit, a Hierarchy of Intelligences, and certain creative impulses active within mankind.

The serpentine form of the symbol of the Devil is also deeply significant; for the characteristic mode of manifestation and manner of expression of the generative power in both Nature and in man is undulatory or serpentine.   This allurement of the Spirit of man from primal innocence to sex experience, and this undulatory current in which the life-force is expressed, are not inaptly described in the allegory of the temptation of Eve and Adam by the serpent in the Garden of Eden and their subsequent " Fall ". As will be noted, this deeply esoteric knowledge could be both incomprehensible and potentially dangerous.   Hence, doubtless, its heavy enveiling in such intricate symbology.[3]

Verses twenty-four and twenty-five of this Chapter of *Genesis* are self-explanatory and therefore do not require any commentary.

---

[1] Monad-Ego—see Glossary.
[2] *Gen.* 2: 7.
[3] q.v.   Glossary—*Kundalini* and *Kundalini Shakti*.

CHAPTER V

THE SERPENT, THE "FALL" AND THE EXPULSION FROM EDEN

Gen. 3: 1. *Now the serpent was more subtil than any beast of the field which the LORD God had made. And he said unto the woman, Yea, hath God said, Ye shall not eat of every tree of the garden?*

2. *And the woman said unto the serpent, We may eat of the fruit of the trees of the garden:*

3. *But of the fruit of the tree which is in the midst of the garden, God hath said, Ye shall not eat of it, neither shall ye touch it, lest ye die.*

4. *And the serpent said unto the woman, Ye shall not surely die :*

1. **Now the serpent** (*no-hash*, Heb., " the activity of the basic element of the human personality, namely selfhood ", symbol of an inward life principle inherent in every human being, the a-moral activity of the self-consciousness of which Adam now becomes aware) **was more subtil than any beast of the field which the LORD God had made. And he said unto the woman, Yea, hath God said, Ye shall not eat of every tree of the garden?**

2. **And the woman** (*aisha*, Heb., " the faculty of will possessed by Adam ") **said unto the serpent, We may eat of the fruit of the trees of the garden:**

3. **But of the fruit of the tree which is in the midst of the garden, God hath said, Ye shall not eat of it, neither shall ye touch** (*thiggehoo*, Heb., " to enter into

anything heart and soul." Adam was not to breathe out his soul into the material substance of the garden) **it, lest ye die.**

4. **And the serpent said unto the woman, Ye shall not surely die** (*moth temuthum*, Heb., " pass from the state of immortal spirit into mortal existence ") :

The symbol of the serpent, here first introduced into the Bible, is of profound significance, as already stated.   The reader is therefore directed to the proffered interpretation in Volume I, Part Three, Chapter I of this work.

Gen. 3: 5. *For God doth know that in the day ye eat thereof, then your eyes shall be opened, and ye shall be as gods, knowing good and evil.*

6. *And when the woman saw that the tree was good for food, and that it was pleasant to the eyes, and a tree to be desired to make one wise, she took of the fruit thereof, and did eat, and gave also unto her husband with her; and he did eat.*

7. *And the eyes of them both were opened, and they knew that they were naked; and they sewed fig leaves together, and made themselves aprons.*

8. *And they heard the voice of the LORD God walking in the garden in the cool of the day: and Adam and his wife hid themselves from the presence of the LORD God amongst the trees of the garden.*

9. *And the LORD God called unto Adam, and said unto him, Where art thou?*

10. *And he said, I heard thy voice in the garden, and I was afraid, because I was naked; and I hid myself.*

11. *And he said, Who told thee that thou wast naked? Hast thou eaten of the tree, whereof I commanded thee that thou shouldest not eat?*

12. *And the man said, The woman whom thou gavest to be with me, she gave me of the tree, and I did eat.*

13. *And the LORD God said unto the woman, What is this that thou has done? And the woman said, The serpent beguiled me, and I did eat.*

14. *And the LORD God said unto the serpent, Because thou hast done this, thou art cursed above all cattle, and above every beast of the field; upon thy belly shalt thou go, and dust shalt thou eat all the days of thy life:*

15. *And I will put enmity between thee and the woman, and between thy seed and her seed; it shall bruise thy head, and thou shalt bruise his heel.*

5. **For God doth know that in the day ye eat thereof, then your eyes shall be opened, and ye shall be as gods, knowing good and evil.**

6. **And when the woman saw that the tree was good for food, and that it was pleasant to the eyes, and a tree to be desired to make one wise** (*l'hashecchil*, Heb., "take one onwards towards perfection"), **she took of the fruit thereof, and did eat, and gave also unto her husband with her** (*imme-ha*, Heb., not another being or a companion but "a quality in the same being. Adam moved by his *na-hash*, Heb., or desire principle willed to enter into material experience and his intelligent self approves of his action." The doctrine of original sin is not to be found in Genesis); **and he did eat.**

7. **And the eyes of them both were opened, and they knew that they were naked** (*aroom*, Heb., "aware that their inward light was extinct"); **and they sewed** (*va-ithepherou* Heb., not sewed even in a figurative sense but "to give birth to") **fig** (*thaeneh*, Heb., "mutual sorrow, plunged into sorrow which is shared or communicated") **leaves** (*aleh*, Heb., a singular word— "covering, protection, overshadowing") **together and made themselves aprons** (*hagoroth*, Heb., not aprons but "a fugitive on account of some contention." Cf. Hagar. Adam and his *aisha*, Heb., realised their lack of guiding intelligence and were covered with mutual grief and confusion, having cast themselves out from

their unity with God and knowing not what to do or where to go. Such is the general meaning of verse seven).

8. **And they heard the voice of the LORD God walking** (not an anthropomorphic Being but the omnipresent Divine Spirit, even the Logos or Voice breathed forth and penetrating to the recesses of the garden or substance of the Universe. A voice can hardly be thought of as walking about!) **in the garden in the cool of the day: and Adam and his wife hid themselves from the presence of the LORD God amongst** (*be-thoch*, Heb., " within ") **the trees** (*etz*, Heb., not plural but singular, " organic substance in general ") **of the garden** (the Spirit of man following the path of forthgoing and " falling " into generation and the physical exercise of the creative power as a single-sexed being is conscious of the privation of spirituality inseparable from this process).

9. **And the LORD God called unto Adam, and said unto him, Where art thou?** (*aicha*, Heb., a question mark expressing questioning interest).

10. **And he said, I heard thy voice in the garden, and I was afraid** (*va-aira*, Heb., " over awed and realising loss of spirituality "), **because I was naked** (*chi-eirom anochi*, Heb., " realised spiritual loss, denudation of spiritual intelligence " and the contrast between himself and the *Elohim*); **and I hid myself.**

11. **And he said, Who told thee that thou wast naked? Hast thou eaten of the tree, whereof I commanded thee that thou shouldest not eat?**

12. **And the man said, The woman whom thou gavest to be with me, she gave me of the tree, and I did eat.**

13. **And the LORD God said unto the woman, What is this that thou hast done? And the woman said, The serpent beguiled** (*hishiani*, Heb., " excited mental disorder or emotional frenzy ") **me, and I did eat.**

14. **And the LORD God said unto the serpent, Because thou hast done this, thou art cursed** (*aroor*, Heb., not cursing as an act of vengeance but "a description of the natural result of the descent into matter and the physical, single-sexed expression of the serpentine creative force." The spiritual essence of humanity has been dragged down to the level of the beasts) **above all cattle, and above every beast of the field; upon thy belly** (*gechon*, Heb., not physical grovelling but "bent, bowed down, inclined earthwards") **shalt thou go** (*thalech*, Heb., not walk about but "act in a lowly manner"), **and dust shalt thou eat** (a figurative term like to lick the dust. At the deepest level, the physical, of the pathway of forthgoing Adam feeds on earthy elements) **all the days of thy life:**

15. **And I will put enmity between thee and the woman, and between thy seed** (*zera*, Heb., "potential fruitfulness. The intellectual and spiritual frustration inseparable from purely physical existence, desire and activity") **and her seed; it shall bruise** (*ishouph*, Heb., "compress or crush") **thy head** (*resh*, Heb., "starting principle", as in *b'resheth*, Heb., *Gen.* 1 : 1), **and thou shalt bruise his heel** (*akeb*, Heb., "impression of heel, footstep, track, consequence of action. The antithesis of the starting principle, the consequences of its expression").

This Chapter of *Genesis* relates allegorically the inevitable defilement of the Monad-Egos resulting from both their immersion in the matter of the worlds below them and the conscious exercise in their physical bodies of their power to procreate.

The final phases of the pathway of forthgoing are therein described. The physical plane has been reached by the divine pilgrim, the densest of man's seven bodies having been assumed. Bone, flesh, blood and the nervous systems constitute the "tomb" in which spiritual Will, Wisdom and Intelligence respectively are "buried". The nerves, dull in the savage, sensitized in the saint, are the doorways and windows through which intellect, at first confined, eventually achieves freedom. The term "the LORD God" must here be interpreted to include Nature herself, the involutionary pressure and all the Hosts of Intelligences (*Elohim*) associated with the forthgoing life-wave bearing its Monadic "seeds" towards physical incarnation. Actually it is these very Agencies which

9

bring about the so-called " Fall " of man.[1] Spiritually regarded, these Intelligences are indeed divine and so are correctly referred to as " the LORD God ". Looked at from below, as forces bringing about the encasement of the human Monad in limiting forms subject to separateness and sensuality, these self-same Agencies can appear devilish, and have therefore been branded as satanic.

THE DEVIL—PERSONIFICATION OF THE INFLUENCE OF MATTER UPON SPIRIT

In this Third Chapter of *Genesis* the serpent, made prominent, represents more especially the intellectual principle. This is nascent in primitive man, but fully awake in those members of the *Elohim* who, as we have seen, undertake to bring the Monad into a mental vehicle and introduce it to individualised, self-conscious mental life. Resistance to the command of God, and personal action at variance with that command, refer to the attainment of individualised self-thought and self-will.

The actual tempting power, also symbolised by both the serpent itself and its influence, is threefold. It consists firstly of the felicity experienced by the mind at the temporary union of opposite polarities in man and woman; for this produces in each of the pair an impression of return to the uni-polarised condition characteristic of Monadic consciousness. Secondly, emotional happiness is felt in the expression of love and the fulfilment of desire. Thirdly, the exercise physically of the procreative power induces pleasurable sensation. This three-fold experience—mental, emotional and physical—of the action of the creative fire in Nature and in man is the triple lure which, as said, the Satanic Hierarchy of Ministers of the Solar Logos or " Word "[2] employs to induce human Monad-Egos to enter upon the human phase of existence.

Even though thus assisted the whole process of " descent ", be it remembered, is a perfectly natural one. For a period it does bring suffering, degradation and shame, but it cannot be truthfully described as a tragic " Fall ".[3] This dogma of " original sin " appears to have arisen from texts in both the Old and the New Testaments referred to in the footnote to this page. The Thirty-nine Articles of Religion of the Church of England state the dogma in the following words:

---

[1] For a fuller exposition of this procedure and these Intelligences see Ch. II of Pt. II and Ch. IV of Pt. III of this Volume.

[2] q.v. *Jn.* 1: 1.

[3] *Gen.* 3: 6; *Ps.* 51: 5; *Is.* 43: 27; *Ro.* 3: 9, 10, 23 and 5: 12; *Gal.* 3: 22.

IX. Of Original or Birth-Sin

"Original Sin standeth not in the following of *Adam* (as the *Pelagians* do vainly talk;) but it is the fault and corruption of the Nature of every man, that naturally is ingendered of the offspring of *Adam*; whereby man is very far gone from original righteousness, and is of his own nature inclined to evil, so that the flesh lusteth always contrary to the spirit; and therefore in every person born into this world, it deserveth God's wrath and damnation. And this infection of nature doth remain, yea in them that are regenerated; whereby the lust of the flesh, called in Greek, *phronema sarkos*, which some do expound the wisdom, some sensuality, some the affection, some the desire, of the flesh, is not subject to the Law of God. . . ."

X. Of Free-Will

"The condition of Man after the fall of *Adam* is such, that he cannot turn and prepare himself, by his own natural strength and good works, to faith, and calling upon God: Wherefore we have no power to do good works pleasant and acceptable to God, without the grace of God by Christ preventing us, that we may have a good will, and working with us, when we have that good will."

The views thus officially stated are hardly acceptable to the student of occult philosophy; for mis-called "original sin" is rather regarded as an inevitable concomitant of the involutionary process, and not as a deliberately committed wickedness for which every human being has ever since been condemned to be born in sin. The stain will be left behind and the fruitage will be preserved in the form of full knowledge of, and capacity to wield, the mightiest of all the powers in Nature and in man— the divine power to create universes and all that they contain. The pains of apprenticeship must be endured by the Monad-Ego in the personality before the state of the Master Builder can be attained.

Èliphas Lèvi writes:

"According to the Kabbalists, the true name of Satan is that of Jehovah reversed, for Satan is not a black god but the negation of the Deity. He is the personification of atheism and idolatry. The Devil is not a personality for initiates, but a force created with a good object, though it can be applied to evil: it is really the instrument of liberty".[1]

The Garden of Eden, Adam, Eve, the serpent, the tree, its fruit and the eating thereof can be variously interpreted. The tree of

---

[1] q.v. *The History of Magic*, Èliphas Lèvi, p. 192.

knowledge of good and evil (leaving aside its ten Sephirothal implications[1]) growing in the midst of the Garden, with its fruit—prescribed
as food—unlike that of the fruit of all the other trees, is the age-old
and universal symbol for the intelligence-imbued life-force of the
Universe.

The roots of this divine " tree " arise from within the substance of
pre-cosmic Space and draw their sustenance from it.   Within every atom
of matter of every grade of density, and within every molecular combination,
both inorganic and organic, the life-force is present as a component
energy.   This is symbolised as the sap absorbed by the far-spreading,
source-tapping roots of the " tree of life ".   It is the atom-forming,
universally manifest, creative energy known in occult science as cosmic
electricity, primordial Fohat[2], the primary atomic product of which is the
Maha-tattva[3].

Diagrammatically this tree grows downwards with its roots in the
heavens, or pre-cosmic and cosmic Space, *Mūlaprakriti*[4] or *Parabrahman*.[5]
The trunk of the tree represents the same divine generative power focused
into an individualised current.   In Nature, the Macrocosm, it is the
specialised life-force of any unit or sub-unit, such as Solar Systems, Planetary
Scheme, Chains[6], Rounds, Globes, and the kingdoms of Nature with their
species, and to each of these there is apportioned an appropriate current
of creative life.

In *The Secret Wisdom of the Qabalah*, pp. 72-73, J.F.C. Fuller writes—
and I fully concur:

" To the student of the occult it will be apparent that these two
trees (the tree of knowledge of good and evil and the tree of life)
closely resemble the letter *Shin*, also the caduceus of Hermes with
its central rod and its two entwined serpents, and also the Ida, Pingala,

---

[1] q.v.   *The Kingdom of the Gods*, Pt. III, Ch. IV, Geoffrey Hodson.

[2] *Fohat* (Tib.)—" Divine Energy ".   The constructive force of cosmic electricity,
polarised into the positive and negative currents of terrestrial electricity; the ever-present
electrical energy; the universal, propellant, vital force.

[3] *Tattva*—q.v. Glossary.

[4] *Mūlaprakriti* (Sk.)—" Undifferentiated substance ".   The abstract, deific, feminine
principle, the *Parabrahmic* root. *Prakriti* (Sk.).   Nature or matter as opposed to Spirit,
the two primeval aspects of the One Unknown Deity.   Root matter.

[5] *Parabrahman* (Sk.)—" Beyond Brahmā ".   The Supreme Infinite Brahmā, the
" Absolute ", attributeless, secondless Reality, the impersonal, nameless, universal and
Eternal Principle.   *Brahman* (Sk.).   The impersonal, supreme and incognisable Principle
of the Universe, from the Essence of which all emanates and into which all returns.
Extracted from *The Theosophical Glossary*, H. P. Blavatsky, and from other sources.

[6] See Glossary—Chain.

and central Sushumna of Hindu Yoga. The whole scheme is symbolized in the Temple of Solomon, the temple itself being the central pillar, whilst its two pylons, Yakhin and Boaz, the white and the black, the right and the left, represent the Tree of the Knowledge of Good and Evil—the eternal complementary forces in life without which nothing can be. This symbolism is an excessively ancient one; thus, in the Norse Mythology we find the mystic tree Yggdrasil, the roots of which are in the material world and the branches of which reach up to Asgard, the happy dwelling of the gods. Again, amongst the Akkadians, Chaldeans, and Babylonians we find the World Tree, or Tree of Life, which 'stood mid-way between the Deep and Zikum'—the primordial heaven above. In Hindu mythology there is also a World Tree—the Lingam— and in Buddhist the Bodhi Tree, or Tree of Wisdom under which Buddha sat in meditation."

THE UNIVERSAL TREE OF LIFE

When the symbol of the tree is used by the allegorists who composed the Scriptures and Mythologies of the world, the serpent is frequently associated with it. The glyph then consists of the tree of life with a serpent or dragon as guardian, as the Argonauts found at Colchis when searching for the Golden Fleece and Hercules in the garden of the Hesperides, where he sought the golden apples.

In Eden the man and the woman complete the representation of the opposite polarities of the electric, *fohatic* energy. The tree is also a symbol of esoteric wisdom, the assimilation of which (allegorically described as eating the fruit) indeed makes man even as a God. Inversely, the misuse of the resultant power can lead to degradation and, as stated above, this may be one reason for God's command to the first pair that they should not eat of the fruit of the tree of life. In Kabbalism, the esoteric wisdom or Theosophy of the Hebrews, the tree of life is a composite symbol of the entire Macrocosm and microcosm. When interpreted, this symbol reveals the whole cosmogonical process and also the relationship between the Universe and man. The Ten Sephiroth, or Emanations concerned with phases of involution and evolution, are represented by circles arranged in a geometric design upon the Kabbalistic Tree of Life.[1] The Garden of Eden with all its contents is thus susceptible of many interpretations, some of which now receive still further consideration.

In the cosmic sense the Garden of Eden describes the condition of potential fruitfulness and productiveness of the combined primordial Spirit-matter. Eve represents original cosmic substance and Adam primordial creative Spirit, whilst the tree of life symbolises the generative current which passes between this pair. The " Fall " describes the involutionary process, whilst the Deity and the Devil represent Spirit and matter respectively—the converse and obverse sides of Nature when once duality has displayed primeval unity.

THE TREE OF LIFE IN MAN

The trunk of the tree, in the microcosmic sense, is represented by the spinal column and cord. The spreading branches are the afferent and efferent nerves in the body, the flowers being represented by the force centres or *chakras*[2] in the etheric and superphysical bodies, together with their associated nerve centres and glands in the physical body.

In man the " fruits " of the tree of knowledge of good and evil are at least twofold. As heretofore suggested, they consist of the natural products of the evolutionary process, and also of the capacity of an occultist to use and express the primeval and manifested life principle at any level of consciousness and through any *chakra* or organ. In Nature the " fruit " represents the varied life-imbued forms which she, with such prodigality, ever continues to produce. Such, in part, is the symbol of the tree.

When man consciously expresses the generative power in procreation, he symbolically partakes of the fruit of the tree of knowledge of good and evil. The statement that he is forbidden to do so by the Deity on pain of death on the same day—a false prophecy, since this did not occur—may be regarded as a cover or blind concealing from the profane a deep esoteric

---

[1] q.v. *The Kingdom of the Gods*, Pt. III, Geoffrey Hodson, and Appendix to this Volume.

[2] *Chakra* (Sk.)—A " wheel " or " disc ". A spinning, vortical, funnel-shaped force-centre with its opening on the surfaces of the etheric and subtler bodies of man and its stem leading to the superphysical counterparts of the spinal cord and nerve centres or glands. There are seven main *chakras* associated severally with the sacrum, the spleen, the solar plexus, the heart, the throat, and the pituitary and pineal glands. *Chakras* are both organs of superphysical consciousness and conveyors of the life-force between the superphysical and physical bodies. q.v. *The Chakras*, C. W. Leadbeater; *The Serpent Power*, Arthur Avalon; *Lecture Notes of the School of the Wisdom*, Vol. I (Rev. ed.), Ch. XI, Geoffrey Hodson.

wisdom. This concerns the existence, the source, the nature and the uses—lowest and highest—of the creative life-force by mankind.

The terms "death" and "to die" have a particular significance in the Symbolical Language. Death can refer to spiritual deadness, a state of becoming cut off from or dead to spiritual awareness and power. In this sense the words "death" and "die" do not connote the finality ordinarily attributed to physical death, but refer only to a temporary loss of the illumination and the wisdom of the Higher Self. Such a reading is somewhat supported by the fact that sexual excess can produce this mental condition, which will remain as long as the error is continued. If, therefore, the "fruit" of the tree of knowledge of good and evil is in part the power to procreate, and the danger of "death" in the above sense exists because of the de-spiritualising effect of excess, then the word "die" in the third verse of the Third Chapter of *Genesis* may also be regarded as a veiled reference to the fact that excesses can produce such a deadening result. Similarly, physical blindness can be used to indicate a state of spiritual blindness, and deafness to indicate inability to respond to the directive "Word" from the Logos of the Soul. The "miraculous" healing by the Divine Master of a person suffering from these two afflictions may be interpreted as an interior action of the Christ Principle to restore responsiveness by the brain-mind to the spiritual light and "Voice" of the Inner Self.

THE TRANSMUTATION OF THE SEX FORCE

Adam alone in the Garden of Eden personifies, as we have seen, the passion-free state of the first physical race of men on Earth who were androgynous, and so self-reproductive. This "innocent" condition of the early human race exists in all humanity from the time of birth to the dawn of puberty. The Garden of Eden itself with its totality of created things—plant, animal and human—together with the indwelling Divine Presence, in one interpretation may also be regarded as a symbol of the physical body of man. Adam and Eve would then represent the oppositely polarised, creative energies, whilst the tree of life symbolises the spinal cord and brain.

In terms of out-poured, formative energy, the tree in the midst of the Garden of Eden is thus emblematic of the triple current of the ever-present electrical energy which plays along the centre of the spinal cord, symbolised by the trunk. In procreation that force plays downwards into the generative organs. When sublimated and consciously directed by spiritually awakened man, it flows upwards into the brain and thence onwards to the Solar Source. When by the action of the will this transmutation is successfully achieved, the brain cells and organs become highly sensitised to superphysical forces and states of awareness. This makes possible, in full waking consciousness, realisation of unity with the Source of all life, the very Lord of Life, the Solar Deity.

One of the secrets of Initiation (every Initiate being symbolically " raised " from a figurative death) concerns the process of this redirection and sublimation of the life-force in man, success in which makes him " immortal " and even as a God.[1] Since that mighty power thus transmuted can be used constructively or destructively, the secret of its nature, control and use is closely guarded within the Sanctuaries of the Greater Mysteries. Whenever referred to in literature which will become available to the general public, the knowledge is invariably revealed—and thereby concealed—in an allegorical and symbolical manner, as in the myth of the Garden of Eden. The supposed command of the Lord, ". . . Ye shall not eat of it, neither shall ye touch it, lest ye die "[2] (quite obviously impossible of fulfilment with regard to the human race) in one of its meanings may be regarded as an example of the method by which the secrecy has been preserved.

Gen. 3: 16. *Unto the woman he said, I will greatly multiply thy sorrow and thy conception; in sorrow thou shalt bring forth children; and thy desire shall be to thy husband, and he shall rule over thee.*

17. *And unto Adam he said, Because thou hast hearkened unto the voice of thy wife, and hast eaten of the tree, of which I commanded thee, saying, Thou shalt not eat of it; cursed is the ground for thy sake; in sorrow shalt thou eat of it all the days of thy life;*

18. *Thorns also and thistles shall it bring forth to thee; and thou shalt eat the herb of the field.*

19. *In the sweat of thy face shalt thou eat bread, till thou return unto the ground; for out of it wast thou taken: for dust thou art, and unto dust shalt thou return.*

20. *And Adam called his wife's name Eve; because she was the mother of all living.*

21. *Unto Adam also and to his wife did the LORD God make coats of skins, and clothed them.*

---

[1] cf. The death and resurrection of Osiris, Persephone, Dionysus, the shepherd boys in Vrindavana and, of course, the Lord Jesus Christ.
[2] *Gen.* 3: 3.

22. *And the LORD God said, Behold, the man is become as one of us, to know good and evil: and now, lest he put forth his hand, and take also of the tree of life, and eat, and live for ever:*

23. *Therefore the LORD God sent him forth from the garden of Eden, to till the ground from whence he was taken.*

24. *So he drove out the man; and he placed at the east of the garden of Eden Cherubims, and a flaming sword which turned every way, to keep the way of the tree of life.*

16. **Unto the woman he said, I will greatly multiply thy sorrow and thy conception** (*heronach*, Heb., "intentions of the will, purposes"); **in sorrow** (*itzebonech*, Heb., "physical obstacles, difficulties in realising desires and purposes") **thou shalt bring forth** (*theledi*, Heb., "generate, produce, realise, not necessarily limited to the maternal function") **children,** (*banim*, Heb., "productions of mind, body or will, ideas, intentions, children in the sense of giving birth to a work of art "); **and thy desire** (*te shoukathech*, Heb., "thy inclination, tendency, attachment". The text does not convey either domination or compulsion of Eve by Adam, or the inferiority of woman to man and her enslavement to him as part of her punishment) **shall be to thy husband, and he shall rule over thee.**

17. **And unto Adam he said, Because thou hast hearkened unto the voice of thy wife, and hast eaten of the tree, of which I commanded thee, saying, Thou shalt not eat of it: cursed is the ground for thy sake ; in sorrow shalt thou eat of it all the days of thy life ;**

18. **Thorns also and thistles shalt it bring forth to thee ; and thou shalt eat the herb of the field ;**

19. **In the sweat of thy face shalt thou eat bread, till thou return unto the ground ; for out of it wast thou taken : for dust thou art, and unto dust shalt thou return.**

20. **And Adam called his wife's name Eve** (*havah*, Heb., " the realisation or materialisation of being or beings "): **because she was the mother of all living.**

21. **Unto Adam also and to his wife did the LORD God make coats** (*che-thanoth*, Heb., " giving bodylike forms, envelopes or coatings " to hitherto superphysical beings) **of skins, and clothed them** (*va-ialebbishem*, Heb., " enveloped, enfolded the spiritual man in appropriate and expressive bodily form[1] ").

22. **And the LORD God said, Behold, the man is become as one of us** (*mimmennou*, Heb., " from us, out of us ". Adam has become individualised for the sake of knowing good and evil.   Not a curse or punishment but a provision for preservation and evolution), **to know good and evil : and now, lest he put forth his hand, and take also of the tree of life, and eat, and live for ever:**

23. **Therefore the LORD God sent him forth from the garden of Eden, to till the ground from whence he was taken.**

24. **So he drove out** (*igaresh*, Heb., not the forcible banishment of a criminal but " remove, put at a distance." To put forth as a tree puts forth shoots and blossoms.   The further descent of the spiritual Soul of man into physical, single-sexed existence, and out of the innocence or Eden of childhood, through puberty into adolescence) **the man ; and he placed** (*va-ischen*, Heb., " cause to be stationed ") **at the east** (*mi-kedem*, Heb., " from the eternity that was before time began ") **of the garden of Eden Cherubims** (*cherubim*, Heb., " symbolic images and living creatures with the cosmic life-forces, angelic powers at work throughout the universe, associated with the outworking of laws and the forth-going into matter of the human soul "[2]), **and a flaming** (*lahat*, Heb , " that which flashes out or gleams ") **sword**

---

[1] Here one may perhaps perceive a reference to the change from the superphysical condition of the first two and a half races of men on Earth to the physical (" coats of skin ") by the third sub-race of the Third Root Race.

[2] q.v.   *The Kingdom of the Gods*, p. 158, Geoffrey Hodson.

(*chereb*, Heb., "the activity and outgoing life-forces of the cherubim ") **which turned every way** (*ha-mithehap-phecheth*, Heb., "whirling ceaselessly on itself, a never-ceasing activity extending in every direction "), **to keep** (*li-shmor*, Heb., "to bring about wise and intelligent relationships, guard, protect ") **the way** (*eth-derech*, Heb., "every path of life ") **of the tree of life.**

Except in the case of very important words and proper names, the process of interpolating Hebrew words and their meanings, as suggested by Hebrew scholars, ceases at this point. Interpretations now follow of those verses alone which seem to offer opportunities for useful commentary.

Racial puberty, like individual puberty, causes allegorical expulsion from Eden, which is regained when the pure innocence of childhood becomes the conscious purity of spiritualised man. Between the innocence of Eden and full redemption or Ascension into Adeptship, man passes through a period of bondage in captivity—subservience to materialism, selfishness and sensuality—with which phase the Old Testament is partly concerned.[1]

SERPENT AND TREE—SYMBOLS OF CREATIVE POWER

The tree of life also symbolises both the creative and inventive capacity of the human intellect and a responsive condition of matter, these being characteristic of an advanced phase of evolution. The life-force active in the human mind, which thus enfired becomes imbued with the generative impulse, is symbolised by the sap of the tree of life. In this interpretation the serpent is the *fohatic* force itself, and the tree of life is human conscious-ness and its vehicles in which that force is active. Together they constitute creative power, Macrocosmic and microcosmic. The serpent by itself is emblematic of the undulatory, *fohatic*, triply polarised formative force in the Cosmos, in a Universe, in all Nature and in every vehicle of man. The tree of life is Spirit-impregnated substance, fructified matter, forming the vehicles of any being at any level from a Logos to an amoeba, charged as that matter is with the universal, propellant, vital force.

When inactive the neutral current by itself—the trunk of the tree—represents the latent divine Presence. When active the positive and

[1] *e.g.*, The bondage of the Israelites in Egypt, the descent of Joseph into the pit and the imprisonment of Samson.

negative, serpentine currents of the Serpent Fire[1] are present and in operation. As previously stated, the symbols for this energised condition are
the serpent and the tree. Sometimes a single serpent is coiled round the
trunk of the tree, whilst at other times two are present, one on either side
of the tree.

The expulsion of Adam and Eve from the Garden as punishment
for their mis-called " sin " of marital union has still other possible significations. After the exercise of the procreative function not only is innocence
or the Edenic condition lost or closed to Adam and Eve (representing
mankind), but the life-force itself becomes temporarily inactive. In this
sense the first parents are away from Eden as a state of consciousness,
whilst for the time being their vehicles are no longer empowered by the
fiery force. Symbolically and allegorically they are expelled by God,
Who in this case partly represents natural law. The term " God " may
also be taken to refer to the Solar Deity, Who is the Source of the Promethean
fire which endows Nature and man with generative potency. It is this
divine power that sends mankind forth from the Presence of God in Eden,
meaning *only* from the condition of pristine purity, into the evolutionary
field for purposes of self-unfoldment and the physical population of a
Universe.

In the fourth and successive Chapters of *Genesis* the children, the
grandchildren and subsequent descendants of Adam and Eve may be
regarded as personifying successive sub-races of the Lemurian or Third
Root Race[2] which, as stated, was the first race of physically embodied
men on Earth.

The members of the Order of Angels known as the Cherubim, which
were placed at the East of the garden of Eden " to keep the way of the
tree of life ", represent a Hierarchy of the *Elohim* associated with the
positive currents of the life-force. As described in the Appendix, kabbalistically the Cherubim are pictured as sphinxes and regarded as Governors
of the four elements in their highest sublimation. They would seem to
correspond to the *Lipika*, the Celestial Recorders or " Scribes ", the Agents
of *Karma* of Hinduism. The Hierarchy is concerned with the initiation
of the whirling motions by means of which primordial atoms or " holes

---

[1] *Serpent Fire* or *Kundalini Shakti* (Sk.). The power of life; one of the forces of Nature.
The occult electricity intimately associated with Azoth of the Alchemists, the creative
principle in Nature, and *Akāśā* (Sk.), the subtle, supersensuous, spiritual essence which
pervades all space. The seven-layered power in the base of the spine of man, composed
of three currents which flow along three canals in the spinal cord, named *Ida* (negative),
Pingala (positive) and *Sushumna* (neutral). These names are sometimes also applied—
erroneously—to the currents of force which flow in these canals. q.v. *The Kingdom of the
Gods*, descriptive matter relating to Plate XXVIII, and Vol. I of this work, Pt. III, under
Serpent, both by Geoffrey Hodson.
[2] q.v. *The Solar System*, A. E. Powell.

in space " are formed, presumably using the force which in Tibetan is called *Fohat*, the essence of cosmic electricity, the ever-present electrical energy and ceaseless formative and destructive power in the Universe, the propelling, vital force, the *primum mobile*, whose symbol is the *svastika*. In Kether[1] are thus said to be the " beginnings of the whirls ", the first stirrings of the divine creative Essence.   One of the chief duties of the members of this Angelic Hierarchy is to receive this Essence in Kether and carry it to the succeeding Hierarchy, the Auphanim or " Wheels ", associated with the second Sephira.

At the beginning of creation—according to occult philosophy— *Fohat*, which arises within the central Source of Life, is directed outwards into space upon the involutionary arc.[2] The consciousness of the Monads follows this fohatic path of forthgoing, being carried by a form of electrical induction outwards from the plane of *Ādi*[3] towards the physical world. On arrival there the Lord God, allegorically speaking, made for Adam and Eve coats of skin, which means that Nature and certain Orders of the *Elohim* produced the physical bodies of men.   Those Orders Who direct the process of forthgoing, and control the activity of *Fohat*, are symbolised by the Cherubim with flaming sword " which turned every way, to keep the way of the tree of life."   In this sense Eden is the first plane of the manifested Cosmos, called in Sanskrit *Ādi*.   Therein the seeds and potentialities of the whole of the subsequent creation exist from the beginning, and indeed throughout all time.   *Ādi* is the plane of the " seeds " (Monads) in their most sublimated state.

RECAPITULATION

Thus the tree of life within Eden, in a limited interpretation, is the life-force in Nature in a state of balance or equipoise.   The serpent associated with it represents the twin currents, positive and negative, with the tree trunk as third, by which the triple creative fire is manifest.   The fruit of the tree is the subsequent development, the harvest accruing from

---

[1] Kether (Heb.).   " The Crown ", the first Sephira of the kabbalistic Sephirothal Tree, which " gives birth to " the nine others, the last or tenth being called Malkuth, the Kingdom, meaning all Nature manifested.   Together the ten Sephira represent the emanation and development of the powers and attributes of Deity.   Each Number is an outward symbol for inner creative forces and processes, and their personifications as Archangels or Builders of the Universe.   See Appendix.

[2] The path of the forthgoing of Spirit-light into matter, in contradistinction to the path of return.

[3] *Ādi* Sk.).   " The first, the primeval ".   The Foundation Plane, the first field of manifestation, " the foundation of a universe, its support and the fount of its life."   The most spiritual level of consciousness.   The subtlest of the seven planes of Nature—Kether in the *Kabbalah*.

the activity of the Divine Life within the matter of the Universe, and particularly the fruitage of the great Monadic pilgrimage of forthgoing and return.

Adam represents both man, the Monad, and the first physical man on Earth, who was androgynous. Adam and Eve as separated entities represent the later stage of man as Monad-Ego clothed in single-sexed, physical personalities. They are personifications of the human race after its division into men and women. Before this takes place, complete innocence or creative inactivity exists. After the separation, procreation begins. Knowledge is thereby gradually gained. Evolution and experience bring that knowledge and its resultant power to the highest fruition, so that man ultimately becomes a God.[1] Therefore the serpent truthfully said: ". . . in the day ye eat thereof, then your eyes shall be opened, and ye shall be as gods, knowing good and evil."[2]

The price to be paid for the development of this deific power is heavy indeed. The Soul of man is encased in matter, wherein he temporarily becomes a prey to the delusion of self-separated individuality, to sex and to the dangers resulting from sexual over-indulgence. Self-degraded as a result, his condition is allegorically described as being condemned by God and driven out of Eden.

---

[1] "Be ye therefore perfect, even as your Father which is in heaven is perfect." (*Matt.* 5: 48—A.V.).

"Ye shall be perfect, even as your Father which is in heaven is perfect." (R.V.).

[2] *Gen.* 3: 5.

PART FOUR

CAIN, ABEL, NOAH, THE ARK, THE FLOOD, THE TOWER OF BABEL AND THE GENERATIONS OF SHEM

CHAPTER I

THE BRAND OF CAIN

Gen. 4. The Birth of Cain and Abel. The murder of Abel. The curse of Cain. Enoch, the first city, built. Lamech and his two wives. Seth and Enos born.

The commentaries on this portion of the Book of Genesis now offered interpret the various stories as allegories of man's first attainment of full physical awareness and the successive phases and developments which, in the course of evolution, followed thereafter; for such would seem to be both the key to the understanding of these otherwise almost incomprehensible accounts and also the intention of the authors who were revealing such knowledge—then secret—in terms of the Symbolical Language.

The account in the Fourth Chapter of *Genesis* of the relationships between the Lord God and Cain and Abel, with all that follows therefrom does indeed present grave difficulties. One may ask, for example, why of the two brothers Abel should be the more favoured of the Lord, Who accepted his sacrifice and rejected that of Cain. Since, moreover, this action provoked the jealousy of Cain, who as a result murdered his brother, would not the Lord God necessarily be partially, if not wholly, responsible for the sequence of events which followed the rejection of Cain's sacrifice?

The episodes being thus unacceptable in their literal form, the idea receives further support that some of the authors of the *Pentateuch* were spiritually instructed men who used the Symbolical Language as a vehicle for the ideas they wished to convey. The occasional introduction of inconsistencies as part of a concealing veil is referred to by Origen in his *De Principiis* in the following words, here repeated from the front of this Volume:

" Where the Word found that things done according to the history could be adapted to these mystical senses, he made use of them, concealing from the multitude the deeper meaning; but where in the narrative of the development of supersensual things, there did not follow the performances of those certain events which were already

10

indicated by the mystical meaning, the Scripture interwove in the history the account of some event that did not take place, sometimes what could not have happened: sometimes what could, but did not."

A famous Rabbi, Moses Maimonedes, Jewish theologian and historian, Talmudist, philosopher and physician (also already quoted) wrote:

" Every time that you find in our books a tale the reality of which seems impossible, a story which is repugnant to both reason and common sense, then be sure that the tale contains a profound allegory veiling a deeply mysterious truth; and the greater the absurdity of the letter, the deeper the wisdom of the spirit."

In pursuance of this method of interpreting the Scriptures, the story of the two brothers is here considered in some detail. It is regarded less as historical and more as allegorical, less as a record of physical events and more as descriptive of processes of evolution and of metaphysical principles, as also of mystical experiences.

If this approach be acceptable, then in conformity with the classical keys of the Sacred Language of Symbols and their use in interpretation— in this case applied to man, the microcosm—Adam, Eve, Cain and Abel may be considered as personifications of the spiritual, the Egoic, the superphysical and the physical parts of man respectively, and the accounts of their mutual relationships as descriptive of the interplay between those constituents of human nature. Adam, for example, being the parent of mankind on Earth, is the first of many successive personifications[1] of the Divine Spark of the Godhead in man, his true Self behind the bodily veil, whilst Eve is its counterpart and expression in the unfolding human individuality, or the spiritual Ego. Of the two brothers who are their sons, Abel (" shepherd ") represents man's more psychical and intuitional aspects, whilst Cain (" tiller of the soil ") personifies his physical nature.

Applying these concepts, the Fourth Chapter of the *Book of Genesis* may be regarded as descriptive of both the subsequent development of humanity after its separation into the two sexes, and also of its successive racial branches and human types. Cain was a tiller of the ground and Abel a shepherd. If interpreted as personifications of the physical and the intuitional principles respectively, Cain represents the positive potency which uses matter for the building of vehicles of consciousness. This

---

[1] In classical Mythology the parent Deities Zeus, Jupiter, Oden, Amun, Ahura Mazda, and each of the three Gods of the Hindu *Trimūrti*, similarly represent the Monad, " The Immortal Germ ", the Dwarf *Purusha*, the Scintilla of the Spiritual Sun.

incarnation of man quickens the evolution of the substance of which his bodies are built and thus gradually prepares it to express, and thereby " produce " (in the agricultural sense) with increasing effectiveness his innate and evolving faculties. As such incarnation in and " tilling " of matter is a positive, active process, Cain may properly be regarded as male. Abel, on the other hand, stands for the guarding, collecting, more feminine spiritual principle. As these two aspects are united in every human being, whilst described in *Genesis* as brothers Cain and Abel might more correctly, perhaps, be referred to as brother and sister.

ADAM, EVE, CAIN AND ABEL

In this microcosmic interpretation, then, Adam personifies the Monadic Ray, Eve the Ego or spiritual Soul in the Causal Body, Cain the physical brain-mind, and Abel the intuitional and emotional principles. Cain, representing the densest and most unspiritual condition, symbolically has his sacrifice rejected—meaning that consciousness, immersed in physical matter and so farthest away from its spiritual Source or the Lord, cannot easily either reach or be reached by that Source. Abel, the psycho-spiritual nature of man, is more susceptible to divine direction, hence his sacrifice is accepted by the Lord. This interpretation is surely preferable to the literal reading in which the Lord God is—quite unacceptably— presented as being capable of favouritism, which in this case provoked jealousy and led to murder. The difficulty is resolved if, as suggested above, the account is read as an allegorical description of psycho-spiritual conditions in man and their effects upon his ability to experience spiritual awareness. Cain, representing consciousness limited to the physical body, in early phases of evolution is unable to reach and to know the interior divine Presence which is his real Self, the God within. In consequence the spiritual part of man, personified by Abel, is temporarily overwhelmed and rendered inactive by its physical vehicle. Symbolically Cain (body consciousness) slays Abel (spiritual awareness).

The actions of the Lord in cursing Cain and putting an ineffaceable mark or " brand " upon him, even if intended to be protective,[1] are also susceptible of an esoteric reading, *sometimes the reverse of the exoteric*. The brand upon Cain may be regarded as the effect or imprint of the spiritual Self (personified by Abel) upon the physical principle; for incarnation in the flesh represents a metaphorical murder, and even burial, of the Monad-Ego until evolution over-comes the deadening effect and evolving man re-attains to spiritual awareness. Both the material Universe and the physical body of man, each symbolised by Cain, forever bear, even

---

[1] *Gen.* 4: 15.

though invisibly, this " brand " or hallmark of the omnipresent, divine Immanence.   Thus, whilst the " brand " upon Cain has come exoterically to be regarded as a sign of shame—the invisible social stigma of a murderer —esoterically the presence of Spirit in matter and of the Soul in the body, of man are implied.

In the Sacred Language, in one interpretation murder is a symbol for the effect of bringing " down " spiritual power and awareness into dense material manifestation.   The consciousness, and so the memory, of the divine nature is temporarily lost or " slain " during the descent of both Spirit into matter and the unfolding human Ego into incarnation upon Earth.   The murder of the Christ and His burial in the rock tomb are susceptible of the same interpretation, as are all symbolical and figurative deaths in the inspired passages of the world's Scriptures and Myths.

THE SUCCESSIVE RACES OF MEN

To sum up—pardon being asked for the repetition, deliberate because of the importance of the subject—according to occult philosophy human life on Earth is divided psychologically and ethnologically into seven major Root Race periods, each in turn being subdivided into seven sub-races.   The spiritual Selves of the first two and a half Root Races were only associated with matter in its more ethereal or tenuous condition. As they proceeded along the path of forthgoing they became clothed in substance of increasing density, eventually reaching in the Third Root Race their point of deepest descent as fully physical human beings. Thereafter the pathway of return was embarked upon, during which both consciousness and vehicles became increasingly less material and more spiritual.

The first men on Earth to be incarnated in bodies with bony structure, as at present, belonged to the Third Root Race.   These, however, were androgynous and are personified by Adam alone in the garden of Eden. The separation of the sexes gradually occurred during this Race, the distinct male and female sexes being personified by Adam and Eve together.   A natural evolutionary procedure is described by the authors of the *Book of Genesis*, the Lord God being made to take Eve out of the side of Adam. The allegory constitutes a typical example of the revelation of occult knowledge—at that time regarded as one of the secrets of the Mysteries— under the veil of a narrative of supposedly historical events.   In order, however, to preserve and also make available the knowledge, it was thus revealed symbolically, Initiates alone possessing the key.   Still deeper truths, knowledge of which can bestow great powers, are also concealed under the allegorical veil.   As mankind further evolves out of its present individualistic and ruthlessly competitive forms of civilisation, and so can safely be entrusted with such knowledge, further keys of interpretation will be made available by the Adept guardians of the Occult Mysteries of this planet.

The Fourth Root Race, still numerically preponderant, has been and still is concerned with the development of self-conscious emotion, whilst the Fifth—the present Aryan peoples—is concerned with the evolution of the mind, concrete and abstract. The Sixth Root Race will unfold the faculties of spiritual intuitiveness and conscious clairvoyance, whilst the Seventh is destined to develop spiritual Will, clairaudience and realisation of oneness with the Source from which at the beginning of manifestation the Monads came forth, and to which at the end they will return.[1]

According to this view of racial evolution, Adam personifies the men of the early third sub-race of the Third Root Race when man's astro-etheric vehicle became " coated " with organic physical matter, " skin "[2], and was androgynous. Adam and Eve represent the two single-sexed types of human bodies after the separation of the sexes had occurred, as previously described.

ENOCH—PROTOTYPE OF THE ADEPT

The generations which are stated to have followed Cain and Abel refer to the principles of both man and Cosmos on the evolutionary arc, culminating in Enoch, which is both a generic title for high Initiates or Adepts (Sages) and a personification of the degree of unfoldment at which the human Ego develops the capacity for abstract thought. This is a most important phase, because the synthesising intelligence makes possible awareness of the innermost spiritual Self, the Divine in man—a mystical experience which can be transmitted to the mind-brain. The Greek word *Enoichion* means literally the inner eye of the Seer, and is a reference to the so-called third or spiritual eye.[3] Entry upon this stage is referred to in the text in the words: ". . . then began men to call upon the name of the LORD."[4]

The evolution of the human mind, with its capacity for both concrete and—later—abstract thought, follows the development of the power of self-conscious emotion and precedes the awakening of the intuitive faculty. Between these two stages Fifth Root Race man achieves mental and Egoic

[1] q.v. *Lecture Notes of the School of the Wisdom*, Vol. I (Rev. Ed.), Ch. XIV, Sec. 2, Geoffrey Hodson.

[2] *Gen.* 3: 21.

[3] Third Eye. The superphysical force-centre or *chakra* (Sk.—" wheel ") between the eyebrows. q.v. *Lecture Notes of the School of the Wisdom*, Vol. I (Rev. Ed.), p. 252, Geoffrey Hodson, *The Serpent Power*, Arthur Avalon, and Glossary to this Volume.

[4] *Gen.* 4: 26.

self-awareness, symbolised by Enoch, the first-born of Cain. The higher intellect (Enoch) is thus rightly said to be the fruit (son) of bodily experience (Cain). The latter, therefore, is correctly described as a tiller of the ground (the physical plane and body), whilst Abel was a keeper of sheep. These symbolise the relatively harmless animal propensities and attributes of the emotional vehicle in the early stages of its evolution, while shepherding refers to the protective service which arises from an intuitive realisation of oneness. The shepherding, disciplinary power in man at that period was the unfolding spiritual Self, the Ego, who awakened in the personality protective love, primarily—and often only—for family and tribe. Admittedly members of later races can also exhibit traits which include a noticeable narrowing of the range of their interests and affections. Such people still put themselves and their families first, leaving the rest of the community to take a decidedly second place.

The shepherd in the Fifth and Sixth Root Races is the human Ego when illumined with intuition, who awakens in the personality that compassion which leads to love and service for the *whole race*. Consequently, when introduced into narratives written in the Sacred Language, shepherds also typify the Members of the Adept Brother-hood, the " just men made perfect "[1], those great, superhuman Beings who guard and inspire humanity—Shepherds of Souls indeed. The first dawning of such spiritual qualities in primitive man, represented by Abel, is also symbolised in the allegory describing the Lord's acceptance of Abel's sacrifice. As previously stated, Cain typifies the physical plane and body in which Spirit is more deeply enmeshed; symbolically his sacrifice was not acceptable.

THE AWAKENING AND DEVELOPMENT OF MIND

The city which Cain built and named after his son Enoch[2] may be regarded as a symbol of the twofold mental principle of man, with Enoch representing the higher or abstract intellect and the city itself the lower or concrete mind. This is in conformity with the use in the Symbolical Language of names to connote qualities. Enoch's great-great-grandson[3] is another example of this form of symbology; for Lamech had two wives, Adah and Zillah. From Adah was born Jabal, father of the nomad, cattle-raising tribes, and his brother's name was Jubal, " the father of all such as handle the harp and organ."[4] Again, the development of mind and the progress of the Fifth Root Race are indicated. The wandering, restless, but highly productive analytical mind is indicated by Jabal and the synthesising, prophetic mind by Jubal, father of musicians. The

---

[1] *Heb.* 12: 23.   [2] *Gen.* 4: 17.   [3] *Gen.* 4: 18.
[4] *Gen.* 4: 21.

Higher Self of man may indeed be likened to a musical instrument upon which the Monad, as master musician, performs continually and with increasing perfection. Thus, in these pregnant verses of the Fourth Chapter of the *Book of Genesis* the evolution of both Cosmos and man is described. The truth is, however, deeply veiled by names, words, numbers, symbols and allegories.

TUBAL-CAIN

Zillah bore unto Lamech the great allegorical figure known as Tubal-cain, described as " an instructor of every artificer in brass and iron ".[1] Since the two metals, brass and iron, are stated to have been associated with Tubal-cain and their symbolical meaning suggested, it is here necessary to introduce the subject of the use of metals in the Sacred Language of Symbols.

According to occult philosophy the whole Universe with all its parts, from the highest plane of Ādi to physical Nature, is interlocked, interwoven, to make a single whole, one body, one organism, one life, one consciousness, cyclically evolving under one law. All the " organs " or parts of the Macrocosm, though apparently separated in space and in plane of manifestation, are in fact harmoniously interrelated and interacting. The whole Cosmos, for example, which includes the Zodiac, many Solar Systems, planets, kingdoms of Nature, planes of Nature, elements and Orders of Beings, is a co-ordinated whole. This is because all these parts of the Cosmos, and also their constituents, are in " correspondence ", harmonious interaction or mutual resonance with each other. Kabbalistically stated, what is below is above, what is inside is outside, and everything interacts with everything else.

Certain " organs " or parts are more intimately grouped together than others. They resonate harmoniously with each other like the notes of a chord, sharing a common basic frequency of oscillation. In Occultism they are said to " correspond ". For example, a particular Zodiacal Sign, one planet, an element, a metal, a colour, a principle of man, a *chakra*,[2] a type of tissue, and a part of the physical body of man will all vibrate on a common frequency. Knowledge of these correspondences provides a key to the understanding of the Universe, of man's place therein and relationship therewith, and of human development. It is therefore also the key to the solution of many human problems, including those of happiness and unhappiness, health and disease.

A profound, fundamental truth concerning man is that in his spiritual, psychical and physical natures he is a microcosm, a miniature replica or

[1] *Gen.* 4: 22.
[2] q.v. **Glossary.**

epitome of the whole order of created beings and things, the Macrocosm. Man is thus a model of the totality of Nature. He contains within himself as a potentiality the collective aggregate of all that has ever existed, does at any time exist, and will ever exist throughout the eternity of eternities.[1]

METALS AS SYMBOLS OF PHYSICAL AND SUPERPHYSICAL BODIES[2]

The authors who used the Sacred Language employed this system of correspondences when choosing metals as symbols of parts of human nature. Thus precious metals such as gold and silver are used as emblems of the more spiritual parts of man, whilst brass and iron refer to the material and mortal vehicles of human consciousness. In Chinese symbology, as also in medieval alchemy, the process of refining and transmuting metals in a furnace represents humanity undergoing the purifying trials of life for the purpose of aiding its evolution. Gold, for example, particularly as the product of transmutation, is generally regarded as a symbol of the Christ nature in man, the divine wisdom in him from which arises his faculty of spiritual intuitiveness. Silver is also a symbol of the natural or mortal man, whilst steel or specially hardened metal, as in spears and swords, refers to the spiritual will, a manifestation of the purest divine Essence (*Ātma*) in him. Copper corresponds to the capacity for abstract thought, a faculty of the synthesising, prophetic intellect. Brass, being an alloy, refers to the blended abstract and concrete minds, whilst iron refers to his emotional nature. Tubal-cain therefore personifies the Inner Self at work on the development and structure of man's mental and emotional natures. As an instructor of artificers in these two metals, he will also be concerned with the force centres (*chakras*[3]) and other channels whereby spiritual attributes and activities reach the physical body and are manifested in it, both consciously and subconsciously.

The Fourth Root Race was especially concerned with the development of man's emotional nature and vehicle. The subtle substances and forces of the mental and emotional planes and bodies were, in consequence, being brought into increasingly intimate relationship with the physical. At the same time the nervous systems—cerebro-spinal, sympathetic and para-sympathetic—were gradually being sensitised so that mento-emotional states of consciousness could be more fully expressed in and through the physical body. Tubal-cain may, in consequence, be regarded as represen-

---

[1] q.v. *Lecture Notes of the School of the Wisdom*, Vol. I (Rev. Ed.), Ch. XIII, Geoffrey Hodson.

[2] q.v. *Lecture Notes of the School of the Wisdom*, Vol. I (Rev. Ed.), Chart facing p. 342, Geoffrey Hodson.

[3] q.v. Glossary.

ting both these processes as well as the Intelligences (*Elohim*) participating in the procedure. The Ego, as master craftsman engaged upon this task, is also represented by Tubal-cain, who thus personifies man's Inner Self occupied with those constructive evolutionary phases which culminate in self-conscious mental and emotional awareness and activity in the physical body.

At the time when the *Book of Genesis* was written, traditionally by a group of high Initiates of the Akkadian, Chaldean and Egyptian Mysteries, this knowledge was revealed directly to fellow Initiates alone, and publicly only under the heavy veiling of the allegories and symbols of the Sacred Language. Interpreted according to this system, Tubal-cain represents man's passage from the stage of egoism or I-am-ness—*Ahamkara*—[1] to ego-less-ness or I-am-all-ness, which in Sixth Root Race man and Fifth Root Race Initiates is one of the results of the attainment of universality of consciousness. This condition is symbolised by Seth, the *later* son of Adam and symbol of Sixth Race man. Before this state of consciousness can be developed prematurely in a spiritually advanced individual, figurative " death " (of the separative and prideful, egotistic quality) must occur. This is not achieved without suffering, as is allegorically revealed in accounts of the painful deaths of divine and semi-divine Beings and the Passion of the Lord Christ. Hence, possibly, the lamentation of Lamech in verse twenty-three of the Fourth Chapter of *Genesis*.

SEVEN A KEY NUMBER

Man's gradual attainment of self-conscious awareness and mastery in each of his seven vehicles of consciousness, gradually achieved during evolution through the seven Root Races, each with its seven sub-races, is indicated, and even positively affirmed, in the revealing but brief twenty-fourth verse: " If Cain shall be avenged sevenfold, truly Lamech seventy and sevenfold." Indeed, it does seem permissible here to discern a revelation of a profound and widely applicable truth by means of a numerical key—the number seven.

> Gen. 2: 26. *And to Seth, to him also there was born a son; and he called his name Enos: then began men to call upon the name of the LORD.*

[1] *Ahamkāra* (Sk.). The first tendency towards definiteness, regarded as the origin of all manifestation. In man the conception of " I ", self-consciousness or self-identity, the illusion of self as a self-separate existence in contradistinction to the reality of the universal all-inclusive One Self. Awareness of this universality is expressed in the words of the Christ: " I and my Father are one " (*Jn.* 10: 30). The illusion of separateness, the " Great Heresy " (Hindu philosophy), is regarded as the source of human sorrow and suffering. Self-emancipation from this delusion is the sure way to happiness and peace.

This closing verse of Chapter Four indicates the critical and supremely important stage in his development at which mortal man, hitherto aware only in and of himself as a physical person, attains to the illumination of his immortality; for the Bible states that at the birth of Enos, the son of Seth, " began men to call upon the name of the LORD." This recognition of and communion with the Lord may be taken to indicate man's attainment of self-awareness as an immortal, spiritual being.

Microcosmically and mystically the " LORD " referred to in this verse is the human Monad. The use of the number seven in verse twenty-four may refer to the fact that Seventh Root Race man will in his physical body have become aware of his " LORD " (Monad), and will be able to call upon " His " Name, thus drawing upon an interior source of its spiritual influence and power. The divine Presence will then become manifest in the fully regenerated physical, emotional and mental principles, these three by that time being wholly blended into a single instrument of action and awareness.

This culmination of human evolution as far as the present Fourth Round of the Earth Chain[1] is concerned, which is both revealed and concealed in the closing verse of Chapter Four of *Genesis*, is also achieved by every Initiate in advance of the normal time period. Such attainment is prophetic, in that it foreshadows and portrays the future condition of the whole race. For this reason Initiates in the Greater Mysteries are said to be " born out of due time ".[2]

The teachings of occult philosophy which are concerned with the evolution of both the Immortal Soul and the mortal personality of man reveal an orderly progression. The basic rule is stated to be that the indwelling, conscious life in the mineral, plant, animal and human kingdoms of Nature advances to the kingdom above during a period of one Chain.[3] Since each Chain is composed of seven Rounds, each Round is expected to be characterised by progress through the subsidiary stages preceding the ultimate attainment for the Chain as a whole. Applied to man, the Monad has evolved Chain by Chain through mineral (First Chain), plant (Second Chain) and animal (Third Chain) into the individualised, self-conscious state characteristic of a human being of the Fourth Chain. This is man's present position, and by the end of each of the remaining Rounds of this Fourth Chain a certain degree of development will have been attained. These stages chiefly concern the unfoldment of capacity for awareness and effective action—spiritual, intellectual, cultural and physical. Thus

---

[1] q.v. Glossary.
[2] 1 *Cor.* 15: 8.
[3] q.v. Glossary.

occult anthropology presents an orderly and systematic scheme of development for the life in all kingdoms of Nature. [1]

At the end of the Seventh Root Race of this Fourth Round on Earth, the mass of humanity will have achieved the level now known as Initiateship or spiritual regeneration, referred to as Christ-consciousness, which includes realisation of the unity of life and the resultant compassion for all living beings—hence its name. At the end of the seventh Round the human race now evolving on Earth is expected to achieve the stature of Adeptship or perfected manhood, " the measure of the stature of the fulness of Christ."[2] The simplicity of the language and the mastery of anthropological and ethnological facts revealed and yet concealed in this Chapter of *Genesis* are worthy of the closest study—and I suggest, the admiration—of the student of occult science.

Gen. 5. The genealogy, age and death of the patriarchs, from Adam unto Noah. The godliness and translation of Enoch.

The Fifth Chapter of the *Book of Genesis* does not appear to lend itself to suggested interpretations verse by verse. In consequence, only the following brief general remarks are offered.

SUCCESSIVE EPOCHS OF MANIFESTATION

Macrocosmically, the nine generations of the descendants of Adam, each named by a male, are a deeply occult recital of the successive minor cycles and their *Elohistic* Logoi by which a major Cycle is completed. Microcosmically, each generation mentioned in the Bible represents a principle of man, a plane of Nature and a phase of human development, as has already been suggested. The age of each Patriarch is the clue which, together with his place in the succession, will reveal to the student the principles which are being symbolised. A period of manifestation or *Manvantara* ends with the entrance of Noah into the Ark. *Pralaya*—the Flood—then follows. When the Flood subsides a new epoch begins; for the emergence of the preserved created beings, human and sub-human, from the Ark on to dry land refers to the re-emanation of the Monads from the divine consciousness and the aura (Ark) of the *Manu* (Noah). Their development then continues from the stage of evolution to which they had attained at the close of the preceding cycle.

[1] q.v. *The Solar System*, A. E. Powell.
[2] *Eph.* 4: 13.

CHAPTER II

" THE WATERS OF THE FLOOD WERE UPON THE EARTH " [1]

Gen. 6. The wickedness of the world, which provoketh God's wrath, and causeth the flood. Noah findeth grace. The order, form, and use of the Ark.

In Chapter Six of the *Book of Genesis* the merging of the cosmogonical with the historical becomes more marked. The engulfing of Universes and their several component Solar Systems within the waters of space at the end of every *Manvantara*,[2] major and minor, and the successive floods by which portions of the Earth have been overwhelmed are allegorically merged in the account of the Flood. Whilst the historicity of stories of local floods is not here discounted, the deluge described in the Sixth, Seventh and Eighth Chapters of *Genesis* is also susceptible of interpretation as connoting the periods of relative quiescence of the objective Universe which intervene between those of creative activity. The verses of this Sixth Chapter will shortly be considered individually, but a general interpretation of the chief symbols—already offered in an abridged version—is here repeated with some additions to serve as an introduction to the more detailed examination of the narrative which will follow in due course.

NOAH AND THE ARK

As a permutation of Jehovah, Noah—considered macrocosmically—represents the masculine creative potency. His presence within the Ark—the feminine aspect—indicates that creative union of which all things are the products. Noah may also be regarded as a personification of *Chokmah*, one of the ten Sephiroth, together with its associated Hierarchy of Archangelic and Angelic Hosts included in the kabbalistic Tree of Life.[3] In one aspect this member of the *Elohim*, is associated with the closing phases

---

[1] *Gen.* 7: 10.
[2] q.v. pp. 53–54.
[3] **q.v.** Appendix, *The Sephirothal Tree.*

of *Manvantara*, his[1] task being to sum up and sublimate into the highest spiritual essence all the fruits of the period which is coming to an end. The Monads and the essential power, life and consciousness of this epoch are symbolised by the family of Noah and by the pairs of the selected animals and birds. These are preserved within the aura (the Ark) of the Representative and Head of the appropriate Order of the *Elohim*.

In the Cosmos as a whole this process of conservation of the seeds of living things throughout *Pralaya* is said to be carried out by an Archangelic Member of the Inner Government of the Solar System. In the case of Chains, Rounds and Globes, however, indications are to be found that this function is performed by a member of the human kingdom of Nature who has attained to a very lofty superhuman stature. Potentialities and seeds are thus preserved in a sublimated state during the period of *Pralaya*, in which all forms disintegrate and their substance loses its individualised vibratory frequencies, returning to the quiescent, pre-creative state symbolised by the waters in flood legends. *Pralaya* ended, the appropriate Member of the *Elohim*, the Seed Manu (Noah), delivers to the corresponding Official of the new cycle the preserved seeds of the preceding epoch which have been in his charge. The great pilgrimage of involution and evolution is then repeated on a higher round of the ascending spiral.

In one sense the rainbow or covenant with the Lord, as described in verse thirteen of Chapter Nine of *Genesis*, symbolises the Office of the *Elohim* in bridging two epochs or cycles of manifestation. The return from simplicity to multiplicity, from the white light to the spectrum, from the One to the many, is also implied.

ERROR, OR WISE VEILING OF POWER-BESTOWING KNOWLEDGE?

The suggestion in verses five, six and seven of the Sixth Chapter of *Genesis* that the Supreme Deity could conceive of an imperfect plan which failed, experience wrath at that failure and then revengefully decide to destroy with insensate cruelty " both man, and beast, and the creeping thing, and the fowls of the air ", in its literal reading is surely quite unacceptable. The assertion that God could be guilty of such actions and could be moved to make the later promise not to " curse the ground any more for man's sake "[2] or " again smite any more every thing living "[2], is either an erroneous attribution to the Deity of conduct of which even man would not be guilty, or else a deliberately constructed blind for the concealment of an underlying truth.

[1] His. The masculine is used for convenience only. Such beings are a-sexual.
[2] *Gen.* 8: 21.

The concept is inconceivable, surely, that there could be in existence a single, extra-cosmic, personal God Who could Himself fail, and then be destructively wrathful at the wicked conduct of a human race which was solely and entirely the product of His own creation.   Such a conclusion is strengthened by the divine proclamation that man was created in God's own image.[1] It is similarly inconceivable that the conjoined *Elohim* (wrongly translated as " God " in *Genesis*), which emerge from and constitute the One Alone, could be capable either of error in the planning and fulfilment of their cosmic functions or of wrath at a failure which was solely attributable to themselves.

In the presence of such affronts to human reason, acceptance of the notion of the use of a special category of literature known as the Sacred Language, as previously defined, is surely preferable to total unbelief in such Biblical inconsistencies and errors as a literal reading necessitates. This could lead to the consequent rejection of the Bible as a whole, with its affirmation of the existence of a Supreme Being as the Directive Intelligence in Nature. The great scientist, Dr. Albert Einstein, evidently felt himself to be under no necessity to make this rejection, for he expressed the view that " That deeply emotional conviction of the presence of a *superior reasoning power* (italics mine, author) which is revealed in the incomprehensible Universe, forms my idea of God." Nevertheless the actions attributed to the Deity in the verses under review certainly do not present Him in the guise of a " superior reasoning power ".

Occult philosophy teaches that the objective Universe is ruled by cosmic law and that under this law *Pralaya* follows *Manvantara*[2] as inevitably as night follows day, for alternation is a law of manifestation. As already stated, the introduction into an account of Cosmogenesis of a capacity for failure and the attribution to the One Law, and the *Elohim* who are its Agents, of the gross and unphilosophical vice of violent and destructive anger, are such notable errors that they must surely be regarded as deliberate blinds. Indeed, the presumedly Initiate authors of the inspired portions of *Genesis*, having already revealed so many sublime truths, would hardly be capable of falling into such a profound mistake. Their complete knowledge, and their skilful use of many components of the entire range of symbols, show them to be highly illumined men. We may therefore regard as fraudulent interpolations, inaccurate translations or deliberate blinds, the suggestion of the visitation of the wrath of God upon Adam and Eve in the Garden of Eden, and later upon the children of men and all living creatures of the succeeding—the Noahian—cycle of manifestation.

---

[1] *Gen.* 1: 26, 27.
[2] q.v. Glossary.

The " bow in the cloud "—the rainbow displaying the seven colours of the spectrum—underscores this interpretation; for the illuminated clouds may be taken to represent the Root Substance into which the positive, creative potency " descends ", changing it from pre-cosmic, virgin (white) matter into its seven gradations of density, thereby preparing it to serve as the field of evolution for the seven kingdoms of Nature. The analogy of the rainbow, produced by the splitting up of white light into the seven colours of the spectrum, aptly presents this idea. In addition, the stretching of a bow across the heavens represents the linking together or bridging of successive cycles, an interpretation seemingly indicated by the Lord's description of the bow as " a covenant ". Furthermore, the speech of the Lord to Noah, giving comfort and command, may refer to the uttered creative " Voice "—the formation of the Universe by sound—implied by the Logos doctrine.[1]

If the account be applied to the physical evolution of the human race on Earth, Noah represents the *Manu* of one of the seven Root Races, an Official in the Hierarchy of the Adepts who is largely responsible for the evolution of a Root Race with its seven sub-races. As will be later expounded, a further function of this Official is to select certain of the more advanced members of the Race under his direction who are to be employed as the physical progenitors of its successor. These are then segregated, their descendants in due course being inspired to emigrate to the country chosen to be the birthplace of a new racial type.

" THE WATERS PREVAILED EXCEEDINGLY UPON THE EARTH "[2]

The following two paragraphs appear in somewhat the same form in the abridged interpretation of the story of the Ark in Part One, Chapter Four.

According to occult philosophy the Flood, its various symbolical meanings apart, was an historical fact. The continent of Atlantis and millions of the bodies of its inhabitants, human and sub-human, are said to have been drowned in four great Floods.[3] Thus, historically regarded, the Flood recorded in *Genesis* was the fourth and culminating cataclysm.

---

[1] Logos doctrine. The universe is first conceived in divine Thought, which is the governing power in creation. The creative " Word " expressive of the idea is then " spoken " and the hitherto quiescent seeds of living things germinate and appear from within the ocean of Space, the Great Deep. q.v., *Lecture Notes of the School of the Wisdom*, Vol. II, Pt. II, Sec. 2, Geoffrey Hodson.

[2] *Gen.* 7: 19.

[3] q.v. *The Solar System*, A. E. Powell, *The Story of Atlantis*, Scott Elliot, and *The Earth and its Cycles*, E. W. Preston, M.Sc.

The Souls, psychical and spiritual, of the Atlanteans were thereby saved from the deeper degradation into which, as practitioners of sorcery and black magic, they were in great danger of sinking. Indeed, very large numbers of the Atlantean peoples did fall into those errors. These are taken by some students of occultism to be the wickedness erroneously referred to as provoking the wrath of the Lord. Members of the Occult Hierarchy of Adepts on Earth are, however, no more capable of wrath than are the *Elohim* of the Universe. Danger to the evolving Souls of men arising from imperfect control of their personalities, which were engaging in deeply degrading black magical practices, alone necessitated occult intervention by the Adept Hierarchy of this planet.

In terms of the sevenfold constitution of man and his successive reincarnations[1] the Ark itself may be interpreted as the Auric Envelope,[2] and more especially the radiance of the body of light severally referred to as the *Augœides* (Gr.), the Robe of Glory (Gnostic) and the Causal Body. This particular vehicle of consciousness both contains and preserves the fruits harvested from each life-cycle or incarnation. In addition, it functions as a vesture for the threefold spiritual Self of man—divine Will, Wisdom and Intelligence. The inhabitants of the Ark, human and sub-human, typify both the fruits of the evolutionary process and the indwelling triune Spirit, and the three storeys refer to the three levels of divine consciousness of the triple Self.

THE FLOOD NARRATIVE AS ALLEGORY OF THE HUMAN LIFE CYCLE

Whilst the student of symbology must ever be on guard against reading into an allegory and its component symbols more than was originally intended or may be justly attributed,[3] descriptions of levels and conditions of human consciousness after the death of the body, with which event the physical part of the life cycle of man is ended, may possibly be discerned in the narrative. Occult science teaches that, having lost its physical instrument by death, the Inner Self of man is thereafter conscious in the emotional world for a time, during which *karma*[4] generated at that level

---

[1] q.v. *Reincarnation, Fact or Fallacy?*, Geoffrey Hodson.

[2] Auric Envelope. The edge and sum total of the substance of the seven human bodies, physical and superphysical, and their subtle radiations. See Glossary under Aura and Auric Envelope.

[3] The necessity for this safeguard is duly recognised throughout this work, and more particularly in the following suggested application of the story of the Flood.

[4] *Karma* (Sk.)—" Action ", connoting both the law of action and re-action, cause and effect, and the results of its operation upon nations and individuals. q.v. *Reincarnation, Fact or Fallacy?*, Geoffrey Hodson.

may be precipitated. This phase is followed by the detachment and disintegration of the substance of the desire nature, after which the Ego is aware in the mental principle. This period—a heaven-like state of happiness consequent upon inability to experience desire[1]—in its turn draws to a close, the Soul being then clothed in its vesture of light, the Causal Body, storehouse of the capacities attained during the life cycle just closed and for the development and expression of the faculty of abstract thought.[2]

If the Flood story be interpreted as an allegorical description of this human experience, a certain fitness may be observed. Water, for example, is used as a symbol of both primordial substance or space and the emotional life of man. The deluge itself might thus be interpreted as the " precipitation " upon the individual, during the first *post mortem* period, of such adversities as were generated during the preceding life. Thus applied to procedures and human experiences immediately after the death of one physical body and rebirth into its successor, the cessation of the rain would symbolise entry into the mental phase of the life after death, whilst the summit of Mount Ararat would represent the purely spiritual condition of Egoic consciousness into which the reincarnating Ray of the Inner Self then withdraws. Emergence on to level ground after descent from the summit represents birth in a new form, with the rainbow as the Egoic bridge or link between two lives. The Causal Body, which is the vehicle of the Ego, is iridescent with all the colours of the spectrum and, being immortal, is also the promise of assurance of safe passage from one cycle to the next. This vesture is therefore also well described as God's covenant with man, since it constitutes the essential link between the spiritual, immortal Self and the more material and decisively mortal personality.

From this preparatory study of the account of the Flood, with consideration given in advance to some of the chief symbols employed, a more detailed interpretation of the narrative is now undertaken. The Sixth Chapter of *Genesis*, with its references to communion and union between the sons of God and the daughters of men—a profoundly occult allegory—will now be examined.

---

[1] In occult philosophy human suffering is said to be caused by desire or, in the words of the Lord Buddha, " craving ". The cessation of human sorrow can only be achieved by the cessation of desire. cf. The Four Noble Truths of Buddhism. Behind desire, however, is the delusion of self-separateness, from which desire itself arises.

[2] q.v. *Through the Gateway of Death*, Geoffrey Hodson.

11

CHAPTER III

"... THE WICKEDNESS OF MAN WAS GREAT IN THE EARTH " [1]

Gen. 6. The wickedness of the world, which provoketh God's wrath, and causeth the flood. Noah findeth grace. The order, form, and use of the Ark.

This Chapter is one of the most wonderful in the Old Testament. So far as the wickedness of early man and the occurrence of a flood are concerned—the affirmed wrath of God is elsewhere considered—historically it is correct for, according to occult ethnology, during the Atlantean or Fourth Race period sin did indeed fall upon the Earth. As we have seen, the Atlanteans were guilty of most grievous wickedness—sorcery and other gross forms of the misuse of psychic forces—the only remedy for which was the destruction of their physical bodies.[2] This was brought about by a succession of floods, four in number, the last of these finally engulfing the Atlantean continent. Certain mountain ranges and peaks have, however, remained above the waters, as evidenced by the various Archipelagos and Islands of the Atlantic Ocean.

A NEW RACE IS FOUNDED

Before the great floods began the *Manu*,[3] personified by Noah, began to draw together those tribes and individuals who were to be the progenitors

---

[1] *Gen.* 6: 5. The reader is referred to Pt. I, Ch. I, of this Volume.

[2] According to occult philosophy the evolution of life and form throughout the Solar System, and so on this planet, is presided over and in some degree directed by Hierarchies of exalted Beings. These " Hosts of the Logos " are said to be represented on Earth by an occult Fraternity of Adepts, some of Whom retain physical bodies on entering the superhuman kingdom of Nature, whilst others do not do so. (q.v. *Lecture Notes of the School of the Wisdom*, Vol. I (Rev. Ed.), Ch. XVI, Geoffrey Hodson). Floods may occur as natural geological catastrophes, but should the necessity ever arise the power is said to be possessed by the Adepts to bring about the destruction of a continent and its people. Hints are to be found in occult literature that this was, in fact, done to cause at least one of the four successive floods, by which the continent of Atlantis was overwhelmed. q.v. *The Secret Doctrine*, Vol. III (Adyar Ed.), pp. 424–427, H. P. Blavatsky.

[3] *Manu*—q.v. Glossary.

of the next Root Race. They were taken to places of safety, one of which was in Arabia and another on the shores of the then existing Gobi Sea. There through hundreds of thousands of years, symbolised by the period within the Ark, the race with its inherent faculties—represented by the human, animal and bird dwellers in the Ark—underwent specialised development. Then, when the time was ripe, the descendants of these specially selected people were liberated from their Arabian and Central Asian homes and charged with the task of settling and populating the chosen countries with the newly established types. Thus arose the first beginnings of the sub-races of the Fifth Root Race. Such, according to occult science and very briefly stated, are some of the chief historical events recorded partly in plain language and partly in allegory in the Sixth Chapter of *Genesis*.

MOUNT ARARAT—SYMBOL OF THE EVOLUTIONARY HEIGHTS

The more advanced phases of the spiritual evolution of humanity to be entered upon during later racial periods are, however, also indicated and with the greatest skill the two accounts are successfully intermingled. In this latter interpretation—the spiritual evolution of man—the process is described of the transmutation of the baser human attributes (the animals) into the fine gold of the nobler qualities of man's Higher Self (Noah and his family in the Ark). This was accompanied by the sublimation of the force behind the grosser, animal passions from its physical (the surface of the Earth) to its mental and spiritual expressions (Mt. Ararat).

The Ark, as symbol of the vehicle of the human Spirit, the Causal Body, is rightly described as having been built by Noah (the Ego) under the direction of the Lord (the Monad). By means of both natural evolution and deliberate self-quickening on " The way of holiness ",[1] the power, the capacities and the attributes of the lower, mortal man were being raised or sublimated to spiritual levels of expression. Simply put, human consciousness—which had hitherto been largely limited to the physical world—was being elevated towards the Egoic level.

THE WINDOW, THE RAVEN AND THE DOVE[2]

The existence of the window in the Ark from which, as later described, the raven (the formal intellect) and the dove (the intuition) went forth,

[1] *Is.* 35: 8.
[2] *Gen.* 8: 6, 7, 8.

portrays the fact that the spiritual Self or Ego of man in its turn is open to supra-mental states of consciousness (the upper air). The window itself indicates that the Ego in the Causal Body always has a means of access to the more lofty spiritual levels of awareness.

The failure of the raven to return indicates that the concrete mind alone cannot receive and reveal full spiritual illumination. This interpretation is supported by the return of the dove with the olive leaf, indicating that the intuition is able to convey illumination because of its oneness with universal life, typified by the olive tree from which the leaf had been plucked. Flight through the air also aptly portrays by allegory the supramental realms from which the intuition flashes into the otherwise darkened mind. The element of air is frequently used in the Sacred Language of Symbols to represent the level of consciousness in which the intuitive faculty inheres and from which it is derived. A similar use of the dove to symbolise spiritual influences and states of awareness is found in the descriptions of the baptism of Jesus in Jordan as given in the three synoptic Gospels. It is recorded that ". . . the heavens were opened unto him, and he saw the Spirit of God descending like a dove, and lighting upon him."[1]

From these considerations of the story of the Flood a return is now made to the beginning of the Sixth Chapter of the *Book of Genesis*. The references to the deluge itself, Noah, the Ark, the raven and the dove were here included in advance of their correct textual sequence in order to present a general intepretation of the event as recorded in the Bible.

> *Gen.* 6: 1. *And it came to pass, when men began to multiply on the face of the earth, and daughters were born unto them,*
>
> 2. *That the sons of God saw the daughters of men that they were fair; and they took them wives of all which they chose.*

In the microcosmic reading the sons of God are the human Monads, whilst the daughters of men represent the personal consciousness of late Third and early Fourth Root Race men. Up to that time humanity as a whole had been unillumined by any spiritual awareness, being conscious only at psycho-physical levels. At the stage of evolution which had then been reached, a further development occurred which consisted of a descent of Monadic influence. In this sense the Monads (the sons of God) " married " the personalities (the daughters of men) and the product was mental—and later Egoic—consciousness. Thus the triplicity of

---

[1] *Matt.* 3: 16.

Monad-Ego-personality was completed, the flesh having then become the vehicle of the Spirit.

In another possible interpretation the sons of God are the Angelic Teachers of the first wholly physical race of men with bony structure (the third numerically). In yet another view they are the *Pitris* or " ancestors ", advanced products of preceding Schemes[1] of evolution who, together with the *Elohim*, constructed the forms of superphysical Nature. These Beings fashioned the first gigantic physical bodies and inducted human consciousness into them.[2]

> *Gen. 6: 3. And the LORD said, My spirit shall not always strive with man, for that he also is flesh: yet his days shall be an hundred and twenty years.*

The threefold nature of man, and the ultimate subservience of his material nature to his spiritual Self, are indirectly indicated in this verse. The stated life period of one hundred and twenty years might indicate that early physical man lived to that age. By numerical integration the number one hundred and twenty becomes three, and this may also imply the first establishment in man of physical, emotional and mental vehicles of consciousness through which the Monadic Ray, itself triple, could be expressed.

> *Gen. 6: 4. There were giants in these days; and also after that, when the sons of God came in unto the daughters of men, and they bare children to them, the same became mighty men which were of old, men of renown.*

In this verse the mystical and the historical are interwoven. Mystically, the Monad-Egos (the sons of God) mingled with the personalities (the daughters of men), which means that they found growing expression in and through them. Historically, the physical bodies of primitive men were gigantic, being at least twice the size of those of Fifth Race man. In addition, the Adept Tutors of the race lived physically amongst mankind and directed them. These were the men of renown, the so-called divine Teachers and Kings of pre-historic periods, giants of intellectual and spiritual power.

> *Gen. 6: 5. And GOD saw that the wickedness of man was great in the earth, and that every imagination of the thought of his heart was only evil continually.*

[1] Schemes. q.v. Glossary, Chain.
[2] q.v. Glossary—*Pitris*.

> 6. *And it repented the LORD that he had made man on earth, and it grieved him at his heart.*

> 7. *And the Lord said, I will destroy man whom I have created from the face of the earth; both man, and beast, and the creeping thing, and the fowls of the air; for it repenteth me that I have made them.*

The process of the incarnation of purely spiritual and immortal Monads—themselves ever unstained and unstainable—into mortal, material, physical personalities involves a measure of temporary degradation for the manifested Race of the Monads. The reference to man's great wickedness is thus allegorical, being actually descriptive of the inevitable staining of pure Spirit by the intimate contact (marriage) of Monads (sons of God) with the desire-charged matter of human physical bodies (daughters of men). The sin referred to is also descriptive of certain experiences associated with the exercise by man of his generative powers.

An allegorical interpretation is further supported by the fact that, as has been previously stated, no sin whatever is involved in the normal exercise by man of the procreative power for the production of children and the continuance of the race. In its literal sense, the idea is entirely unacceptable that the Creator of those human beings who exercised a power with which they had been divinely endowed were guilty of wickedness. The further statement that this completely innocent action evoked the wrath of God, and led to His vengeful act of total destruction, with the exception of the inhabitants of the Ark, is also an affront to the intellect. If by the Lord God of the *Book of Genesis* is implied the Supreme Deity, the one Conceiver, Fashioner, Preserver and Transformer of Universes as a whole, then " He " must be assumed to be endowed with the attribute of omniscience. This power would include complete foreknowledge— even in transcendence of the restrictions of time—so that in the consciousness of such a Being full awareness of the total product of His " creation " from beginning to end must be presumed to have been present. If this be so, then the Lord God would from the outset have been fully aware of every forthcoming event and, in consequence, could in no sense have been surprised or aggrieved by any action of His sons whom He had created in His own image. Once again, therefore, acceptance of the literal reading of this, as of so many other passages, becomes an impossibility.[1]

---

[1] I am aware that references to the total incredibility of many parts of the Bible in their literal form frequently appear in this work, involving what might be regarded as undue repetitiveness. This repetition, however, is quite deliberate, being considered necessary in order to correct the degradation of the idea and ideal of the Supreme Deity, as in this instance; to support the concept of the existence of a Symbolical Language; and to assist those who find themselves disturbed, and even repelled, by the all-too-frequent unacceptable statements occurring in the Scriptures.

The statement that God repented of having created man must either be rejected or regarded as a blind to enveil knowledge of the deeply occult process of involution, partly described in allegory by the Christ in His parable of the Prodigal Son.[1] The " descent " of the Ray of the human Monad from the realm of pure Spirit, through the intervening planes into physical incarnation, is also implied. The stories of the salvation of Noah and his family,[2] of the raising of Joseph from the pit[3] and his ultimate attainment of high office under Pharoah,[4] of the liberation by Moses of the Israelites from bondage in Egypt,[5] of their eventual arrival under Joshua at the Promised Land,[6] and of the spiritual salvation of all men by the Redeemer—all these both veil and reveal the process of evolution, or the returning ascent of the Monadic Ray to the purely spiritual state.

God, whether as Law or as the Source, Emanator and Director of the creative impulse in Nature, neither rejoices nor repents. Completely impersonal, the creative Power and its Archangelic and Angelic Intelligences (*Elohim*) skilfully operate the vast cosmic machinery throughout alternating *Manvantaras* and *Pralayas*, the former with their innumerable sub-cycles of forthgoing and return. As suggested above, the attribution of human limitation to the Deity is to be regarded as either complete error or part of the veil of allegory which must be drawn aside if the concealed spiritual verities are to become known, just as the veil of matter must similarly be removed from the eyes and minds of men if full realisation of spiritual truth is to be attained.

[1] *Lk*. 15.   q.v. *The Hidden Wisdom in the Holy Bible*, Vol. I, Pt. IV, Geoffrey Hodson.
[2] *Gen*. 6, 7 and 8.
[3] *Gen*. 37.
[4] *Gen*. 41.
[5] *Ex*. 14.
[6] *Joshua* 3.

CHAPTER IV

"BUT NOAH FOUND GRACE IN THE EYES OF THE LORD "[1]

Gen. 6: 8. *But Noah found grace in the eyes of the Lord.*

> 9. *These are the generations of Noah: Noah was a just man and perfect in his generations, and Noah walked with God.*

> 10. *And Noah begat three sons, Shem, Ham, and Japheth.*

In one meaning as we have seen, Noah is a personification of the holder of an Office (*Manu*) in the Spiritual Government of Solar Systems, Chains, Rounds, planets and races. Noah more particularly represents the Root and Seed *Manus*, whose vocation it is to absorb and preserve within their auras (arks) during *Pralayas* (flood) the seeds of living things and the Monads of men. These they deliver to their successors at the opening of the next *Manvantara* (post-diluvian dispensation).

In the mystical interpretation Noah represents the Monad-illumined Ego which, though limited and even stained in its mortal manifestation in the physical body, nevertheless in its own essential nature remains unstainable and unstained. Thus " Noah found grace in the eyes of the Lord " and " was a just man and perfect in his generations, and Noah walked with God." In this interior sense the term " God " refers to the human Monad, of which the Ego is a product and with which it is ever at one. The three sons of Noah personify man's mental, emotional and physical bodies, their wives representing the expressed powers and attributes thereof—in Sanskrit *shaktis*. Noah and his family thus stand for the whole nature of man.

> *Gen.* 6: 11. *The earth also was corrupt before God, and the earth was filled with violence.*

> 12. *And God looked upon the earth, and, behold, it was corrupt; for all flesh had corrupted his way upon the earth.*

[1] *Gen.* 6: 8.

> 13. *And God said unto Noah, The end of all flesh is come before me;*
> *for the earth is filled with violence through them; and, behold, I*
> *will destroy them with the earth.*

Historically these verses refer to the degradation or corruption into which early Fourth Root Race men fell. The maximum materialism which occurs during all fourth phase manifestations, when compared with the spirituality typical of both earlier and later epochs, is also indicated. The fourth phase of a sevenfold cycle[1] of forthgoing and return represents both the deepest level of descent and the beginning of ascent. It is marked by the maximum " degradation " of Spirit produced by embodiment in densest matter, and a life and consciousness by incarnation in mortal vehicles. Here it may be repeated that according to occult philosophy the corruption of the Atlantean (Fourth Root Race) people was an historical fact, as also was the destruction by drowning of great numbers of physical bodies. The flood legends of the Scriptures of other ancient civilisations are also partly based upon these events.

> Gen. 6: 14. *Make thee an ark of gopher wood; rooms shalt thou make in the*
> *ark, and shall pitch it within and without with pitch.*
>
> 15. *And this is the fashion which thou shall make it of: The length*
> *of the ark shall be three hundred cubits, the breadth of it fifty*
> *cubits, and the height of it thirty cubits.*
>
> 16. *A window shalt thou make to the ark, and in a cubit shalt thou*
> *finish it above; and the door of the ark shalt thou set in the side*
> *thereof; with lower, second, and third stories shalt thou make it.*

THE SYMBOL OF THE ARK

Regarded as a symbol, the ark is susceptible of numerous interpretations. In general as observed, it is any vehicle of consciousness, whether of Cosmos, Solar System, sun, planet, race or individual. The arks and ships of the Allegorical Language employed by the Initiates of the Mystery Schools of early civilisations all refer to containing vehicles of consciousness of whatever dimensions and at whatever level, including cosmic matter when formed into Universes, as also the Spiritual or Causal Body of man, his Auric Envelope[2], the animal and human wombs, the enclosing membrane of a cell and the " wall " of an atom.

---

[1] For a full exposition of cycles of forthgoing and return see Vol. I, Pt. IV of this work.

[2] *Aura* (Gr. & Lat.). A subtle, invisible essence or fluid that emanates from human, animal, and even inanimate, bodies. A psychic effluvium, superphysical and physical,

The outer hull is the " Ring-pass-not "[1] of Universes, the Auric Envelope of man and the skin of his physical body. The inner lining, symbolised by pitch, is the hardened, protective substance which forms at the edge of the sphere of manifestation, enclosing the creative forces with their distinctive frequencies of oscillation. As pitch keeps out water, so do these vibrating energies render impossible any intrusion from the sea of space outside by forces and Intelligences foreign to those within. The division of Noah's Ark into rooms describes the establishment of the various planes of Nature in the Cosmos, the vehicles of consciousness in man, the constituent parts of the embryo and the cell, and the differently charged particles of the chemical atom.

THE DIMENSIONS OF THE ARK

The number of cubits in each direction, namely three hundred in length, fifty in breadth and thirty in height, may be regarded as referring to cycles and phases of development. In this sense the three hundred cubits in length may indicate the plant kingdom of Nature, for that number reduced becomes three and plants consist of three principles, namely the physical form, the vital force and the dawning sensitivity or feeling. The stated breadth of fifty cubits, which by reduction is five, refers to the animal kingdom wherein exists the potential development of a fifth principle, the Higher *Manas*,[2] which will bestow separated individuality or Ego-hood. The thirty cubits in height similarly gives three and thus designates man who, whilst including all preceding development, is in two senses a threefold being; for the Inner Self is triple, a trinity in the likeness of its Creator, whilst the total man, as distinct from the members of all the sub-human kingdoms, consists of highest Spirit (Monad) and lowest matter (physical body) united by intellect.

including the electro-vital emanations from the physical body in the case of man. It is usually oviform or egg-shaped and is the seat of the Monadic, spiritual, intellectual, mental, passional and vital energies, faculties and potentialities of the whole sevenfold man.

Auric Envelope. The whole aura as defined above, with reference to both the edge or extreme range of the auric radiations (envelope) and the presence of germinal powers, particularly those retained in the immortal vesture of the triple Self known as the Causal Body. This vehicle is more especially symbolised by the arks of the Flood legends of the Scriptures of ancient peoples, and by boats introduced into other allegorical narratives such as those of the ships built by Argus and Deucalion (Greek mythology), that built for Vaivasvata (*Mahābhārata*, the *Purānas* and the *Brāhmanas*), and that upon which Christ performed the miracle of the stilling of the tempest. (*Matt.* 8: 23–26). q.v. *Lecture Notes of the School of the Wisdom*, Vol. II, Pt. I, Sec. I, Geoffrey Hodson.

[1] q.v. Glossary.

[2] *Manas* (Sk.). " Mind ". Generally used in reference to the planes of Nature built of mind-stuff and to the mental faculties of man.

Noah (the Monad-Ego), his wife (the Causal Body), and Shem, Ham and Japheth (the three vehicles of the personality—mental, emotional and physical) personify the component principles of man. The Noah's Ark symbol with its carefully indicated dimensions, structure and inhabitants, thus accurately represents man himself at his present evolutionary position on this planet. The Flood narrative is also of universal significance; for it applies equally to the planet Earth, to its Fourth Root Race, and to the Fourth Round of the Fourth Chain of our Planetary Scheme. Since it portrays a basic creative principle, the allegory must apply to all Schemes, Solar Systems and Cosmoi.

THE WINDOW

The window of the Ark, placed in its upper portion, points to the fact that man's faculty of abstract thought, which is a function of the Ego in the Causal Body (the Ark), constitutes a window or opening to metaphysical states of consciousness. In the physical body the " window " is the *anterior fontanelle*, and in the etheric and superphysical bodies it represents the *Brahmarandhra* (Crown) *chakras* or force-centres.[1]

THE DOOR

The oft-used symbol of the door is susceptible of at least two meanings. In one it represents the possibility of an entrance into the mind of power, light and inspiration from supra-mental levels. In this sense the door symbolises a means of access for spiritualising influences through the abstract to the concrete mind. Such influences are sometimes in their turn personified by a Great Teacher. Jesus would appear to use the symbol in this sense in His words: " I am the door: by me if any man enter in, he shall be saved, and shall go in and out, and find pasture."[2] In another meaning the door is a symbol of the possibility of an entrance into the mind of certain forces and predilections from lower levels, particularly those of the emotional and purely physical parts of human nature.

> *Gen.* 6: 18. *But with thee I will establish my covenant; and thou shalt come into the ark, thou, and thy sons, and thy wife, and thy sons' wives with thee.*

[1] q.v. *The Chakras*, C. W. Leadbeater.
[2] *Jn.* 10: 9.

19. *And of every living thing of all flesh, two of every sort shalt thou bring into the ark, to keep them alive with thee; they shall be male and female.*

20. *Of fowls after their kind, and of cattle after their kind, of every creeping thing of the earth after his kind, two of every sort shall come unto thee, to keep them alive.*

21. *And take thou unto thee of all food that is eaten, and thou shalt gather it to thee; and it shall be for food for thee, and for them.*

These verses, despite their brevity, describe long continued processes of evolution in which during preceding races, plants, Rounds and Chains the four kingdoms of Nature had become established on the Earth. By the time the present fourth Chain had been reached, adequate vehicles of consciousness (arks) for each kingdom had been developed.[1] In the interpretation of Noah as *Manu* the Flood refers, as we have seen, to the period between cycles of manifestation.

THE UNIVERSALITY OF THE FLOOD LEGEND

The Flood legend also appears in the Assyrian Tablets, the Hindu Scriptures, Greek mythology and the so-called *Troano Manuscript* of the Mayans. *The Chaldeo-Babylonian Tablets* describe a flood as having lasted for " six days and nights (during which), the wind, deluge and storms overwhelmed (the Earth). On the seventh day in the course was calmed the storm and all the deluge which had destroyed like an earthquake, quieted. The sea he caused to dry, and the wind and deluge ended. . . ."

In the Hindu version found in the *Mahābhārata*, the *Purānas* and the *Brāhamanas*, Vaivasvata, the Hindu Noah, saved a little fish which proved to be an *Avatār* (descent or manifestation on Earth) of Vishnu, the Second Aspect of the *Trimūrti*. The fish warned him that the Globe was about to be submerged and that all that inhabited it must perish. It ordered him to construct a vessel in which he was to embark with his family. When the ship was ready and Vaivasvata had entered it with his family, together with pairs of all animals and the seeds of plants, the rain began to fall. The fish, now become gigantic and having developed a horn to which the *Manu* tied the ship, guided it through the raging elements— and when they were calmed landed it on the summit of the Himalayas.

---

[1] For a fuller exposition of this concept of evolution through the kingdoms of Nature, Chain by Chain, see *The Solar System*, A. E. Powell, and *Lecture Notes of the School of the Wisdom*, Vol. I (Rev. Ed.), Ch. XIV, Sec. I, Geoffrey Hodson.

In Greek mythology when Zeus had resolved to destroy mankind, which had become degenerate, Deucalion, the Greek Noah, and his wife Pyrrha were on account of their piety the only mortals to be saved. Deucalion built a ship in which he and his wife floated to safety during the nine days of flood which destroyed all the other inhabitants of Hellas. At last the ship rested on Mount Parnassus in Phocis. Thereafter, by very strange magical actions, the human race was restored.

The *Troana Manuscript*, which appears to have been written about 2,500 years ago among the Mayans of Yucatan and has been translated by Le Plongeon, gives the following description of the submergence of a continent in the Atlantic, presumably the Poseidonis referred to by Plato:

" In the year of 6 Kan, on the 11th Muluc in the Zac, there occurred terrible earthquakes, which continued without interruption until the 13th Chuen. The country of the hills was covered by mud, the land of Mu was sacrificed; being twice upheaved it suddenly disappeared during the night, the basin being continually shaken by volcanic forces. Being confined, these caused the land to sink and to rise several times and in various places. At last the surface gave way and ten countries were torn asunder and scattered. Unable to stand the force of the convulsions, they sank with 64,000,000 of their inhabitants 8,060 years before the writing of this book."

In a later find of an ancient Mayan manuscript known as *The Book of Chilam Balam*, discovered by A. M. Bolic, a flood is referred to thus: " and then in one watery blow, came the waters . . . the sky fell down and the dry land sank."

Flood narratives, in addition to their historical bases, are also susceptible of the interpretation applied to the Biblical account of the Noachian deluge. As heretofore advanced, the uniformity and universality of these and many other legends, myths and allegories characteristic of such remnants of the literature of ancient peoples as are preserved, may be regarded as indicating both a single source of all of them and a similar system of symbology. Occult philosophy affirms that source to be the Hierarchy of Adept Sages, still existent on Earth, the " just men made perfect."[1] The similarity of the symbols employed to denote the same ideas is explained by the use of the Language of Allegory and Symbol in which world Scriptures and Mythologies have been written.

---

[1] *Heb.* 12: 23 and 1 *Cor.* 2: 6.

CHAPTER V

THE ARK ENTERED AND THE RAVEN AND DOVE RELEASED

Gen. 7: *Noah, with his family, and the living creatures, enter the ark. The beginning, increase, and continuance of the flood. All flesh destroyed.*

Gen. 7: 1. *And the LORD said unto Noah, Come thou and all thy house into the ark; for thee have I seen righteous before me in this generation.*

2. *Of every clean beast thou shalt take to thee by sevens, the male and his female: and of beasts that are not clean by two, the male and his female.*

3. *Of fowls also of the air by sevens, the male and the female; to keep seed alive upon the face of all the earth.*

4. *For yet seven days, and I will cause it to rain upon the earth forty days and forty nights; and every living substance that I have made will I destroy from off the face of the earth.*

The mention of the seven pairs of clean beasts and of the fowls of the air may refer to the numerous septenates[1] throughout all Nature, physical and superphysical. Amongst these are the deeply occult classifications known as the Seven Rays[2] into which all created things are divisible. The seven Sephiroth, also named the Seven Mighty Spirits before the Throne, the *Elohim* or primary Agents of the one creative Will, are as seven gateways through which the Monad-bearing life-wave passes on its

---

[1] q.v. *The Hidden Wisdom in the Holy Bible*, Vol. I, Pt. III, Ch. II, Geoffrey Hodson.

[2] The Seven Rays. A term used in occult philosophy for the seven main classes of Monads and the powers, qualities and weaknesses by which they are expressed in the seven differing types of human beings. q.v. *The Seven Rays*, Ernest Wood, and *The Seven Human Temperaments*, Geoffrey Hodson.

way out—in terms of the physical three dimensions only—from the one Source into the field of evolution. In consequence, the currents of that life and every Monad carried with them receive the impress of the quality of that One of the Seven Sephiroth through which they pass. This fact is presumably referred to by the Lord in His instructions to Noah concerning the selection of the types to enter the Ark. It was essential that the animal representative of each of the Seven Rays should be present, preserved throughout the Flood (period of creative quiescence), and thereafter released in order to ensure the perpetuation of each main Ray type in the animal kingdom.

From the point of view of the unity of the one life present in and evolving through all beings, the classification of the animals as clean and unclean would seem to be artificial and erroneous. *All* such creations are " clean " in the sense that they are vehicles for unfolding consciousness and evolving life. The Jews, however, following very old traditions, had designated certain animals as unclean.[1] Such division was doubtless based on the fact that some beasts are earth-eaters, and even dung-eaters, and this includes the whole of the porcine tribe. Their flesh was forbidden because their diet was presumed to render it unfit for consumption. The classification is also hygienic. The flesh of such animals is more likely to contain poisons and dangerous bacteria, the absorption of which into the human body could generate conditions favourable to disease.

The fact that all animals, whether supposedly clean or unclean, were ordered to be taken into the Ark demonstrates that all were valued by the Lord. This implies that Nature herself and Her creative Intelligences, from the lowest to the highest, regard both categories of creatures as included within the plan of evolution. The Jews, however, especially those outside the old original Sanctuaries of Chaldea, desired to give to the so-called unclean beasts less value than the so-called clean animals. Habit and human hygiene were most probably the chief deciding factors when once the original instructions to partake of a vegetarian diet[2] were disregarded.

Gen. 7: 6. *And Noah was six hundred years old when the flood of waters was upon the earth.*

The six hundred years of the age of Noah (by reduction six) may indicate the approaching end of both a second ternary and a sevenfold period of manifestation—the close of *Manvantara.* If so, this would support a dual reading of the allegory—terrestrial and cosmic. The various time

[1] *Lev.* 11.
[2] *Gen.* 1: 29; 9: 4.

periods referred to in the remainder of this Seventh Chapter of the *Book of Genesis* may thus have a chronological significance applicable to the major and minor cycles of activity and quiescence. Since, however, full consideration has already been given to this subject in preceding Chapters, in order to avoid undue repetition I have decided to resume proffered interpretations of the narrative of the Flood from the beginning of the Eighth Chapter of *Genesis*.

> Gen. 8: 1. *And God remembered Noah, and every living thing, and all the cattle that was with him in the ark: and God made a wind to pass over the earth, and the waters assuaged.*

In Chapter Eight of *Genesis* the symbolism of numbers is also largely employed. In the purely human sense the subsiding of the Flood, the emergence of the occupants from the Ark and the beginning of the post-diluvian era have two possible significations. One of these refers to the beginning, at birth, of a new reincarnation of the Inner Self, whilst entry upon " The way of holiness "[1]—a spiritual rebirth—is also allegorically described. In addition, racial, planetary and supra-planetary *Manvantaric* dawns are referred to, these microcosmic and Macrocosmic phases of existence being intimately related.

In this first verse the statement that " God remembered Noah " may allude to the fact that each new manifestation, whether of a single life or of a Cosmos, is a repetition of its predecessor but at a higher level. The *contents* of the new dispensation—the Monads and the harvested fruits of evolution in all the kingdoms of Nature—are always the same, but their *condition* is different. Each Monad begins the new cycle at that point to which it had previously attained and continues to advance therefrom; for the ascent of Spirit, life and consciousness through a succession of *Manvantaras* and *Pralayas* follows a circular path, each cycle closing at a point higher than that at which it began. Occult philosophy thus teaches that the path followed by cosmic life is not a circle, but a series of rounds in an ascending spiral.

The words " God remembered " are of especial interest, for the occult teaching is that the Solar Creative Deity does not initiate and bring into existence an entirely new creation. At the dawn of every cycle there emerges or is transmitted from Universal Intelligence the " memory " or record of the attainments of its predecessor. Thus the Eighth Chapter, allegorically considered, rightly opens with the statement that " God remembered Noah, and every living thing, and all the cattle that was with him in the ark."

---

[1] *Is.* 35: 8.

THE GREAT BREATH BREATHED UPON THE GREAT DEEP

The first creative act is described in the latter part of this first verse in the words: ". . . God made a wind to pass over the earth, and the waters asswaged."[1] Just as in the second verse of the First Chapter of *Genesis* " the Spirit of God moved upon the face of the waters " and then God spake, so now at the opening of a later cycle God made a wind (the Divine Breath) to pass over the Earth, which is said to have been entirely covered by water.[2] This breath or " wind " is used as a symbol for the outpoured creative energy proceeding as a verbal command from the " mouth " of the Deity. As in so many cosmogonies,[3] the divine Voice or " Word " constitutes the first act of " creation ".

The sequence of so-called " memory " and the causing of a wind thus conform to the procedures described in other Scriptures. Each re-emergence of a Solar System or a Cosmos first originates in the Mind of the Logos wherein, as we have seen, the Archetype[4] or divine " idea " of the Universe-to-be has been formulated. This concept includes all that was contained in its predecessors, together with the preserved essence of the evolutionary products of the last cycle of activity. The next succeeding phase consists of the projection of the Archetype by the emission of a spiritual energy of the quality of sound. This has the effect of causing hitherto quiescent substance to begin to assume forms expressive of the original design. Thus, as said, the Logos is referred to as " the Great Breath " which is breathed upon " the Great Deep " and in *Genesis* God (*Elohim*) speaks, saying " Let there be light ". The first five verses of the Gospel according to St. John, in which the Logos is referred to as the " Word ", enunciate the same cosmogonical concept.

Plato contributed the word " idea ", his philosophy being that of idealism in which the perfect original is said to pre-exist in the supra-sensual world and that this perfect Archetype alone exists, the earthly copy being only apparent. From God, as the First Cause, proceeded all creation concepts. The visible Universe, he taught, is a copy of the image of the perfect Archetype which alone exists, the earthly appearance being relatively illusory. In Hindu philosophy also, that alone which is changeless

[1] The reference here is to the Logos doctrine, which includes the formation—according to the Archetype or " Idea "— of Universes by the potency of " sounds " emanating from the Logos as the divine " Breath " or " Voice ". Thus it is written : " The Great Breath breathed upon the Great Deep."

[2] *Gen.* 7: 19; 8: 9.

[3] q.v. *Lecture Notes of the School of the Wisdom*, Vol. II, Pt. II, Geoffrey Hodson, where a number of cosmogonies are quoted.

[4] Archetype (Gr.)—" First-moulded " or stamped. The ideal, abstract or essential design. The divine conceiving from which arises the divine " idea " of the whole Universe in time and space; the governing Power in creation.

and eternal is called " the Real ".   All that is subject to change through
differentiation and decay, and which therefore has a beginning and an
end, is regarded as *maya*—illusion, " the unreal ".   Thought is thus elevated
towards a supernal world of absolute values.

Plato likewise taught the doctrine of the reincarnation of the unfolding
spiritual Soul of man.   In this procedure of Nature only the physical body
of the child is a new creation, the reincarnating Ego having pre-existed
and preserved within its vesture of light, the Causal Body, the evolutionary
fruits of all preceding life cycles.   In this microcosmic sense too the words
" God remembered " are appropriate.

The waters of the Flood symbolise the virgin boundless sea (*mare* or
Mary)[1] of equi-polarised space within which is contained the potentiality
of all life.   This substance, when fructified by creative Spirit, is the material
from which every form—from the cosmic to the physical atomic—is to be
built.

The period of one hundred and fifty days, after which the waters were
abated, by reduction gives the figure six.   This is the final number of the
second ternary and therefore indicates the approaching close of a cycle,
in this case of quiescence or *Pralaya* (Flood).   These numbers also refer to
Sephirothal Powers and Intelligences (*Elohim*)[2] associated with such periods.

> Gen. 8: 4. *And the ark rested in the seventh month, on the seventeenth day of
> the month, upon the mountains of Ararat.*

The seventh month indicates the end of the first septenary, whilst
mountains[3] are generally used by authors writing in the Language of
Symbols to typify exalted states of waking consciousness in which lofty
Intelligences abide and which are entered by illumined men.

This highly spiritualised state is not inaptly represented by mountains.
Parnassus, Mount Olympus, abode of the gods of Greece, the Himālayas,
Kailāsa, Meru,—a fabulous mountain in the navel or centre of the Earth,
the heaven of Indra, containing the cities of the gods and the habitations
of celestial spirits—Sinai where Moses received the tablets of the law, Ararat
where the Ark rested, Carmel where Elijah made his sacrifice, Moriah
where Abraham prepared to sacrifice Isaac, Olivet from which Christ
made His Ascension—all these as stated above typify lofty planes of
Nature and the levels of consciousness attained by those exalted Beings

---

[1] In a cosmic interpretation of the Nativity of Jesus, His Mother Mary typifies the
virgin sea of Space.   She is, in consequence, referred to as the Virgin Mary.   (*Matt.* 1: 18;
Lk. 1: 27).

[2] q.v. Appendix, *The Sephirothal Tree*, and Glossary.

[3] q.v. *The Hidden Wisdom in the Holy Bible*, Vol. I, Pt. III, Ch. I, Geoffrey Hodson.

who are said to dwell upon or enter them. The Egyptians wrote of the
" Gods of the mountains " and the " Gods of the mountain of the Hidden
Land ", these Gods being regarded as the off-spring of Ra Himself, having
emerged from His eye. (*Egypt. Heaven abd Hell*, Volume III, p. 110,
E. A. Wallis Budge, M.A., Litt.D.).

In conformity with this method of symbolism the Ark of Noah is
correctly made eventually to have rested upon Mount Ararat; for this
mountain represents that spiritual level of existence between periods of
objective activity at which the seeds of all living beings and things are
preserved, and from which successive creative epochs are initiated. In
this cosmic interpretation Noah, in his turn, personifies the Official
responsible for the preservation of the seeds within His aura (Ark) during
periods of quiescence (Flood).

Gen. 8: 6. *And it came to pass at the end of forty days, that Noah opened
the window of the ark which he had made:*

7. *And he sent forth a raven, which went forth to and fro, until the
waters were dried up from off the earth.*

To the student of symbology the statement that it was a bird which
first emerged is of interest. In general the bird symbolises the triple
Creative Deity, the first Trinity, the highest Sephirothal Triad.[1] The
bird form—triple with body and two wings—makes the choice singularly
apt. The fact that birds are oviparous also renders them suitable representations of the threefold Deity as source of the divine " idea ", the germ of
worlds-to-be and all they will ever produce. The egg-shell, in its turn,
appropriately typifies the newly marked out boundary, the Ring-pass-not[2],
within which the divine " idea " is to become objectively manifested or
" hatched out ".

The egg thus becomes a symbol of the Cosmos in its original, abstract
conception, the Archetype in its innermost state of existence, prior to the
periods and processes of involution and evolution. Thus the emanation
(involution) of a Universe begins from the simplest state of substance on
the highest plane from which Spirit commences to express its qualities
through matter. These attributes are germinal within the divine Consciousness before involution begins, and culminate in their densest (physical
mineral) manifestation. Evolution, in its turn, progresses from the lowest
material condition to the attainment of the highest degree of development
of form and the loftiest spiritual condition of consciousness.[3]

[1] Kether, Chokmab and Binah.   q.v. Appendix.
[2] q.v. Glossary.
[3] q.v. *The Hidden Wisdom in the Holy Bible*, Vol. I, Pt. **IV**, Geoffrey Hodson.

Aquatic birds are frequently used as symbols for the Creative Logos and are described as laying their eggs upon the waters, representing the sea of space upon (actually within) which germination and development thereafter occur.   According to *Manu, Hiranyagarbha*, (" Golden Egg " or " Golden Womb ") was a name of *Brahmā*, the first male Deity, Who was formed by the indiscernible, eternal First Cause in a golden egg resplendent as the sun.   *Brahmā* is also referred to as the Supreme Spirit, the active Creator of the Universe, Who sprang from the mundane egg deposited by the First Cause and is the Father of all creatures and the Progenitor of all worlds.   Over this " egg ", or germ of Universe-to-be, the divine " bird " broods maternally to bring about its hatching as a Monad-filled Cosmos, each Monad in its turn being a reproduction of the Parent, a manifested triple Deity-in-the-becoming.   The symbol of the bird thus also applies to the human Higher Triad, the threefold divine Self or Ego[1] in man.

The raven was possibly chosen by the authors of *Genesis* because it is black.   The highest Triad of all, the first creative Trinity, is above and beyond all objective light, and so to beings limited to that light it would be invisible or dark.   It would also be unsubstantial, its motion or vibrating frequency being far too rapid for human perception and comprehension.   The first Triad does not descend below its own level, only reproductions of itself emanating into the deeper densities.   These concepts may have been in the minds of the authors of *Genesis* when they made the raven to fly to and fro over the landless waters, neither returning to the Ark nor settling on dry land.

THE BIRD AS SYMBOL OF THE SPIRITUAL SOUL OF MAN

Microcosmically interpreted, this Chapter is not without profound psychological revelations.   Admittedly great care should always be taken neither to over-stress a possible symbolical significance nor to read into a narrative more than is inherent within it or was presumably present in the minds of the authors.   Nevertheless, useful ideas may arise when certain passages are considered and interpreted as allegories portraying both cosmic and microcosmic verities.   Throughout this work, therefore, as if exploring a mine or vein of precious metal, I have not hesitated to interpret the Scriptures and Mythologies of ancient peoples from this symbolical point of view and often, I hope, with valuable results.   Thus the incident of the raven may also be susceptible of interpretation as a reference to the right uses of the limitations of the human mind.   In the course of man's later evolution the separative, analytical mentality, in

---

[1] q.v. Glossary.

Norse Mythology symbolised by the raven, is first developed and later discarded as a means of discovery and comprehension of ultimate truth. The symbol of the raven was also possibly chosen because certain of the attributes of this bird may aptly be applied to the human mind. For example the raven has a glossy sheen, is omnivorous, somewhat predacious, intelligent, mischievous when tamed, can learn to speak, was formerly an object of veneration and superstition, and was used on statues of the Vikings and on coats of arms—perhaps because ravens were sacred to Odin, who had two which were actually called Hugin (reflection) and Mugin (memory). He would send them out (somewhat Noah-like) at the dawn of each day and each evening receive from them accounts of the actions of men.

The Ark, microcosmically interpreted, stands for the Auric Envelope of spiritually awakening man, and with its contents may even be regarded as a symbol of man himself. The liberation of the raven represents man's first uses of the formal intellect in the search for knowledge, whilst the bird's non-return suggests both the inadequacy of logic alone for that purpose and its eventual transcendence. The formal, concrete, analytical and individualistic thinking principle, by itself incapable of perceiving and assimilating abstract spiritual truth, is symbolically blind, dark or unillumined by the light of such truth. A black raven therefore aptly portrays the formal mind of man whilst, as we have seen, its non-return to the Ark refers appropriately to the inevitable failure of attempts to conceive by purely mental processes alone truths which are eternal and infinite.

The dove later released by Noah symbolises the higher or abstract mind of man in which the intuitive principle is active as both divine light and divine love, well represented by the light grey, softly cooing and supposedly amorous bird which was associated with Venus. By means of intuitive perception alone may living truth, symbolised by the leaf of the olive tree be perceived. This is indicated by the return of the bird to the Ark with the leaf in its mouth.

Gen. 8: 8. *Also he sent forth a dove from him, to see if the waters were abated from off the face of the ground;*

9. *But the dove found no rest for the sole of her foot, and she returned unto him into the ark, for the waters were on the face of the whole earth; then he put forth his hand, and took her, and pulled her in unto him into the Ark.*

10. *And he stayed yet other seven days; and again he sent forth the dove out of the ark;*

> 11. *And the dove came in to him in the evening; and, lo, in her mouth was an olive leaf pluckt off: so Noah knew that the waters were abated from off the earth.*

> 12. *And he stayed yet other seven days; and sent forth the dove; which returned not again and unto him any more.*

The dove in its turn, together with all birds, is used as a symbol of Deity, as heretofore suggested. From here on the narrative includes the drying up of the Flood waters, the resting of the Ark upon Mount Ararat and the subsequent emergence of its contents. These may be interpreted as descriptive of the opening of a new period of creative activity and, in the eternal succession of cycles, the projection once again of Archetypal influences in the fashioning of Nature's material forms. The deliverance from the Ark thus allegorically describes the entry of the hitherto quiescent Monads into the new dispensation or period of involution and evolution.

In Cosmogenesis the dove represents the second divine Triad,[1] which carries the formative impulse on into the deeper densities and is responsible for the actual production of the final mould. The three departures and the two returns of the dove are, in their turn, of special interest. The first of these symbolises the supra-mental stages of the creative process. No objective forms have yet appeared, though the *Elohim* have already become active in the projection of the Archetypes. As this process had not then produced physical Nature, including either trees or solid earth, involution not yet being complete, " the dove (in consequence) found no rest for the sole of her foot." It is therefore said to have returned to the Ark or gestative condition. Eventually material structures imbued with spiritual life appeared. These are portrayed by the olive tree (the kabbalistic Tree of Life) from which the leaf was plucked and carried to the Ark on the second return of the dove. Thereafter physical Nature appeared with its myriad shapes in which the divine life became embodied.

On its third flight from the Ark the dove found the plant kingdom to be sufficiently developed to provide adequate shelter and food; it therefore did not return. This may imply that in the new dispensation, or post-diluvian era, the newly awakened creative impulses had by that time brought into existence Archetypes, mental forms and the first conditions of fruitful physical substance, symbolised by the olive tree. Thereafter the Monads (the inhabitants of the Ark) entered their prepared evolutionary field. The Ark, whether as symbol of the feminine aspect of Deity, of the aura of a *Manu*, of the human Auric Envelope or of the physical womb, is delivered of its contents and the activity of the new epoch is established right down to the physical world.

---

[1] q.v. Appendix, *The Sephirothal Tree*, and also the literature of the *Kabbalah*.

CHAPTER VI

DRY LAND APPEARS, AN ALTAR IS BUILT AND NOAH GOES FORTH FROM THE ARK

Gen. 8: 13. *And it came to pass in the six hundredth and first year, in the first month, the first day of the month, the waters were dried up from off the earth: and Noah removed the covering of the ark, and looked, and, behold, the face of the ground was dry.*

14. *And in the second month, on the seven and twentieth day of the month, was the earth dried.*

15. *And God spake unto Noah, saying.*

16. *Go forth of the ark, thou, and thy wife, and thy sons, and the sons' wives with thee.*

17. *Bring forth with thee every living thing that is with thee, of all flesh, both of fowl, and of cattle, and of every creeping thing that creepeth upon the earth; that they may breed abundantly in the earth, and be fruitful, and multiply upon the earth.*

18. *And Noah went forth, and his sons, and his wife, and his sons' wives with him:*

19. *Every beast, every creeping thing, and every fowl, and whatsoever creepeth upon the earth, after their kinds, went forth out of the ark.*

The number six hundred and one by addition totals seven, which numerically represents transition from a completed septenary cycle to its successor. According to the symbolism of numbers[1] the first month and the first day of the month in which the waters were dried up indicate, by the use of the number one, the beginning of a new epoch.

---

[1] q.v. *The Hidden Wisdom in the Holy Bible*, Vol. I, Pt. III, Ch. II, Geoffrey Hodson.

DIVINE COMMANDS AS INDICATIONS OF NATURAL PROCEDURES

As is not unusual in the Sacred Language—doubtless to aid those for whom abstract thought was difficult—supposedly Divine commands are employed in order to enunciate and describe impersonal procedures and laws of Nature. This would seem to be exemplified in verses fifteen to nineteen of this Eighth Chapter of *Genesis*, when an apparently personal Deity is said to give instructions to a human being acting under His direction. Cyclic progression and the succession of the seasons are, however, to be regarded as continuing processes of Nature. When, in the course of time, a Universe, a star and a Scheme of planetary evolution[1] reach their appointed end, they dissolve and their substance returns to the void or " Deep ", meaning virgin Space (Flood). The seeds of living things are, however, carefully preserved by Nature, as has heretofore been indicated. When in obedience to impersonal, cyclic law their re-emergence, further manifestation and development are to be continued a new Universe, a star or a Planetary Scheme gradually appears. Similarly Spring, Summer and Autumn are followed by the relative quiescence of Winter. Spring returns in its natural sequence and the cycle of regeneration and reappearance automatically follows, as partly affirmed in verse twenty-two of the Eighth Chapter of *Genesis*.

Occult philosophy indicates the similar application to the unfolding spiritual Self of man of this principle of progression. During each succeeding reincarnation the new personality as foetus, infant, adolescent and adult carries development a stage further. Nature then provides for the ultimate dissolution of the personality and a period of Egoic quiescence. This, in its turn, is followed by the physical conception, gestation and birth of a new personal incarnation of man's divine Self. Thus, for both Universes and men such cyclic progression is a law of Nature rather than a process initiated by a personal Deity. It is, moreover, stated to be eternal; for occult philosophy states that " this stupendous development has neither conceivable beginning nor imaginable end."[2] As stated above, this evolution is the product of universal forces and not the result of intrusion by a divine Intelligence.

Since, however, the human mind—particularly in its formal aspect—is unable easily to conceive such abstract ideas, to assist during this phase of human development the Sages of old personified as Deities what actually are natural laws and processes. The supposed interminglings and resultant progeny of the gods and goddesses of ancient Mythologies are allegorically and symbolically descriptive of the interplay of Nature's forces and its consequent effects.

[1] See footnote to p. 190 and Glossary.
[2] q.v. *The Secret Doctrine*, Vol. I, p. 115, H. P. Blavatsky.

Gen. 8: 20. *And Noah builded an altar unto the LORD; and took of every clean beast, and of every clean fowl, and offered burnt offerings on the altar.*

21. *And the LORD smelled a sweet savour; and the LORD said in His heart, I will not again curse the ground any more for man's sake; for the imagination of man's heart is evil from his youth; neither will I again smite any more every thing living, as I have done.*

In these verses, also, universal Law, Power, Life and Consciousness are personified by a single personal Deity. Furthermore, the Lord is described as enjoying the smell of burning flesh and as promising neither to curse His own creation (including man made by Him in His own image) nor ever again to destroy every living thing, as He in His great anger had previously done.

Here again, as we have seen, one is confronted with the extreme difficulty of accepting a literal reading of such Biblical passages. Evidently the Bible consists of a strange blend of spiritual and philosophic revelations, presumed and actual history, and statements which are incredible, impossible, repellant and obscene. Many minds and hands must have contributed, and whilst some of these authors were wise and illumined men, others were evidently ignorant and primitive people. The latter tended to describe God in terms of a bloodthirsty, tribal fetish who ordained and enjoyed massacres and blood sacrifices. It is thus apparent that the inspired Prophets were not able completely to control the choice of the subject-matter of the Hebrew Bible. Other hands added other material. On occasion, it would seem, the Sages of old made use even of otherwise undesirable statements as possible allegories veiling a hidden wisdom. The passage under consideration may permissibly be regarded as an example of this admixture of primitive anthropomorphism and of pseudo-history with allegory and symbol.

ANIMAL SACRIFICES SYMBOLIC OF SELF-PURIFICATION

Nevertheless the ritual sacrifice of animals as a religious act, whilst admittedly performed, is in itself not without a possible mystical significance. It may, for example, typify the burning out and the surrender of the animal propensities in man. The " sweet savour "[1] rising up to the nostrils of the Lord could indicate the result of this act of self-spiritualisation; for the energy or driving force which hitherto has been directed into physical

[1] *Gen.* 8: 21.

and sensual gratification becomes sublimated and is eventually received as spiritual and intellectual creativeness by the spiritual Self of man, personified in the text by the Lord.   In this sense the supposedly pleasant odour from the burnt sacrifice may be taken to symbolise the transmuted energy, whilst the pleasure of the Lord is represented by both the purification and consequent sensitisation of the bodily person and the evolutionary progress of the divine Self which is thereby produced.   Complete success in this transmutation of the " base metal " of animality into the fine " gold " of spirituality—the true objective of alchemists and fire philoso- phers—brings about the conscious realisation of immortality.   The promise by the Lord God not any more to destroy living things may in its turn possibly be described as an allegory of this great achievement.

If the mystical, racial and cosmogonical interpretations of the narrative of the Flood and of the symbols of the Ark and the burnt offerings are acceptable, then their blending in the story is seen to be extremely skilful. In the racial sense primitive man, for example, was relatively mindless, being guided largely by instinct.   More advanced man developed the intellect, and eventually the mind itself (the non-returning raven) will come to be renounced as the sole instrument of guidance, and abstract thought and intuition (the dove) be adopted as the true source of knowledge, inspiration and mystical realisation.   In due course, the Ageless Wisdom teaches, man will become spiritually self-conscious and in harmonious relationship with his Monad (God).   Thereafter his whole life will be lived in surrender and sacrifice (the mystical burnt offerings) to the divine purpose and the divine will.   He will then have become a perfected man— an occult Sage, an Adept.   Whilst this knowledge has been made generally available to mankind in more recent times, in olden days it formed part of the secret teaching of the Mysteries, being revealed to their Initiates alone.   When referred to in the literature of the time it was always heavily veiled by use of the Language of Allegory and Symbol.

THE RULE OF LAW

> Gen. 8: 22. *While the earth remaineth, seedtime and harvest, and cold and heat, and summer and winter, and day and night shall not cease.*

Although in this verse the Lord is affirmed to be ordaining the unbroken succession of the seasons and of day and night, as already observed these sequences follow naturally from the inception of the Macrocosmic creative— or rather emanative—procedure.   Deity in this sense signifies law—the very law of existence, in fact—administered by hosts of highly evolved spiritual Beings, *Elohim* (God).   This verse therefore, cannot be accepted in its literal meaning; for no individual Intelligence, however lofty, is personally responsible for seasonal changes and their products, for variations of temperature or for the alternations of night and day. The law is that, in an eternal succession of quiescence and activity, Universal Spirit fructifies Universal Substance, the product being a life-filled Universe populated by innumerable beings (the Ark and its contents).

Occult philosophy thus elevates the concept of Deity far above that of a tribal fetish who produces natural phenomena and who is adored through fear, being potent to destroy. Rather is God revealed as the self-existent, creative Spirit emanated from the Absolute under that impersonal law which rules all manifestations of the equally impersonal life. Alternation is the underlying basis of all objective manifestation, regularity the unbroken rule and an evolutionary ascent the unfailing result. Such is the key to the mystery of life. Such, the Sages teach, is part of the revelation of the Scriptures of the world.

The reader of the Bible who is able to accept and apply such an approach will be preserved from much confusion and the tendency to discard the whole of a wonderful book because parts of it appear to " pile the impossible upon the incredible."[1] The deliberately constructed veils[2] will then no longer hide from him the wisdom which they conceal.

> *Gen.* 9: 1. *And God blessed Noah and his sons, and said unto them, Be fruitful, and multiply, and replenish the earth.*
>
> 2. *And the fear of you and the dread of you shall be upon every beast of the earth, and upon every fowl of the air, upon all that moveth upon the earth, and upon all the fishes of the sea; into your hand are they delivered.*
>
> 3. *Every moving thing that liveth shall be meat for you; even as the green herb have I given you all things.*
>
> 4. *But flesh with the life thereof, which is the blood thereof, shall ye not eat.*
>
> 5. *And surely your blood of your lives will I require; at the hand of every beast will I require it, and at the hand of man; at the hand of every man's brother will I require the life of man.*

---

[1] I nevertheless leave room for the possibility that these passages may have a deep significance as parts of a perfect edifice, as if the *Pentateuch* were a living and organic whole with its vital organs, each possessing its own sublime meaning—a kabbalistic idea.

[2] Veils—partially or wholly inaccurate statements either allowed to remain in the original manuscript or composed and added in order to conceal from the profane potentially power-bestowing knowledge.

6. *Whoso sheddeth man's blood, by man shall his blood be shed; for in the image of God made he man.*

7. *And you, be ye fruitful, and multiply; bring forth abundantly in the earth, and multiply therein.*

As earlier stated, Adam alone in Eden is made to represent the first physical race of men in their primeval, androgynous condition, and Adam and Eve together personify the same race after the separation of the sexes. Ethnologically, therefore, Noah and his family, referred to in the first verse of the Ninth Chapter of the *Book of Genesis*, typify the race which followed. The next four verses indicate the evolutionary position— physical, intellectual and spiritual—of man in relation to the sub-human kingdoms of Nature.   The suggestion of man's divinely ordained dominion over the lower creation, of his right to exploit its members and of their decreed fear of him—*surely a further example of the unacceptability of a literal reading of the Bible*—is rather an indication of the respective evolutionary positions of animals and men than an imposed lordship and subordination. This status refers not only to their physical bodies, but also to the indwelling principle or " Soul " evolving within those bodies.   The Ageless Wisdom refers to an ascending ladder of evolving life, the indwelling Spirit embodied in the mineral kingdom being on the lowest rung.   This stage is followed by incarnation in the plant, animal and human kingdoms successively. In the last of these self-consciousness is attained—hence alone, I submit, the idea of the superiority of man over the sub-human kingdoms of Nature.

THE " BIRTH " OF THE SOUL OF MAN

In exposition of this idea the word " Soul " is of necessity used with two distinct meanings.   Soul (Gr. *nous*) spelt with a capital " S " is defined in occult philosophy as the unfolding and relatively immortal spiritual Self of man, the triple Self of will, wisdom and intellect in a vesture of light (Gr. *Augoeides*) constructed of the substance of the subtler sub-levels of the mental world.   This is the " Robe of Glory " of the Gnostics[1] and the Causal Body (a translation from the Sanskrit term *Kārana Sharīra* as used in Hindu philosophy) of theosophical nomenclature.   The word " soul " (Gr. *psyche*) with a small " s " is used to indicate the psychical nature (mind and emotion) of animate beings, whether animals or men.

Animals differ from men in that, unlike men, they have not yet attained to self-conscious individuality.   Each animal is not, in consequence, a single spiritual being composed of inter-related body, self-conscious Soul and pure Spirit.   Animals have souls, but according to occult philosophy

---

[1] **q**.v. *The Hymn of the Robe of Glory*, G. R. S. Mead, in the series *Echoes From the Gnosis*.

are animated by group consciousness, herd instinct, arising from within a mass of soul essence or a group soul and not from a single spiritual Soul. In the course of evolution, out of this group soul a number of individualised human Egos or unfolding, self-conscious Souls become differentiated.   In this way the indwelling and unfolding life in Nature, having evolved during vast ages through the mineral, plant and animal kingdoms, attains to the status of manhood, or enters the human kingdom.   This natural procedure is termed " individualisation ".[1]

Unlike the animal, therefore, man is a threefold being composed of body, Soul and Spirit, with an unbroken interior Ray which is the connecting link, the true " covenant " referred to in later verses, between the bodily man (Noah in this particular instance) and his innermost spiritual Self (God).   This is symbolised by the rainbow, for it also is built of light and constitutes that " bridge "[2] over which one day the Soul of man will pass from separated self-consciousness into full realisation of its unity with the life-essence of the Universe and with the Supreme Lord of Life.   In Hinduism this is referred to as *Moksha* or Liberation, in Buddhism as *Nirvāna* or Absorption, and in Christianity as Salvation or Ascension to the right hand of God.   Unfortunately, however, the verses under consideration have been misinterpreted to indicate a divine enactment bestowing upon man the right to use, misuse, and even cruelly exploit, members of the animal kingdom of Nature.   In consequence, the second verse of Chapter Nine of the *Book of Genesis* has proved to be prophetic of the fear which many animals naturally feel towards human beings.   This fear is indeed justified, for man has long been their greatest enemy.

Whilst the interpretations which follow might read as a criticism of meat-eating and a recommendation to adopt the vegetarian way of life, I wish to make it clear that such ideas are included solely in relation to the injunction against meat-eating contained in the fourth verse.   This book is written as an impartial interpretation of the Bible, and any moral of ethical implications which it may seem to contain are only advanced because they arise naturally from the text and therefore cannot be ignored.

The fourth verse—" But flesh with the life thereof, which is the blood thereof, shall ye not eat "—unmistakably corrects the misinterpretation, particularly concerning the infliction of the suffering which is inseparable from the use of animal flesh for food.   This verse clearly indicates that man was not created by divine law to be a flesh-eater and a blood-drinker. As the anatomy and physiology of his body also proclaim, he is designed

---

[1] q.v. *The Causal Body*, A. E. Powell; *First Principles of Theosophy*, C. Jinarājadāsa; *A Study in Consciousness*, A. Besant; *Lecture Notes of the School of the Wisdom*, Vol. I (Rev. Ed.), Ch. II, Sec. IV, Geoffrey Hodson.

[2] q.v. *Mundaka Upanishad*, II, ii, 5; St. Catherine of Siena, *Revelations*, LIX; Boehme, *Mysterium Magnum*, p. 207.

to be a plant feeder.[1] The result of man's departure from the way of life ordained in the fourth verse is stated in verses five and six, for in them the resultant operation of the law of retribution is clearly enunciated.

The existence of this law is also affirmed by the Lord Christ; for in the Fifth Chapter of *Matthew*, verse eighteen, we read: " For verily I say unto you, Till heaven and earth pass, one jot or one tittle shall in no wise pass from the law, till all be fulfilled," and by St. Paul in the Sixth Chapter of *Galatians*, verse seven: ". . . God is not mocked: for whatsoever a man soweth, that shall he also reap."

---

[1] Carnivora have claws, pointed molar teeth as fangs for tearing, acid saliva and urine and a skin without pores. The stomach is simple and roundish and the intestinal canal is three times the length of the body. There is no ptyalin ferment in the saliva for changing starch to dextrose. The colon is smooth and the food is flesh. Herbivora, on the other hand, have no claws and possess blunt molar teeth, alkaline saliva with ptyalin, alkaline urine, a stomach with duodenum as second stomach, a skin with millions of pores and an intestinal canal twelve times the length of the body. The colon is convoluted and the food is grass, herbs, plants, fruit and nuts. Man has no claws and also has blunt molar teeth, saliva containing copious supplies of ptyalin and alkaline to a considerable degree, a skin with millions of pores and a stomach with duodenum. The intestinal canal is twelve times the length of the body and the colon is convoluted. Man, therefore, is anatomically constructed to be herbivorous and frugivorous.

CHAPTER VII

THE BOW IN THE CLOUD

Gen. 9: 8. *And God spake unto Noah, and to his sons with him, saying,*

9. *And I, behold, I establish my covenant with you, and with your seed after you ;*

10. *And with every living creature that is with you, of the fowl, of the cattle, and of every beast of the earth with you; from all that go out of the ark, to every beast of the earth.*

11. *And I will establish my covenant with you; neither shall all flesh be cut off any more by the waters of a flood; neither shall there any more be a flood to destroy the earth.*

12. *And God said, This is the token of the covenant which I make between me and you and every living creature that is with you, for perpetual generations;*

13. *I do set my bow in the cloud, and it shall be for a token of a covenant between me and the earth.*

14. *And it shall come to pass, when I bring a cloud over the earth that the bow shall be seen in the cloud ;*

15. *And I will remember my covenant, which is between me and you and every living creature of all flesh; and the waters shall no more become a flood to destroy all flesh.*

16. *And the bow shall be in the cloud; and I will look upon it, that I may remember the everlasting covenant between God and every living creature of all flesh that is upon the earth.*

17 *And God said unto Noah, This is the token of the covenant, which I have established between me and all flesh that is upon the earth.*

THE RAINBOW

The very important symbol of the rainbow introduced into these verses is susceptible of a number of interpretations. Several of these are considered in some detail in this Chapter, which is largely devoted to the subject. An allegorical reading is enforced by the fact that rainbows are natural phenomena formed in rain or spray by the rays of the sun or the moon. Rainbows must have appeared from the time when the first condensations and precipitations of moisture took place on the Earth. The laws under which they appear are well-known and provide a complete explanation of their visibility. There was, therefore, neither need nor place for such a special creative act to be performed by the Deity to establish the fact of an objective covenant of this nature between God and man, for rainbows would have appeared in any case. Furthermore, the relationship or bond between the Supreme Deity and the Spirit of man, the human Monad, is *interior* since an inseparable unity exists between them, the human body being in this sense a temple of God, as St. Paul more than once affirmed.[1] Admittedly early man—indeed, all men without mystical experience of the divine Presence within them—could not be expected to be aware of this unity and the strangeness and beauty of the rainbow might well have been used to draw attention to and serve as a reminder of the " God which worketh in you "[2]. Verse sixteen, interpreted literally, suggests that God Himself needed a reminder of the everlasting covenant, and set His bow in the heavens for that purpose also—a *reductio ad absurdum*.

THE TRUE COVENANT BETWEEN GOD AND MAN

In this the Monadic interpretation, the covenant also indicates the assurance of the ultimate regeneration of man; for by virtue of the divine Monadic ray or " silver cord "[3]—the *sūtrātma* or " thread-self" of Hindu philosophy—an unbreakable link exists between the Monad, its Egoic expression and their successive bodily individualities during their physical lifetimes. As the rainbow exhibits the seven colours of the spectrum, so the Monadic " bridge " or Ray is composed of the inherent sevenfold power of the Monad. In this reading the everlasting remembrance and covenant which the Supreme Deity has promised to establish between Himself and man is regarded as affirmation of the existent, inseparable unity of God with man and man with God, and not as a covenant newly · established immediately following the recession of the waters of the Flood. Our Lord affirmed His realisation of this oneness in His words: " I and

[1] I *Cor.* 3: 16; II *Cor.* 6: 16.
[2] *Phil.* 2: 13; *Col.* 1: 27.
[3] *Eccl.* 12: 6, 7.

my Father are one "[1]—Christ and man being identical in this respect[2]—and St. Paul wrote: ". . . work out your own salvation with fear and trembling. For it is God which worketh in you. . ."[3]. The custom is here followed by the ancient writers of enunciating a principle or a law in the form of a decision, a command or an action of a personal Deity. Actually the unity is inherent in both Universe and man, the latter having been made in God's image[4] and therefore being eternally divine in his essential nature. The aptness of the symbol is further evidenced by the fact that even as both ends of a rainbow reach to Earth, and the uppermost arc of the bow is in the heights above, so the spiritual light shines from the " highest " to the " lowest " levels of divine manifestation.

Applied racially, the rainbow as a covenant between God and man may be interpreted as a statement of the existence of an imperishable, unifying, spiritual Presence within each of its members which assures continuity of identity from one race to the next. This indwelling Divinity forms a spiritual " bridge " along which the Egos of humanity in their successive incarnations pass from nation to nation and race to race in an unending spiral ascent.

Cosmically the rainbow in the cloud symbolises the spiritual link between all cycles major and minor. It is the " bridge " whether universal or planetary, over which the emanated Monad-bearing life-wave[5] crosses from an old to a new dispensation. The material manifestation of such life is indicated by the symbol of the rainbow; for by its emanation the white light of unmanifested Spirit is split up into the seven component hues. In his *Adonais* Shelley thus expressed this idea:

" Life, like a dome of many-coloured glass,
    Stains the white radiance of Eternity."   (St. 52).

The rainbow is also a symbol of hope and there is some philosophic justification for this popular view; for mystically interpreted the rainbow indicates the absolute certainty of safe passage by the Monad-Ego[6] across the " ocean " of manifested existence to the " further shore ". This journey of the Soul takes man through successive physical incarnations and throughout that journey the ever-present Monadic Ray is his assurance

---

[1] *Jn.* 10: 30.   [2] *Jn.* 14: 20.   [3] *Phil.* 2: 12, 13.   [4] *Gen.* 1: 26.
[5] q.v. *First Principles of Theosophy*, Ch. IX, C. Jinarājadāsa.
[6] Monad-Ego. A dual term used in this work to connote the individualised manifestation of the human Monad as triple Spirit, the Higher Triad, in a vesture of light or " Robe of Glory ", the Causal Body. The Monad is described as the Divine Spark or Dweller in the Innermost, which in the course of evolution has attained to self-conscious individuality as man (Ego) and during life on Earth is embodied in vehicles of mind, emotion and flesh. q.v. Glossary—Monad.

of both safety and the ultimate attainment of Adeptship, which implies realisation of unity with the Godhead.

AN AFFIRMATION OF LAW

As we have seen, although depicted as a personal Deity Who Himself decrees a certain sequence of cause and effect, in assuring Noah of the Covenant the Lord is actually affirming the existence and operation of an impersonal, immutable, natural law. Thus in affirming in verse six of Chapter Nine of the *Book of Genesis* that " Whoso sheddeth man's blood, by man shall his blood be shed. . .", God is most seriously warning mankind of the retributive effects that under this law would accrue to the race and to every individual as an inevitable result of the unnecessary shedding of blood.

Since such a sequence is not always clearly discernible in the same physical incarnation in which the action is performed, and the law would therefore seem to be either inoperative or faulty, another factor must be presumed to apply if human life is in truth ruled by law. This factor is provided by the theory of reincarnation and if this doctrine be true the precipitation of the effect of a causative action could be held over until a later life. This is the concept of *karma* as found in Hinduism and Buddhism, which religions teach the evolution of man to perfection through successive lives on Earth, justice being assured—even if possibly postponed—under the inviolable law of cause and effect. As a rider, it is also conceived that actions intermediate between " sowing " and " reaping "[1] modify the ultimate consequences. *Karma* is thus presented as flexible, as a modifiable rather than as a fixed decree.[2]

---

[1] *Gal.* 6: 7.

[2] q.v. *Reincarnation, Fact or Fallacy?*, Geoffrey Hodson.

CHAPTER VIII

NOAH, HIS WIFE, SONS AND GRANDSON PERSONIFY COMPONENTS OF HUMAN NATURE

THE SONS OF NOAH

Gen. 9: 18. *And the sons of Noah, that went forth of the ark, were Shem, and Ham, and Japheth: and Ham is the father of Canaan.*

19. *These are the three sons of Noah: and of them was the whole earth overspread.*

20. *And Noah began to be an husbandman, and he planted a vineyard:*

21. *And he drank of the wine, and was drunken; and he was uncovered within his tent.*

22. *And Ham the father of Canaan saw the nakedness of his father and told his two brethren without.*

23. *And Shem and Japheth took a garment and laid it upon both their shoulders and went backward and covered the nakedness of their father; and their faces were backward, and they saw not their father's nakedness.*

24. *And Noah awoke from his wine, and knew what his younger son had done unto him.*

25. *And he said, Cursed be Canaan; a servant of servants shall he be unto his brethren.*

26. *And he said, Blessed be the LORD God of Shem; and Canaan shall be his servant.*

27. *God shall enlarge Japheth, and he shall dwell in the tents of Shem; and Canaan shall be his servant.*

28. *And Noah lived after the flood three hundred and fifty years.*

29. *And all the days of Noah were nine hundred and fifty years: and he died.*

In these verses it would seem that a further esoteric revelation is being made by means of allegory, symbol and patent incongruity. Indeed, a literal reading might be regarded as destructive of the whole basis of the story of Noah and the Ark; for if so read the Lord's choice of Noah as being the only man amongst the whole multitude of the human race worthy of being saved is shown to be founded upon a complete misjudgment of the true character of the Patriarch. Two alternatives therefore present themselves to the reader. The passage must either be dismissed as unworthy of serious consideration, or else be carefully studied in order to discover whether a significant truth is concealed behind otherwise unacceptable statements. Remembering the exhortation of the author of the *Zohar* quoted in the opening pages of this Volume: " Woe to the man who sees in the Thorah, i.e. Law, only simple recitals and ordinary words!"; recalling also the kabbalistic idea that the Thorah is an organic whole with all its parts essential to the understanding of the total work; and in order that an important revelation should not be missed, the story will now be interpreted by use of the classical keys.

On examination the verses may possibly be read as a definition and description of the true nature and make-up of man. In the human interpretation, Noah represents a projected Ray (*Ātma*) of the essential spiritual unit of human existence, the Monad.[1] His wife personifies the evolving human Ego,[2] a threefold manifestation of the Monad as Will, Wisdom and Intelligence, in its vehicle of abstract thought or Higher *Manas* (Sk.). The Ark is a symbol of that vehicle, variously referred to as the " Vesture of Light ", the *Augœides* (Gr.), and the Causal Body. Noah and his wife together, as Monad-Ego, are said to have had three sons—Shem, Ham and Japheth. Ham in his turn had a son called Canaan. This genealogy may be interpreted as an allegory of the four mortal principles of the human personality—the mental body or lower *Manas*[3] (Shem) the emotional body[4] (Ham), the vital body[5] (Japheth) and the physical body (Canaan), " offspring " and vehicles of the Monad-Ego.

---

[1] q.v. *Lecture Notes of the School of the Wisdom*, Vol. I (Rev. Ed.), Ch. I, Geoffrey Hodson, and Glossary.

[2] q.v. *ibid*, Ch. II.

[3] q.v. *ibid*, Ch. V.

[4] q.v. *ibid*, Ch. IV.

[5] q.v. *ibid*, Ch. III.

INTOXICATION—SYMBOL OF SPIRITUAL EXALTATION

The drunkenness of Noah—like that attributed to the Initiates of the Bacchic and Dionysian Mysteries in their original, pure forms—may indicate the spiritual exaltation, or God-intoxication, experienced when unity with the Monad is attained. The possession of a vineyard and the occupation of husbandman symbolise the fact that the seeds of all deific powers reside in the Monad. The meaning and purpose of human existence in the material world (vineyard) are to manifest (grow) and develop to perfection (ripeness) the inherent (seedlike) human faculties. In order to do so, vehicles of consciousness as instruments of awareness and action are essential. These vehicles are frequently personified as father, mother, children and grandchildren.

NAKEDNESS—SYMBOL OF SPIRITUAL PURITY

The nakedness of Noah describes the natural condition of the Monad-Ego *in its own world of pure Spirit.* There it is unstained by desire, unsullied by contact with matter and the world and unreservedly open to universal light and truth. When, in an allegory, the symbol of nakedness is applied to the mortal man, it implies freedom from traditional and imposed modes of thought and belief and the complete and faithful exposure of the mind to truth itself. The Monad-Ego, by its very nature, abides perpetually in this condition. In conformity with such symbolism Noah is said to have been naked.

THE FAMILY OF NOAH AS PRINCIPLES OF MAN

If an attempt be made to explain the apparent anomalies in these verses by regarding the three sons and the grandson of Noah as personifications of the four mortal principles of man, then these constitute the denser coverings or vestures of the threefold Monad-Ego. In this sense—as we have seen—Shem, the mental body, and Japheth, the vitality-conserving etheric double[1], actually clothe or embody the Ego. Ham, personifying the emotional principle of man, functions rather as a conveyor of the life-force than as a vehicle or " covering " for the Ego.

The supposed modesty of Shem and Japheth may be interpreted as portraying the fact that these two vehicles of mental and etheric-physical substance are those in which matter and form predominate over life. In consequence they do not readily and naturally respond to and manifest spiritual impulses from the Monad-Ego. Nevertheless it is they who are rightly said to " clothe " the Ego, since they serve as its vehicles in the denser worlds and so " cover " its purely spiritual nakedness or

[1] q.v. *Lecture Notes of the School of the Wisdom,* Vol. I (Rev. Ed.), Ch. III, Geoffrey Hodson.

natural condition in its own world. Strangely, and indeed unjustly if the literal reading be followed, since both brothers performed the same act, the son of Ham (Canaan—the physical body) was cursed and condemned to be " a servant of servants " to his brethren. Shem, on the other hand, was blessed and Japheth promised enlargement (doubtless of his affairs) whilst dwelling in the tents of Shem.

CANAAN AS THE PHYSICAL BODY

In what sense could such inexplicable behaviour on the part of a grandfather be justified? Consideration of the suggested personifications offers an answer. The physical body, for example, is by its very nature both the temporary " curse " and the ultimate " blessing " of man. It is the curse in that it is the instrument which most deeply imprisons, even entombs, the Ego. Because, however, the incarnation of the Spirit of man in the densest of all its sheaths, the physical body (Canaan), is essential to the full unfoldment and " perfection " of its innate powers and faculties, that vehicle must be regarded as also of very great importance. Thus if Canaan be interpreted as a personification of the body, then his position as grandson in the family of Noah harmonises with this view; for in the successive development of the four mortal bodies of the Monad-Ego throughout the ages, the mental, the emotional and the etheric bodies *precede* the development of the physical.[1] In this sense—the sequence of development and the process of incarnation—the physical body is the latest of the series to be formed and entered. In conformity with the practice of authors writing in the language of symbols, Canaan is therefore not inaptly described as the grandson.

This Ninth Chapter of the *Book of Genesis* is thus both chronological and ethnological for it brings the story of the descent of the Monad-Ego— both of the race as a whole and of every individual—to the stage at which all the seven principles of man have been formed and are used as instruments of consciousness and action. A complete sevenfold human structure has come into existence. Over and above all is the Lord God, the Logos Who " speaks " to Noah, the Source of life, the Emanator of all beings and the Agent for the manifestation of cosmic Mind and universal law. To sum up, if such a reading be permissible, the personifications of the principles of man are: Noah, *Ātma* or projected Ray of pure spirit; his wife Higher *Manas*, abstract intelligence, who is also the potential source or mother-to-be of *Buddhi* or intuitive wisdom as yet unborn; Shem, the lower *Manas* or reasoning mind; Ham, the *kāmic* or desire principle, seat of the emotions;

---

[1] q.v. *The Miracle of Birth*, Geoffrey Hodson; *First Principles of Theosophy*, Ch. XIII C. Jinarājadāsa; *A Study in Consciousness*, especially Ch. XI, A. Besant.

Japheth, the etheric body; Canaan, the physical body. The fact is of interest that in this present era only five " planes "—components of the fivefold Universe—are entered and used by man as the field of his evolution. They are the *Ātmic*, the *Buddhic*, the dual *Mānasic* the emotional and the physical levels of consciousness and degrees of density of substance. If such an approach to the subject be justifiable, then a careful examination rather than a dismissal of the passage under consideration will prove to have been of considerable value.

KNOWLEDGE IS POWER

One might, however, be forgiven for questioning the necessity for the veiling of the information concerning the constitution of man which the interpretation is presumed to have revealed. In reply, it may be pointed out that such knowledge is indeed power-bestowing and therefore susceptible of misuse, to the grave detriment of those falling into such an error and of all whom it affects. Once a man learns that there is a divine Principle within him, and by the requisite practices contacts that Principle, then the power of the Universe is at his disposal. His will-force and his capacity to hypnotise and otherwise influence the conduct of others by concentrated thought and by oratory, for example, can make of him either a God or a devil. To guard against his becoming the latter, the more esoteric aspects of the Ageless Wisdom have from the remotest times been carefully veiled. Nevertheless, those who teach humanity by this means can in no sense be accused of deliberately keeping it in ignorance, since the knowledge is actually available to those who are able to meet the conditions necessary for its discovery.

The closing verses of Chapter Nine states that the age of Noah at his death was nine hundred and fifty years. By theosophic reduction the number fourteen—and thus five—is obtained, giving a numerical summing-up and restatement of the teaching of the latter portion of the Chapter. In terms of the symbolism of numbers this may be interpreted as a statement of the fivefold constitution of the Universe referred to above. All basic numbers in symbology have at least two significations. They refer to the successive sub-cycles and phases of the major cycle, and also to principles and levels of consciousness of both Universe and man.

THE CHALDEO-EGYPTIAN ORIGIN OF HEBRAISM ACCORDING TO OCCULT DOCTRINE

Chapter Ten of *Genesis* is largely historical, telling of the nations and tribes which originated in and around the basin of the Euphrates and constituted the Chaldean and Babylonian population; for the Old

Testament, with its multiplicity of authorship, oscillates in somewhat disconcerting fashion between the esoteric and the exoteric, the philosophic and the historical.   The racial history and development of the Jewish peoples have here become blended with the occult revelations from the Sanctuary.   The occult thread is, however, present and distinctly discernible under the veil of interwoven symbology, allegory and history.   A digression is therefore now made in order to consider the subject from an occult viewpoint.

The Jews drew their religion from Chaldea, and a great deal that is esoterically true in the Mosaic books is of Chaldean origin with a later admixture from the Egyptian Mysteries.   According to occult philosophy the original Semites who arose from the Fourth or Atlantean Race lived largely, but not entirely, in the regions between the Levant and Eastern Persia, now Iran.   They became blended with the emigrating central Asian Āryans to produe a branch of the Chaldean sub-race.[1]

THE CHOSEN PEOPLE

Abraham and Moses were high Initiates who assisted in the development of the Hebrews into Semitic Āryans, instructing them to preserve through several generations a certain purity of blood.   This instruction gave rise to the concept that the Hebrews were a specially chosen people[2] who must not mingle with the Gentiles.

Occult philosophy teaches that the evolution of both life and form in all the kingdoms of Nature is guided throughout each of its successive cycles and their various phases by Officials of superhuman stature.   These Beings are members of a Hierarchy of ministrants and servants of the Will of the Solar Logos.   This Solar Hierarchy is represented on Earth by the Great White Brotherhood of Adepts.   Fully conversant with the evolutionary plan and both its intermediate and ultimate objectives, They are able to assist the development of the species according to that plan, or " idea " in the Platonic sense.   One of these Officers is referred to in Sanskrit as the *Manu* (personified by Noah) Who, in addition to extraterrestrial activities, guides the evolution of the races and sub-races of men on Earth.[3]   In order to preserve the purity of the racial type[4] the Lord *Manu* transmitted through agents of the Brotherhood instructions prohibiting for a time intermarriage with members of other tribes.

---

[1] q.v. *The Solar System*, A. E. Powell, and *The Earth and its Cycles*, E. W. Preston, M.Sc.
[2] *De.* 7: 6.
[3] q.v. *Lecture Notes of the School of the Wisdom*, Vol. I (Rev. Ed.), Ch. XVI, Geoffrey Hodson.
[4] *De.* 7: 1–3.

THE SONS OF THE PROPHETS

Certain of the Prophets of Israel were employed as representatives of the *Manu*. These included—doubtless among others—Moses, Jeremiah, Nehemiah, Elijah, Elisha and Samuel who, according to occult tradition, were Initiate Members of the Greater Mysteries. The School or Secret College of the Prophets may be regarded as representing the Ancient Mysteries which had been established amongst the early Hebrews and included the Official Grades or Degrees in both the Lesser and Greater Mysteries. This School is still in existence, the original Kabbalists and Essenes being its earlier and the Druses its later heirs and descendants.

The esoteric Druses are described as an occult community who jealously guard their traditional secrets.[1] They preserve one of the Sanctuaries of the Greater Mysteries which is still operating today and is used largely by Semitic peoples and their racial offspring. It is a unique and very stern School of Occultism, with a symbology and ceremonial brought down from ancient times. The old Akkadian, Chaldean, Hittite and Syrian occult teachings are blended to form the esoteric doctrines and Rites of the Druses.

The subject-matter of Chapter Ten of the *Book of Genesis*, consisting wholly of the genealogy of the sons of Noah, does not offer opportunity for occult commentary. I therefore pass on to Chapter Eleven, which is full of interest to the student.

---

[1] I am able to confirm this, having visited the religious Head of the Druse Sect at his home in the hills of Lebanon. Conversation with him revealed his knowledge of and belief in certain occult doctrines. Those included the existence of perfected men, whom he referred to as " the Sons of Light ", and the evolution to perfection of the Soul of each man through successive incarnations under a law of cause and effect. I also discovered the existence of a secret knowledge dealing with matters which he and other Druses whom I met were not willing to discuss with me. q.v. *Secret Sects of Syria and the Lebanon*, Bernard H. Springett, Chs. 3 and 21 (Geo. Allen & Unwin Limited) and *Researches into the Religions of Syria*, Rev. John Wortabet, M.D., London, 1860.

CHAPTER IX

THE TOWER OF BABEL

Gen. 11:   *One language in the world.   The building of Babel, and confusion of tongues.   The generations of Shem, and of Terah.   Terah goeth from Ur to Haran.*

1. *And the whole earth was of one language, and of one speech.*

2. *And it came to pass, as they journeyed from the east, that they found a plain in the land of Shinar; and they dwelt there.*

3. *And they said one to another, Go to, let us make brick, and burn them thoroughly.   And they had brick for stone, and slime had they for mortar.*

4. *And they said, Go to, let us build a city and a tower, whose top may reach unto heaven; and let us make us a name, lest we be scattered abroad upon the face of the whole earth.*

5. *And the LORD came down to see the city and the tower, which the children of men builded.*

6. *And the LORD said, Behold, the people is one, and they have all one language; and this they begin to do: and now nothing will be restrained from them, which they have imagined to do.*

7. *Go to , let us go down, and there confound their language, that they may not understand one another's speech.*

8. *So the LORD scattered them abroad from thence upon the face of all the earth: and they left off to build the city.*

9. *Therefore is the name of it called Babel; because the LORD did there confound the language of all the earth: and from thence did the LORD scatter them abroad upon the face of all the earth.*

A REASON FOR ENVEILING

The Bible is indeed a difficult book to understand, and this partly because of the almost inextricable admixture and juxtaposition of the esoteric, the exoteric and the pseudo-historical. Because of the multiplicity of authorship and the numerous interpolations and disfigurements, the original revelation is deeply veiled. Pure occultism and plain history, the latter often mistold, stand together in Chapter after Chapter. Allegory and fact are presented side by side, with nothing to distinguish them, save the intuition of the reader and some knowledge of the keys of interpretation. Nevertheless passages of the purest wisdom shine like jewels in the morass and it is these which catch the eye and evoke the gratitude of the student in search of truth.

Thus, between two long genealogies is placed the allegory of the Tower of Babel with its unacceptable exoteric suggestion that the Lord God, in order to restrict their power, deliberately cast His people into confusion by breaking their unity and destroying their common language. Since from such an action a great many of the subsequent sorrows of the so-called sons of Noah—supposedly the whole of mankind—arose, the attribution of this conduct to the Supreme Deity is unthinkable.

THE SOURCE OF SUFFERING AND ESCAPE FROM IT

In the Hindu Scripture, *Yogavāsishta*, we read:

" As the source of all waters is the ocean, so the idea ' I am this ' and ' this is mine ' is the cause of all our suffering. The thought of the ego is the cause of our fatal bondage. He gets bound himself who imagines a limit within his Self which is immeasurable and infinite. We are deluded and undergo terrible experiences of the world, because we feel ourselves as different or separate from Brahman, in spite of having our being in the ocean of Brahman. Trust in perishable things is known to be the source of numberless troubles. The individual becomes liberated when he gives up the attributes of mind and acquires the attributes of Brahman. The individual becomes liberated when he perceives without distinction the Self in all beings and all beings in the Self."[1]

In *Reign of Religion in Contemporary Philosophy*, Dr. Radhakrishnan writes:

" So long as we feel ourselves to have individualities of our own, we will be beset with conflicts and contradiction, pain and pleasure, but when once we disinterestedly give ourselves up to the Whole, there is an end to all discord. . . We can never completely break the shell of egoism

---

[1] Adapted from *Yogavāsishta and Modern Thought*, B. L. Atreya, M.A., D.Litt. Vasishta was one of the seven great Rishis and a most celebrated Vedic sage.

and attain the infinite if we remain in the finite universe, giving a substantial existence to our own individual self.   The release from this world of trouble, risk and adventure can be had only by losing the separate self."

In *Book of Meditations*, James Allen states:

" Seeking to save his personal life, man forfeits the greater impersonal life of truth; clinging to the perishable, he is shut out from the knowledge of the Eternal. . . Love of self shuts men out from Truth, and seeking their own personal happiness they lose the deeper, purer and more abiding bliss. . . He who has yielded up that self, that personality that most men love, and to which they cling with such fierce tenacity, has left behind him all perplexity, and has entered into a simplicity so profoundly simple as to be looked upon by the world, involved as it is in a network of error, as foolishness. . .

" The spirit of man is inseparable from the Infinite, and can be satisfied with nothing short of the Infinite, and the burden of pain will continue to weigh upon man's heart, and the shadows of sorrow to darken his pathway until ceasing from wanderings in the dreamworld of matter, he comes back to his home in the reality of the Eternal.   As the smallest drop of water detached from the ocean contains all the qualities of the ocean, so man, detached in consciousness from the Infinite, contains within himself its likeness; and as the drop of water must, by the law of nature, ultimately find its way back to the ocean and lose itself in its silent depth, so each man, by the unfailing law of his nature, at last returns to his source, and loses himself in the heart of the Infinite."

In one possible interpretation, however, the narrative may be read as an allegory describing normal processes of evolution, and by the term " the Lord " should be understood the creative and evolutionary impulses and the laws governing their manifestations in Nature and in man.   As recently observed, a full knowledge of the existence of this irresistible, propellant power and of the laws under which it finds expression in all kingdoms of Nature, including the human, would bestow very great theurgic and hypnotic powers upon its possessor.   Evil-minded men, as history reveals, grasping at this knowledge and not hesitating unscrupulously to misuse it and, to some extent, divert Nature's purposes to their own personal ends, could pervert the character of individuals—and even of nations.   Under such almost demoniacal misuse of power-bestowing knowledge, people who have hitherto been reasonably harmonious members of the family of nations can temporarily be changed into active and cruel enemies of the human race, as is demonstrated by wars of aggression— notably the First and Second World Wars.   The evils of the Nazi regime, the hysterical and slavish national acclaim of its leader and his immediate associates, the embarkation upon an unprovoked war of aggression upon a vast scale, the extermination of some six million members of the Hebrew

Race and the horrors of the Nazi concentration camps—all these afford examples of the danger resulting from the possession of even a modicum of occult knowledge. With such events frequently recorded in history and occurring in living memory, the motives of the authors of the Scriptures and Mythologies of ancient peoples in veiling their esoteric knowledge in the Language of Allegory and Symbol proves—as has frequently been pointed out in this work—to be more than justified.

AN UNVEILING OF THE ALLEGORY

How, then, may the story of the Tower of Babel be interpreted ? It may, I suggest, be regarded as descriptive of an epoch in the history of man as an individual and as a race, whilst the allegory is also susceptible of a cosmic interpretation. Pursuing these ideas, pre-Babel or primitive man may be presumed to have been largely motivated by relatively mindless tribal consciousness, his actions being largely guided by herd instinct, Post-Babel man, on the other hand, had begun to develop the mind. As mentality later entered in, displacing instinct by reason, individuality began to be born. The Tower of Babel—as already suggested in the abridged interpretation which appears in Part Two of this Volume—is thus a symbol of man's *natural* evolutionary ascent from the first purely physical race through the development of instinctual and emotional states of consciousness, on to that of the capacity for free personal choice based upon the conscious exercise of the intellect. The subsequent sorrows of mankind are traceable to the misuse for gain often at the cost of others, of this power of self-centred thought and action. In Oriental philosophy, as quoted above, such individualistic attitude of mind is called " the heresy of separateness ".

The city of Babel with its Tower is aptly described as unfinished[1] because human evolution was at that time, and still is, incomplete. The erection of the symbolic Tower will, however, be continued by the Sixth and Seventh Races, which will develop the capacity to use intuitive perception and the spiritually inspired and reinforced power of the will. This latter is to be man's greatest and most Godlike attainment; for, recognising the identity of his own interior Spirit-Essence with that of the Deity, he will share in increasing degree in the divine omnipotence. This will be the pinnacle of the as yet unfinished " Tower " of Babel.

THE BRICKS

The Tower is thus both a symbol and a chart of the evolution of man's consciousness. Its foundations are rooted deep in the earth and represent

[1] *Gen.* 11: 8.

the androgynous Adam (earth) Race, the first truly physical humanity which existed on Earth and evolved through some millions of years in a state of both mental and desire-free torpor, symbolised by Adam's sleep.[1] The later appearance of Eve beside Adam, or of single-sexed male and female humanity with its self-conscious experience of emotion as sex desire and its resultant gratification in the procreative act, represents the first layer of bricks above the ground, as it were. The sex desire of the first men and women on Earth, as earlier observed, is portrayed by the temptation of Eve in the Garden of Eden by the serpent (symbol of the Serpent Fire or universal, creative life-force), whilst Adam's reponse is allegorically indicated by the actions of receiving and sharing the fruit of the tree of knowledge of good and evil.

THE CLAY

The clay of which the bricks were made is a symbol of primordial substance. The sun which dried and baked the bricks represents creative Spirit which fructifies matter and, on the involutionary journey of forthgoing,[2] produces forms according to their Archetypes.[3] Gradually, on the downward arc, these creative " ideas " are projected from Universal Mind to become manifest as physical forms. Symbolically, the clay is hardened and the bricks are baked. Eventually the different species developed, to culminate in the emergence of man. Slowly, as the Third Race was followed by the Fourth, the great Tower or racial symbol arose. Since this progress occurred in man and was the result of human experience and effort, the narrative correctly states that the Tower of Babel was built by man.

THE DEVELOPMENT OF INDIVIDUALITY

The allegory is carried no further than the discontinuance of the erection of the city and its Tower and the scattering of the people " upon the face of all the earth ". This progressive change from pre-Babel instinctual, tribal unity into post-Babel individualism, and consequent separation, was not the result of action by a personal Deity but came about through the natural development of the human mind. The seeds of disunity, divided activity and competitiveness then germinated and began to produce their first fruits. The unifying, cohesive influence of the herd instinct, which had hitherto held the people together in families and tribes, thereafter began to lose its hold.

---

[1] *Gen.* 2: 21. This subject is more fully considered in Pt. III, Ch. IV, of this Volume.
[2] q.v. Pt. IV of Vol. I of this work.
[3] Archetype—q.v. Glossary.

A spirit of enquiry and a search for knowledge also became evident, and these led individuals and groups to explore the Earth and gradually to emigrate from the original racial centres of civilisation. Through vast ages, as the analytical and separative attributes of the mind developed, differences of language and custom accentuated a growing diversity. This culminated in the production of the entirely distinct races and nations characteristic of humanity at the present time.

The change from unity to diversity was thus inevitable—completely necessary, indeed—for the evolution of man. Despite its grievous results, destined to endure far on into the Fifth Root Race (the present time), it was an essential phase of the process of the unfoldment of human life and consciousness. It might even be said that Nature demanded it as the price of the triumph to follow and the crown to be won. The triumph will consist of a conscious, self-chosen return to unification, and the crown will be the realisation of the unity of the life within all the diversities of form.

FROM MATTER TO SPIRIT, FROM EARTH TO HEAVEN

Macrocosmically, the incarnation of the one life into many forms, and the expression of the one creative " idea " through its innumerable manifestations in Nature, are allegorically described. From this cosmic point of view the building of the Tower of Babel might symbolise entry on the pathway of return from matter to Spirit, or from Earth to Heaven. The unfinished state indicates a continuing process as yet incomplete, whilst the limitless regions of the sky above suggest an infinity of potential attainment.

The whole story of the city and Tower of Babel may be said to portray progression by the one life from unity (pre-Babel and Babel)[1] through diversity (post-Babel)[2] towards unity again. It is thus entirely symbolic, and is one of the many flawless jewels of wisdom which are scattered in prodigal abundance throughout the pages of the Bible.

An indirect reference may possibly be perceived to the Sacred Language of the Mystery Schools, the significance of which was—and still is—the same for all peoples. In olden days this cryptic tongue was employed universally as the literary vehicle for occult knowledge. Later the primeval Wisdom Religion and its hierogrammatic language were forgotten by the masses, who had become restricted to the several tongues of the different nations of the world.[3]

---

[1] *Gen.* 11: 1.
[2] *Gen.* 11: 7, 8.
[3] q.v. *The Secret Doctrine*, Vol. V (Adyar Ed.), p. 185, H. P. Blavatsky.

THE GENERATIONS OF SHEM

Although verses ten to thirty-two of the Eleventh Chapter of *Genesis* are largely genealogical, they also serve to indicate the general expansion and growing diversity of the early races of men, and particularly of the Semitic peoples.   They close with the introduction of those two momentous figures, Terah and his son Abram, whose deeply allegorical adventures begin in Chapter Twelve.   Racially and historically Abram represents the father and leader of the Aryo-Semitic peoples, and his experiences are those of one selected branch, the Palestinian.

PART FIVE

AN INTRODUCTION TO THE STUDY OF THE ABRAMIC CYCLE IN THE HISTORY OF THE JEWISH PEOPLE

AN INTRODUCTION TO THE STUDY OF THE ABRAMIC CYCLE IN THE HISTORY OF THE JEWISH PEOPLE

THE Fifth Part of this Volume largely consists of commentaries upon Chapters Twelve to Fifteen inclusive of the *Book of Genesis*. A departure is, however, made from the method earlier employed of suggesting possible interpretations of verses in their consecutive order. A more general purpose is here being pursued, namely to offer a review of the life stories of the chief characters in the great drama of the founding under Abraham of the Hebrew nation as described in the Chapters mentioned above. In addition, some interpretations of certain dramatic events and remarkable symbols are included. Readers will, in consequence, discover that the continuity is broken at Chapter Twelve, the succession being resumed at Chapter Sixteen. The more detailed verse-by-verse interpretation is recommended at Chapter Twenty. It has been thought desirable, however, first to present general expositions of ideas contained in occult philosophy which are pertinent to these particular passages. In addition, reference is made to the Symbolical Language in general, and more particularly to the more important symbols employed in the Abramic narrative.

Since a vast period in the history of the whole human race is also found to be allegorically described in this portion of the *Pentateuch* interpretations of each separate verse have not seemed to be desirable. The central figures which successively occupy the stage may, I suggest, be regarded as both representing directive Intelligences in Nature, including spiritual Guardians of Races[1] and—in accordance with the Law of

---

[1] *Manus*—q.v. Glossary.

Correspondences[1]—personifying powers, principles and vehicles of man. In the latter, microcosmic sense the Lord God typifies the Monad, and His human agents on Earth personify the divine, evolving, spiritual Self of man, the Ego. Consorts and offspring, in their turn, stand for man's mental, emotional and physical bodies.

Such, in general, is the theme of the Fifth Part of this book, which mainly concerns the early history of all mankind although the apparent purpose of the authors[2] of the *Book of Genesis* was to write a history of the Hebrew Race alone. The following Chart epitomises, and is here offered as a key to, the teachings of occult philosophy concerning past and present races of men :[3]

RACE	ERA	NAME	SENSE	LEVEL OF CONSCIOUSNESS	
1	Eocene	Polar	Hearing	Finer-etheric	⎫
2	Oligocene	Hyperborean	Touch	Denser etheric	⎬ Downward arc
3	Miocene	Lemurian	Sight	Physical—" coats of skin "	⎭
4	Pliocene	Atlantean	Taste	Emotional	
5	Pleistocene	Aryan	Smell	Mental	
6	Future		E.S.P.	Intuitional	⎫ Upward arc
7	Future		E.S.P.	Realisation of Oneness	⎭

As we have seen heretofore, the members of the first two Root Races did not possess entirely solid physical bodies of flesh and bone, and therefore left no discoverable traces. Since the *Pentateuch* deals with the history of

---

[1] *The Law of Correspondences*: The harmonious co-ordination or mutual resonance between the many apparently separate parts of the Universe and corresponding parts of the constitution of man. Occult philosophy teaches that all components of both Macrocosm and microcosm are interwoven and interactive according to a universal system of vibrational interchange. In his spiritual, intellectual, psychical and physical make-up man is regarded as a minature replica or epitome of the whole Order of created beings and things, a model of the totality of Nature. He is said to contain within himself the collective aggregate of all that has ever existed, does at any time exist and will ever exist throughout the eternity of eternities. The Chinese philosopher Lao Tzu expressed this in his words: " The Universe is a man on a large scale." Eliphas Levi quotes from the *Kabbalah*: " The mystery of the earthly and mortal man is after the mystery of the supernal and immortal one." This view is indeed basic to Kabbalism, which affirms that man may be regarded as a symbolic transparency through which the secrets of the Cosmos may be discerned. In the Bible one reads: ". . . God said, Let us make man in our image, after our likeness . . ." (*Gen.* 1-26). Inspired allegories may, therefore, and indeed should, be equally understood in both the Macrocosmic and the microcosmic senses. For a fuller exposition of this important subject see *Lecture Notes of the School of the Wisdom*, Vol. I (Rev. Ed.), Ch. XIII, Geoffrey Hodson.

[2] Whilst generally attributed to Moses, scholars agree upon a composite authorship, one reason being the inclusion of a description of the death of Moses.

[3] For a fuller exposition see *Lecture Notes of the School of the Wisdom*, Vol. I (Rev. Ed.), Ch. XIV, Geoffrey Hodson.

physical man on Earth, no reference is made to pre-physical man. The first fully embodied men with " coats of skin " were androgynous and are represented by Adam alone in the Garden of Eden, itself emblematic of the innocent, passionless state. A separation of the sexes occurred later in this race and the resultant male and female human beings are represented by Adam and Eve, as is advanced in the interpretations of the First Chapter of *Genesis* offered in Parts Two and Three of this book. Later developments and divisions into different nations and civilisations (" confusion of tongues "[1]) form the chief subjects of the Chapters now to be considered.

CHAPTER I

THE ORIGIN OF THE SEMITIC PEOPLE

THE BIBLE AN INSPIRED BOOK

SINCE the Mosaic Books recount—largely in allegorical form, I submit—both the spiritual and physical beginnings and the early history of the Levantine branches of the Jewish people, a restatement of the sources and the keys of interpretation of the Sacred Language would seem to be desirable at this point.

In conformity with ancient custom the authors of the *Pentateuch* also revealed by means of the Symbolical Language the occult wisdom of their Sanctuaries. This is the heart of Judaism, the *Kabbalah*[1] being its exegesis. The real *Kabbalah* is said to have been lost, or perhaps deliberately withdrawn. Inspired teachers have, however, discovered parts of it and have revealed them as the true *Kabbalah*. Initiates alone amongst the Jews have been permitted to receive the full doctrine, and then only under vows of secrecy. Nevertheless certain teachings of the occult wisdom are to be found in both the Old and the New Testaments.

From *Genesis* to *Revelation* the Bible contains inspired passages, but not in the sense in which either orthodox Jews or Christian theologians interpret the word " inspired ". As suggested earlier, many of these passages have become overlaid and distorted by later unillumined writers who added accounts based upon tribal superstitions and primitive standards of morality *not included in the original*—and now lost—inspired revelations. Apart from lofty morality, and language of great beauty as in the King James version of the Bible, deep interior illumination is but rarely to be found in the purely literal reading or " letter " alone. It is, however, nearly always to be discerned in the " spirit ". This is as true of the New Testament as of the Old, and particularly of the Four Gospels and *The Revelation of St. John the Divine*. If the treasures of wisdom in the Bible, as in other authentic world Scriptures, are to be discovered they must be searched for by means of meditation and the use of the appropriate keys.

---

[1] q.v. *Zohar* and Appendix to this Volume.

THE SEVEN KEYS OF INTERPRETATION

He who thus searches will find the Bible to be as a casket of jewels with seven compartments, the possession and use of the keys to each of them being necessary for the finding of the hidden treasure. A description of these keys refers to them as: the cosmogonical; the solar, which includes the planetary and racial; the microcosmic, dealing with the inter-relationships between man and Cosmos; the psychical and spiritual, referring to the superphysical nature and evolution of man; the occult which concerns the life and wisdom of the Sanctuary; the numerical; and lastly the verbal, giving the interpretations of the cyphers· hierograms and cryptograms of which the Sacred Language partly consists.

These keys, and the wisdom to which they give access, are not deliberately kept away from humanity. Indeed, knowledge is never denied to those who seek it earnestly and with a pure heart. In the Scriptures of the world truth can be discovered by the investigator who will work humbly and in conformity with valid methods of occult research, keeping that open mind which alone can receive the light of the hidden wisdom, " the mystery of the kingdom of God ",[1] the *gnosis*, *Theosophia*. The Adept[2] Teachers of the Race, Themselves having discovered the Sacred Wisdom, preserve and make available to enquiring minds the knowledge which They have undertaken to guard throughout all ages and to deliver to sincere seekers amongst mankind.

REASONS FOR SECRECY

The Adept Brotherhood cannot, I repeat, justly be charged with undue secrecy, and least of all with selfishness in guarding that knowledge which is power. The destruction of the whole human race could be brought about by the appropriate means—nuclear energy, for example.[3] Lesser catastrophes and cataclysms could also be produced by those who are sufficiently informed. The destructive potential of the human will, directed by a mind armed with the necessary knowledge, is almost without limit, and this is the chief reason for secrecy. Immensely injurious though such devices can be, their effects are limited to the physical world. Occult knowledge, however, which can include equal and even greater possibilities for construction and destruction, bestows capacities for injury affecting the superphysical planes of Nature. If harmfully used the damage would penetrate into and affect the *psyche* of man, not only for one physical incar-

[1] *Mk.* 4: 11.

[2] q.v. Glossary.

[3] Since this passage was originally written, science has discovered a fusion device known as the thermo-nuclear bomb (H-bomb).

nation but even extending to its successors. Sorcery, necromancy, mental and emotional domination and enslavement are examples of the damage which could be—and indeed has been—brought about by these means, hence the need for secrecy. Actually humanity has every reason to be grateful to, rather than to indict, the Members of the Great White Brotherhood for the care with which such knowledge has been guarded.

An occultist of the white (wholly selfless) order can inspire, illumine and heal both individuals and whole communities, so great are the natural forces available when once the means of tapping them and using them have been discovered. Similarly an occultist of the dark (wholly selfish) order can both mentally blind and physically destroy individuals and communities, as has several times become evident during this twentieth century. He who would first win knowledge and then rightfully employ it must therefore range himself irrevocably upon the side of those who, with self burned out of them, live but to serve humanity and obey the behests of the One Will in Nature, which ever moves to assist the evolution of the human race. This, it has always been taught, is the spirit in which the aspirant should approach the Scriptures of the world, including the Bible. Purified of self and applying the classical keys, he will then discover the power-bestowing truths.

THE HEBRAIC MYSTERIES

During their residence amongst the Chaldeans, Terah and the great Jewish patriarchs, Abram, Lot and others unnamed in the Bible came, according to occult tradition, under the influence of the Sanctuaries of the Chaldean Mysteries[1] (said by Hesiod to have been founded by Semiramis, the mother of Nimrod), which at that time were highly developed as Centres of occult and spiritual life. The Brotherhood of the Adepts established and maintained these occult schools in all of the civilisations of the sub-races of the Aryan Race. The Mysteries[2] were the heart of the national life and religion, both temporal direction and spiritual impulses emanating from them. Candidates for Initiation were admitted and, when worthy, passed through their successive Grades. As in all " valid "[3] Temples of the Ancient Mysteries, Initiates were instructed concerning, and trained to perceive direct, those cosmic laws, processes, forces and Intelligences which, for reasons of safety and security, were only revealed to the uninitiated

---

[1] q.v. *Philosophy of History and Traditions*, Molitor, Howitt's Translation, p. 285; *Caberiria*, Anthon; *Phaedras*, Plato; *Herodotus*, Book I; *Babylonian Magic and Sorcery*, L. W. King, p. 117; *Assyrian Religion*, T. G. Prinches, p. 100. See also Plutarch, Sophocles and Pindar.

[2] The Mysteries—q.v. Glossary.

[3] " Valid "—founded by the Great White Brotherhood of Adepts.

by personifications, symbols and myths. For thousands of years the Chaldean Sanctuaries thus served the second, the Iranian, sub-race of the Aryan Race,[1] and in addition gave the primary impulses from which it was hoped a great Aryo-Semitic civilisation would develop.

Occult tradition also tells that the original Atlantean Semites had colonised the region of Mesopotamia and were the progenitors of the indigenous population. The whole area was their national home, they being a branch of the Semitic or fifth sub-race of the Fourth Root Race. Mesopotamia, which stretched from the mountainous border of Baluchistan to the north-east, along the coastal regions of the Persian Gulf to the Euphrates Valley, was the site of one of the very oldest civilisations known to man. Neolithic peoples—village-dwellers, fishermen, farmers and craftsmen—were attracted to this fertile land. The first Sumerians were followed by ancient Semitic peoples—the Akkadians and others.

Chaldea was the name given to Babylonia, the later Semitic kingdom built upon Sumeria, the ruling class in Babylon being called the Chaldeans. The Semites who had assimilated the civilisation of Sumeria, culminated their complete control of Babylonia with a Chaldean dynasty in the seventh century B.C.[2] The *Manus* of the Fourth and the Fifth Races had chosen them, it is said, to be the forefathers of certain sub-races of the Aryan Race. In addition, they were expected to transmit the Mystery teaching known as the *Kabbalah* to the Western humanity which was then waiting to be born. They were drawn into Mesopotamia and more or less segregated there long before either the coming of the original Iranians from Central Asia or the departure under Abram of selected families from the City of Ur.

These original Semites had their own Mysteries established for them by their Masters, the Adepts of those days, and all the real mysticism and occultism, including the *Kabbalah* of Judaism stems from a blending of the Hebrew and the Chaldean Mysteries. The general populace of those early times followed the monotheism characteristic of that religion, but later became guilty of anthropomorphism, animism and superstition. The esoteric and the exoteric are found to be blended in the ancient records, particularly in the *Pentateuch*, though also in later Books of the Old Testament.

From the Sanctuary, then, came the great Jewish Patriarchs though their historians, often writing from oral tradition many centuries later, in some cases produced travesties of the real figures and the actual events. Nevertheless, as these Volumes are designed to show, the two streams of thought—the occult and the historical—are traceable in the ancient records.

---

[1] q.v. *The Solar System*, A. E. Powell, and *Lecture Notes of the School of the Wisdom*, Vol. I (Rev. Ed.), Geoffrey Hodson.

[2] For fuller information see *The Wisdom of Chaldea*, Charles A. Muses.

Under the orders of the Hierophants of the Sanctuary, however, much true occultism is interpolated, if under the veil of pseudo-history, allegory and symbol.

The genealogies are important to the Jews because they affirm and preserve the unbroken lines of descent from the original spiritual leaders, the inspired Agents of the Brotherhood of the Adepts, as also from the Patriarchs and progenitors of the nation. In the writing of the *Pentateuch* the ancient custom was followed of combining history with allegory, and of using numerical and other classical symbols in order to hand down to posterity the hidden wisdom of the Sanctuaries.

The bounden duty was laid upon the Initiates and Hierophants of the Ancient Mysteries both to preserve and to hand on to their successors such truths as could be valuable for human progress and development. These illumined men of old had themselves plunged deeply into occult research, had made their own physical, metaphysical and spiritual discoveries, and had also become recipients of the wisdom and knowledge of their forerunners, the Adepts of preceding Ages.

THE DIVINE DIRECTION OF THE SEMITIC PEOPLES

The Old Testament, however disfigured, is one of the relics of that glorious past when the Wisdom Religion was universally recognised by men. The Sanctuaries of Initiation were in those days open to humanity, and the guidance of their Hierophants was given to its leaders. Thus from the Sanctuaries there quite frequently came to the ancient Patriarchs those orders and instructions which are described in the Old Testament as being " the word of the Lord." The angels and the unnamed men who appeared as messengers from God—apart from their possible psychological significance in the microcosmic interpretation—were none other than Initiate or Adept Representatives of the Brotherhood of the Adepts. By these means constant guidance and direction were maintained, especially in the early beginnings of nations and civilisations.

Unfortunately the Jewish portion of the great programme for the development of the Aryan Race failed of complete success, qualities of character having emerged which limited the usefulness of the Semitic contribution. Amongst these were mental rigidity and excessive and separative pride of nationhood, which prevented the planned admixture of Hebrew characteristics—particularly also the wisdom of the *Kabbalah*— from being transmitted to the fourth (Celtic) and fifth (Teutonic, Nordic and Anglo-Saxon) Aryan sub-races.

CHAPTER II

THE ISRAELITES AS A CHOSEN RACE [1]

OCCULT PHILOSOPHY AND THE HEBREW PEOPLES

THE history of the Jews as a chosen people is so narrated in the Bible as to make it also descriptive of the trials, tribulations and triumphs of every Initiate who treads " The way of holiness ".[2] As has been earlier stated, the Sacred Language is thus especially adapted to fulfil such a dual, even threefold, purpose. The history of a nation or a personage can be so recorded as to apply to the evolution and life story of the whole human race, of each human being and of those man and women who are treading the pathway of hastened evolution, having already entered in " at the strait gate "[3] and chosen the narrow way.

If some repetition will be excused, historically the original Jewish peoples—the Atlantean and Akkadian Semites—were selected because of certain Egoic, psychological and physical characteristics. They were chosen by the Adept directors of evolution upon this planet to receive and to deliver to posterity deeply occult aspects of the One Wisdom Religion. Their mission has to some extent been fulfilled; for the *Kabbalah* and the Old Testament are their magnificent gifts to humanity, however deeply veiled in allegory and symbol the underlying esoteric wisdom may be. Their virile physical health, for the attainment and preservation of which they received special guidance, was shared with those Gentiles with whom they permitted themselves to intermingle. The detailed instructions, recorded chiefly in *Leviticus*, concerning religious practices and communal and hygienic customs are imperfectly preserved memories of the ancient directions which had been imparted to them.[4]

The Jewish nation, it was apparently hoped, would become one of the trusted repositories of the Secret Wisdom, as also one of the great dispensers of that Wisdom to mankind. The succession of great Initiates (sons of the Prophets[5]) who incarnated amongst them, and the establishment

---

[1] *Ex.* 19: 6; *Lev.* 20: 24–26; *De.* 7: 6; *Is.* 61: 6.
[2] *Is.* 35: 8.
[3] *Matt.* 7: 13.
[4] cf. *The Laws of Manu, Sacred Books of the East*, Vol. XXV.
[5] II *Kings* 2: 5.

of training Centres (Schools of the Prophets) all refer to both the occult assistance and the esoteric knowledge given to the Jews to aid in the fulfilment of their true mission on Earth.

Unhappily the spiritual and the occult gradually became outweighed by the material, the innate wisdom being clouded by the quality of pride and the sense of superiority over other nations which the fact of their being referred to as the chosen people aroused in the Hebrew people. A remarkable recrudescence occurred in the early Middle Ages when a group of Kabbalists residing in Spain produced many books on the subject, some of which are still extant, including the *Zohar* itself. As material ambition increased so the theosophy and the degree of occult instruction declined, until now—with due respect to a great nation—some Jews are known primarily for the first-named whilst the last two are almost lost. This may well be part of the tragedy of the Jewish nation, which arose with so much promise but later fell, generating under the law of *karma* most grievous adversities in the process. To be specially chosen and in a wonderful degree to receive spiritual and occult wisdom and direction are very great privileges. Correspondingly heavy, one presumes, must be both the responsibility and the danger to the recipients.

ABRAHAM—HISTORICAL AND MYSTICAL

The epoch of the Patriarch Abraham was one of great spiritual and material promise, hence the many prophecies of Israel's immeasurable fruitfulness and of the advent of a Messianic Age. Abraham must surely be regarded as a real and not a mythological personage, being one of the original Patriarchs of the Levantine Jews. His journey from Ur of the Chaldees[1] and his subsequent activities as recorded in *Genesis* actually occurred, though the narrative reveals but a small part of the full history. Even that, I submit, is related in the allegorical language. The earliest records of the Semitic people reveal them as desert nomads moving down the Euphrates and settling north of the land of Sumer where they seized the city of Opis. Ur of the Chaldees was located in the extreme south of the country not far from the mouth of the river. The Semitic settlers bore the name of Akkadians. In the late Twenty-sixth Century B.C. the warrior chieftain named Sargon made himself lord of all the plain of Shinar from whence he later led his army—including the swift Akkadian archers—westward to the shores of the Mediterranean and northward into Asia Minor. Sargon thus built a powerful Semitic nation in Western Asia.

---

[1] *Gen.* 11: 31.

These conquests brought about great changes in the manner of life of the nomadic tribes who foresook their tents, built houses of sun-dried brick and learned from the Sumerians to write, to cut seals and to manage communal affairs. They also adopted the Sumerian calendar, weights and measures, numerals and business methods. Thus the Semites and the Sumerians became blended, and Abraham is believed by the Hebrews to have been a citizen of Ur.[1]

Sir Charles Leonard Wooley writes: " We must radically alter our view of the Hebrew patriarch when we see that his earlier years were passed in such sophisticated surroundings. He was the citizen of a great city and inherited the traditions of an old and highly organised civilisation. The houses themselves reveal comfort and even luxury. We found copies of the hymns which were used in the services of the temples and together with them mathematical tables. On these tables were anything ranging from plain addition sums to formulae for the extraction of square and cube roots. In other texts the writers had copied out the old building inscriptions to be found in the city and had compiled in this way a short history of the temples. . . ."[2]

Abraham was no simple nomad, therefore, but a son of a great city of the second millenium B.C. who was destined to become the father of a great race. Esoterically regarded, however, he is found to be a highly complex figure. The Bible presents him as a spiritually developed man acting under the direction of the Lord God. This may signify that his colonising journey was carried out under the direction of a Sanctuary of the Greater Mysteries. He may also be seen as a personification of both the Logos of a Solar System and the Monad-Ego of man. Even in this latter view of him—fully considered elsewhere in this Volume—although he displays characteristics attributable to a man following the pathway of normal evolution, later in his life he would appear to be pursuing the path of hastened progress towards Adeptship. In addition, as is the case with many leaders whose lives are related in allegorical writings, the account of his life also mirrors phases of the manifestation of the indwelling power, life and consciousness of Solar Systems and Cosmoi. If this interpretation be applied, then Abraham's forthgoing from the parental home refers to the descent into matter of the divine life with its latent potentialities, whilst his attainment and death portray the return or ascent of that life to the original Source[3] with those innate powers fully developed. Thus the four threads—the historical, the occult, the psycho-spiritual and the cosmic— would seem to be interwoven in the great epic.

[1] After Breasted, *Ancient Times*.

[2] q.v. *Abraham, Recent Discoveries and Hebrew Origins* (1936) and *Ur of the Chaldees* (1954) Quoted from *The Bible as History*, Werner Keller.

[3] **q.v.** *The Hidden Wisdom in the Holy Bible*, Vol. I, Pt. IV, Geoffrey Hodson.

Drawing upon certain teachings of occult philosophy, one assumes that Abraham was acting under the orders of a Hierophant of the Chaldean Sanctuary, of which he was an Initiate. If this be so, it would appear that he was chosen as the leader of a small group of Chaldean Semites selected by the Adept Government of the planet for purposes of racial development and evolution. The instructions given by the Lord,[1] and the visitations by angels and divine men,[2] may be regarded as referring to his continual receipt of direct guidance from these spiritual sources.

Abraham's personal experiences, his domestic life and the events which occurred around him, in some of which he was a participant, thus have their psycho-spiritual significance and also, as we have seen, portray experiences and developments of the human Soul when treading the Path. As an example of this, his wife Sarai is barren until her name is altered to Sarah, this change being of deeply occult significance. Sarai is the formal mind, half-sister and wife of the abstract mind, represented by Abraham. Intuition (the son) cannot reach the lower mind as long as it retains its original characteristics of marked separative individuality and critical analysis implied in the given name Sarai (" contentious "); for in the symbolical language the name of a person is descriptive of their characteristics, as also of their innate powers and capacities.

When once the limiting aspects of the mentality are changed, it becomes susceptible of impregnation (is no longer " barren ") by the spiritual will (Terah) of the Monad (the Lord) through the higher or abstract mind (Abraham). The reception (" birth ") of intuitive wisdom and vision (Isaac) then becomes possible. The change, however, is not in the basic character of the mind, but only in the use to which existent faculties and attributes are put.

CYCLES AND SUB-CYCLES OF FORTHGOING PORTRAYED BY THE JOURNEYS OF TERAH, ABRAM AND SARAI[3]

If the different characters in the story are regarded as personifications of the principles of man, thereby adhering to the microcosmic interpretation, three cycles of forthgoing are found to be indicated by the travels of Terah, Abram and Sarai. The first is from Ur into Haran, where Terah dies. The second is from Haran to Canaan and Bethel, and the third is from Bethel to Egypt, made in order to escape the famine (another symbolical reference to the barrenness of Sarai). Egypt thus regarded represents the

---

[1] *Gen.* 12: 1.

[2] *Gen.* 18 and 19.

[3] The names first used for them in the Bible.

physical plane, where the descent into incarnation reaches its deepest point. Thence the cycle of return is entered upon, being indicated by the journey back to Bethel (" the house of God ") and referring to the spiritual state of awareness of the Inner Self of man, sometimes named Causal consciousness.[1]

Three cycles or stages in the forthgoing of man the microcosm are thus indicated. The first concerns the primordial emanation of the Monad (Terah) into the field of evolution. The second, the projection of the Ray of the Monad (Kabbalistically " light of the inexhaustible light ") is symbolised by the departure to Canaan. The third describes the forth-going of the Ego (Abraham) into successive incarnations in physical bodies, portrayed by the journey into Egypt, the deepest point of descent.

EGYPT AS SYMBOL OF SPIRITUAL BONDAGE

Egypt—except when a visit to its Mystery Schools for purposes of Initiation is implied, as in the case of the supposed flight of Jesus—is also used as a topographical symbol of a condition of captivity and bondage. When eventually freedom has been won, the narrators indicate by their account that benefits have been gained from the enforced residence in the land of Khem. This is true of both the Israelites and Joseph. The former return to their own land of Canaan, where the race multiplies and prospers, whilst the latter rises to pre-eminence.

Microcosmically, Egypt represents the Inner Self incarnated in its three mortal vehicles—mental, emotional and physical. The Ruler, Pharaoh himself, typifies the reincarnating Ego, and his palace the mental body, vehicle of analytical thought. The waters of the River Nile symbolise both the emotional nature and body and the creative life-force within the physical body. The source of the River refers to the superphysical reservoir of creative energy or *kundalini*[2] and its force-centre or *chakra*[3] situated at the sacrum or base of the spine. The delta corresponds to the crown *chakra*, and the Mediterranean Sea to the condition of freed and universalised consciousness attained when that *chakra* is opened and consciously used. The country itself, however, symbolises more especially the physical body of man, and the restricted state of human consciousness when mainly directed towards the physical world.

---

[1] The normal condition of awareness of the spiritual Self of man, which includes universalisation of consciousness and experience of oneness with God, and through Him with all that lives.

[2] q.v. Glossary.

[3] q.v. *The Chakras*, C. W. Leadbeater, and Glossary.

THE SYMBOL OF THE UNION OF UPPER AND LOWER EGYPT

At this point, in illustration of the method of concealing and revealing occult knowledge by means of allegory and myth, and to offer some suggested interpretations, a digression is made. Consideration of the story of Abraham is resumed on page 229.

The oft-used Egyptian symbol, exoterically supposed to represent the fusion of the two kingdoms of Upper and Lower Egypt, is susceptible of interpretation as representing the three currents of *kundalini* in the spinal cord of man, as also does the Greek Caduceus which it somewhat resembles. The stalks of the papyrus and the lotus flower in the symbol of union typify the channels for the two oppositely polarised currents of the Serpent Fire, known as *Ida* and *Pingala*, whilst the central rod portrays the channel, known as *Sushumna*, for the equipolarised stream of spinal energy. The breasted but otherwise male figures are holding the two stalks. These they intertwine and knot around an upright rod, which would indicate the dual polarity (male-female) of the Serpent Fire and its winding and intertwining pathway of ascent along the spinal cord. Support for this interpretation is gained from one form of the Egyptian symbol in which the central line is marked with regular crossbars, causing it closely to resemble the spinal column and vertebrae. The supposed vessel out of which the plants seem to be growing is aptly shaped like the human pelvis.

One of the results of this sublimation of the creative energy consists of realisation of unity with the one life in all beings and all things. In this sense the Upper and Lower Nile (as also Egypt itself) as topographical symbols represent the spiritual and personal Selves respectively. These are fused in the Initiate, as is suggested by the binding of the two flower stalks in the symbol of union, bestowing upon the brain-mind a universalisation of consciousness. The blending of the Crowns of Upper and Lower Egypt after their unification is susceptible of the same interpretation.

The shape and position of the land area of Egypt in relation to the Mediterranean Sea, and the annually flooding River Nile with its source in a lake and its outlet in a sea, together symbolise man—physical, superphysical and spiritual—the land itself representing the physical body. The River Nile corresponds to the spinal cord and its nerve and other fluids, with the delta as brain. The absolute Monarchy, represented by successive Pharaohs, portrays the presiding divine Presence, the Inner Self of man. The ordinary Temple life of the people symbolises both exoteric religion and the normal exercise of the procreative function. The Sanctuaries in their turn typify nerve, glandular and superphysical force-centres or *chakras*, which are aroused into hyper-activity when the sex force is sublimated and its energy turned upwards into the region of the head, particularly after the Rite of Initiation has been conferred by a Hierophant of a Sanctuary.

A similar system of symbology is applied to certain of the ancient cities of India, each with its implied correspondence with physical organs, superphysical force-centres or *chakras*, and the particular type of energy and consciousness associated with each of them. These associations are given as follows[1]:

Ayōdhya	—	corresponding to the		crown	*chakra*
Mathura	—	„	„	„	brow „
Māyā	—	„	„	„	throat „
Varānasi	—	„	„	„	heart „
Conjeevaram		„	„	„	solar plexus *chakra*
Avantika	—	„	„	„	spleen *chakra*
Dvāraka	—		„	„	sacral „

Thus as was proclaimed by both the Hierogrammatists of old and in modern days, by the poetess Elizabeth Barrett Browning:

" Earth's crammed with heaven
And every common bush afire with God;
But only he who sees, takes off his shoes; "[2]

This view is, indeed, the very heart of the concept of the Sacred Language and applies more especially to the use of topographical symbols. The wise men of old, with their open vision, saw that in very truth Earth mirrors Heaven.

THE CYCLE OF RETURN

As the phase of forthgoing is succeeded by that of return, the consciousness and power of the Immortal Self are gradually awakened in the mortal personality. The mind (Sarah) then becomes purified (is rescued from Pharaoh) and the spiritual mode of life is entered upon. This is allegorically revealed by the narrative of the departure of Abraham and Sarah from Egypt, their arrival at Bethel and the building at that place of an altar to the Lord. Whilst the interpretations suggested above concern the general processes of emanation and withdrawal, forthgoing and return, involution and evolution, the journey from Bethel to Egypt and back to Bethel again may also be read as descriptive of each single cycle of descent into incarnation or birth and ascent after bodily death. On its return journey, after the physical body has been laid aside, the Egoic Ray (Abraham) is withdrawn through the astral plane, where it experiences the operation of *karmic*

[1] q.v. *Esoteric Writings of T. Subba Row*, B.A., B.L.
[2] q.v. Poems of Elizabeth M. Browning, Bk. 7.

15

adjustment (Pharaoh's wrath). Thereafter consciousness is further with-drawn through the mental plane, at which stage the heaven life is entered (riches and gladness at being free), and on into Egoic self-awareness (Bethel).[1]

Thus, I suggest, is allegorically portrayed the oft-repeated minor cycle of birth and death as a component of the major cycle of the age-long evolution of the Monad-Ego. All accounts of such journeys of forthgoing and return appearing in Scripture and myth are susceptible of similar interpretations. The Parable of the Prodigal Son is one outstanding example of this method of revelation by means of allegory.[2]

THE MYTH OF PERSEPHONE [3]

The story of Persephone, which formed the metaphorical basis of the Eleusinian Mysteries, is a magnificent example of the portrayal of these profound truths by means of allegory and symbol. Since this is the case, it may be appropriate at this point to include the story and some of its possible interpretations.

Persephone was the daughter of Demeter (called Ceres by the Romans), one of the great divinities of the Greeks, who was regarded as the protectress of agriculture and of all the fruits of the earth. She was the daughter of Cronus and Rhea, and sister of Zeus, by whom she became the mother of Persephone. Zeus, without the knowledge of Demeter, had promised Persephone to Aidoneus (Pluto); and while the unsuspecting maiden was gathering flowers in the Nysian plain in Asia, the earth suddenly opened and she was carried off by Aidoneus. After wandering in search of her daughter, Demeter learnt from the Sun that it was Aidoneus who had carried her off. Thereupon she quitted Olympus in anger and dwelt upon Earth among men, conferring blessings wherever she was kindly received and severely punishing those who repulsed her. In this manner she came to Celeus, at Eleusis. As the goddess still remained angry, and did not allow the earth to produce any fruits, Zeus sent Hermes into the lower world to fetch back Persephone. Aidoneus consented, but gave Persephone part of a pome-granate to eat. Demeter returned to Olympus with her daughter, but as the latter had eaten in the lower world she was obliged to spend one-third of the year with Aidoneus, staying with her mother for the remainder of the year. Thereafter the earth brought forth fruit again.

---

[1] q.v. *Through the Gateway of Death*, Geoffrey Hodson.

[2] q.v. *The Hidden Wisdom in the Holy Bible*, Vol. I, Pt. IV, Geoffrey Hodson, and Charts on p. 46 of this Volume.

[3] q.v. *The Hidden Wisdom in the Holy Bible*, Vol. I, Pt. II, where an interpretation also appears.

This is the ancient legend as preserved in the Homeric hymn.[1] The Latin poets place the scene of the rape near Etna, in Sicily. Ascalaphus, who had alone seen Persephone eat anything in the lower world, revealed the fact and was in consequence turned into an owl by Demeter. One meaning of the legend is fairly obvious. Persephone, who is carried off to the lower world, is the seed-corn which remains concealed in the ground part of the year; Persephone, who returns to her mother in this context represents the corn which rises from the ground and nourishes men and animals.

A solar allegory is also unfolded, the time spent underground in Hades being the Wintertime in the Northern Hemisphere, when the sun lacks power for some three to four months of the year. Applied to the Cosmos as a whole, the myth tells of the divine Consciousness which descends from its lofty spiritual state deeper and deeper into matter, until at last the deepest depths are reached—the mineral kingdom—symbolished by the Underworld. Then in the course of evolution consciousness begins to win free from the domination of matter, to shake off the shackles of materiality and ultimately to become spiritualised. At the close of the cycle that which has been embodied and imprisoned is freed and returned to its source. Allegorically, Persephone is reunited with her Mother. Cycles follow cycles, each with their arcs of descent and ascent. Persephone must therefore go down into the Underworld again and again.

Recurrent phases of generation and regeneration are also portrayed by other symbols, such as those of the serpent which regularly sloughs its skin, the scarab which rolls the ball of mud in which it has enclosed its eggs, and the Phoenix which rises new-formed from the ashes of its body, deliberately burnt every five hundred years.

In the microcosmic or human interpretation of the myth Zeus personifies the Monad, Demeter the Ego, and Persephone the portion or " daughter " of the Ego which is incarnated in the body (Hades). Before birth the Ego sends a ray or portion of its life—Persephone—down from the Causal world, through the realms of mind and emotion (the upper air) into the physical world to be born on Earth (Hades) and marry Pluto, who partly personifies the elemental bodily desires. Each time a reincarnating Soul is born to live in this darkened, material, physical body and world, Persephone—who personifies that Soul or Ray of the Ego—has allegorically returned to the Underworld.

An occult interpretation of the myth is also possible. The personal soul can prematurely win freedom from total imprisonment in the physical body if, at the command of Zeus (the Monad), symbolically Hermes with his staff can be found to come and rescue it. The nature and structure of

---

[1] q.v. *Homeric Hymns.* Introduction to the *Hymn to Demeter,* Sykes and Allen.

this staff give the key to the process of self-liberation; for in one interpretation, the human, the Caduceus represents very accurately the aroused serpentine, triple, creative power in man. As I have earlier written, when no more used for procreation this power is transmuted or turned upwards until the two serpents' heads, or two oppositely polarised serpentine currents of creative fire, and the central rod or neutral current, enter the head. They then illumine and enfire the brain-mind, thereby made responsive to superphysical powers and states of consciousness, or ·" freed " from the imprisoning limitations of the physical body. Hermes with his staff has then metaphorically liberated Persephone from the Underworld. At the command of Zeus (the Monad) and with the submission of Pluto (the disciplined body elemental), Persephone (the personal soul) is restored by Hermes (the Serpent Fire) to her Mother (the Ego in Causal Consciousness). From these human interpretations it will be seen that, as in the microcosmic meaning of every inspired allegory, the *dramatis personae* represent aspects of one individual and the whole drama is enacted *within* man as an interior experience.

Such are some of the possible interpretations of this traditional story from the Eleusinian Mysteries, of which many of those who now find themselves deeply interested in Occult Science may have been members; for, in their outer garb, the Eleusinia were public spectacles and every distinguished citizen of Athens could become an Initiate of the Outer or Lesser Mysteries. At first they merely received and enacted the symbolic glyph. As they passed from the Outer or Lesser to the Inner or Greater Mysteries, allegory gave way to reality. Then, as the Initiating Hierophant touched the Candidate with the Wand or Rod of Power, the Thyrsus, the interior, spinal forces symbolised by the Caduceus began to awaken. The Initiate was thereby freed from the body, which became entranced and was placed in the care of the Priests. The Initiated soul, symbolised by Persephone freed, could then ascend into Egoic consciousness or become one with Demeter, its Goddess Mother.

The Caduceus has another meaning. That which I have already given is its possible dynamic significance, but it is also suceptible of a philosophical interpretation, as are all the great symbols. In this latter interpretation the two serpents represent the pairs of opposites, such as success and failure, heat and cold, pleasure and pain, happiness and despair, love and hate, health and disease, presence and absence, activity and inertia— all the opposites, in fact. Before man can be perfected and fully liberated, he must have become equipoised in consciousness between all the pairs, being equally indifferent to either of their components. This attainment is called in Hindu philosophy *vairāgya* (desirelessness, detachment) and *upeksha*, another Sanskrit word meaning the poise of indifference, the dynamic balance between all pairs of opposites. The whole nature has then been brought into perfect equipoise, dynamic equilibrium, and has in consequence become relatively immovable, stable like the gyroscope. Thereafter, touched as it were by the staff of Hermes, the soul (Persephone) is no longer a prisoner of Pluto (bodily desires and other limitations) but is liberated, free. Such, in outline only, is a portion of the mystery of the Caduceus, such the story of Persephone, told only in the earliest of the *Homeric Hymns.*

COSMIC CYCLES PORTRAYED BY THE LIFE STORY OF ABRAHAM

Consideration of possible applications of these principles to the story of Abraham is now resumed.

In the cosmogonical interpretations of the dramatic narratives which are included in the Scriptures and Mythologies of ancient peoples the out-poured, Monad-bearing life-wave, personified by leading characters in the stories, flows forth from its spiritual Source into Cosmos, Solar System, Scheme, Chain, Round, Planet and Race.[1] In this process of forthgoing the Monads enter and become embodied in planes and levels of consciousness which are successively more material. Such, it is suggested, is the first Biblical account of a major cycle of manifestation as told in the story of Abraham. A second account—which is simply a successive phase in which the whole is repeated—is portrayed in the story of Isaac. The close similarity between the two narratives suggests that both are presented as allegories of the same general principle; for Isaac's wife was also lent to a King, Abimelech, after being passed off as a sister.[2] A third account is given in the still later cycle of Jacob, in which the portrayal of the evolution of both life and form in general, and of the human Ego in particular, is carried to a further stage.

SUB-CYCLES PORTRAYED BY LOT, HAGAR AND ISHMAEL

Phases of the evolution of particular principles of Cosmos and man are also, and with the greatest skill, allegorically described in the stories of Lot, Hagar and Ishmael. Terah, as has been suggested, is the Monadic Ray. Abram is that Ray individualised in a Causal Body, symbolised

[1] q.v. Glossary—Chain.

[2] The stories of the journeys and adventures of Ulysses, the Argonauts, Perseus, Theseus, Hercules and other heroes may be regarded as further examples of this allegorical method as employed in Greek Mythology. The life stories of Jesus the Christ, Shri Krishna, Shri Rāmachandra, the Lord Gautama Buddha and Shri Shankarāchārya may be similarly interpreted as descriptions of major and minor cycles of forthgoing and return, macrocosmic and microcosmic.

by the land of Canaan. Bethel is the Monadic Centre within the Causal Body, the interior Divine Presence, " the living God. "[1] Sarai, before her name is changed, is the unillumined (barren) lower, concrete, analytical mind embracing the higher, abstract, synthesising mind (married to Abram). She has not as yet brought forth the still nascent intuition (Isaac-to-be). In such an interpretation Sarai is correctly described as both wife and sister of Abram. The higher and lower minds may indeed be regarded as husband and wife, because of their intimate relationship and mutual use of the same power and principle—that of thought. Sarai might also be regarded as Abram's sister since both higher and the lower aspects of mental activity share a common source—the human intellect.

Lot represents the reincarnating, unfolding spiritual Self or Ego of man, whilst in one possible interpretation[2] of the incident in which his wife (shakti)[3] was turned into a pillar of salt,[4] she personifies *kundalini*—the creative fire resident in the spinal cord of man and so, in this particular case, of Lot himself. Her petrification after looking back at the stricken, sinful cities—undesirable continuance of a practice pertaining to an earlier evolutionary phase—refers to the loss of the fruits of the sublimation of this great power or *shakti* caused by its over-expression in sexual indulgence, and even perversion.[5] The inspiration and genius which result from its successful transmutation are unable to find expression in a brain and a nervous system which are habitually bedulled by excess. Symbolically this power in Lot (his *shakti* or wife) is petrified, or turned into a pillar of salt. Although presented as man and wife or two separate people, in accordance with the method employed in the Sacred Language they are in fact one. The male partner represents the divine Self and the female, wife or consort, his active expression as power. Brahma-Vāch[6] constitutes an example drawn from the Hindu pantheon.

THE SYMBOL OF THE PILLAR

If interpreted microcosmically, pillars, trees, staves, wands and rods are, in addition to other meanings, used as symbols for the spinal cord of man. When serpents are associated with any of them, as so often occurs,

---

[1] II *Cor.* 6: 16.

[2] Others are suggested on p. 269–70.

[3] *Shakti* (Sk.), " ability ", " power ", capability, faculty, strength. The outgoing energy of a god is spoken of as his wife or *shakti*. Thus, although a Deity or a central personage and his consort or wife are prescribed as two separate people, the latter (wife) actually personifiess attributes or powers of the former (husband). In consequence, as said above, the supposed pair in reality represent one being.

[4] *Gen.* 19: 26.

[5] *Gen.* 13: 13; *Jude* v. 7.

[6] *Brahma-Vāch* (Sk.), q.v. Glossary—*Vāch*

a reference to the presence of *kundalini* or the creative Serpent Fire in the spinal cord is intended. Notable examples are; the serpent and the tree of knowledge of good and evil in the Garden of Eden;[1] the turning of Aaron's rod into a serpent before Pharaoh;[2] the elevation of a serpent upon a pole healed the Israelites from the " bites " of serpents (extremes of egoism and sensuality);[3] the Egyptian Goddesses Nekhebet and Uatchit[4] holding upright flower stems with serpents entwined round them; the Caduceus or staff of the Greek God Mercury or Hermes; and the trees upon which in Grecian mythology the Golden Fleece was hung in Colchis guarded by the serpent or dragon, and on which the golden apples of the Hesperides grew, also guarded by a dragon—in this case Ladon.

In another interpretation the hidden treasure of supreme bliss—symbolised by the Golden Fleece and the golden apples of Greek mythology—is said in Hinduism to be guarded by a very powerful and terrible " snake " (*ahamkara*, Sk. " egoism "), which envelops the self with its three heads (the *gunas*,[5] Sk. or three attributes of matter—activity, rhythm and inertia). The wise man is able to enjoy the hidden treasure of bliss only after cutting off these three heads and destroying this serpent with the great sword of spiritual knowledge.[6] One is here reminded of the second labour of Hercules, in which he killed the nine-headed Hydra of Lerna by cutting off all its heads and thereafter searing the neck of each with fire.

Lot is rightly (the Ego being a manifestation of the Monad) made to be a relative (nephew) of Abram and to share in the riches gained from the descent into Egypt, meaning the fruits of evolutionary progress resulting from physical incarnation. This is also indicated by Lot's choice of the plain of Jordon, well watered and fruitful.

RIVERS IN SYMBOLOGY

In the Symbolical Language rivers in those countries in which the events recorded in Scriptures and myths are said to take place may have several meanings. One of these is the evolutionary pathway followed by the Soul of man. As rivers generally rise from sources higher than the countryside through which they pass, and not infrequently in mountain ranges, so the source of both cosmic and human life exists at highly

---

[1] *Gen.* 3: 1–7.

[2] *Ex.* 7: 10.

[3] *Lu.* 21: 8.

[4] q.v. *The Gods of the Egyptians*, E. A. Wallis Budge, Vol. I, pp. 438 and 440.

[5] *Gunas*—q.v. Glossary.

[6] Adapted from *Viveka-Chūdāmani*, " Crest-Jewel of Wisdom", *Shloka* 302, Sri Śankara-chārya, translation by Mohini M. Chatterji.

etherialised states of matter and exalted levels of divine consciousness.[1] The river is also used as a symbol of both the divine life itself and its out-pouring from its spiritual origin towards and into the material Universe and the mortal self of man, appropriately symbolised by the plains irrigated and made fruitful by that life. Rivers are also symbols of those interior canals through which truths perceived in uplifted states of awareness can flow into the mind-brain.

As stated in Volume I of this work the River Jordan, like the Nile in Egyptian symbology, is also used throughout the Scriptures as a topographical symbol for the current of creative fire playing along the *sushumna nādi* (Sk. " tube ") in the centre of the spinal cord. The Dead (salty) Sea into which the Jordan flows symbolises the physical body, and especially, the sacrum at the base of the spine. The Mountains of Lebanon, where the waters of Jordan rise and flow down to the plain below, aptly represent the spiritual source whence the divine, creative fire arises and flows along its appointed channels in both Nature and man. Other examples of this form of symbology are the Rivers Jumna, Ganges, Godavari, Eridanus, and the four Rivers of Eden. The Rivers Alpheus and Peneus of Greek mythology are of special interest, since they can be related to the canals and currents of *kundalini* known as *Idā* and *Pingala*; for it was by the redirection of these two Rivers that Hercules cleansed the Augean stables. The sublimation, and so redirection, of *kundalini* as the sex force brings about the transmutation of desire and the purification of the bodily life (the Augean stables).

Valuable instruction may be gained from such an interpretation of the fifth labour of Hercules; for he did not purify the stables by digging out the huge accumulation produced during the preceding thirty years by the herd of 3,000 oxen owned by Augeas. Indeed, this would have been an almost impossible task, even for Hercules, or at any rate a very prolonged one. Instead, with great wisdom he went to higher ground and diverted the two streams, Alpheus and Peneus, making them flow through the stalls, which were thus cleaned out in a single day.

Similarly, long established undesirable habits and addictions cannot be overcome by attempting to attack them direct in a conflict of will-thought. Success can best be achieved by withdrawing attention from them and entering those higher levels of human consciousness (the source of the two Rivers) at which pure and spiritualising currents of force exist, thereby causing the indulgences and their debasing effects (animal excretions) to disappear, die out, or symbolically be washed away. Earth mirrors heaven and, as in this case, in their use of topographical symbols

---

[1] In Hindu cosmogony this is given a *Sanskrit* name, *Ādi*, meaning the first and " highest " of the seven planes of Nature.   q.v. Glossary.

the illumined authors of the Scriptures and myths of ancient peoples skilfully used that fact to portray and deliver to man their treasures of spiritual wisdom.

" AN HORROR OF GREAT DARKNESS " [1]

In verses nine to seventeen of Chapter Fifteen of the *Book of Genesis* certain very strange supernormal phenomena are described. After the Lord had encouraged Abram and promised him a son and numerous seed, the land of Canaan is again assured to him. This covenant is said later to have been confirmed by a sign and a vision. Sacrificial animals and birds were offered, the sun set and a deep sleep fell upon Abram. As in a dream, whilst the sun was setting, " an horror of great darkness" descended upon him and the Lord uttered the dire prophecy that the Israelites would be strangers in foreign land, in which they would be afflicted throughout a period of four hundred years. This prophecy was later fulfilled by the captivity and bondage of the Israelites in both Egypt and Chaldea.[2] Thereupon, apparently still in the dream, after the sun had set, a smoking furnace appeared in the darkness and a burning lamp passed between the various portions of the sacrifice.

This episode, and especially the " horror of great darkness " which enveloped Abram, are susceptible of interpretation as allegories of the mental darkness and doubt by which mystics are on occasion assailed. The very divinity, immortality, and even significance, of the individual and the Universe are then doubted. Spiritual blindness assails the aspirant. Matter, symbolised by the dark smoke of the furnace, temporarily obscures the vision of the Higher, Immortal Self which normally functions as a centre of consciousness in the mortal personality. Nothing then seems true; all things appear false, or at best uncertain and doubtful. In this ordeal the neophyte sees only the material Universe with all its unreliability, uncertainties and dangers (the horrors of great darkness)—as it appears to him in his mentally darkened state.

OFFERINGS AS SYMBOLS OF SURRENDERED INDIVIDUALITY

Abram, by virtue of his sacrificial acts, emerged successfully from his nightmare of horror. Similarly, the problem arising from periods of darkness and spiritual aridity can be solved by the sacrifice of self-centredness. The solution, given allegorically in this Chapter of *Genesis*, consists of the renunciation of I-am-ness and the offering of the whole nature to

[1] *Gen.* 15: 12.
[2] *Ex.* and II *Kings*, XXV.

the great purposes of life, whatever they may prove to be.   If this interpretation is acceptable, then the nature of Abram's sacrifice is found to be
allegorically descriptive of the wholeness of the act of self-surrender.   The
heifer, the goat and the ram, for example, being restricted to the surface
of the Earth, represent the three vehicles of form—mental, emotional and
physical—whilst the turtledove and the pigeon,[1] which can rise freely into
the air, represent those of life—intuitional and spiritual.   The female and
male creative elements and powers in the body (the heifer and the ram)
and the mind (the goat) must all be sublimated and sacrificed as far as
separated self-individuality is concerned.   The two life principles of
intuition (the turtledove) and spirit (the pigeon or ordinary dove[2]), in
recognition of their universal, divine origin, must similarly be surrendered
as purely personal attributes.

Sunset brought the miracle of the passage of the smoking furnace
and the burning lamp amidst the components of the sacrifice.   If in the
dark night of the soul, and despite that darkness, the great surrender of
I-ness can be made and sustained, then all dross is burnt out of the lower
nature.   The whole man, thus purified, then becomes illumined by the
light of the Higher Self, the Monad-Ego in the Causal Body, symbolised
by the flame and the burning lamp respectively.   Thus, even in the midst
of surrender and renunciation the infinite power of the God within is realised,
and the knowledge is born that all aspirations will one day be fulfilled.
The completeness of this consummation throughout the whole make-up
of man is allegorically indicated in the last four verses of this Chapter; for
in them the Lord makes a covenant with Abram and names the Twelve
Tribes (microcosmically man's inherent zodiacal attributes) which shall
be his fruit and seed.

Whilst admittedly the names differ from the Biblical account, the
following correspondences between the Twelve Tribes of Israel (omitting
Ephraim and Manassah but including Joseph and Dinah) and the twelve
zodiacal Signs and their attributes have been deduced by astrologers from
the words addressed by the dying Jacob to his sons, and from his prophecies
of the future of each Tribe:[3]

Reuben	Aquarius	" Unstable as water.... "
Simeon and Levi	Gemini	A close fraternal association.
Judah	Leo	The strong lion of his Tribe, " a lion's whelp.... "
Zebulun	Pisces	" ....shall dwell at the haven of the sea.... "

[1] *Gen.* 15: 9.
[2] cf. *Matt.* 3: 16.
[3] *Gen.* 49.

Issachar	Taurus	" ....a strong ass couching down ", and therefore associated with stables, byres, etc.
Dan	Scorpio	" ....a serpent by the way, an adder in the path, that biteth...."
Gad	Aries (ruled by Mars)	" ....a troop shall overcome him; but he shall overcome at the last. "
Naphtali	Capricorn	" ....a hind (deer) let loose...."
Joseph	Sagittarius	" ....his bow abode in strength.... "
Benjamin	Cancer	" ....shall raven as a wolf.... "
Asher[1]	Libra	..
Dinah[2]	Virgo	The only daughter of Jacob.

An astrological interpretation is also implied by the use of two symbols (Aries the Ram and Capricorn the Goat) for the components of the offerings and to represent the principles of man. The Twelve Tribes thus closely correspond to the twelve Signs of the Zodiac, the powers of which are inherent in the human Monad. As a result of the involutionary and evolutionary processes[3] these powers will gradually develop and ultimately be made fully manifest.

The supreme " promise " made by " Life " (the Lord God) to the spiritual Self of every human being (Abram) is that within the Monad reside all the powers of the Cosmos, and that in due course those powers will be unfolded and consciously wielded by perfected man. As long, however, as one clings to the illusion of separated self-individuality, so long will the fulfilment of the purposes of life be delayed. As soon as self-separateness is wholly and finally renounced (as indicated by the allegory of Abram's sacrifice), so soon will darkness be banished, light attained and perfection achieved.

This great truth of fulfilment through renunciation is, indeed, inculcated throughout the Bible. It is the burden of the Sermon on the Mount and is revealed in various Biblical allegories of the temporary rejection of a certain stone and its ultimate recognition as the chief corner-stone.[4] The

---

[1] *Gen.* 30: 13.

[2] *Gen.* 30: 21. Dinah is generally included by astrologers in order to complete the twelve Signs of the Zodiac, although she is not referred to in the Bible as the head of a Tribe.

[3] q.v. *The Hidden Wisdom in the Holy Bible*, Vol. I, Pt. IV, Geoffrey Hodson.

[4] *Matt.* 21: 42; *Ps.* 118: 22; *Acts* 4: 11; *Eph.* 2: 20.

darkness, conflict and ultimate surrender of Jesus in Gethsemane,[1] followed by His Resurrection and Ascension, portray the same great truth. Renunciation is thus adduced as the keynote of the spiritual life and self-sacrifice as the first step. Self-personality, together with acquisitiveness and possessiveness, must be renounced. Paradoxically such surrender brings not loss, but gain. Indeed, life *is* fulfilled by renunciation.

---

[1] *Matt.* 26: 39.

PART SIX

ABRAHAM, SARAH, ISAAC AND REBEKAH

CHAPTER I

ABRAM JOURNEYETH THROUGH CANAAN TO EGYPT

FROM consideration of some general principles concerning the Hebrew nation, the Allegorical Language and a number of symbols, a return is now made to the interpretation of particular incidents in the life-story of Abram.

Gen. 12: 1. *Now the LORD had said unto Abram, Get thee out of thy country, and from thy kindred, and from thy father's house, unto a land that I will shew thee:*

In his book, *The Bible as History*, Werner Keller writes:

" The country of which the Bible is speaking in this case is Haran. Terah, his son Abram, his daughter-in-law Sarai, and his grandson Lot lived there. (*Gen.* 11: 31). What was actually meant by Haran was until recently almost entirely unknown. We knew nothing of its early history. All the old Babylonian documents were silent about the middle reaches of the Euphrates, Mesopotamia, the land between the rivers, where Haran once stood....

" The excavations of Tell Hariri brought a wealth of new discoveries to a chapter of the history of the ancient East that is still unwritten. No one yet knew how close a connection the finds at Mari would prove to have with quite familiar passages in the Bible... Mari lay at the intersection of the great caravan routes from west to east and from north to south. It is not surprising, therefore, that the traffic in goods, which extended from Cyprus and Crete to Asia Minor and Mesopotamia, necessitated a lively correspondence on clay concerning imports and exports....

" On other clay tablets the Assyriologists dealing with these reports of governors and district commissioners of the Mari empire came across, one after another, a whole series of familiar sounding names from Biblical history—names like Peleg, and Serug, Nahor, and Terah and Haran. ' These are the generations of Shem, ' says *Gen.* 11. '....Peleg lived thirty years and begat Reu....And Reu lived two and thirty years and begat Serug....And Serug lived thirty years and begat Nahor....and Nahor lived nine and twenty years and begat Terah.... And Terah lived seventy years and begat Abram, Nahor, and Haran.'

" Names of Abraham's forefathers emerge from these dark ages as names of cities in northwest Mesopotamia. They lie in Padan-Aram, the plain of Aram. In the centre of it lies Haran which, according to its description, must have been a flourishing city in the nineteenth and eighteenth centuries B.C. Haran, the home of Abraham, father of the patriarchs, the birth-place of the Hebrew people, is here for the first time historically attested, for contemporary texts refer to it. Further up the same Balikh valley lay the city with an equally well-known Biblical name, Nahor, the home of Rebecca, wife of Isaac....

" The road from Haran, the home of the Patriarchs, to the land of Canaan runs south for more than 600 miles. It follows the River Balikh as far as the Euphrates, thence by a caravan route thousands of years old via the oasis of Palmyra, the Tadmor of the Bible, to Damascus, and from there in a south-westerly direction to the Lake of Galilee. It is one of the great trade routes that have always led from the Euphrates to Jordan, from the kingdoms of Mesopotamia to the Phoenician seaports on the Mediterranean and the distant Nile lands in Egypt. "[1]

From these references to the findings of modern archaeology a return is made to consideration of the Biblical text. In making a personal and racial covenant with Abram and his people, Jehovah changes in character from the universal, creative " God " (*Elohim*) to the deity of a single tribe. Implicit behind the first of these concepts must be the unknown, incognisable Deity, the one Infinite God, Source of Creation as a whole, the One Alone. The adoption by the Israelites of the Supreme Deity as their own tribal god was, in consequence, an unjustifiable appropriation; for the *Book of Genesis* and the Supreme Creator (Emanator) revealed within it are above all things universal. The first " creation " (*Gen.* 1: 1-25) is of the Universe as a whole, whilst the second (*Gen.* 1: 26, 27) may be presumed to be pertaining to the humanity of our Solar System. The further limitation of the One Uncreate to become the deity of a single tribe, who exhibits the human and even sub-human weaknesses of a jealous, wrathful and blood-loving tribal fetish, has led to much confusion and also to the appalling degradation of the idea of the Supreme Deity.

ABRAM—HISTORICAL AND MYSTICAL

Abram was the son of Terah, with whom he journeyed from the city of Ur of the Chaldees. The name " Abram " may possibly provide further information concerning his origin, and this view may perhaps usefully be here advanced. Etymologically it suggests that he may have been an

---

[1] q.v. *The Bible as History*, pp. 42, 45, 48, 51, 52 and 53, Werner Keller.

ex-Brahman who, having repudiated his caste, became Abram or " No-Brahman. " This finds support from the tradition that some of the very early ancestors of the later Jews are said to be descended from the Chandālas of India, many of them being ex-Brahmans who sought refuge in Chaldea, in Scinde (Sind) and in Aria (Iran) and were truly born from their father A-Bram (Sk. No-Brahman) some 8,000 years B.C.[1]

The word Abram is also said to be derived from *Arba* or *Abhra*, the " clouds " or the bosom of the Eternal One. This translation of the word *Arba* leads one's thoughts to the New Testament, where a mystical reference to the great Patriarch is made. In the Parable of the rich man and the beggar related by the Lord Christ,[2] the bosom of Abraham[3] may be regarded as referring to the state of consciousness in which the spiritual Self of man perpetually abides and to which, by means of contemplation, the mortal personality can attain. This metaphysical experience includes full realisation of union with God, of man-Spirit with God-Spirit and through That with all that lives. In Hinduism this state is called *Moksha*[4] (Liberation), in Buddhism *Nirvāna* (the Supreme Goal), and in Christianity Salvation. In the Parable, the phrase " carried by the angels into Abraham's bosom " allegorically describes realisation of unity with God. The reference to the disciple John leaning on the bosom of Jesus[5] is susceptible of a similar interpretation, implying the attainment by John of mystical union with the Christ.

In this method of Biblical study the characters—divine, semi-divine, patriarchal and human—are thus regarded as personifications of principles and powers of both Nature the Macrocosm and of man the microcosm. This is supported by St. Paul, who writes: " Now these things happened unto them for ensamples.... " [6] and again: " For it is written, that Abraham had two sons, the one by a bondmaid, the other by a freewoman....Which things are an allegory.... "[7]

Since the *Book of Genesis* may thus be regarded as being of an allegorical nature, it is not unreasonable to assume that the same could also be true of the other inspired Books of the Bible. One might even go further than this and assert that the practice of studying the Scriptures of the world in their literal, " dead-letter " meaning and as records of actual historical events *alone* can, as we have seen, lead to both confusion of mind and a degradation of the concept of Deity. This is indeed of very great importance; for the presentation on Scriptural authority of the Supreme

---

[1] q.v. *The Secret Doctrine*, H. P. Blavatsky, Vol. III, Adyar Ed., p. 205, and Vol. VI, Glossary—Abram.

[2] *Lk.* 14: 19–30. [3] *Lk.* 16: 22.

[4] *Moksha* (Sk.)—" To release ". The state attained when a man becomes a *Dhyān-Chohan*. One who is thus released is called a *Jivanmukta* (Sk.), " freed " spirit. Liberation from the delusion of self-separateness (Hinduism).

[5] *Jn.* 13: 23. [6] I *Cor.* 10: 11.

[7] *Gal.* 4: 22, 24.

16

Emanator of the Universe and Embodiment of its Life, Law and Intelligence as the anthropomorphic God of the Jews has indeed turned otherwise religious minds to agnosticism, and even atheism. Furthermore, the orthodox Christian teaching of man's complete reliance, with all its morally weakening influence, upon an external Redeemer alone instead of also upon an interior redemptive power, may legitimately be regarded as one of the consequences of this profound error of anthropomorphism.

If, however, the Scriptures are studied as being both allegorical and historical, these and other unfortunate mistakes can be avoided. Such an approach is also found to be supported in the text of the Bible itself. St. Paul writes of the essential redemptive Presence and Power within man as follows: " ....Christ in you, the hope of glory ",[1] "....work out your own salvation with fear and trembling. For it is God which worketh in you.... "[2] and " Know ye not that ye are the temple of God, and that the Spirit of God dwelleth in you? ".[3] Thus St. Paul is found to be using the terms " Christ " and " God " as personifications of principles and powers which are present *within* every human being. Abram's wife, Sarai, may be similarly regarded though not, of course, as an interior divine Being and Presence, since she herself was still human.

THE STORY OF SARAI

Sarai, according to Biblical history, was the beautiful but barren wife of Abram, who made her pose as his sister in order that later she could become a concubine of Pharaoh. Abram's deceitful action caused Pharaoh and his people to be plagued, and the imposture when discovered aroused the King's wrath. Read literally, Abram's action is most repellant to the mind, especially since he is presented as a man of God, His chosen agent in the founding of the Hebrew nation and its settlement in the land of Canaan. The incongruity—one amongst a great many in the Old Testament—disappears, however, if the supposed episode be interpreted as an allegory descriptive of evolutionary stages through which humanity passes, particularly the development of the intellect. I consider this idea to be of sufficient interest and importance to justify the fuller consideration of it which now follows.

The conception of Isaac in Abraham's old age, after the changing of Sarai's name to Sarah, provides in part a key to the symbology. As stated above, she represents a phase in the evolution of the human mind, which remains barren of intuition until Egoic experience (Abraham in his old age)

---

[1] *Col.* 1: 27.
[2] *Phil.* 2: 12, 13.
[3] I *Cor.* 3: 16.

makes her fruitful by union with him as a personification of the synthesising, prophetic intelligence. The birth[1] of Isaac refers to the succeeding phase in the evolution of the mind when it becomes illumined by the intuition.

A reference to the total sevenfold nature of man must here be advanced in order to make clear the interpretation which follows of the relationship between Abram and Sarai. In occult philosophy man is regarded as a threefold spiritual being, a manifestion of divine Will, divine Wisdom and divine Intelligence. For purposes of self-expression and evolution this triple Self is incarnated in four mortal, material bodies—the mental, the emotional, the etheric and the physical. Chapter Twelve of *Genesis* is interpreted as consisting chiefly of allegorical descriptions of the evolution of the human intellect. The higher and the lower mind together are represented by Sarai. Her marriage in youth to Abram refers to the first emergence of the reasoning faculty in early man, as also in every child. The vehicle of thought may be taken as the outer form of Sarai, and the higher conceptual faculties as her Soul. In earlier phases of human evolution these powers are but nascent. Symbolically, Sarai is for a long time barren. A relationship with the inner Ego (marriage to Abram) is as yet unfruitful.

The germs of all intellectual powers and activities are, however, potentially present within both the Ego (Abram) and the new-formed vehicles (Sarai). Before they can be fructified (in the allegory the marriage) and develop as pure reason, and ultimately intuition (personified by Isaac), much bodily experience is necessary. This is referred to in the story by departure from famine-stricken Canaan (the unawakened, unfruitful state) and entry into the rich and fertile country of Egypt. The land of Khem is here used as a symbol of the physical plane into which Sarai, representing the nascent mind, is admitted or incarnated, implying its close association with the physical world and its indwelling consciousness. This experience stimulates and arouses into activity the hitherto dormant mental faculties, whilst Sarai's admittance to Pharaoh's house and her life there typify certain experiences which from below, as it were, awaken, draw out and develop the powers of the mind.

THE SUBTERFUGE

The supposed deceit, in the dead letter reading, places Abram in a very unfavourable light. It may, however, possibly be regarded as an allegorical reference to the natural relationship between the Ego and its vehicles rather than as a record of a most reprehensible act of which it

[1] In all inspired allegories marriage symbolises the union between the spiritual and the material parts of human nature, whilst the resultant motherhood refers to the development of the intuitive faculty, personified by the offspring.

is difficult to believe the great Patriarch could have been guilty. Examining the former approach—the allegorical—the spiritual, abstract intelligence and the formal, analytical mind (personified respectively by Abram and Sarai) are, in fact, more nearly as brother and sister[1] than as husband and wife; for they are of the same substance and arise from the same source, the Universal Mind. This reading, which may indicate that the subterfuge has a special significance, is confirmed in verse twelve of Chapter Twenty, where Sarai is made to be Abram's half-sister.

Furthermore, the inner, spiritual Self of man (Abram) in the Causal Body, in which vehicle are garnered the fruits of mental, emotional and physical awareness, can only obtain fully realised immortality or be saved ("they will kill me"—verse twelve) as a result of repeated incarnation.[2] In other words, as earlier stated, Sarai as the manifestation of the spiritual Self in terms of the formal mind must enter the physical body (the house of Pharaoh) before the Ego (Abram) can attain to liberation, or save his life. The fruits—power, wisdom, knowledge and faculties garnered during successive lives on Earth—are represented by the riches which Abram gained as a result of his residence in Egypt. These he was later able to take with him back to the land of Canaan, "the Promised Land", symbol of the abode of the Immortal Self of man.

THE RESULTANT PLAGUES

The wholly inconsistent punishment of Pharaoh by plagues because of his perfectly innocent acceptance of Sarai was either a grave injustice or was included in the narrative to serve as a blind for an underlying truth. In its psychological significance the record of the incident may also indicate the discipline, the trials and the difficulties which the burgeoning mind brings to man in his daily life. Animals, which are guided largely by instinct, are free from the many difficulties and errors, born of faulty reasoning, which " plague " mankind up to the time when the human mind is fully developed and in control. Pharaoh does not slay Abram for the seeming deceit and the plagues, as would have been both justifiable and within his power as an absolute Monarch. This unusual clemency towards an exposed criminal, which was out of character if one may trust Egyptian history, tends to support the view that the story is indeed not intended to be taken literally, but rather as an allegory describing certain fundamental procedures of Nature designed to produce out of primitive humanity a

---

[1] *Gen.* 12 : 13.
[2] q.v. *Reincarnation, Fact or Fallacy*, Geoffrey Hodson.

race of perfected men.[1] Clearly, then, the whole story is to be regarded as an allegorical description of the nature of man, and more particularly of the development of the human mind (Sarai herself) through bodily experience (entry into Egypt and Pharaoh's house). If this view be regarded as acceptable and in harmony with the purposes of the authors, the distasteful character of the episode and the slur upon Abram himself are removed. The recognised custom of those who wrote in the Symbolical Language, of concealing power-bestowing truths beneath a veil of incongruity[2], supports this approach.

As earlier stated, knowledge of the constitution of man—particularly of his spiritual nature and its almost infinite potentialities—can indeed bestow theurgic and hypnotic powers upon its possessor. Such knowledge was in olden days reserved for the Initiates of the Ancient Mysteries. Even today, when the information is more freely available, it still needs to be translated into personal experience before it can be fully used as a source of self-empowerment.

THE BIRTH OF ISAAC—PSYCHOLOGICAL, UNIVERSAL, RACIAL

The apparent miracle of the change from barrenness to mother-hood late in Sarai's life indicates the result of evolutionary progress. In a microcosmic interpretation it is of interest that her name was changed to Sarah from this time onwards.[3] Isaac, the first-born son, partly personifies the faculty of reason, the development of which was the supreme attainment of the most advanced Fourth Root Race men. Its further unfoldment into direct intuitive perception is the work of the later sub-races of the Fifth Root Race,[4] the Aryan.

With the other wives of great Biblical figures from Eve onwards, Sarai or Sarah also Macrocosmically symbolises Universal Space, and that root substance [5] in its later guise as Nature herself, the mother or womb whence all creation (personified in this case by Isaac) is " born ". Since the Macrocosm is reflected in the microcosm, Sarah—and indeed all mothers in inspired allegories and myths—also represents the human womb.

---

[1] cf. St. Paul: " Till we all come in the unity of the faith, and of the knowledge of the Son of God, unto a perfect man, unto the measure of the stature of the fulness of Christ." (*Eph.* 4: 13).

[2] Incongruous only according to modern standards of morality, which were not necessarily applicable in those days.

[3] *Gen.* 17: 15.

[4] q.v. The Chart included in the Introduction to Pt. V of this book.

[5] *Mūlaprakriti* (Sk.), " Undifferentiated substance ", q.v. Glossary.

RECAPITULATION

Thus far in *Genesis* the racial story has been carried from the Third Root Race (Adam and Eve) to the close of that epoch. The Flood and the emergence from the Ark represent the transition into the Fourth Root Race. The account continues into the later sub-races, notably the fifth—the Semitic—of the Fourth Root Race, personified by Abram and his immediate descendants. In these sub-races the mental faculties (Sarai) first began to develop as a result of both a spiritual impulse (marriage to Abram) and a physical experience (entry into Egypt and Pharaoh's house).

The history is also told of the Jewish nation which scripturally sprang from Adam, Noah and Abram, and which was ultimately taken to its national home, the land of Canaan. The great Official (*Manu*)[1] in the Adept Order Who is responsible for the evolution of races is personified by both Noah and Abram, whilst Terah refers to a predecessor, an Adept of still higher rank in the great Order.

ABRAM, FATHER OF A NATION

At the appointed time the *Manu*, Who is referred to as the father of the Root Race under His charge, leads it from its birth-place into its future homeland. Thus Abram, the first Patriarch of the Jewish nation, who under divine inspiration leads its progenitors out of Ur of the Chaldees into the land of Canaan, typifies this great Being.

The rest of the Old Testament combines with a supposed history of the Jewish race an allegorical description of cosmic, planetary, racial and individual phases of evolution and their fruits. The two are thus blended, often with great skill, the former being used as the basis for the allegories by means of which the latter are both revealed and concealed. From this present point onwards the narrative, whilst often descending to mere tribal quarrelling, superstition and primitive standards of morality, gradually reveals both profound spiritual truths of universal application and also aspects of the history of the Hebrew nation. Abram is presented as the father and inspired leader of that branch of the Jewish race which settled in Palestine, somewhat as described in Chapters Thirteen, Fourteen and Fifteen of the *Book of Genesis*. These Chapters are more historical than allegorical, though not entirely without application to the spiritual, intellectual and physical development of man as both a race and an individual.

Abram and Lot, the two leaders enriched by residence in Egypt, returned to the very place from which their journey had begun, namely Bethel. Here again an evolutionary cycle and its fruits are suggested. The name " Bethel " means " the House of the Lord ", and thus could perhaps be taken as an allusion to the Causal Body in which the Monad-Ego resides,

[1] *Manu.* See. Pt. II of this Volume, and Glossary.

In this microcosmic interpretation the Egyptian adventure is descriptive of incarnation in the flesh and the resultant Egoic enrichment. In the larger sense all journeys of forthgoing and return, including those of cosmic life itself, are indicated.[1]

THE MASTER KEY—THE PRINCIPLE OF FORTHGOING AND RETURN

Knowledge of the principle of major and minor cycles of involution and evolution was and is a profoundly occult revelation, the full significance of which has ever been reserved as a secret of Initiation. Exoterically, the doctrine has been made known by means of mythological stories of epic journeys of forthgoing and return completed by Saviours and heroes. The Lord Christ presented this theme in the Parable of the Prodigal Son[2]. The story of His own life—the historicity[3] of which does not here come into question—from His Nativity, to His death and burial in a rock tomb (the forthgoing divine life, personified by the Christ, becomes incarnate in the mineral kingdom), followed by His Resurrection and Ascension to the right hand of God, may be regarded as itself an allegory of the same great truth. Indeed, this knowledge provides one of the master keys to the understanding of life itself and to the evocation, use, and possible misuse, of occult and spiritual powers; hence, I repeat, its general presentation in the form of parable and myth and its full revelation to pledged neophytes alone.

This statement of some general principles is now followed by a more detailed consideration of the Biblical narrative, using particularly the method generally employed in the interpretation of allegories. This consists of regarding the *dramatis personae* from two points of view. One of these is that they stand for powers in Nature and their interactions. The other is to regard people in the stories as personifications of levels and vehicles of consciousness of man, and their conduct as representing phases of human evolution. The account of the relationships between Abram, Sarai, Hagar and Ishmael is therefore now considered from these points of view—particularly the latter.

At the beginning of Part Five of this Volume the reader was informed that the Chapters of *Genesis* recording the life of Abram would not be taken seriatum. At all places regarded as appropriate, however, interpretations are offered of the more important incidents described in omitted passages. The consideration of each Chapter in succession is now resumed.

---

[1] See Charts facing p. 55.

[2] q.v. *The Hidden Wisdom in the Holy Bible*, Vol. I, Pt. IV, Geoffrey Hodson.

[3] q.v. *Aspects of the Christ* and *Esoteric Christianity*, Annie Besant; *The Hidden Wisdom in the Holy Bible*, Vol. I, Pt. V and *Lecture Notes of the School of the Wisdom*, Vol. II, Ch. VII, Sections 3 and 4, Geoffrey Hodson.

CHAPTER II

THE BIRTH OF ISHMAEL

SARAI, HAGAR AND ISHMAEL

Gen. 16. Sarai, being barren, giveth Hagar to Abram. Hagar fleeth from her mistress, is sent back by an angel to submit to her. Ishmael is born.

The lustful aspect of emotion, personified by Hagar, is the most difficult of all the human principles to subdue. History apart, Ishmael represents the psychological effect (son) of the unregulated activity of the desire nature, personified by his mother Hagar, whose relationship with Abram was irregular. Sarai, who gave Hagar to Abram, represents the mind which serves as a link between the Ego (Abram) and the emotional nature. The mind of itself, despite its beauty and brilliance, is barren. To be fruitful it must become the vehicle either for intuition or its reflection as certain lofty aspects and activities, such as pure devotion and universal love. At first desire predominates; the handmaid or bondswoman becomes the focus and centre of interest. The jealousy of Sarai indicates the deprivation which the mind suffers during emotional activity, and the whole episode portrays with great psychological insight and subtlety these phases and experiences of human development.

The reaction of the mind under such circumstances takes the form of the determination to banish desire. Thus, at the instance of Sarai, Hagar is sent into the wilderness in disgrace. Nevertheless she represents the life principle of the personality, its generative power and its reproductive urge. For her to be found by the Monad (the angel of the Lord) beside a fountain of water[1] (emblem of emotion) is therefore symbolically correct.

ISHMAEL—THE CHILD OF BONDAGE

Desire alone, whilst fruitful, can become antagonistic to the welfare and progress of the unfolding spiritual Self. Both racially and individually

[1] *Gen.* 16 ; 7.

over-accentuated sensuality is a barrier to Egoic unfoldment, especially
if the centre of consciousness is artificially placed in the feelings for too
long a time.   This is particularly true when the need for sensual experience
has begun to be outgrown.   Ishmael, whose hand is against every man
and against whom every man's hand is turned, represents the result,
the inevitable *karma*, of undue submission to desire.   Emotion is, however,
an essential form of self-expression, is indeed a great driving force.   Ishmael
is therefore rightly made to dwell among his brethen[1] (the other principles
of man).

The Lord's command to Hagar through an angel, to return and submit
herself to her mistress, if interpreted allegorically points out the one sure
way to the co-ordination of the emotional nature with its many aspects
and faculties.   The harmonious performance of its function as an instrument through which the Inner Self manifests is also indicated.   Ultimately
the previously outcast lower emotions become both the honoured vehicle
for the highest feelings and the conveyor of the noblest impulses from the
Monad-Ego to the man in his physical body.   This sublimated function
is indicated by the communion between the Lord (the Monad) and
Hagar (the life principle in the mortal personality) at the well " between
Kadesh and Bered ", which was called Beer-lahai-roi.

If, as St. Paul indicates[2], the narrative be thus regarded as an historical
metaphor, Chapter Sixteen of *Genesis* may be taken as allegorically descriptive of both the evolution of the capacity of feeling and the eventual
transcendence of desire itself.   The name Ishmael[3] is variously translated
as " God hears " and " God shall hear ", suggesting intercommunion
between the Divine and the human aspects of one individual.   This close
relationship can only occur after the grosser emotions have been sublimated
and the personal nature consequently sensitised to spiritual influences.
Such attainment of conscious communion with the divine Principle in
man bestows almost limitless power.   This is part of the reason for its
revelation by allegory and symbol rather than in plain language.   In the
Greater Mysteries the consciousness of the Initiate was illumined by this
knowledge and assisted in the transmutation of desire into will.   As recently
stated, outside of these deeply occult Institutions, such teachings were only
conveyed—as in the Bible, for example—under the veil of allegory, symbol
and myth.[4]

Whilst the narrative is thus analysed and possible interpretations
and applications to human evolution are suggested, the fact is not overlooked that the whole procedure of offering one's handmaid to one's husband
for purposes of procreation is immoral according to modern standards.

[1] *Gen.* 16 : 12.   [2] *Gal.* 4 : 22 *et seq.*   [3] *Gen.* 16 : 15.
[4] *Mk.* 4 : 11.

Such passages, of which there are a number of counterparts in the Old Testament, may also be read as indications of the outlook of earlier peoples, particularly wandering tribes, upon such human relationships. Indeed, this has already become apparent in the action of Abram in offering his wife Sarai as a concubine to Pharaoh. Whilst repellant to modern monogamist society, such conduct—as we have already seen—may not necessarily have deeply offended the moral standards of those days, particularly when polygamy may have been customary. Admittedly the story in its literal reading is not a very elevating one. The student of symbolism may, however, permissibly see in the manner in which this incident is described an illuminating commentary upon a particular phase (the sublimation of sexual desire in this case) of human development, both racial and individual. This view would seem to be supported by the institution of the practice of circumcision at that time, the full significance of which will be considered later.

Such an approach is, indeed, indicated both by the intervention of the Supreme Deity of the Universe, the Lord God, into purely mundane, human affairs and by the introduction into a Book of supposedly Divine revelation of passages which, to say the least, are of doubtful morality. These two characteristics of the Symbolical Language are, in fact, part of the method employed by writers using this particular category of literature, and are regarded by those—Origen and Moses Maimonides, for example—who interpret world Scriptures allegorically as hints or clues directing the mind of the reader to deliberately concealed undermeanings.

Gen. 17. The covenant is renewed. Abram's name changed. Circumcision instituted. Isaac with a numerous issue is promised.

Whilst Chapter Seventeen of *Genesis* continues the history of Abram and his family, it can also be read as descriptive of the further psychological development of man. Abram at the age of ninety-nine, which by reduction becomes nine, received from the Lord the promise of exceeding fruitfulness. Here, as in many other passages in the Bible, certain numbers are introduced, some of them being susceptible of symbolic interpretations by means of which undermeaning in the text may be discerned.

The science of numbers is of the remotest antiquity. Among the Aryans, the Greeks, the Assyrians and Egyptians, indications are found of a development which gave to numbers a mystical value and employed them in a system of symbolism which referred to something more than enumeration alone. Under this system[1] nine is regarded as indicating regeneration, a

---

[1] q.v. *Lecture Notes of the School of the Wisdom*, Vol. II, Ch. I, " The Sacred Language of Allegory and Symbol " (Sec. 4, " The Symbolism of Numbers ") and Vol. I of *The Hidden Wisdom in the Holy Bible*, Pt. III, Ch. III, both by Geoffrey Hodson.

new birth, enterprise, extension, and the completed manifestation in a given cycle of that which was innate in the digit one. This latter is said to indicate the Manifestor of the Infinite and Unmanifest, the Logos, the synthesis in unity of all that is to appear, and the epoch of the initiation of the process of emanation. The number nine, in its turn, indicates the completion of the work and its summing up into its highest essence in readiness for entry upon the succeeding cycle, indicated by the number ten which follows. This macrocosmic significance given to numbers by the Ancients[1] is said also to apply to man as microcosm.[2]

In addition to the Lord's promise of exceeding fruitfulness, Abram also received the Divine affirmation and instruction: " ....I am the Almighty God; walk before me, and be thou perfect. And I will make my covenant between me and thee, and will multiply thee exceedingly. "[3] Thereupon ....God talked with Abram, again promising fruitfulness.[4] As we have seen, the number nine indicates the approach to the culmination and perfection of any cycle. For advanced man it refers to the final Initiation which leads to Adeptship. The unfolding Inner Self (Abram) has by that time entered into intimate relationship with the Monad (the Lord)—a possible mystical reason for the change of name—and the fruits of that spiritual " marriage " will consist of the full illumination of the whole intellect (the name of Sarai is accordingly changed to Sarah) by the light of spiritual intuition (a son is conceived and " born ").

---

[1] *e.g.* " The world is built upon the power of numbers." Pythagoras.

". . . some philosophers hold that ideas and numbers are of the same nature and amount to ten in all." Aristotle, *Metaphysics*, vii, F. Also Kabbalism.

[2] " Here is wisdom, Let him that hath understanding count the number of the beast: for it is the number of a man; and his number is Six hundred threescore and six." *Rev.* 13 : 18. (By reduction 666 equals 18 equals 9—G.H.).

[3] *Gen.* 17: 1–2.

[4] *Gen.* 17: 3–9. Support for a symbolical reading of the Bible is gained by comparison of the promises of perpetual prosperity and divine protection made by God to Abraham and his successors with the subsequent defeats by invaders, exile under their commands in Babylon and Egypt, and the destruction of the Temples of King Solomon and King David. To these misfortunes may be added the later fate of the Hebrew people, including their miseries and homelessness since the *Diaspora* and the holocaust of German Jews under Nazi rule. This marked divergence between divine assurances and promises on the one hand and what actually happened on the other provides strong grounds for a non-literal reading of the Scriptures.

The alternative of a total rejection of the *Pentateuch* as being, on the surface, unworthy of serious consideration would, I suggest, involve the loss of invaluable treasures of wisdom which are revealed when the veil of allegory and symbol is removed. (*Gen.* 17: 2, 5–8; 26 : 2–5; 28 : 13–16).

ISAAC—THE CHILD OF PROMISE[1]

Isaac, who was symbolically promised by the Lord, thus personifies the fully developed intuitive faculty and vehicle, sheath for the Monadic power, life and consciousness. As stated earlier, the interpretation of the narrative as an account of human evolution written in terms of historical metaphor is suggested and supported by the introduction into it of the Lord God, the Supreme Deity of the Cosmos as a whole. However important—for their own sake as also for the welfare of the human race—the Israelites were at this time in their history, this would seem to have been hardly sufficient to necessitate such special intervention in the affairs of a small tribe by so inconceivably vast a Being, particularly when it is remembered that the evolution of all life, all form and all beings continues uninterruptedly according to the operation of impersonal law. St. Paul would seem to have advanced this view in his adjuration to the Philippians: " ....work out your own salvation with fear and trembling. For it is God which worketh in you.... "[2]   Indeed, if the repetition be pardoned, the introduction of the person of Deity and of supernatural and miraculous events is found to have been part of the method of the writers of inspired allegories which was used in order to indicate, and encourage the search for, a hidden meaning in the supposedly historical narrative. The death of Sarah and Abraham—their names being so spelt by that time—soon after the birth of Isaac, in addition to being natural because of their old age may also reveal that the limitations imposed by the past and by the normal activities of the mind are outgrown by the Inner Self of the high Initiate who approaches the stature of the Adept, as personified by Abraham.

Thus read, the account of Abraham's later years may be interpreted as being descriptive of passage through the Fourth of the Five Great Initiations, also symbolised by the Crucifixion of Christ.[3]   The deaths and burials of heroes, leaders and Saviours are to be regarded as figuratively portraying the " death " of all sense of separated individuality. Thus the Christ affirmed: " I and my Father are one. "[4]

After the change of Abram's name to Abraham there came the instruction that every man child, whether born in Israel or adopted therein,[5] should from then onwards be circumcised when eight days old. This ordinance may have had its spiritual[6] as well as its admitted hygienic

---

[1] *Gen.* 17 : 19.

[2] *Phil.* 2 : 12, 13. (Neither divine guidance nor the interior descent of divine grace are intended to be here denied—Author).

[3] q.v. *The Hidden Wisdom in the Holy Bible*, Vol. I, Pt. VI. (The Nativity, Baptism and Transfiguration portray the first three Initiations, and Ascension the Fifth).

[4] *Jn.* 10 : 30.

[5] *Gen.* 17 : 12, 13.

[6] This view receives support from the following Biblical texts: *De.* 30: 6, *Jn.* 4: 4, *Rom.* 2 : 29, *Col.* 2 : 11.

significance. For the Jews it was a tribal badge, a mark of consecration according to Mosaic law. As "Abraham's seal" it represented the covenant between the great Patriarch and Jehovah.

If this view be acceptable then the rite of circumcision, the obvious hygienic purpose apart, may also be taken as a physical symbol of the dedication of the highest power of man—procreation—to the service of God. The *prepuce in situ* would thus symbolise the enclosed or individually exercised creative power, whilst its removal would indicate both the sanctification of the organ through which it is expressed and the renunciation of separated individuality, particularly in the exercise of the highest spiritual and physical functions. Discipline, sublimation, self-spiritualisation and universalisation of consciousness in the exercise of the creative process—these are all possibly symbolised by this rite. In this sense the instruction may have indicated that the Jewish people were originally intended—and were offered the opportunity—to be a race of Initiates who would receive and deliver to later generations pure spiritual wisdom and power.[1]

THE HEBREW NATION—A RACE SET APART

To digress briefly, according to an occult tradition the Jews were offered the privilege and opportunity of performing the dual function of receiving and delivering spiritual wisdom to the Aryan Race and of providing bodies and secluded environment for reincarnated Initiates. The wisdom—or body of private teachings—is known as the *Kabbalah*, which is described as an unwritten oral tradition, the esoteric doctrine of the Jewish religion, the theosophy of the Hebrews. The word *Kabbalah* is derived from the root QBL, "to receive". Included in the meaning of the word, therefore, is the practice of transmitting secret knowledge by word of mouth.[2] Such, according to both the Bible and occult tradition, was the high office to which the Jews were originally called and it was largely, if not entirely, for this purpose that they became a chosen race. Indeed, their great Patriarchs and Prophets appeared amongst them in fulfilment of this plan. The Hebrew Schools of the Prophets provided the nation with both spiritual Centres and trained occultists known as "sons of the prophets".[3] Thus the many prophecies of future greatness may have been not of temporal dominion, but rather of the fulfilment of a far greater spiritual office amongst men.

The provision of the physical body of Jesus as He is named in the New Testament, though known to the Hebrews as Jeshu Ben Pandera,[4] repres-

---

[1] The Lord spoke to Moses, saying: "And ye shall be unto me a kingdom of priests, and an holy nation. . . ." (*Ex.* 19 : 6). Also *Le.* 20 : 24-26, *De.* 7: 6 and *Is.* 61 : 6.

[2] See Appendix. [3] II *Kings* 2: 5.

[4] q.v. *Sepher Toldos Jeshu*, a Rabbinical work.

ented the highest fulfilment of the national mission, though other Initiates and Adepts have been born of the race. Amongst these, however, Jesus alone is regarded in occult philosophy as having been the vehicle for the " incarnation "[1] of the Cosmic Christos, or the Second Aspect of the Blessed Trinity.[2] In addition, through its Scriptures Israel actually has delivered the spiritual wisdom to mankind, however much it may have become distorted and however heavily it may have been veiled. Nevertheless, if one may presume to say so, it is unhappily true that the full promise has not as yet been fulfilled.

In its occult rather than its psychological interpretation, the story of Abraham tells of the choice of the Hebrew peoples for the spiritual and racial purposes already described, and of the instruction which the ancient Patriarchs received from the appropriate Adept Officials in the Inner Government of the World, the Great White Brotherhood,[3] the august Assembly of " just men made perfect ".[4] Thus many threads are interwoven in the story, which relates both the psycho-spiritual evolution of every human being and the spiritual and physical histories of the Jewish peoples.

THE PROMISE OF THE FUTURE

The story of the Hebrew nation is far from being ended. In their boundless virility the Jews will doubtless continue to make their unique and striking contribution to the cultural and spiritual progress of humanity. Esoteric Judaism—the *Kabbalah*, or theosophy of the Hebrews—still lives, is still taught and practised, if as yet but to a limited extent. If a Gentile may be permitted to comment, the day may yet come when the light and wisdom in the *Kabbalah* will be shed upon the world by its Hebrew proficients, as it has continued to be transmitted in other languages and systems of symbology.[5] A complete physical and intellectual apocalypse has yet to be achieved; for surely a very great future must lie ahead of the descendants of Abraham.

Heavy, indeed, is the price which they have paid since the *Diaspora* for their presumed failures and their transgressions, and especially for their

---

[1] Incarnation, *Avatāra* (Sk.)—" Descent ". The incarnation of a Deity, especially Vishnu, the Second Aspect of the Hindu *Trimūrti*. q.v. Glossary.

[2] q.v. The Gnostic tradition as collected in *Fragments of a Faith Forgotten*, G. R. S. Mead.

[3] The Hierarchy of the Initiates and Adepts of this planet. q.v. *The Inner Government of the World* and *The Masters*, A. Besant; q.v. *Lecture Notes of the School of the Wisdom*, Vol. I, (Rev. Ed.), Ch. XVI, Geoffrey Hodson.

[4] *Heb.* 12: 23.

[5] This is already occurring. The reader's attention is drawn to the works of Gershom G. Scholem, Professor of Jewish Mysticism at the Hebrew University in Jerusalem, indebtedness to whom is here gratefully acknowledged, without in the slightest degree suggesting that he concurs in any of the views presented in this work of mine.

departure from the service of the Sanctuary to which they had been called[1]. As they return to that service (many individuals amongst them having already done this), so will the race arise in greatness and a measure of the ancient promise be fulfilled. Indeed, an Israeli nation has already come into being and has been established in a national home in Palestine, now known as Israel. Though beset by many difficulties, and even dangers, the new Republic gives evidence of both survival and progress.

---

[1] *Ex.* 19: 6, *Le.* 20 : 24–26, *De.* 7 : 6 and *Is.* 61: 6.

CHAPTER III

THE DESTRUCTION OF SODOM

Gen. 18. Abraham entertaineth three angels. Sarah reproved. Destruction of Sodom revealed to Abraham: he intercedes for it.

Whilst the early verses of this Chapter of *Genesis* read somewhat ambiguously, particularly concerning the number of Abraham's visitors, verse twenty-two makes it clear that there were four, namely the Lord God and three men, for it reads:

> " And the men turned their faces from thence, and went toward Sodom: but Abraham stood yet before the Lord. "

The relationship between these four visitors and the significance of the human attendants upon the Lord is, however, not made very plain. If, following St. Paul's affirmation,[1] Abraham's story continues to be read metaphorically, then it can be interpreted as an allegory descriptive of a spiritual experience. If this view be adopted and the rules governing interpretation of the Sacred Language be obeyed, then Abraham at the door of his tent on the plains of Mamre would personify man spiritually illumined whilst in a state of waking, physical consciousness (the plains). Because he is at the doorway or entrance he is capable of attaining to spiritual awareness or using the consciousness of his vesture of light, the *Augoeides* or Causal Body. Entering that lofty condition he is aware of himself as the Higher Triad, the divine Self as spiritual Will, spiritual Wisdom and spiritual Intelligence (the three men accompanying the Lord) The Lord Himself personifies the Source of this triplicity, the divine Spirit-Essence, the Dweller in the Innermost, the human Monad.

The horror of great darkness[2] has passed and the outer man has entered into full realisation of unity with his own divine nature, the immortal God within. Abraham's invitation to his visitors to partake of food (admission to an intimate relationship), to rest and to have their feet washed, indicates the true attitude of spiritualised man to divine visitations, whether external

---

[1] *Gal.* 4: 24–26.   [2] *Gen.* 15: 12.

or interior—namely responsiveness and humility. Thus the allegory is descriptive of that stage in human evolution in which the individuality has become self-identified with the innermost Self, their close communion being symbolised by the hospitality and service offered to the visitors. The universal nature of the experience is indicated by the fact that it all occurred under a tree,[1] the mystic Tree of Life, symbol of the one omnipresent, protean, creative life-force.

At first consciousness, restricted to the concrete mind (the tent), because of its analytical and critical attributes does not fully participate in this mystical exaltation and is not able wholly to ascend and surrender to the spiritual experience. This is symbolised by the fact that Sarah (personification of the mind), who was *within the tent*, laughed scornfully at the promise of fruitfulness (the birth of a child).[2]

A TWO-EDGED INSTRUMENT

The tendency for the aspect of the mind which is limited to material logic—in certain of its functions valuably so—to be incapable of perceiving abstract, transcendental truth is well illustrated in this incident, as also in that of the scornful thief on Calvary.[3] The untrustworthiness of the thinking principle alone as an instrument for the attainment of spiritual understanding is also shown in the denial of Sarah that she had laughed at the words of, the Lord.[4] A parallel passage occurs in the New Testament where Peter, also representing the concrete mind, is made to deny his Master.[5] His confession that Jesus was the Christ, his[6] presence at and ability to perceive the Transfiguration,[7] his repentance,[8] his liberation from prison (the separative sense) by an angel[9] (the innermost Self), his instruction by a vision not to despise the Gentiles[10] (to rise above racialism into a universalisation of consciousness) and other events in the Apostle's life, all indicate that eventually he rose above the limitations imposed by the ratiocinating mind. Indeed, the recorded incidents in Peter's life—as in the lives of many other personifications of principles of man—so accurately portray phases of human evolution as almost to force one to the conclusion that such indeed was the purpose of the authors. The presumption which prompted Peter openly to rebuke the Christ, evoking the response " Get

---

[1] *Gen.* 18: 4.

[2] *Gen.* 2618 : 12. cf. Occult Philosophy: " The mind is the great slayer of the Real. Let the disciple slay the slayer." (*The Voice of the Silence*, translated H. P. Blavatsky).

[3] *Lu.* 23 : 39–43.

[4] *Gen.* 18 : 15.

[5] *Matt.* 26 : 69–75.

[6] *Matt.* 16 : 16.   [7] *Matt.* 17.   [8] *Matt.* 26 : 75.

[9] *Acts* 12.   [10] *Acts* 10 : 9–16.

17

thee behind me, Satan ",[1] Peter's denial of the Christ in the darkness of the night when he was away from the direct Presence, and his later remorse at daybreak,[2] for the student of symbology constitute " cameos " of such forms of revelation by allegory. The surrender of Pilate to the demand of the multitude for the crucifixion of Christ, and the washing of his hands[3] (failure), followed by his later refusal to alter the inscription[4] (recovery) to be placed over the head of Christ upon the Cross, may be similarly interpreted.[5]

THE SYMBOL OF DECAPITATION

The killing of Goliath (excessive mental arrogance) by means of a small white stone (intuition) taken from the brook (the " Stream "—a mystical symbol for the River of Divine Life, realisation of unity with which comes passage through the First Great Initiation) and his decapitation by David[6] (the Higher Mind), the beheading of John the Baptist,[7] the martyrdom of Peter foretold by Christ[8] and the suicide of Judas Iscariot[9] by hanging, may all be read as indications of complete self-emancipation from purely mental restrictions upon consciousness and from inhibitions preventing spiritual intuitiveness. The cutting off of the human head (concrete mind) of Ganesha, the elder son of the Lord Shiva, and its replacement by that of an elephant (wisdom), the slaying by decapitation of the serpent-haired Medusa (misused procreative energy and inordinate sexual indulgence, also personified by Salome[10]) by Perseus (the Higher Mind), and the striking off of the head of the Hydra of Lerna by Hercules as his second labour—all these carry a similar significance, with variations according to accompanying circumstances. The symbol of decapitation, then, refers to the fact that in this method of killing the head is severed from the body, indicating the removal of the power of the concrete mind to limit—as by excessive analysis, argument and criticism—entry into transcendental spiritual experience. Killings and deaths in inspired allegories, it may be repeated, are generally used to indicate the " death " of such mental inhibitions, particularly those arising from a marked sense of separativeness, whilst resurrections and reappearances indicate that these barriers to spiritual illumination have been transcended.

---

[1] *Matt.* 16 : 22, 23.
[2] *Matt.* 26 : 69-75.   [3] *Matt.* 27 : 24.
[4] *Jn.* 19 : 22.
[5] q.v. *The Hidden Wisdom in the Holy Bible*, Vol. I, Pt. V, Geoffrey Hodson.
[6] *I Sam.* 17 : 51.   [7] *Matt.* 14 : 10.
[8] *Jn.* 21 : 18.   [9] *Matt.* 27 : 5.
[10] *Matt.* 14.

As suggested heretofore the knowledge, and therefore the power attained when the limitations of the mind and of the desire nature are over-ridden, can be most gravely misused and even perverted—hence the enveiling of such knowledge in allegory and symbol.

JUDGMENT DAYS—THEIR OCCULT SIGNIFICANCE

Returning to the text of Chapter Eighteen of *Genesis*, now under consideration, the incident of the bargaining of Abraham with the Lord for the safety of the city of Sodom should fifty, forty-five, forty, thirty, twenty, or even ten, righteous men be found within the city,[1] is of significance to the student of occult philosophy. Applied to the human race as a whole, this compact can be read as portraying the principle of periodic assessments of evolutionary progress—the esoteric meaning of " judgment days "[2]— made at critical epochs in the lives of individuals, of races, and of the whole population of a planet. (An interpretation of the particular numbers specified in the text is offered later on in this Chapter).

Theosophy includes the idea that the evolution of life " has neither conceivable beginning nor imaginable end. "[3] No " day of judgment "— actually an assessment of progress in deciding the cycle of further evolution on which the unfolding spiritual Selves of men will proceed—is regarded as final. There cannot be a *last* judgment for any eternal, immortal, spiritual Soul—the true Self of each human being. From this it follows that there can be no eternal damnation for anyone. The successive numbers from fifty to ten indicate, in part, careful numerical selection of those who pass successfully through these so-called " judgment days ". In this sense the term " righteous "[4] men refers to those who have attained to the necessary evolutionary level for that epoch, and are therefore capable of benefiting by advancement to its successor.

The Lord's promise to Abraham not to destroy the cities of Sodom and Gomorrah if certain numbers of righteous men should be found therein has also its microcosmic significance. In general it is a warning to all mankind against the danger of excessive sexual indulgence. A message is also conveyed to those who aspire to find and enter in at the " strait gate " and tread the narrow way.[5] For these the destruction is not a disaster, but

---

[1] The very absurdity of the idea of such a bargaining between the Supreme Deity and the leader of a small tribe, as also of all such transactions, must surely suggest to the unbiassed mind either perfound ignorance or the intention of the authors to convey a hidden truth. G.H.

[2] q.v. *The Solar System*, A. E. Powell; *The Secret Doctrine* (Adyar Ed.), Vol. I, p. 192, H. P. Blavatsky.

[3] q.v. *The Secret Doctrine*, Vol. I, p. 115.

[4] *Gen.* 18: 25.

[5] *Matt.* 7: 13, 14.

rather a symbol of that burning out of desire which must precede successful progress on the Path and passage through the first of the Great Initiations. In this particular interpretation—the Initiatory, in which such reversals of meaning frequently occur—success, and not failure, is indicated by destruction; for in this deeply occult sense the death and extinction of the grosser attributes (Sodom and Gomorrah) refer to both the loss of their power to degrade and ascent to consciously realised immortality and the resultant regeneration of the whole man. Because enhanced powers of will and thought can result, the power-bestowing knowledge is revealed only by allegory.

ABRAHAM'S INITIATION

At this point it is desirable for purposes of continuity to refer back to the Fourteenth Chapter of *Genesis*, verses twelve to sixteen. By theosophic or numerical reduction the three hundred and eighteen servants with whom Abraham (then named Abram) defeated the Sodomites and freed Lot become three,[1] representative of the three-fold spiritual Self by whose might victory over the lower nature is gained. This achieved, an upwelling of spiritual power and an expansion of knowledge occur, making the Initiate ready for further interior progress and for assistance from a Hierophant of the Greater Mysteries. Appropriately, therefore, Melchizedek, King of Salem, the Priest of the Most High God, is now introduced into the story; for he represents the Hierophant or Adept Initiator, whilst the Order of his Priesthood refers to the "just men made perfect",[2] the Great White Brotherhood of the Adepts and Initiates of this planet. In support of this view, Abram is stated to have received from Melchizedek bread, wine, blessing and tithes.

THE MYSTICAL MELCHIZEDEK

Interpreted microcosmically, Melchizedek is the fully awakened, Christ-nature of man from which the " gifts " of regenerative power (bread), realised oneness, wisdom and spiritual intuitiveness (wine), insight (blessing) and Christlike ministration born of compassion for all sentient beings (tithes), flow or " descend " into the purified mind and body of advanced man. Together these symbolise both the new powers welling up within the Inner Self from the Monad (Melchizedek) and the fruits of Initiation. The gifts of gold, frankincense and myrrh received by the Christ-child (or Initiate) at the hands of the Eastern Kings are of similar significance. Bread symbolises the regeneration of life from the seed, and gold the

---

[1] $3+18=21=3$.
[2] *Heb.* 12 : 23.

increase of wisdom, vitality and power. Both wine and frankincense indicate increase in spiritual knowledge, perception and comprehension. Blessing and myrrh are emblems of added evolutionary stature, beauty, bliss and grace. The receipt by Abram of tithes from the people also refers to the drawing up of the whole of the powers of the lower nature into the higher, the mental into the Immortal, and to entry upon a new phase of development.

The attainment of God-consciousness in the present epoch is " out of due time "[1] or in advance of the natural entry by the race into that state.[2] This transmutation of purely human attributes into their spiritual expression is, therefore, not achieved without intense effort and much suffering in which the fetter of doubt, amongst others, is keenly felt and must be cast off. The " horror of great darkness ",[3] previously interpreted, into which Abram had descended symbolises this inescapable experience of every Initiate when darkness temporarily engulfs the soul. Christ in Gethsemane[4] and on the Cross[5] also entered into this experience.

THE SYMBOLISM OF NUMBERS

Six differently numbered groups of righteous men, referred to earlier in this Chapter, are considered as justifying a change in the decision of the Lord to destroy Sodom and Gomorrah. Fifty may be taken to refer to the principle of spiritual will, and forty to that of the abstract mind. Forty-five, being midway between the two numbers and partaking of the numerical value of both, represents the interlinking principle, bridge or *antah-karana* between the divine and the human in man. The number thirty is the formal mind, which is the third principle of the mortal personality, counting the physical body as number one. Twenty stands for the more refined emotions and ten the unification of those five principles to form the superphysical vestures of the Monad-Ego, personified by Abraham.

These views are advanced here because some systems of religious mysticism are thus based upon numerals. In such systems the succession of numbers begins with 1 and ends with 10, the 0 being the symbol of the infinite and boundless circle which represents the Universe. All intervening numbers, however combined, added or multiplied, exemplify philosophic ideas relating either to a moral or a physical fact. According to Pythagoras, from the Monad or Unity emanated the Duad, thus forming the Trinity, the *Tetraktys* (Gr.) or the *Tetrad* (the three-sided pyramid) constituting the

---

[1] I *Cor.* 15 : 8.   [2] See Chart on p. 212.
[3] *Gen.* 15 : 12.
[4] *Mk.* 14.   [5] *Mk.* 15 : 34.

" Sacred Four " by which the Pythagoreans swore, this being their most binding oath.   In these and other ways numbers are said to be keys to the views of the ancients on cosmogony in its broad sense, on man, on all beings and on the spiritual and physical evolution of the human race.   The number 7 was evidently regarded by the ancient philosophers as the most sacred of · all; for everything of importance—ideas and localities—was calculated by and fitted into this number.   Examples are the sevenfold golden candlestick (*Ex.* 25: 31-37), the seven Churches of Asia and the seven Spirits before God's throne (*Rev.* 1: 4), seven golden candlesticks (*Rev.* 1: 12), seven stars in God's right hand (*Rev.* 1: 16 & 20) and seven plagues and seven golden vials (*Rev.* 15: 6, 7 & 8).

This numerical form of symbolism is but one of the methods of conveying occult wisdom, another being that of the personification of principles of Nature and of man by a succession of divine, semi-divine and human personages in the narratives.   For examples, the Lord, Melchizedek, and now Lot, all personify the Monad.   In this latter method, as we have seen, Sarah (the mental principle), hitherto barren and scornful of a divine prophecy of motherhood (unillumined by spiritual intuitiveness and pure wisdom), conceives (or is fructified by a Ray, the divine " Word " and promise) from the Monad (the Lord), and Isaac (the Christ-nature) is later born (begins to influence increasingly the attitude and activities of the mind).   Renunciation of egoistic individuality has by that time been attained and complete surrender made to spiritual law.   This is later portrayed by the readiness of Abraham to sacrifice Isaac, and by angelic intervention followed by the appearance of the ram in the thicket as an immediately available substitute.   As indicated earlier in this Chapter, decapitation is also used as an allegory of the transcendence of the separative attribute of the mind.

CHAPTER IV

LOT, HIS WIFE AND THE TWO CITIES

Gen. 19. Lot entertaineth two angels. The vicious Sodomites stricken with blindness. He is directed to flee to the mountain. Sodom and Gomorrah destroyed. Lot's wife punished. Origin of Moab and Ammon.

Modern archaeological research contributes to an understanding of the phenomenon of the destruction of Sodom and Gomorrah; for geological investigation has shown that this may have been due to natural causes. In *The Bible as History* (pp. 79-81) Werner Keller writes:

" The American expedition under Lynch in 1848 produced the first information about the prodigious drop of the Jordan on its short course through Palestine. This plunging of the river bed until it is far below sea level is, as later investigation established, a unique geological phenomenon...

" The Jordan Valley is only part of a huge fracture in the earth's crust. The path of this crack has meanwhile been accurately traced. It begins far north, several hundred miles beyond the borders of Palestine, at the foot of the Taurus Mountains in Asia Minor. In the south it runs from the south shore of the Dead Sea through the wadi el-Arabah to the Gulf to Aqabah and only comes to an end beyond the Red Sea in Africa. At many points in this vast depression signs of intensive volcanic activity are obvious. In the Galilean mountains, in the highlands of Transjordan, on the banks of the Jabbok, a tributary of the Jordan, and on the Gulf of Aqabah are black basalt and lava.

" Together with the base of this mighty fissure, which runs precisely through this area, the Vale of Siddim, including Sodom and Gomorrah, plunged one day into the abyss. The date of this event can be fairly accurately established by the geologists. It must have been soon after 2000 B.C.

" 'Probably it was about 1900 B.C. that the catastrophic destruction of Sodom and Gomorrah took place', wrote the American scholar Jack Finegan in 1951. 'A careful examination of the literary, geological and archaeological evidence leads to the conclusion that the corrupt " cities of the plain " (*Gen.* 19: 29) lay in the area which is now submerged beneath the slowly rising waters of the southern section of the Dead Sea, and that their destruction came about through a great earthquake which was probably accompanied by explosions, lightning, issue of natural gas and general conflagration.'

(This occurred) " about 1900 B.C.—that is in the time of Abraham.

" The subsidence released volcanic forces that had been lying dormant deep down along the whole length of the fracture. In the upper valley of the Jordan near Bashan there are still the towering craters of extinct volcanoes; great stretches of lava and deep layers of basalt have been deposited on the limestone surface. From time immemorial the area around this depression has been subject to earth-quakes. There is repeated evidence of them and the Bible itself records them. "

The discrepancy between the Biblical account and the evidence provided by " geological and archaeological evidence " concerning the cause of the destruction of the two cities need not unduly disconcert the student of the Bible. Rather may the former be read as a description of a historical event told in such a manner as also to use it as a vehicle for the conveying of psychological and spiritual truths. I now propose experimentally to investigate this possibility, but before presenting interpretations of the incidents of this Nineteenth Chapter of *Genesis* in detail consideration will be given to some general principles.

The chief characters and the two cities may be studied both as symbols of levels of consciousness and the vehicles through which they are expressed, and as portrayals of stages in human evolution. Lot, for example, personifying the highly evolved Monad-Ego[1] incarnate in emotional and physical bodies, sits not *in* the city of Sodom but at its gate; for Sodom and Gomorrah represent the deepest degree of material manifestation (philosophically a " degradation ") of the creative life-force and consciousness of Cosmos and man. Even though forced thus to " descend ", the Monad is never sullied, being unstained and unstainable. Symbolically, Lot remains only *at* the gate of the city.

After the phase of deepest descent of the life-wave has been reached on the pathway of forthgoing, that of return is entered upon. For man this is marked by an increasing responsiveness to the elevating influences of the threefold Self, the divine Presence, and is portrayed in the story of Lot by the visitation of the two angels, who personify spiritual wisdom and spiritual intelligence. Until a certain degree of evolutionary progress has been attained, the mortal man is unresponsive to interior illumination. Ultimately, however, the " lower " nature becomes refined, and in consequence sensitised to spiritual influences. Lot thus becomes aware of the presence of the two angels and rises up to meet them, bowing himself with his face toward the ground.[2]

---

[1] q.v. Glossary.   [2] *Gen*. 19: 1.

BRIMSTONE AND FIRE FROM HEAVEN

On the upward arc, when man becomes elevated by the influence of the Monad-Ego (the two divine men), sublimation of the procreative impulse naturally occurs. The grosser forms of sexual indulgence which precede this stage are symbolised by the two cities, as is evidenced by the reputation which they are given in the Bible. The fact that they are erroneously described as having been destroyed by brimstone and fire which the Lord rained upon them,[1] may be interpreted as an indirect reference by the authors (using the Symbolical Language) to the destruction of the hindrances imposed by physically expressed desire upon the ascending consciousness of aspiring man (Lot and his wife). In other words, the burning of the cities by brimstone and fire allegorically refers to both the destructive nature (to the higher attributes) of gross sensual indulgence and the burning up, when transmutation occurs, of both sexual passions and the *karma* resulting from their excessive expression.

The two cities are emblematical of the emotional and physical bodies of man during the cycle of deepest density, housing as they do the evolving Monad-Ego and his creative powers (personified by Lot, his wife and the other inhabitants). Brimstone and fire from a heavenly source may represent the sublimated creative fire and the Monadic will by which lust and the vehicles of its expression are burnt out when the way of return has been traversed to the appropriate evolutionary phase. The advanced Monad-Ego, however, eventually lifts the individual out of these lower stages, and when transformation is completed it is most important that the indulgences of the past should be finally forsworn and forgotten. Symbolically, Lot and his wife (the Inner Self and its expressed energy) must not look back as they depart from the burning cities.[2] Unfortunately this is what Lot's wife is said to have done, thus being obliged to pay the penalty of the loss (petrification) of her spiritual powers, as will be expounded later in this Chapter.

SODOM AND GOMORRAH—NADIR OF THE CYCLE

In addition to representing the personal soul and body of every human being, Sodom and Gomorrah have also their racial significance as symbols of the period and state of consciousness of mankind in which sexual self-degradation occurs. This happens when the Monad is passing through the most material phase of its pilgrimage of forth-going and return. Homosexuality, which is suggested as the chief vice of those cities, symbolises the unnatural exercise, in an entirely selfish and totally non-productive manner

---

[1] *Gen.* 19: 24.
[2] *Gen.* 19: 17.

of the procreative power with which man is endowed.[1] Thus the major plan for the continuance of the race is frustrated, the creative power is diverted from its intended use and the seed is wasted and lost. This is a grievous " sin "[2] indeed, an offence against the Logos Itself, particularly when the creative force is regarded as a purely reproductive, race-perpetuating power. Elsewhere in the Bible this " sin " is referred to and denounced.[3] In another possible meaning the brimstone and the fire descending from heaven indicate the deliberate and excessive turning downwards of the creative fire and the sterility, destruction and death which are its inevitable results.

The incident of the supposed bargaining between God and Abraham for Sodom and Gomorrah may also be interpreted as descriptive of both a phase of evolution and of readiness for Initiation. In this sense the two cities represent the desire body and the physical body of man, with their inherent attributes. The righteous men, so carefully numbered, refer to the higher spiritual principles which, if active in and through the two lower bodies, preserve and redeem them. Bereft of their influence, however, the mortal personality is spiritually " dead ". In the allegory, without a sufficient number of righteous men Sodom and Gomorrah were to be destroyed.

In the deeper sense unreadiness, or the pre-Initiatory state, precludes the attainment of " immortality " by the emotional and mental bodies of the personal self or individuality. At this stage, after physical death the body and the vehicles of emotion and concrete mind successively disintegrate, the three more spiritual vehicles alone being preserved.[4] After the First Great Initiation,[5] as a result of the preponderance of the power and influence of the Higher Self over the lower, a relative immortality of the latter is attained.

The allegory of the petrification of Lot's wife has been interpreted as indicating the loss of mental and spiritual awareness and creativeness and also of the enfired condition of the spinal cord, which metaphorically is " petrified ".[6] This tragedy can arise when an advanced or initiated person " falls into sin " meaning in this case a return to past sexual indulgences (looking back at Sodom and Gomorrah). When, however, this

---

[1] I am aware of the views now gaining some support that homoexuality in private between consenting adults is not justly to be regarded as perversion, and that a homosexual is a sick person in need of psychiatric treatment.

[2] Philosophically the term " transgression through ignorance " is preferable to me. G.H.

[3] De. 23: 17 and I Kings 14: 24.

[4] q.v. Through the Gateway of Death, Geoffrey Hodson.

[5] Into the Greater Mysteries.

[6] The column or pillar is universality used as a symbol of the spinal cord of man. q.v. Pt. III of Vol. I of this work—Pillars.

error is avoided—as in the case of Lot himself—then the fiery creative life-force, the Serpent Fire, resident in the physical body is sublimated, thereby producing elevation of consciousness. As said above, should this mighty power become debased, as in its excessive sensual and physical expressions, the energy plays downwards to cause the temporary loss of spirituality in both the mento-emotional and the physical man. This profound truth is allegorically revealed by the account of the burning of Sodom and Gomorrah, which refers to the disintegrating effects of an exclusively sexual expression of the creative fire.

ALLEGORIES AS REVELATIONS OF OCCULT TRUTHS

This approach to the Bible and these suggested interpretations of supposedly historical—in this case now disproven as such—episodes may possibly seem to be somewhat arbitrary. At this point, therefore, a brief restatement is made of the origin and purpose of the Sacred Language. The custom of introducing into historical records apparently supernatural happenings, divine interventions, and even the actual presence on Earth of the Supreme Deity in visible form and displaying human attributes, clearly suggests an allegorical significance.

Many of the dramatic stories which are included in the Mosaic Books are regarded by symbologists as having been composed by inspired Seers, Kabbalists and Initiates, who wrote from within a Sanctuary of the Ancient Mysteries. As stated in the Introduction to this work, actual physical events were by these authors given a miraculous character. Super-sensual and physical happenings were said to be caused by the intervention of the Lord. History thus recounted became also a revelation of spiritual and occult truths. Power-bestowing knowledge of the true nature of man as a sevenfold being, and of the relationship of each of his seven parts to its corresponding plane of Nature, was both concealed and yet revealed under the veil of symbolism, allegory and historical metaphor. A master key of interpretation consists of knowledge of the seven principles of man and of their correspondences with planets, Universes and the Cosmos as a whole.[1] In addition, their mutual inter-relations and their parallel evolution through-out seven progressive cycles were revealed, particularly by means of numerical symbology.

The Canaanite Jews, whose history is partially related in the Old Testament, are assumed to have been at this period under the direction of the Initiates of the Sanctuary who had been appointed for that purpose. The numerous recorded interventions by the Lord, Who frequently appeared in human guise, may in addition to their possible mystical meaning—

[1] q.v. Glossary—Law of Correspondences.

awareness of the divine Presence within every man—also be interpreted as referring to visitations by Initiates as messengers of the Hierophant or Head of the Temple and his Inner Council. Much of this had become legendary when the so-called Mosaic books were later written, not only by Moses[1] but also by a group of tribal historians, with interpolations by a succession of Initiates.

The intention was to place on record cosmogonical, macrocosmic and microcosmic knowledge in order that it might not be lost when the Chaldean and Babylonian Sanctuaries and civilisations disappeared. A supposed history of the foundation of the Canaanite Jewish Race was chosen as the vehicle for this purpose, and the Old Testament with its many supernatural and magical passages is the result. Much of it was written by unpractised hands. Some of it is pure history, some mere legend. Nevertheless the light of occult wisdom shines brilliantly in a great many of its Chapters and verses. The *Pentateuch*, more particularly, thus constitutes one of the spiritual treasures of mankind.

After this digression—an admitted repetition of my basic theme—a return is now made to the study of the Nineteenth Chapter of *Genesis*.

THE ANGELS WARN LOT

The two angels appearing to Lot at his house in Sodom are greeted and offered hospitality by him. At first they refuse this, but later accept under pressure and consent to eat unleavened bread. Thereafter they save Lot, smite his attackers with blindness and warn him to depart because of the oncoming destruction of the two cities, Sodom and Gomorrah. The angels are deeply symbolical figures. Readers who are members of certain ceremonial Orders, especially those of an occult character, will readily perceive a correspondence between these two angels and the assistant Officers who have charge of a Candidate for Initiation, accompany him throughout his ordeals, and serve him in the ways symbolically referred to in this story.

Mystically interpreted these messengers, who appear to Lot in the form of men, are personifications of the power or influence of the two highest human principles—those of spiritual will and spiritual wisdom. By the aid and action of these two awakened interior powers, man is regenerated after his long journey through matter and his so-called " fall ". Allegorically stated, man's innate spiritual will and wisdom reach (visit) the now regenerated personality (Lot) and share (accept hospitality) increasingly in its life. The effect of the influence of these two inner, spiritual principles

---

[1] This is evidenced by the inclusion of an account of his death which is given in *The Fifth Book of Moses, Called Deuteronomy,* 34: 5.

is to free the outer man from the limitations of physical and emotional consciousness and experience (the two cities) and render the vices and habits (enemies) of his pre-Initiate period impotent to hurt him any more.   Symbolically, the angels blind Lot's attackers.   This is an accurate portrayal by means of allegory of certain results of man's evolutionary advancement; for these two interior powers of man, gradually increasing in effectiveness, both warn him against the dangers of retreat into earlier habits of thought and conduct and advise him in the further stage of his evolution.   Thus the angels warn Lot, saying: ". . . neither stay thou in all the plain (ordinary waking consciousness); escape to the mountain (supra-mental states of awareness), lest thou be consumed. "[1]

In accordance with the practice followed by those who write in the Symbolical Language, in which the characters portray attributes and characteristics of all men, Lot, his wife and two daughters *each personify an aspect of one person*—man himself.[2]   If the family be thus analysed, Lot represents the threefold innermost Self during physical incarnation.   His wife typifies the mento-emotional nature or *psyche*, whilst the two daughters personate the vital or etheric and the dense physical bodies.   Thus the whole sevenfold man is by these means portrayed by Lot and his family.   The two angels are the spiritualising influences of the two highest principles of man.   Illumined—indeed forced—by them, he forsakes forever all his pre-illumination indulgences (Sodom and Gomorrah) and moves on to the next stage in his evolution, which is the attainment of spiritual awareness (entrance into the city of Zoar and later ascent of the mountain).   The Initiatory Rite is distinctly indicated in the words: " The sun was risen upon the earth when Lot entered into Zoar. "[3]   The sun is also a symbol of the influence of the Monad of man upon his mortal nature, particularly as the power of spiritual will.   The Initiate is one who has reached the evolutionary stage at which the will (sun) is in the ascendant or has " risen upon the earth ".   Thereafter he is empowered and illumined by the light of the " sun " which is within him.   This, as will be shown later, is the Initiatory significance of the supposed but impossible action of Joshua in making the sun stand still " in the midst of heaven ".[4]   Thus Freemasonry, a survivor of the Ancient Mysteries, affirms that the sun is always at its meridian when the Rite of Initiation is performed.

THE SYMBOL OF PETRIFICATION

The turning of Lot's wife into a pillar of salt is susceptible of at least two interpretations.   One of these, referring to the stagnation of the

[1] *Gen.* 19: 17.
[2] q.v. Pt. I, Ch. II.
[3] *Gen.* 19: 23.   [4] *Joshua* 10: 13.

creative power or *kundalini* in the spinal cord,—symbolised by a pillar—which is caused by a return to past excessive sensual indulgences (looking back at Sodom and Gomorrah), has already been advanced. This error does occur; for old habits die hard, old pleasures and indulgences leave their marks upon the very substances of the emotional and the physical bodies. In consequence, sheer habit can and does still make its claims. If these are gratified (Lot's wife looks back), the powers of pre-Initiate man far advanced on the upward arc, and even of the Initiate of th Sanctuary, can be temporarily " petrified ".

In such cases the *siddhīs*,[1] including the power of seership, become inactive. Symbolically, the enfired spinal cord or rod becomes as a pillar of salt, or returns to pre-Initiate insensitivity and purely material automatic function. From another point of view, however, which does not negate the above, the petrification can indicate that the illumined Ego has finally deprived (petrified) the mental and emotional principles of all power to initiate action apart from the Egoic will. Actually neither the mental faculties nor the creative power (*kundalini*) are ever really petrified. They are only rendered inactive as purely material functions and sublimated to their spiritual expression.

The wisdom concealed beneath the veil of allegory and symbol is frequently found to exist in lay rs. Penetrating into these the student sometimes discovers that a deeper layer reveals a teaching which reverses, though not necessarily contradicts, an idea contained in an upper one.

LOT ASCENDS THE MOUNTAIN

A further remarkable allegory[2] follows, descriptive of the more advanced phases of spiritual development and experience. Lot leaves his first resting-place of Zoar, ascends the mountain and takes up residence in a cave, where he is made drunk and seduced by his two daughters on two successive nights, thereby perpetuating his family line. The first-born or elder daughter took the lead in this procedure, and then counselled her younger sister to follow her example. Both conceived, the first-born bearing a son, Moab, father of the Moabites, whilst the younger bore a son, Ben-ammi, father of the Ammonites, two tribes which played significant parts in later Jewish history.

Whilst this incident is offensive according to modern standards of morality, its acceptance as history need not necessarily be ruled out. According to the literature of contemporary and later peoples, the practice of incest and sexual intercourse in undesirable forms has by no means been

---

[1] *Siddhīs* (Sk.)—" Occult powers developed by *yoga* ".
[2] *Gen.* 19: 30-38.

uncommon. When reading such allegories, studying such symbols as the *lingam*[1] and observing statues indicating procreative union, the student of symbology sees nothing immoral in them. He perceives the universal laws, principles and energies that they are intended to symbolise and is therefore reverent in their presence. The Biblical passages under consideration do, however, contain a number of classical symbols which make possible an allegorical reading. Amongst them are the plain, the mountain, the cave, wine, intoxication and procreative intercourse. Such symbols are generally and respectively translated as: normal waking consciousness (plain); a more advanced and exalted state of awareness (mountain); withdrawing into relationship with one's spiritual nature and Inner Self (cave); imbibing spiritual wisdom—the product or ferment of life's experiences (wine); exaltation into God-consciousness (intoxication); the blending or union of the more spiritual and the more material aspects of human nature, sometimes called " the heavenly marriage " (procreative intercourse). The human participants in this drama may be regarded as personifying aspects of human nature, such as principles of man and vehicles of his consciousness, whilst the actions described portray symbolically their varied inter-relationships.

Thus interpreted, the narrative may be read as a description of the experiences of the advanced Soul (Lot) as it enters upon new phases of evolution which have been gradually attained. Lot's elevation into spiritual awareness (as of the Higher Mind within the Causal Body) is indicated by his leaving the plain, ascending the mountain and entering the cave. As this is achieved an upliftment occurs of the whole individuality of the illumined one, including the *psyche* or conjoined mental and emotional natures and the two physical principles—the etheric and the solid physical bodies (the two daughters).

THE OUTER MAN PARTICIPATES IN THE ADVANCEMENT OF THE INNER SELF

The psychical and the physical consciousness of the mortal man must participate in the experiences and attainments of the Immortal Self throughout its evolution to Adeptship. Thus regarded, the whole story of Lot relates in allegorical form this ascent from the human into the superhuman kingdom, during which progression all the powers attained must be brought to full fruition and made manifest in and through the whole nature of man—spiritual, intellectual and physical (Lot and his two daughters). The drunkenness by which Lot was supposedly overcome symbolises the state of

---

[1] *Lingam* (Sk.). Physically, the phallus. A symbol of abstract creation and of the divine, masculine, procreative force.

exaltation experienced by illumined man. The raptures into which the
Initiates of the Bacchic, Dionysian, Orphic and other Mysteries, as also
those who participated in certain Gnostic Rites, were said to have been
elevated, have been misinterpreted as drunkenness pr. duced by ir dulgence
in alcoholic beverages. Whilst these Mysteries may in their later days
have degenerated into drunken orgies, in their original forms they were
skilfully designed to produce in Initiates or *Mystae* the raptures of bliss or
God-intoxication experienced by those who attain to realisation of unity
with God.

REPELLANT PASSAGES AS ALLEGORICAL REVELATIONS OF SPIRITUAL TRUTHS

Since the subject is both interesting and important, I propose at this
point to advance a certain theory concerning the inclusion in sacred literature
of so many passages which cannot fail to be offensive to the modern mind.
I suggest, for example, that in writing the story of Hebrew and other peoples,
certain authors recorded as history such actions as those which are ascribed
to Lot and his daughters. Initiates of the Sanctuary, Sages, Seers and
Prophets, whilst not free wholly to delete such passages, later recast and
added to them, thereby making the stories also descriptive of both spiritual
states of awareness and phases of the evolution of the human Soul. The
Bible, as also certain other Scriptures, is sometimes criticised on the grounds
of their inclusion of accounts of alcoholic intoxication, adultery, incest
and enforced sexual intercourse. If, however, such narratives are regarded
as allegories of states of consciousness, evolutionary processes and Initiatory
attainments, then they may be interpreted in a new light and so lose some
of their repellant implications.

Readers of the Old Testament may, however, and not without reason,
take exception to the numerous passages attributing to the Lord God and
His human agents on Earth exceedingly cruel and flagrantly immoral conduct.
It must be remembered, however, that it was the original historians who
wrote the chief narratives of which the Bible consists and attributed to the
Deity and to the people concerned their described actions, thereby bestowing
upon them their resultant characters. Doubtless such authors believed
that Abraham, as also Lot's daughters, had actually conducted themselves
in the manner recorded.

If this is so, then the original occultists who decided to use the rather
crude stories as vehicles for their wisdom were obliged to accept these as
already written, make the best of such situations, and interpolate into the
narratives as much philosophic and symbolical material as in their view
was possible. Those who made such additions may not have felt themselves
justified in altering locally recorded history in order to clear the good names

of people who are said to have been guilty of immoral, and even criminal, conduct.

Statements may also be found in occult literature to the effect that, although repellant, certain portions of the Scriptures and myths of ancient peoples were nevertheless useful in serving as additional blinds or covers for more deeply hidden and potentially dangerous information. By such means it was hoped that valuable knowledge would be preserved from complete loss during the Dark Ages which cyclically descend upon the world. With their profound insight, the Sages of old foresaw the coming eras of spiritual blindness during which humanity would tend to accentuate materialistic and egoistic concepts of life and so suffer the manifold disasters which history records. They wished to ensure the preservation of the Ageless Wisdom and thus couched it in terms which would convey abstract ideas in concrete forms, whilst at the same time preventing the premature discovery of its more potentially dangerous aspects. The darkness having passed, those who sought the hidden truth could, with their developed intuition and the use of the keys of interpretation, then bring forth into the light of day the knowledge thus preserved. This approach offers an explanation of the numerous accounts of immoral conduct on the part of divine, semi-divine and heroic characters recorded in World Scriptures and Mythologies.

THE SYMBOLS OF STERILITY AND FERTILITY

Applying this view, barrenness and fruitfulness may be regarded as symbols used in the Sacred Language to describe conditions of human consciousness. Thus translated from a physical to a mental condition, barrenness portrays the unresponsiveness of the formal mind (the wife) to the fructifying Rays of spiritual and intellectual light shining forth from the Inmost Self (the husband). Inversely, fruitfulness represents the evolutionary stage at which this has been remedied, the outer personality being thereafter illumined by the light of the imperishable soul. In consequence, a son (spiritual intuitiveness) is conceived and born in the supposed old age (advanced evolutionary stature) of a hitherto barren (unevolved) wife, as in the cases of Sarah and Abraham, Rebekah and Isaac, Rachel and Jacob, Elisabeth and Zacharias, and other wives and husbands in the Bible.

Since all the chief characters in inspired allegories are personifications of principles and attributes of a *single* human being, the husband is affected by this evolutionary change from mental " barrenness " to mental " fruitfulness ". Childless until it occurs, he becomes a father when the fruitful state has been achieved. As we have seen, once this is understood frank Biblical references to legitimate or illicit procreative activity lose their repulsiveness; for such " marriage " is not physical, but psycho-spiritual. Actually, marriage and the woman partner are used as symbols, and some

18

times in two different ways. In one of these the woman is the abstract mind and its vehicle the Causal Body, whilst marriage refers to the descent of the fructifying Monadic Ray as a result of which the Higher Mind becomes pregnant with the intuitive faculty and the power to perceive the oneness of life amidst diversity of form. When these capacities are developed to the degree at which they are consciously realised and expressed, a " son " is said to be born. Such is an Initiatory interpretation, which applies to all major Nativities as of Saviours, demi-gods and heroes. Classical mythology is replete with such allegories, as in the cases of Leda and the swan (the triple Deity of Universe and man), Danae and the shower of gold (pure Spirit), and Io whom Zeus visited in the form of a cloud (container of the " Waters of Life "). Castor and Pollux, Perseus and Epaphus were the sons of these respective unions.

In a second meaning the woman is the outer personality, and more especially its formal mind. Marriage portrays the phase in human development at which the mentally fructifying influence of the inner Self, through the abstract intellect, is finding a response in the hitherto wholly analytical, concrete mind, which is therefore likely to be barren as regards intuitive perception. In consequence the faculty of abstract thought is added to those of analysis and deduction (conception). Thereupon a son (intuition) is said to be born.

OUTRAGES TO MORALITY AS CLUES TO A HIDDEN MEANING

The student of the Sacred Language, whether finding the above interpretations acceptable or not, will doubtless be ready to regard this Scriptural account of incidents in the life of Lot and his contemporaries as one of the most remarkable examples of allegorical revelation in any Scripture. The fact that in its literal reading the story of Lot, Sodom and Gomorrah is wholly unacceptable—is, indeed, an affront to both the intellect and the moral sense, in common with much other supposedly historical material in the Bible—gives strong support to an allegorical approach to the Scriptures, hence its repetition here. Of three choices before the reader—to discard unacceptable portions and retain the remainder, to reject the whole as unworthy of serious consideration, or to seek for possible deeper meanings—the last-mentioned is surely preferable. This is the view taken by the learned Rabbi Moses Maimonides who, as quoted earlier, wrote:" ....the greater the absurdity of the letter, the deeper the wisdom of the spirit. " The Analogeticists[1] of old, as also those who have since

[1] The Neo-Platonic School, founded in 193 A.D. by Ammonius Saccas, included Alexandrian philosophers who sought to interpret the Bible according to a system of allegory, analogy and symbol and were, in consequence, named Analogeticists.

followed in their footsteps, perceived this " deeper wisdom of the spirit " in the Scriptures and Mythologies of ancient peoples and fortunately recorded their several interpretations.   The destruction of Sodom and Gomorrah, the personal intervention of the Supreme Deity, the turning Lot's wife into a pillar of salt, Lot's readiness to offer his virgin daughters as prostitutes to the peoples of the city, the daughters' subsequent incestuous intercourse with their father after having rendered him intoxicated—these and other events do, indeed, strain to the utmost one's ability to accept a dead letter reading of such Biblical narratives.   Happily, as stated above, an alternative exists; it is to regard the Bible as an allegorical work, apply the keys of interpretation, and thereby discover the rich treasures of wisdom which lie hidden, layer upon layer, beneath the veils of incongruity, allegory and symbol.

followed in their footsteps, perceived this deeper wisdom of the spirit
in the Scriptures and Mythologies of ancient peoples and fortunately

CHAPTER V

ABRAHAM AND SARAH JOURNEY INTO EGYPT

Gen. 20. *Abraham denieth his wife, and Abimelech taketh her: he restoreth
her with presents.*

1. *And Abraham journeyed from thence toward the south country,
and dwelled between Kadesh and Shūr, and sojourned in Gerär.*

2. *And Abraham said of Sarah his wife, She is my sister: And
Abimelech king of Gerär sent, and took Sarah.*

In this Chapter of *Genesis* the Bible once again presents as history
accounts of most reprehensible conduct which, read literally, cannot
but be offensive to the reader. If, however, they are not read literally
but allegorically, then a concealed wisdom may possibly be discerned. In
pursuit of this idea, as throughout this book, I offer the results of an application of the keys of interpretation to the stories here recounted. Abraham
for example, may be taken as personifying the immortal Self of man
expressed through the higher, abstract intellect, whilst Sarah represents
the lower, concrete mind. She is thus not incorrectly described as his
sister since both are manifestations, as intellect, of the one Monadic Ray
(Terah). When physically incarnate, the inner Self of man is related to
its mortal personality (Abimelech) through the medium (by the loan) of
the concrete, analytical portion of the mind (Sarah). Thus the account of
an apparently offensive action performed by Abraham, in again passing
off his wife as his sister to the King of a country which he is visiting, could
possibly be read as a description of both the complete constitution of man
and the means whereby the spiritual Self becomes manifest in the physical
body and brain of a highly evolved individual.

THE DREAM OF ABIMELECH

Gen. 20: 3. *But God came to Abimelech in a dream by night, and said to him,
Behold, thou art but a dead man, for the woman which thou
hast taken; for she is a man's wife.*

The appearance of God to Abimelech, who is innocent of wrong, indicates that phase in human evolution at which the outer person begins to enter into communion with the divine Presence *within* him. Conscience, personified by God, is thus said to have intervened, although Abimelech may have sinned in thought with Sarah. Physically, however, he was entirely blameless, first because he had not touched Sarah and secondly because she had come to him as Abraham's sister, and not as his wife.

> Gen. 20: 4. *But Abimelech had not come near her: and he said, Lord, wilt thou slay also a righteous nation?*
>
> 5. *Said he not unto me, She is my sister? and she, even she herself said, He is my brother: in the integrity of my heart and innocency of my hands have I done this.*

These verses read somewhat like accounts of vocal interchanges typical of certain Initiatory ceremonials in which Candidates are questioned and tested in order to demonstrate that they have come properly prepared for the solemn Rite of Initiation, or is *Mer Kheru*[1] or *Gotra-bhu*.[2]

> Gen. 20: 6. *Ana God said unto him in a dream, Yea, I know thou didst this in the integrity of thy heart; for I also withheld thee from sinning against me: therefore suffered I thee not to touch her.*

This verse states that due preparation and good report had given assurance of the Candidate's preparedness. His purity and his innocence, even under temptation to give way to sensual indulgence, are proven. The introduction of the Supreme Deity into a supposedly historical narrative, and " His " intervention, may be read as an indication that more than history is intended. In consequence, the reader's attention is arrested and directed to a search for an under-meaning, a revelation of eternal truths by means of the allegorical method of describing events in time. Thus God appears to Abimelech in a dream.

> Gen. 20: 7. *Now therefore restore the man his wife; for he is a prophet, and he shall pray for thee, and thou shalt live: and if thou restore her not, know thou that thou shalt surely die, thou, and all that are thine.*

[1] *Mer Kheru* (Egyptian). " True of voice "—a judgment pronounced by Tehuti when the soul has passed successfully the test of the supposed weighing of his heart against a feather in the Hall of Judgment. Probably an allegorical presentation of *karma*.

[2] *Gotra-bhu* (Pali)—Amongst the Buddhists one sufficiently evolved to receive Initiation.

The restoration of Sarah—personifying the formal, analytical mind—to her position as wife of Abraham—the abstract, synthesising intellect—draws attention to the fusion of the two aspects of the mind characteristic of the illumination attained when this union has been achieved. The warning of the Lord to Abimelech that if he fails to restore Sarah both he and all his people will die, truly indicates that without this union and enlightenment the outer, personal man is metaphorically without life, meaning unillumined by spiritual light and unsustained by an inward power. In the Symbolical Language such a condition is described as death. Miraculous resuscitation, in its turn, allegorically refers to the recovery of spiritual insight and illumination.[1]

Otherwise expressed, in a dream (superphysical awareness) Abimelech realises that the two attributes and activities of the mind are really one, that actually Sarah *is* Abraham's wife. Abimelech, King of Gerär, whither Abraham had journeyed, represents the evolving personal consciousness and his country the component vehicles, including the physical—the land itself. The story thus portrays the evolutionary phase at which man frees himself from the limitations of the lower, purely analytical mind and attains to the universality typical of the synthesising, prophetic mind. Since this achievement will be normal only in later races Abraham personifies one who has anticipated normal evolutionary progress and attained spiritual awareness in advance of the race.

The reader is here reminded that in allegorical narratives each of the more prominent people portray *an aspect of one person*. Terah, for example, personifies the human Monad, and Abraham its manifestation as a spiritual individuality, an interior divine Presence. Sarah represents the formal mind, and Abimelech the *psyche* and the physical aspects of the mortal man. The whole nature of each and every man is in fact present, being represented by different personages, and the drama of the evolution of the Soul—and sometimes of certain of its parts—is described by means of pseudo-historical metaphor.

If the narrative be thus read—and surely this is preferable to a literal reading, in which the Lord and Abraham appear to combine in an action which is both deceitful and flagrantly immoral—then the offensiveness disappears, possibly, having been included deliberately in conformity with the custom of concealing certain power-bestowing truths under a veil, sometimes repulsive in its literal form. The three principles of man—the spiritual intelligence, the more material mind, and the body with its brain—must achieve union before full illumination can be attained. Symbolically the mind is lent to the body (Sarah to Abimelech) as part of this procedure, which is described as a kind of marital drama, or even mystery play. This

---

[1] cf. Christ's raising of Lazarus (*Jn.* 11) and the daughter of Jairus (*Matt.* 9: 18).

is another example of a skilfully delineated psychological development through which the whole race will eventually pass, as also will Abraham, both as symbol of the racial Monad-Ego and as an illumined historical character.

HUMAN EVOLUTION—NORMAL AND HASTENED

The Twentieth Chapter of *Genesis* thus tells the story of the descent of the Ray of the Monad (Terah) into incarnation (family emigration to Canaan), and also of the ultimate illumination of the personal consciousness (Sarah) by the spiritual light of the innermost Self (Abraham).   This evolutionary phase is entered upon naturally after a sufficient number of physical incarnations, and enforcedly as a result of three significant experiences.   These consist of interior awakening, official entry upon the Path of Swift Unfoldment,[1] and passage through Initiatory Rites in the Lesser and Greater Mysteries.

Throughout the whole narrative Sarah, as has been previously stated, represents the linking, formal mind—that intellectual principle of man which unites the unfolding inner Self or Ego and the outer physical personality.   The mind of man is dual, as correctly portrayed by Sarai who, as the lower mind, is spiritually " barren ", meaning ineffective as a link between the spiritual and the physical man.   Her duality is displayed when her name is later changed from Sarai to Sarah, indicating that the two aspects of the mind—the formal and the abstract—were becoming blended.   In consequence of this fusion the level of mental activity becomes raised to that of the Higher Mind, or abstract, synthesising, intelligence in man.   Thereafter Sarah, as the illumined formal mind, is no longer " barren ".

The account of Sarai's residence in the Palace of Pharaoh in Egypt on an earlier occasion, and the statement that concubinage did not occur either then or in this later episode associated with Abimelech, is also significant.   The former experience indicates the enmeshment of the personal consciousness within the lower mentality (Sarai).   The latter portrays the more advanced phase at which the desirable activities and powers of the lower mind have been used and developed and the hypercritical, prideful and separative attributes (Sarai's laughter in the tent) forsworn.   Thereafter the mortal personality is appropriately depicted as the servant, or sometimes the handmaiden or bondswoman, of the Higher Self.

> Gen. 20: 14. *And Abimelech took sheep, and oxen, and menservants, and womenservants, and gave them unto Abraham, and restored him Sarah his wife.*

[1] q.v. *The Hidden Wisdom in the Holy Bible*, Vol. I, Pt. VI, Geoffrey Hodson.

15. *And Abimelech said, Behold, my land is before thee: dwell where it pleaseth thee.*

16. *And unto Sarah he said, Behold, I have given thy brother a thousand pieces of silver: behold, he is to thee a covering of the eyes, unto all that are with thee, and with all other: thus she was reproved.*

If mystically interpreted, this action of Abimelech may well refer to that phase of human evolution at which the outer, personal nature is at last wholly surrendered to its Higher Self and the spiritual laws to which it is obedient. If this be accepted, then the forgiving and unresentful attitude of mind of Abimelech towards Abraham, even after the supposed subterfuge was discovered indicates a recognition of that which Abraham represents in the microcosm, namely the inspired inner Self for which the mortal man is but a vehicle. Up to a certain evolutionary phase the latter is ignorant even of the existence of its own divine nature, and in consequence is in conflict with the ideals which it represents. These verses show that this former phase has come to an end and indicate recognition of and surrender to the Divine, together with the sacrifice of the material motives and objectives of man's physical nature and life.

Sheep and oxen may well be emblems of those emotions which had already become " tamed ", since these are domestic animals. Men and women servants would represent mere bodily attributes, whilst Sarah, who was returned to Abraham, is as we have seen, emblematic of the purified mind, now duly prepared to be unified with the abstract intelligence. Silver, in the symbology of metals, generally denotes the mortal man, as also does the moon, with which in occult philosophy silver is associated.[1] Thus again, by reference to a gift of this metal, surrender of the personal self to the immortal soul is allegorically referred to. The number 1000, which by reduction may be regarded as 10, implies both the completion of one cycle and more especially preparation for embarkation upon its successor.

Examining the component figures, 0 stands for infinite, boundless Being, the Source of all existence, whilst the number 1 symbolises both manifestation and the manifestor of the Infinite and Unmanifest. It is also the unit of individual, spiritual life, the 0 made manifest. Together, then, these two numbers (10) represent re-emergence after the closing of a cycle of manifestation, with absorption into the boundless Source, as represented by the cipher (0). The addition of ciphers in numerical symbology, as in this case of 1000 pieces of silver, is said to indicate the dimensions involved.

[1] q.v. *Lecture Notes of the School of the Wisdom*, Vol. I (Rev. Ed.), Ch. XIII, Geoffrey Hodson, and Chart preceding Part V of this book.

In this sense 10 would represent a minor cycle, 100 a still greater period, whilst 1000 could be read as referring to a total period of divine manifestation and suggests a macrocosmic interpretation.[1]

> *Gen.* 20: 17. *So Abraham prayed unto God: and God healed Abimelech, and his wife, and his maidservants; and they bare children.*
>
> 18. *For the LORD had fast closed up all the wombs of the house of Abimelech, because of Sarah Abraham's wife.*

In the Symbolical Language, as previously stated, fertility, fructification, conception and birth are used as symbols for both a state of consciousness and a phase of evolution. The state of consciousness is one of self-illumination as the result of a descent of power and light from the innermost Self, and phase of evolution is that at which this can be consciously received, an expansion of awareness occur, and the faculty of spiritual intuitiveness begin to manifest itself, or be " born ". Thus, remembering that the whole drama is descriptive of experiences of one individual and that each actor personifies a part of that one individual, the opening of the wombs of the wife and maidservants of Abimelech, and their later bearing of children, indicate that these experiences had been entered upon and this phase had become outwardly manifest. Mystically stated, an Annunciation (God's answer to Abraham's prayer) and a Nativity (the birth of children) had occurred to Abimelech, who personifies the consciousness of the mortal man.

This Twentieth Chapter of *Genesis* may thus legitimately be regarded, I submit, as more than a strange story concerning Abraham, Sarah and Abimelech, in which almost incomprehensible, even immoral actions were contemplated and partially performed; for it is susceptible of interpretation as a description by means of allegory of the experiences of the mind and Spirit of the human being who has entered upon the pathway of return and attained to the mystical " birth ".

---

[1] q.v. Vol. I of this work, Pt. III, Ch. III.

CHAPTER VI

THE BIRTH OF ISAAC—A MYSTICAL NATIVITY

Gen. 21. *Isaac is born. Hagar and Ishmael cast forth. An angel comforted her. Abimelech makes a covenant with Abraham.*

SOME PRINCIPLES OF INTERPRETATION

Before embarking upon a detailed commentary upon this Chapter of *Genesis*, it may be useful to remind the reader of some of the keys of interpretation, at the same time and once again requesting kind indulgence for seemingly undue repetitiveness. All the *dramatis personae* included in allegorical literature represent the several principles, attributes, characteristics, capacities, strengths and weaknesses of *one* human being. The deeds performed by the different people are descriptive of activities and transformations occurring within both the human and the divine nature of the same person. Phenomena and events are designed to portray the results of these actions and changes, whilst the end product or conclusion of the story—whether marriage, parenthood, productivity and progress, or decline, decay and death—allegorically describes the consummation of a phase of human evolution.

These interpretations can severally apply to an ordinary human being living a normal life, to a Candidate for Initiation, and also to Initiates of successive Degrees from the First to the Fifth, at which Adeptship is attained. In the larger sense the many happenings apply equally to a single nation, to a race, and to humanity as a whole. Macrocosmically they apply to Solar Systems, Universes and Cosmoi. In the human sense, however, the master key is that *all happens within one individual person.* When interpreting the *dramatis personae*, however, as representing principles of the Universe and of man, it is found that the personifications vary somewhat according to the themes of the stories.

NATIVITIES AS MYSTICAL EXPERIENCES

The Nativity of Christ is one example of this personification of human principles and of variations in possible interpretations. The narrative introduces Gabriel (the Monad); the Annunciation (the monadic Ray or *Ātma*); Mary (the Higher Self in the Causal Body, or Higher *Manas*) the Christ child (spiritual wisdom and intuitiveness, or *Buddhi*); Joseph (the mature, formal mind); domestic animals whose presence is assumed (the docile emotions or disciplined *kāma*); the manger (the etheric double[1]); the stable (the physical body and the Auric Envelope).[1] As not infrequently occurs in both the Old and the New Testaments, the *dramatis personae* of a story are found to be seven in number. Whilst this may be mere coincidence, it would seem to be more reasonable to regard the enumeration as deliberate, particularly if the view be accepted that the authors of certain parts of the Old Testament and the Evangelists were instructed Kabbalists and therefore veiled, whilst also revealing certain power-bestowing aspects of their wisdom.

Similarly, in the stories of the divine Annunciation to Abraham concerning the hitherto barren Sarah,[2] followed by her conception, the later birth of Isaac, the Annunciation to Hagar by an angel,[3] the treatment later meted out to Hagar and Ishmael and their subsequent experiences—all these describe transformations occurring *within one person*. Allowances must, however, be made for differing correspondences necessitated by the stories themselves. For example, Abraham sometimes stands for the Monad and at other times, as in the story of Abimelech, the Monad individualised as the reincarnating spiritual Self or Ego.

Accordingly, in reference to the conceptions of Ishmael and Isaac, Abraham's story includes: the Lord God (the Monad); the Lord's promise of conception, and Abraham himself as the divine agent (the monadic Ray or *Ātma*); Sarah (the formal mind now unified with the abstract intelligence); Isaac (spiritual wisdom and intuitiveness); Hagar (the desire-enfired mind); Ishmael (the will-force first expressed as desire and later sublimated when Ishmael becomes an archer); Abraham's home (the physical body and Auric Envelope); the wilderness of Paran (the renunciation of desire and the sense of emptiness at first experienced); the thirst (the beginning of aspiration for the spiritual heights which leads to sublimation); the bottle of water given by Abraham to Hagar (personal, possessive desire); the well in the wilderness disclosed by the angel (the vision of universal love); the water in the well (universality and impersonality of life, love, thought and will); and the wife from Egypt (spiritual wisdom derived from a Sanctuary of the Greater Mysteries).

In the Initiatory interpretation the higher Self in its Causal Body (Abraham—Sarah) renounces personal and desireful self-expression (the expulsion of Hagar and Ishmael) in favour of spiritual fulfilment (the

---

[1] This interpretation is more fully expounded in Pt. V of Vol. I of this work.
[2] *Gen.* 18: 10.
[3] *Gen.* 16. 7–11.

conception and birth of Isaac). The personal nature, suffering for a time as Hagar and Ishmael did, is eventually empowered and initiated into the Greater Mysteries, having passed through the philosophic death and resurrection known as Initiation. Ascents from plains to mountains, visitations of the Lord and surrenders to His will, all indicate that the centre of consciousness is being slowly lifted past and above the formal, material, acquisitive outlook of the personal nature into that recognition of and surrender to spiritual law which is characteristic of the Initiate's attitude towards life.

Astrological symbolism is also frequently employed, this being the custom in Chaldea. The substitution of the ram (Aries) for Isaac as a sacrifice, the supplying of a pitcher of water (Aquarius) to Hagar in the wilderness and the presentation of Ishmael as an Archer (Sagittarius), refer respectively to the Zodiacal attributes and qualities within and to influences playing upon the race.

After this brief reconsideration of some classical symbols and the principles of their interpretation, a return to the Biblical text is now made. The Twenty-first Chapter of *Genesis* is so full of occult allusions that it will now be considered verse by verse.

Gen. 21: 1. *And the LORD visited Sarah as he had said, and the LORD did unto Sarah as he had spoken.*

In the Sacred Language old age signifies that phase of evolutionary maturity at which occult development is far advanced. Thus Abraham as the spiritual Self, and Sarah as the now unified abstract and concrete mind, have reached the stage of unfoldment at which the intuition is to be awakened and developed. Here the allegorical method is followed of describing this birth of intuitive perception as a Nativity. The Lord is the Monadic *Ātma* which visits Sarah, the creative agency being twice referred to in the first verse as speech or the spoken " Word " of God. A similar practice is followed in the Annunciations by Archangels to the parents of John the Baptist and Jesus the Christ foretelling their respective births. The symbolism also applies to the Macrocosm, with a reference to the divine, creative power as the *Logos* or *Verbum*, the emitted fructifying energy of the masculine spiritual principle, which is described as being of the order or quality of sound—in Sanskrit *ākasa*.[1]

---

[1] *Ākāsā* (Sk.). " The subtle, supersensuous, spiritual essence which pervades all space. The primordial substance erroneously identified with ether. But it is to ether what spirit is to matter. . . . It is, in fact, the Eternal Space in which lies inherent the Ideation of the Universe in its ever-changing aspects on the planes of matter and objectivity, and from which radiates the *First Logos* or expressed thought. This is why it is stated in the *Purānas* that *ākāsā* has but one attribute, namely sound, for sound is but the translated symbol for *Logos*—' Speech ' in its mystic sense." q.v. *The Theosophical Glossary*, H. P. Blavatsky.

Gen. 21: 2. *For Sarah conceived, and bare Abraham a son in his old age,*
at the set time of which God had spoken to him.

In consequence of the action upon the feminine principle (Sarah)
of the fructifying male energy (the voice of God) a third is born, symbolised
by the son (Isaac). Macrocosmic and microcosmic creative processes are
correctly allegorised in these remarkable verses and in the former, as said
above, it is the Universe which is born out of the Great Deep (Sarah) as
a result of the action of the Great Breath, Voice or spoken " Word ". In
the microcosmic interpretation the Monad-Ego embarks upon a new phase
of existence when once it has self-consciously and actively entered the plane
of pure wisdom, become aware of the essential unity of all life and developed
the faculty of the intuition (the son).

Gen. 21: 3. *And Abraham called the name of his son that was born unto*
him, whom Sarah bare to him, Isaac.

4. *And Abraham circumcised his son Isaac being eight days old, as*
God had commanded him.

Macrocosmically, the eighth day indicates that a minor or component
cycle or *Manvantara* has passed through its seven phases and so ended, a
new one, an eighth, having begun. Since evolution is not an eddy but a
spiral ascent, this new creation will be more refined and more spiritual
than its predecessors. Symbolically Isaac, representing the Macrocosm,
is circumcised on the eighth day. Microcosmically, the eighth is the first
" day " of the new phase of Egoic evolution that is entered upon when the
birth of the intuition occurs. In this phase the procreative power, which
has been previously brought under control, is now sublimated to the spiritual
and intellectual purposes of the Monad-Ego.

The universalisation of consciousness attained and experienced at
that level is also symbolically implied in the removal of the *prepuce* or covering
of the male creative organ. In offering this interpretation, I repeat that
the purely hygienic purpose of the practice is not overlooked. The skin
of man is, however, a symbol for the accentuated sense of separated individuality or I-am-ness. Piercings of the skin, woundings, flayings and
circumcisions occultly imply that this sense of separateness has been outgrown
and that a more universal outlook upon life has been entered upon as a
new cycle begins—symbolically on the eighth " day ". Circumcision thus
symbolises both universalisation of consciousness and the power attained
by the practice of continence.

In the more exoteric sense circumcision represents renunciation of the
worldly, secular mode of life and the adoption of the ideal of self-discipline

and service. This includes the so-called putting away of the flesh, or the adoption of chastity. Philo Judaeus, the great Alexandrian sage, wrote: " The circumcision of the skin is said to be a symbol, indicating that it is proper to cut away all superfluous and extravagant desires, by studying continence and religion. "[1] In this symbolical sense the uncircumcised state indicates uncontrolled desire which resists the discipline of the inner will, renders the person unfitted to receive the gifts of the Spirit, and kills out the higher impulses which must precede spiritual rebirth.

> Gen. 21: 5. *And Abraham was an hundred years old, when his son Isaac was born unto him.*

By reduction the number 100 becomes 10 and 1. The first two—100 and 10—imply the final summation into synthesis and unity of all powers and products of a cycle at its close. The number 1, a phallic symbol, refers to the opening of a relatively major (100) and relatively minor (10) new creative cycle. Also implied by these numbers is, Macrocosmically, the initiation of and entry upon a new order of universal existence (*Mahā-Manvantara* or cosmic cycle), and microcosmically the attainment of a new level of consciousness by man.

> Gen. 21: 6. *And Sarah said, God hath made me to laugh, so that all that hear will laugh with me.*

The earlier laughter of Sarah referred to in the twelfth verse of the Eighteenth Chapter of *Genesis* was sceptical, and even scornful, of the words of the Lord. Thus described, such derision indicates mental blindness, an unillumined state of mind. Sarah's laughter described in this verse, however, is clearly of an entirely different character being expressive of an interior experience in which all mankind might share. In the Sacred Language such laughter, in the macrocosmic sense, symbolises the joyous response of the recipient maternal principle to the impulse and influence of the paternal " Voice ". The laughter is the rippling echo of the creative " Word " as it resounds from the Great Deep, or basic substance (Sarah), which has been changed from quiescence to vibratory and productive activity.

Microcosmically, however, Sarah here represents the synthesising, prophetic mind, or rather the total mental unit, concrete and abstract, now blended into one. When awareness is centred in this vehicle, exaltation and bliss are experienced. Poets and philosophers have borne testimony

---

[1] Philo Judaeus, *Works*, Vol. IV, p. 451, Bohn.

to this condition of harmonious happiness, serene ecstasy, indescribable
" Brahmic " bliss. Thus Dante wrote:

" That which I was seeing seemed to me a smile of the universe,
for my inebriation was entering through the hearing and through the
sight. O joy! O ineffable gladness! O life entire of love and of
peace! O riches secure without longing! "[1]

Jacob Boehme says on the same subject:

" Earthly language is entirely insufficient to describe what there is
of joy, happiness, and loveliness contained in the inner wonders of
God. Even if the eternal Virgin pictures them to our minds, man's
construction is too cold and dark to be able to express even a spark
of it in his language. "[2]

Edward Carpenter wrote: " All sorrow finished. " " The deep, deep
ocean of joy within. " He describes this aspect of spiritual awareness as:
" being filled with joy " and " singing joy unending. "[3]

Such spiritual upliftment affects the entire nature of man. All
the seven principles are gradually brought into vibratory response, so that
the whole being is pervaded by a serene bliss. Symbolically, ". . . all that
hear will laugh with me. " Sarah, at the stage described in this verse,
represents the intelligence aspect of the three-fold[4] Inner Self of Initiated
man experiencing the bliss of *Buddhic*[5] or Christ consciousness and sharing
it with, or transmitting it to, all the other vehicles.

> *Gen.* 21: 7. *And she said, Who would have said unto Abraham, that Sarah*
> *should have given children suck? for I have born him a son in his*
> *old age.*

---

[1] q.v. *The Divine Comedy—Paradiso*, Dante, trans. C. E. Norton.

[2] q.v. *The Life and Doctrines of Jacob Boehme*, Franz Hartmann.

[5] q.v. *From Adam's Peak to Elephanta*, Edward Carpenter.

[4] In occult philosophy the immortal Self of man is conceived as threefold, being a
reflection and representation in miniature of the Three Aspects or " Persons " of the Blessed
Trinity. In man the First Aspect is present as spiritual will (Sk. *Atma*), the Second Aspect
as spiritual wisdom (Sk. *Buddhi*) and the Third Aspect as spiritual intelligence (Sk. *Manas*).
The spiritual man is thus made in the image of his Creator. In the Symbolical Language
the *dramatis personae* typify one or more of these component parts of man, sometimes at
particular stages of evolution. In addition the formal mind, the emotions, the vital forces
and the physical body are sometimes personified by characters in an allegory, as we have
just seen.

[5] *Buddhi* (Sk.). The sixth principle of man, that of intuitive wisdom, vehicle of the
seventh, *Atma*, the supreme Soul in man.

If, in its turn, this episode be translated from the personal or micro-cosmic to the universal or macrocosmic application and regarded as descriptive of Cosmogenesis, then the maternal principle (Sarah) becomes vocal and reiterates that which the paternal principle (the Lord via Abraham) had promised. The interplay between the two is symbolised by vocal response.

Centre and circumference, sun and " Ring-Pass-Not ",[1] are implied in the macrocosmic interpretation of these first seven verses of Chapter Twenty-one, which by their content constitute a miniature account of Cosmogenesis. Abraham is the point or centre and Sarah is the circum-ference of the sphere of differentiated substance, which responds creatively to the Great Breath or " Word ". The occult potency of sound is indicated in all verses except the fifth by the references to words spoken.

> Gen. 21: 8. *And the child grew, and was weaned: and Abraham made a great feast the same day that Isaac was weaned.*

Here the new-born child and its development form the subject matter. Weaning is a symbol of the attainment of full self-consciousness at the level concerned, just as birth symbolises the first entry upon that level. The former constitutes an important attainment, and symbolically is made the subject of rejoicing and celebration.[2]

> Gen. 21: 9. *And Sarah saw the son of Hagar the Egyptian, which she had born unto Abraham, mocking.*

Five persons are included in verses eight and nine—Abraham, Isaac, Sarah, Ishmael and Hagar, Ishmael being the one who mocked. In terms of the principles of the microcosm, man, but in " descending " order, these members of the family of Abraham, the Monad, personate respectively the Christ consciousness (Isaac), abstract intelligence (Sarah), the emotions (Hagar) and the physical mind-brain (Ishmael). Typically the conjoined analytical, hypercritical mind, focused almost exclusively upon the physical world and worldliness, jeers or mocks at spiritual, intuitive and prophetic activities and claims. Similarly Goliath (the arrogant formal mind) issued a jeering challenge to the Israelites, and particularly to the young shepherd boy, David (spiritual intuitiveness), armed only with a sling. In the New Testament one of the two thieves who were crucified with the Christ mocked Him.

[1] q.v. Glossary.
[2] q.v. *The Hidden Wisdom in the Holy Bible*, Vol. I, Pt. IV, Geoffrey Hodson—more especially the interpretations of the Feast and the Fatted Calf in the Parable of the Prodigal Son.

As previously suggested the birth of Isaac when applied to the evolution of the Monad (Abraham), as with all other Nativities, allegorically refers to the birth of the Christ consciousness and the profound interior regeneration associated with passage through the Great Initiations. Whilst eventually the whole experience is transmitted fully to the successive mortal personalities, this spiritual Nativity is at first obstructed by the not unnatural action of the prideful, materialistic aspect of the human mind (Goliath and Ishmael).

> Gen. 21: 10. *Wherefore she said unto Abraham, Cast out this bond-woman and her son: for the son of this bondwoman shall not be heir with my son, even with Isaac.*

Read literally, Sarah's action can only be characterised as unjust, even though not unnatural; for it was Sarah who originally suggested to Abraham his association with Hagar, since she herself had up to that time failed to produce a son. Interpreted as a portrayal of experiences which follow spiritual regeneration, and accepting the respective personifications suggested earlier, Sarah's action may be read as descriptive of the results of evolutionary progress; for it naturally follows in due course that the unspiritual attributes of the outer personality are outgrown and left behind. Allegorically, Sarah demands the expulsion of Hagar and Ishmael from the family. As a result of this development the outer man is deprived of all power to distract and limit at the physical level the intelligence and activity of the new-born intuitive faculty (Isaac). These transformations and achievements are described in the story of Ishmael's mocking and Sarah's demand for the banishment of both mother and son into the wilderness.

If the repetition be permitted, despite the fact that a number of people are introduced into an allegory descriptive of normal human evolution and sometimes of the attainment of spiritual and occult powers, nevertheless each of the persons involved is a personification of one or more of the seven component powers, principles or parts[1] of *one* individual—the hero or central figure. Thus it is Abraham himself, as the unfolding Monad of man, who is passing through the experiences associated with evolutionary progress. Whilst it is not argued that none of the people in the story had an actual existence—quite probably they did—at the same time the story of their actions and experiences is so related as to apply to the development not only of the central figure, but of every human being who has passed through or will pass through the same evolutionary phases.

Thus Typhon, King Kamsa and Herod (the acquisitive, power-seeking mind) endeavour to destroy Osiris, Shri Krishna and the new-born Christ-

---

[1] q.v. Footnote 3, p. 287.

19

child respectively. Thus, also, they inevitably fail, since the spiritual Self of man, being divine and immortal, cannot be finally defeated by any material power. Even if a figurative death is described, resurrection always follows.

> Gen. 21: 11. *And the thing was very grievous in Abraham's sight because of his son.*

The story of the actions of Sarah and Abraham, the abandonment and suffering of Hagar and Ishmael and the intervention by the Lord God may be regarded as one of the many cameos or portrayals in miniature of the passage of advanced Souls through certain phases of evolution. The experience includes the stress, mystical wounds and " passion "which must accompany efforts to take the Kingdom of Heaven by storm, or in advance of the epoch at which such progress will naturally occur.

As indicated earlier, it frequently happens that narratives which when read literally contain unpleasant and even repellent subject matter prove on close examination to be revelations of spiritual truth and abstract ideas beneath a veil of symbolism. Abraham's apparently cruel treatment of Hagar and Ishmael may indicate that old habits die hard and that the past is not renounced without the necessity for determined effort. Egoic detachment and dispassion must ultimately be attained. Symbolically, the mento-emotional nature (Hagar) and its products—feeling, desire, sensuality—must be banished and rendered impotent lest at some future time they become unduly active. The petrification of Lot's wife may illustrate the effects of this error. Therefore Hagar and Ishmael are symbolically sent into the wilderness to perish.

> Gen. 21: 12. *And God said unto Abraham, Let it not be grievous in thy sight because of the lad, and because of thy bondwoman; in all that Sarah hath said unto thee, hearken unto her voice; for in Isaac shall thy seed be called.*
>
> 13. *And also of the son of the bondwoman will I make a nation, because he is thy seed.*

Every experience ultimately proves to be fruitful, none being wasted. All that happens plays its enlightening and educative part upon the inner Self, pure wisdom being eventually attained. If other undesirable attributes have been outgrown, the critical faculty of the mind and its power of detailed analysis remain as valuable, even necessary, assets; for ultimately all ideas and all truths realised by the exercise of the intuition must be justified at the bar of the intellect. Thus Thomas was not rebuked for demanding sensory proof of the risen Christ,[1] and St. Paul advises: " Prove all things; hold fast that which is good. "[2] Thus, also, the Lord God promised Abraham that his son Ishmael was to " make a nation ".

Gen. 21: 14. *And Abraham rose up early in the morning, and took bread, and a bottle of water, and gave it unto Hagar, putting it on her shoulder, and the child, and sent her away; and she departed, and wandered in the wilderness of Beer-sheba.*

This conduct of Abraham towards Hagar and Ishmael appears on the surface to be extremely cruel, and even out of character, for a great Patriarch and a servant of the Lord. A mystical meaning would, however, seem also to be conveyed; for when a certain advanced phase of evolution is reached by the evolving Spirit of man (Abraham), the restrictive mental and emotional influences of the mortal personality begin to be reduced to a minimum. Symbolically Hagar and Ishmael, representing these influences, are banished. Nevertheless the dispassion and detachment thus implied do not involve either the death of the mortal personality or the complete cutting off of the inner Self from the outer man. Reincarnation in physical bodies must still occur, the Higher Self directing them increasingly by will, thought and experience (bread) and vitalising them with spiritual life-force (water).

Bread, in the allegorical language, is a symbol of the regeneration of life from the seed and of the fruits of the activity of the higher intellect, especially those of perception of principles and comprehension of truth. Water, in this sense, symbolises the intellectual and spiritual refreshment and vivification which the personality (Hagar-Ishmael) receives when nourished by the higher nature (Abraham). From this and preceding verses it may be deduced that the power to restrict the spiritual Self is " banished " from the lower nature, which in its turn receives Egoic illumination.

Gen. 21: 15. *And the water was spent in the bottle, and she cast the child under one of the shrubs.*

16. *And she went, and sat her down over against him a good way off, as it were a bowshot: for she said, Let me not see the death of the child. And she sat over against him, and lifted up her voice, and wept.*

17. *And God heard the voice of the lad; and the angel of God called to Hagar out of heaven, and said unto her, What aileth thee,*

[1] *Jn.* 20 : 24–28.   [2] I *Thes.* 5 : 21.

> *Hagar: fear not; for God hath heard the voice of the lad where he is.*
>
> 18. *Arise, lift up the lad, and hold him in thine hand; for I will make him a great nation.*
>
> 19. *And God opened her eyes, and she saw a well of water; and she went, and filled the bottle with water, and gave the lad drink.*

The personality of even an advanced Soul is still prone to materialism, selfishness, indulgence and the loss of the spiritual impulse—a state which is represented in the Sacred Language by a desert, a wilderness, and the experiences of hunger and thirst. Recovery and recuperation are always possible by the action of the Higher Self, symbolised in this case by the angel of the Lord God, Who removes the veil of ignorance from the eyes of the mind and reveals the omnipresence of the divine life, typified by both the tree and the well with its contents.

The change from the possession of water contained in a bottle to the discovery, consequent upon divine illumination, of water in a well, may be read as signifying a liberation of consciousness from the restrictions of acute self-personality (bottle) and possessiveness to universalisation and the recognition that the one life (water) is available to and shared by all creatures. In this sense the bottle of water given by Abraham refers to that highly personal individualism which in the course of evolution must give place to recognition of unity and development of the capacity to draw upon the universal Source, symbolised by the well. Thus, as verse nineteen reads, " ....God opened her eyes, and she saw a well of water.... " When evolutionary progress is deliberately quickened, as by Candidates for Initiation and—until Adeptship is attained—by Initiates themselves, this universalisation is achieved by arduous self-training. The prophecy of the Lord concerning Ishmael is in due course amply fulfilled; for he becomes the father of a nation, twelve princes being included amongst his sons.[1]

CHAPTER VII

THE SYMBOLISM OF THE BOW AND THE ARROW

Gen. 21: 20. *And God was with the lad (Ishmael); and he grew, and dwelt in the wilderness, and became an archer.*

Here the symbolism is most direct. The lower nature has become spiritualised and its creative capacities adapted and sublimated. The archer in the Sacred Language personifies the manifested powers of the Logos or " Word ". These powers are threefold, being positive (the bow), negative (the string) and, before shooting or the utterance of the " Word ", neutral or equipolarised (the arrow).

The arrow itself reproduces the whole symbolism, since by its construction it also is threefold, consisting of point, shaft and feathered end with nick to engage the string. Thus the arrow resting on the strung bow represents the inherent creative life of universal Spirit-matter, symbolised by the bow and the string respectively. If the analogy is not being pressed too far, then the act of stringing not inaptly represents the state of tension which precedes the action of the Spirit of God in moving upon the face of the waters.[1]

THE LOGOS AS ARCHER

The act of shooting by the Divine Archer, the Primordial Logos—the flashing forth of the arrow—represents the emanation into matter (the target) of the divine life-force or *Fohat*. This action of the *Demiurgos* initiates the involutionary phase of manifestation. In a later phase, the evolutionary, when the organic kingdoms have come into being, the creative fire descends into them to provide the energy for processes of fertilisation, generation and regeneration.

THE DIVINE ARCHER WITHIN MAN

In the human kingdom the Monad is the archer and the Monadic will-force (*Ātma*) is the arrow which is shot into the spiritual Soul to bring

[1] *Gen.* 1 : 2.

about the fertilisation and development of the inherent capacity for spiritual awareness and intuition. This same power is also wielded by the Hierophant of the Greater Mysteries when he performs the Rite of Initiation, bringing about a profound interior regeneration accompanied by a philosophic death and ascension.

The arrow may also be regarded as a symbol of the spiritualising power which the inner Self " shoots " into the mind-brain of its mortal personality. This greatly stimulates the evolution of the mental, emotional and bodily natures. One further effect of this is the destruction of the less desirable mental and emotional qualities. The bow by itself portrays the bridge between Spirit and matter in the Universe, and between the inner and the outer selves of man. The arrow is also a symbol of ardent adoration and aspiration directed towards the one divine Source of all that exists. As this " arrow " strikes its target, so does the spiritual Self as human archer become one with the Supreme.[1]

THE IMMACULATE CONCEPTION

The First Logos, " born " (shot forth) as Universal Light from the first parental Pair, primordial Spirit-matter, is itself a triplicity as symbolised by the threefold arrow (point, shaft and feathered end with nick). Objectively active, the " Mindborn Son " enters or flashes forth into the awakened or atomised substance of the Universe-to-be. This creative union brings about the immaculate conception of the Cosmic *Christos* within the Virgin *Mare* or " sea " of primordial space.

In the Cosmogony of Hinduism, using *Sanskrit* terms, the bow would symbolise *Purusha*, the Great Breath, the string is *Prakriti*, the Great Deep, and the arrow is *Fohat*, the " Word " -force or emitted creative energy. The Archer is the active, universal Intelligence, *Mahat*, and His target is the differentiated area in *Prakriti* wherein He will produce the localised Universe-to-be. The point of impact and penetration becomes the first centre or " heart " of the Universe, the physical sun-to-be. The symbology is thus cruciform in design; for the arrow rests upon the bow, its shaft at right angles to the string. Also, when the target is penetrated after the shot a second cross is formed. All phallic, cosmogenetic symbology is based upon the impact of the *fohatic* " arrow ", the emitted vertical, creative fire of Spirit, upon the horizontal substance to be impregnated—universal space.

---

[1] " Having taken the Upanishad as the bow, as the great weapon, let him place on it the arrow, sharpened by devotion !. Then having drawn it with a thought directed to that which is, hit the mark, O Friend, namely, that which is Indestructible! Om is the bow, the Self is the arrow, Brahman is called the aim. It is to be hit by a man who is not thoughtless, and then as the arrow becomes one with the target, he will become one with Brahman." *Mundaka Upanishad*, II.

THE SYMBOL OF THE BROKEN BOW

The arrows of Eros, the God of Love, are said to inflame their victims with love-desire. In the spiritual sense the awakened love of God is implied, for it is this which ultimately leads the " victim " to the experience of oneness. On " The way of holiness "[1] personal love and desire are transmuted into universal love and realisation of unity with the life in all beings, instead of in the one chosen beloved alone. The breaking of the bow symbolises both victory over sensuality and desire and the sublimation of the life-force from its personal to its spiritual and universal expression. Thus Shri Krishna breaks the bow of his uncle, Kamsa. This bow is described as resembling the rainbow in size and colour, and as being guarded by many men, worshipped, and adorned with beautiful ornaments. Shri Krishna took it by force into his hands and strung it in a moment, breaking it as he did so. The sound of the breaking is said to have filled all space, including Heaven and Earth as well as the cardinal points.[2] Similarly at the Court of Janaka, King of Videha, who had offered his lovely daughter Sīta to anyone who could bend the magical bow, Prince Rāma not only bent but broke the bow and thus won the hand of the Princess, who became a most devoted and virtuous wife.[3]

THE ARROW AS THE SERPENT FIRE

After the sublimation of the sex force as portrayed in these allegories, the procreative fire—*Fohat-Kundalini*—is turned or " shot " upwards from the physical body, through the superphysical vehicles and into the Higher Self. The brain and the mind then become enfired and sensitised by the passage of this " arrow " of fire. In consequence the evolving spiritual Self—the mystic Archer—itself receives an enhancement of its intellectual faculty, which overflows as genius into the personal nature thus prepared. The story of Ishmael becoming an archer is therefore also susceptible of interpretation as an allegory of the successful sublimation of the creative force in man.

SAGITTARIUS, THE ARCHER

In Astrology Sagittarius is the ninth zodiacal Sign, and those born with the sun in this Sign are said to be endowed with typical Sagittarian characteristics. The mind, for example, is both penetrative and accurate in " hitting the mental mark ". When illumined, and even on ordinary occasions, Sagittarians readily pierce illusions, perceive essential verities,

[1] *Is.* 35: 8.
[2] q.v. *Bhāgavata-Purāna*, Sk. X, Chs. 41 and 42.
[3] q.v. *Ramayana*, Valmiki.

" hit the nail on the head ".   In addition, the influence of the active Logos is accentuated in them, and the flashing fire (arrow) of their highly perceptive intelligence fructifies those areas or regions of the mind which, according to temperament and activity, thereafter become intellectually fruitful.   This Sagittarian aspect of human nature and of divine activity is expressed as the faculty of inventiveness.

THE ARCHER IN THE WILDERNESS

Drawing together these various interpretations of the symbols of the bow and the arrow, macrocosmically the *fohatic* fire (the cosmic arrow) descends creatively into matter to produce the Universe of form.   Microcosmically the monadic *Ātma* (the arrow of man's spiritual will-force) descends into the higher and lower natures of man, awakening and stimulating both of them to greater activity.   When this process is quickened by the Rite of Initiation, the divine Fire is brought down by the Hierophant into the Ego and personality of the Candidate, who is thereafter spiritually empowered and illumined.

The wilderness in which Ishmael dwelt with his mother, Hagar, and where he became an archer, represents a condition and mode of life which is arid only to worldly-minded men.   The monastic life may appear fruitless, restrictive and devoid of happiness to those absorbed in normal everyday living.   The ascetic and the hermit may appear as emaciated and emasculated human beings to those who know nothing of the joys of solitude, and who would be incapable of living alone.   This apparently unproductive life in the wilderness can, however, be spiritually fruitful to a high degree. Whilst in its general meaning the wilderness is a symbol of mento-spiritual aridity, nevertheless in the Initiatory sense it indicates a condition of solitude and interior abstraction, " the quiet desert of the Godhead. "[1]   Elijah, though mentally in despair or in the wilderness state of consciousness, later received two visits by an angel (the spiritual Self), and the miracle was twice performed of the provision of food (mental illumination), the first time under a juniper tree,[2] representing the kabbalistic Tree of Life. In the wilderness, also, Jesus confronted and defeated Satan—the emblem of egoism, pride and desire.

In general, then, Ishmael's receipt of the water of life from a well by the aid of the Lord God symbolises the universalisation of consciousness, whilst his adoption of the calling of an archer typifies the sublimation of the procreative power which is achieved by the Initiated Monad-Ego (Abraham).

---

[1] q.v. *The Inner Way*, p. 233, Tauler.
[2] I *Kings* 19 : 4–8.

CHAPTER VIII

ABIMELECH MAKES A COVENANT WITH ABRAHAM

Gen. 21: 21. *And he dwelt in the wilderness of Paran: and his mother took him a wife out of the land of Egypt.*

History apart, a number of spiritualising experiences are allegorically described as affecting the consciousness and life of Ishmael. Amongst these are: responsiveness to the spiritualising influence of the Monad (the favour of the Lord God);[1] withdrawal from normal worldly life and renunciation of egoism, pride and personal possessions, these no longer providing either happiness or satisfaction, having been outgrown (living in the wilderness); and the sublimation of the creative force (becoming an archer). In consequence of these interior changes the illumined mind (Hagar) seeks and finds a Sanctuary of the Greater Mysteries.[2] There the personal nature (Ishmael) participates in the Rite of Initiation and becomes illumined by direct knowledge (marriage) of the esoteric wisdom (the woman of Egypt). Admittedly this interpretation appears to attach to a simple narrative a disproportionately deep and complex meaning. Nevertheless such a reading bestows upon an otherwise uninteresting story about unknown people of ancient times a significance and a value to seeking men and women of modern days, and especially to aspirants to spiritual illumination—hence its inclusion.

Thus regarded, the narrative describes by means of allegory and symbol the purification of the personal nature, the sublimation of the creative power, the expansion of consciousness and the attainment of Initiation into the Greater Mysteries. This way of life, which has been chosen and followed to its consummation from time immemorial, continues to be chosen and followed by the occultists of today. A story of an event occurring in ancient time is here so recounted as also to reveal continuing experiences of man, thereby lifting the historical account out of the limitations of time and space.

[1] Always a suggestion of the interpolation of secret knowledge into historical narratives.

[2] Indicated by the reference in the text to the land of Egypt, then an active Centre of the Ancient Mysteries.

Gen. 21: 22. *And it came to pass at that time, that Abimelech and Phichol the chief captain of his host spake unto Abraham, saying, God is with thee in all that thou doest:*

23. *Now therefore swear unto me here by God that thou wilt not deal falsely with me, nor with my son, nor with my son's son: but according to the kindness that I have done unto thee, thou shalt do unto me, and to the land wherein thou hast sojourned.*

24. *And Abraham said, I will swear.*

Advanced phases of human evolution and further developments in preparation for passage through the Grades of the Greater Mysteries are allegorically described in the narrative of those episodes in the life of Abraham which followed the birth of Isaac and the banishment of Hagar and Ishmael. The profound interior regeneration experience by Initiates includes the integration into wholeness (covenant) of the complex and sometimes warring components of the make-up of man. This summation into unity of man's seven vehicles of consciousness,[1] their irradiation by spiritual light (" God is with thee ") and their harmonious blending (the mutual oaths) to become an increasingly effective instrument of the Monad of the Initiate, are of profound significance. As described in the verses quoted above, these three phases of spiritual development—unification, irradiation and harmonious blending—are associated with events leading up to the covenant between Abimelech and Abraham. Abimelech personifies especially the mortal, personal vehicles, and more particularly the attributes and consciousness of the mental and physical bodies (the *psyche*) in their masculine polarity. The presence of Phichol, the Captain of the army, suggests the positive virtues of will, courage and discipline.

The allegory may thus be regarded as descriptive of a stage of human evolution at which man has experienced spiritual awakening. In consequence, he has surrendered his hitherto self-seeking and aggressive desires to control by the divine Self within. The allegory appropriately opens with the statement that Abimelech spake unto Abraham, acknowledging him to be under divine protection. Here it is implied that the brain consciousness has become illumined by Egoic light, and that the personality has recognised and been brought into harmony with its Higher Self. It is noteworthy that the approach is made from below, or by Abimelech, indicating that ardent aspiration has been aroused in the personal conscious-

---

[1] Physical, etheric, emotional and concrete mental, the fourfold mortal personality (Abimelech), abstract mental (Sarah after the conception and birth of Isaac), intuitional (Isaac) and purely spiritual (Abraham).

ness for union (the covenant) with its own divine nature, and through that with God.

> Gen. 21: 25. *And Abraham reproved Abimelech because of a well of water, which Abimelech's servants had violently taken away.*

Before spiritual awakening the personality (Abimelech and his servants) had absorbed and used exclusively for its own purposes the sustaining spiritual life-force drawn from universal sources. This vitalising energy (*prāna* or divine life-breath) is symbolised by the water in the well (not the well itself) which the servants are said to have violently taken away. This implies that hitherto both truth and the inner, sustaining life of God had been diverted from spiritual to material purposes, thereby bringing down reproach from the inner Self (Abraham). The fact of the receipt of such reprimand indicates entry upon an evolutionary phase at which communion between the immortal and mortal selves (Abraham and Abimelech) was beginning to be established. In such a case the reproof—prick of conscience —would be keenly felt, since the personality had grown responsive to the inner " Voice ". Such a rebuke is not at first received without protest and the excuse that the personal nature, being at the time unillumined by the Ego, was not responsible for the offence. Under not dissimilar circumstances Pilate washed his hands.

THE SYMBOL OF THE WELL

In the universal sense water is a symbol for both the matter of space and the sustaining life by which all forms are preserved. As a well holds the supply of water which is essential to physical existence, so it may aptly be regarded as a representation of the containing vehicle for the spiritual " waters of life ". This thought may, perhaps, here be usefully enlarged upon. A physical well can, for example, be compared to the ever-renewed " well " from which the Logos perpetually pours forth His life that all created beings and things may live. Indeed He is said to " empty " Himself (Gr. *Kenosis*), and this concept of the divine outpouring is at the heart of Christian Mysticism. St. Paul's *Epistle to the Philippians*, Chapter II, verses 6 and 7, is thus translated by Lightfoot:

> " Though he (Christ) pre-existed in the form of God, yet he did not look on equality with God as a prize which must not slip from his grasp, but he emptied[1] himself, taking upon him the form of a slave, being made in the likeness of man. "

[1] Also in the Revised Version of the Bible and *The Concordant Version of the Sacred Scriptures*, with a restored Greek text, with various readings based upon a Standard English equivalent for each Greek Element. (The Concordant Publishing Concern).

Here we are led to think of Christ in His macrocosmic Self as the Logos Who continually pours out from within Himself His own life, and by that outpouring the worlds are ever nourished and sustained.   Of Him as Logos it is said: " Thou didst breathe forth Thine own Divine Life into Thy Universe......By that self-same sacrifice Thou dost continually uphold all creation......dying in very truth that we might live."[1]   He who would more swiftly reach the spiritual heights is directed to put into practice the ideal of self-sacrifice, self-emptying of self (undue self-centredness), in imitation of the Supreme Lord of Life.   This is also inculcated by the Christ in His words:

" ....Except a corn of wheat fall into the ground and die, it abideth alone: but if it die, it bringeth forth much fruit.

" He that loveth his life shall lose it; and he that hateth his life in this world shall keep it unto life eternal. "[2]

Whilst in the Eleusinian Mysteries the bestowal of ears of wheat upon the Candidate (notably Triptolemos, for example) supposedly refers to a command by Demeter to spread order, civilisation and agriculture throughout the world, some writers ascribe to the Initiatory action a mystical significance.   Aristophanes, for example, in his drama *The Frogs*, wrote: " O! Demeter, thou who hast nourished my soul, make me worthy of thy Mysteries. "   These Mysteries may well have included instructions to Candidates in the more advanced Grades to forsake self (let the husk die) in order to enter into knowledge of Life Eternal.   Evidently the aspirant must become " the wheat of Christ " and, as Ruysbroek said, there is then " attained the immediate contact with the Divine. "

The improvement in the relationship between Abraham and Abi-melech may well indicate that the latter was becoming spiritually illumined and able to adopt this more universal point of view.   Mention of the existence of a well implies a process of digging, and in one possible inter-pretation this action may refer metaphorically to the laborious process whereby the material nature becomes spiritualised, the unredeemed personality regenerate, the consciousness universalised and the lower nature, in consequence, refreshed by the upwelling " waters " of spiritual life and truth.   In mystical literature the terms " son of that Spring which gushes forth out of the depths—the wisdom of God ", and " son of the wells " are applied to those who have thus achieved.[3]   The Path of Swift Unfoldment

---

[1] q.v. *Lecture Notes of the School of the Wisdom*, Vol. I (Rev. Ed.), Ch. XV, p. 465, Geoffrey Hodson.
[2] *Jn.* 12: 24, 25.
[3] *Commentary on John*, Book II, Ch. I, Origen.

and the well of universal life are thus referred to by Omar Khayyam in his
Rubaiyat:

> " A moment's halt—a momentary taste
> Of Being from the Well amid the waste, [1]
> And Lo! the caravan has reach'd
> The Nothing[2] it set out from, Oh! make haste. "

Both Ego and personality must engage in a process of " digging ", since
only so can the encrustations, clogging substances and all the material
tendencies and proclivities of human nature be cleared away.

THE ETHERIC CANALS IN THE PHYSICAL BODY OF MAN

A well is a shaft sunk in the ground, generally cylindrical, in which
water drained from surrounding sources is stored. An interpretation of
the symbol of the well from the point cf view of occult physiology would
therefore seem to be pcssible: for a well and irrigation channels may
suggest the canals (Sk. *nādis*) in the spinal cord and the etheric body along
which the creative life-force (Sk. *Kundalini*)[3] inherent in matter, and so
present in the physical body of man, may be drawn up into the brain
consciousness. When this sublimation has been fully achieved by the outer
man, self-awareness as an immortal, spiritual being is attained. In somewhat similar terms the Lord Christ uses water as a symbol for the interior,
spiritual life-force in the Higher Self. When received through Self-realisation, this symbolical water bestows upon the devotee the experience of
deathlessness, immortality. Thus Christ said: " But whosoever drinketh
of the water that I shall give him shall never thirst; but the water that I
shall give him shall be in him a well of water springing up into everlasting
life. "[4]   In still another possible interpretation the whole personal nature—
and especially the physical body and its experiences in the material world—
is as a well or source from which the unfolding inner Self acquires wisdom
and attains to understanding and power.

THE MACROCOSMIC " WATERS OF LIFE "

In a more general sense the earth itself, and particularly the country
or field where the well is dug, represents pre-cosmic matter in which, when

---

[1] Waste—the arena of purely material life.

[2] Nothing—from the point of view of finite intelligence, the kabbalistic *Ain Soph*,
" No-thing ", the Absolute.   q.v. Glossary under *Parabrahm*.

[3] q.v. Glossary.

[4] *Jn.* 4: 14.

once the process of emanation has begun, Spirit creatively " digs holes " or sets up whirlpools, which in occult philosophy are regarded as the first, the primordial atoms.[1] The Source of the outpoured (well-digging) life force is within the creative Logos, Who is thus in Himself as a well-spring of life.

> Gen. 21: 27. *And Abraham took sheep and oxen, and gave them unto Abimelech; and both of them made a covenant.*

ANIMALS—SYMBOLS OF DIVINE POTENCIES

Eventually, in either the normal process of evolution or as a result of spiritual awakening, the grosser desires are outgrown so that indulgence in them ceases. In due course the personality, having surrendered self-will, becomes illumined by the light and wisdom of the spiritual Self (the gifts of and covenant with Abraham). Thus this verse allegorically indicates that a harmonious relationship between the inner and outer man, personified by Abraham and Abimelech respectively, had been established, a covenant having been made between them.

Since sheep and oxen are universally used in the Sacred Language, an apparent digression may perhaps here be permitted in order to present some aspects of this form of symbology. In scriptural Cosmogenesis the ram is used as a symbol for the masculine, deific, creative potency and life-force, the positive current of the divine " Breath ".[2] Sheep, on the other hand, particularly ewes, represent the feminine creative potency and the negative current therein. At first then, as has been heretofore observed, there was a duality in unity: the " Word " which was God, the masculine, creative Principle—Spirit—on the one hand, and on the other the feminine, creative Principle—matter. Both positive and negative potencies pre-existed, the eternal poles, Spirit-matter (the ram and the ewe, as also the bull and the cow).

" THE LAMB SLAIN FROM THE FOUNDATION OF THE WORLD "

Upon the vast ocean of space, the Great Abyss, during the long " Night " which in Sanskrit is called *Pralaya*—rest—there was darkness which brooded upon the face of the Deep. All slept. Boundless space was dark and quiescent to any finite intelligence. A change then occurred. The Spirit of God emerged from Absolute Existence and " moved upon

---

[1] q.v. *The Secret Doctrine* (Adyar Ed.), Vol. I, p. 203, H. P. Blavatsky.
[2] q.v. *Occult Powers in Nature and in Man*, Introduction and Pt. I, Geoffrey Hodson.

the face of the waters "[1] of space. Then God spake, saying " ....Let there be light: and there was light. "[2]   *Mahā-Pralaya*—cosmic rest—gave way to *Mahā-Manvantara*—activity. The emanated Logos thus becomes an active Creator. This submission to finiteness and self-manifestation in the Universe is looked upon as a sacrifice on a cosmic scale; for the boundless freedom of infiniteness is surrendered to the imprisoned state of finiteness. The symbol of the lamb—the sacrificial animal[3]—is used to represent the First Logos, more particularly as the Cosmic *Christos*, in relation to His metaphorical death in order that the Universe may live.

In pursuance of the symbology used in verse twenty-seven, the lamb naturally personifies the product of the union of the masculine potency (the ram) and the feminine potency (the ewe). Macrocosmically, the lamb is a symbol of the first creative Logos. St. John, who introduces much cosmic symbolism in his Gospel, as is evidenced by the first five verses of its First Chapter, evidently regarded the Christ as a manifestation of the Logos or " Word ". Later he refers to the Christ as " the Lamb of God "[4] and as " the Lamb slain from the foundation of the world. "[5]   The lamb is thus used as a symbol of divine sacrifice. The Logos, having been emanated from the Absolute, limits His nature by manifesting through material forms, and in the cosmic " Calvary " is " slain " that the Universe may live. Microcosmically, the indwelling divine life (the slain lamb) gradually dissipates all undesirable qualities by the so-called " blood of the Lamb ", freeing the Soul from bondage to matter. The pure wisdom and the divine power of the Christ Principle, the Logos of the Soul, the Monad, when received by the mind and the heart purify the lower nature of man.

Oxen are susceptible of a similar interpretation, so that—historicity apart and not here challenged—Abraham's gift of oxen and sheep to Abimelech symbolises the downpouring of wisdom and power from the Monad (Abraham). These are received by the personality (Abimelech) when it is purified of selfishness and has surrendered to and become harmonised with (the covenant) its inner Self.

Gen. 21: 28. *And Abraham set seven ewe lambs of the flock by themselves*

The bestowal of seven gifts to a representative of the material and mortal self (Abimelech) by any personification of the spiritual and immortal Self of man (Abraham in this particular story) allegorically portrays the downpouring of spiritual powers. Their conscious reception symbolises the manifestation of those powers throughout the whole nature of man, and

---

[1] *Gen.* I: 2.   [2] *Gen.* I : 3.
[3] *Gen.* 22: 7, *Ex.* 12, *Le.* 3 : 7–8.
[4] *Jn.* 1: 29, 36.   [5] *Rev.* 13 : 8.

304 THE HIDDEN WISDOM IN THE HOLY BIBLE

particularly by his hitherto erring, mortal personality. The seven ewe lambs set apart from the flock are therefore the sevenfold divine powers of every individual Monad, each being a microcosmic individualisation of the seven corresponding macrocosmic powers or manifested energies of the Logos.[1]

The study of these verses as historicised metaphor is justified, I suggest, by the inclusion into the narrative of the direct influence of the Lord God. In addition oxen and lambs, the number seven and the covenant are all symbols which are universally used in the Sacred Language. Admittedly the account may be read as a simple record of actual events occurring at a critical period in early Hebrew history; nevertheless its allegorical character is sufficiently indicated to justify the suggested analysis of the symbolism. A parable, be it remembered, is designed to convey abstract truths in more easily comprehensible, concrete form.

Gen. 21: 29. *And Abimelech said unto Abraham, What mean these seven ewe lambs which thou hast set by themselves?*

30. *And he said, For these seven ewe lambs shalt thou take of my hand, that they may be a witness unto me, that I have digged this well.*

31. *Wherefore he called that place Beer-sheba; because there they sware both of them.*[2]

32. *Thus they made a covenant at Beer-Sheba; then Abimelech rose up, and Phichol the chief captain of his host, and they returned into the land of the Philistines.*

33. *And Abraham planted a grove in Beer-sheba and called there on the name of the LORD, the everlasting God.*

34. *And Abraham sojourned in the Philistines' land many days.*

The conversation between Abimelech and Abraham may be interpreted as representing the interchange of power between the mortal man and the immortal, divine Self respectively. If so, then the direct statement in verse thirty-two that both Abimelech and Phichol " rose up " refers to the regeneration of the lower nature and the sublimation of its powers. Abraham's actions of naming a district and planting a grove signify the

---

[1] The Logos manifested in and through all the septenates in Nature. This is also indicated, I suggest, by the seven-branched candlestick or *Minorah*.

[2] Beer-sheba (Heb.)—" well of the oath."

establishment throughout the individuality of the spiritually vivifying power of the universal life, frequently symbolised by trees. Throughout the Bible the Philistines are portrayed as warlike enemies of Israel. They personify and their land typifies the lower, personal nature of man with its material, acquisitive and militant attributes.

Even so, the reincarnating Monad-Ego must dwell amongst the Philistines for a time (be incarnated in a body). It must also be temporarily overcome by them, eventually triumph over them (spiritualise bodily propensities) and, as in the case of Samson, ultimately destroy them (eliminate all power of the mental personality to inhibit full spiritual awareness). In general the many battles between the Israelites and the Philistines and all their other enemies symbolise the perpetual conflict between Spirit and matter, life and form, consciousness and vehicles, Ego and personality; for this is the microcosmic Armageddon.

CHAPTER IX

ABRAHAM'S RENUNCIATION ON THE MOUNT

Gen. 22:   *Abraham offering Isaac, is stayed by the Angel: he is blessed*
         again. Generation of Nahor unto Rebekah.

1. *And it came to pass after these things, that God did tempt Abraham, and said unto him, Abraham: and he said, Behold, here I am.*

2. *And he said, Take now thy son, thine only son Isaac, whom thou lovest, and get thee into the land of Moriah; and offer him there for a burnt offering upon one of the mountains which I will tell thee of.*

Read literally, these two verses show the Supreme Deity of the Universe to be capable of instructing a trusted and faithful servant to sacrifice a dearly loved son as a burnt offering to Himself. Whilst such a character might be given to a tribal god, no civilised person would be capable of attributing such conduct to the Most High God.[1] If, however, the verse be read as an allegory veiling a profound spiritual truth, the repellant nature of the command disappears, and with it the implied concept of the unworthy character of the Deity. This revealed truth would seem to be that renunciation of possessive desire and of the objects of its gratification brings not loss, but gain. In other words, life is fulfilled by renunciation.

ABRAHAM—SYMBOL OF MAN APPROACHING ADEPTSHIP

In order that this apparently self-contradictory idea may be acceptably presented, the evolutionary position of Abraham himself must first be con-

---

[1] Attention is here drawn, however, to the inclusion—in a supposedly historical narrative—of the personal appearance of the Supreme Deity of a Universe and His guidance to the head of a small family. Students of history are not usually asked to give credence to such supernormal happenings. Indeed, they can hardly be expected to do so. The frequent appearance in *propria persona* of the Supreme Deity in the Biblical account of Jewish history is, I suggest, an indication of the presence of an under-meaning.

sidered. The life story of Abraham is being interpreted in this Volume from more than one point of view, but mainly as an allegory of the passage of an advanced human being through phases of psycho-spiritual regeneration and successive Initiations. If this approach be provisionally adopted, then the sacrifices demanded of Abraham—as also of all who embark upon " The way of holiness "—are those of the sense of self-separateness from the rest of humanity and of the quality of possessiveness as portrayed by Abraham's parental love for Isaac. These are two of the most natural of human attributes, and therefore very difficult to eliminate. Nevertheless, the time does inevitably come when all the powers wrested with such difficulty from the experiences of life and developed or " born " within the Soul must be renounced as individual possessions.

On the Path of Swift Unfoldment all personal possessiveness must be outgrown and relinquished. Even the faintest trace of egoism can so greatly limit the manifestation of the faculties of abstract thought, intuition and spiritual will as almost to nullify them. No illusion of self-centred individuality must remain and, above all, no personal pride of power and attainment must sully the perfect purity of mind and heart. This necessity is made clear by such instances in the life of Jesus as His submission to the divine will in Gethsemane,[1] the fact that He did not call upon either His own theurgic powers or the legions of angels which He stated were available to Him[2], and symbolically by the piercing of His skin (symbol of self-separateness) by whips, nails and thorns. Only under such conditions of absolute surrender of individual selfhood and possessiveness can principles be perfectly perceived, knowledge of them conveyed to the mind, and the aspirant—being " pure in heart "—see God.[3]

Ultimately a third and still greater renunciation is made, when even the Monadic centre of awareness disappears flame-like within the Great Flame. Then, and then only, may the One Will, the One Life and the One Law completely occupy the field of awareness, the illusion of individuality having been finally dispelled. Thereafter the fullness of unity is known and this is the crown, the summit, the goal, of human evolution. No one need be deterred, however, from the great spiritual adventure. The achievement is said to be less difficult than it might seem, for, as spiritual awareness with its deepening realisation of unity with the life in all beings increases, so personal self-separateness naturally decreases.

Abraham, as indicated by his readiness to sacrifice Isaac at the command of the Lord,[4] had already evolved to the renunciation of Egoic selfhood, as have all those high Initiates of which he is allegorically the pattern and the prototype. The Monad, in this case personified by the Lord, spoke to

---

[1] *Matt.* 26: 42. [2] *Matt.* 26: 53.
[3] *Matt.* 5: 8. [4] *Gen.* 22, particularly, v. 10.

the Ego (Abraham), inwardly inspiring both ascent to the highest states of consciousness (Mount Moriah) and the final surrender there (as a burnt offering) of all the powers, faculties and qualities (Isaac) that with so much effort had been acquired.

> Gen. 22: 3. *And Abraham rose up early in the morning, and saddled his ass, and took two of his young men with him, and Isaac his son, and clave the wood for the burnt offering, and rose up, and went unto the place of which God had told him.*

Much symbology is contained in this verse. Abraham represents the Ego in an inspired state (early in the morning), but not yet at the full height of his illumination (generally symbolised by the hour of high noon). The ass, as a docile beast of burden, is a symbol of the lower quarternary or mortal personality, consisting of mind, emotion, vitality and physical body. The change of the proverbial stubbornness of the ass into readiness to serve indicates the tamed, trained and obedient emotions. This is further indicated by the presence of the two young men, presumably servants, who personify the conjoined mento-emotional and the physical principles now rendered subservient to the Egoic will. Isaac, as indeed all new-born sons in allegories, represents the dawning faculty of spiritual intuitiveness. It should be noted that Sarah does not participate in this experience, which means that the purely intellectual attribute is left behind when the sense of separated individuality is outgrown; for the states of full spiritual awareness and realisation of oneness are necessarily supra-menta. Thus Sarah does not accompany Abraham in the ascent of Mount Moriah.

> Gen. 22: 4. *Then on the third day Abraham lifted up his eyes, and saw the place afar off.*

A lofty state of Egoic consciousness, that of realisation of identity with the One Will, is here indicated. This is a prerequisite for the still later attainment of full perfection, reaching which the sense of selfhood finally dies. These stages of development, associated with Initiations into the Greater Mysteries, are also allegorically portrayed in the life of Christ. At the Nativity—the First Initiation—unit with the Spirit, Life and Consciousness of the Universe begins to be experienced. At the Baptism—the Second Initiation—the potentiality becomes more active. At the Transfiguration on the Mount—the Third Initiation (possibly referred to in this verse by reference to the third day), a further evolutionary phase is entered upon, that of spiritual illumination and self-surrender, as in Gethsemane.[1]

---

[1] *Matt.* 26: 39.

At the Crucifixion—the Fourth Initiation—self finally dies, and at the Ascension—the Fifth Initiation—all human limitations are finally and completely outgrown and every potentiality is at last fully developed and made manifest in Adeptship. This attainment is described in the New Testament as follows " Till we all come in the unity of the faith, and of the knowledge of the Son of God, unto a perfect man, unto the measure of the stature of the fulness of Christ. "[1]

The epic of the life of Abraham from the time of his departure from Ur of the Chaldees up to the receipt of the divine blessing and the promises that his seed should multiply as the stars of the heaven and the sand upon the sea shore and in his seed should all the nations of the earth be blessed,[2] may be similarly interpreted. Indeed, the narrative contains indications that it is so written—or perhaps recast— by inspired hands as to reveal by means of allegory and symbol the same great story of the hastened evolution of the Soul to the stature of perfected manhood.

> *Gen, 22: 5. And Abraham said unto his young men, Abide ye here with the ass; and I and the lad will go yonder and worship, and come again to you.*

In the ascent of consciousness into the state of spiritual awareness (the mount) the limitations of the personality are transcended. Nothing that is external to the spiritual Self (Abraham) can be carried up into the Mount of Transfiguration. The young men and the ass are therefore left behind or, as stated in the Gospels, the disciples are asleep.[3]

> *Gen. 22: 6. And Abraham took the wood of the burnt-offering, and laid it upon Isaac his son; and he took the fire in his hand, and a knife; and they went both of them together.*

This verse also may suggest a comparison with the story of the life of Christ; for just as Jesus is made to bear the Cross upon which he is to be crucified,[4] so Isaac is made to carry the wood of the burnt offering, the altar upon which he is to be sacrificed (all the *dramatis personae*, be it remembered, personify principles of one individual). Thus it has been said, and with deep mystical significance, that every Initiate must symbolically carry his own cross, for if he casts it down it will crush him in its fall.

---

[1] *Eph.* 4: 13. A study of the life of Christ from this point of view is to be found in *The Hidden Wisdom in the Holy Bible*, Vol. I, Pt. V, and also in *Lecture Notes of the School of the Wisdom*, Vol. II, Ch. VII, Sec. 7, Geoffrey Hodson.

[2] *Gen.* 22: 17, 18.

[3] *Matt.* 24: 40.

[4] *Jn.* 19: 17. Admittedly the other three Gospels state that the Cross was carried by Simon of Cyrene.

Abraham, however, carries the fire and a knife. The fire symbolises the attributes of the creative and regenerative spiritual fire which must, at whatever cost, be brought to bear upon the nature and the life of the aspirant. The knife, in its turn, symbolises that steel-like will and iron resolution which are essential to success in both ascending the spiritual heights and making the great renunciation of self.

Gen. 22: 7. *And Isaac spake unto Abraham his father, and said, My father: and he said, Here am I, my son. And he said, Behold the fire and the wood: but where is the lamb for a burnt-offering?*

8. *And Abraham said, My son, God will provide himself a lamb for a burnt-offering: so they went both of them together.*

THE SYMBOL OF SACRIFICE

Macrocosmically, the lamb used as a burnt offering symbolises the Logos, either of the Universe as a whole or of a major cycle. If the repetition be pardoned, the offering of a lamb upon an altar allegorically portrays that surrender which the Logos of a Universe continually makes in order that the components of that Universe may live, evolve and attain. Clearly this divine surrender is made at an infinitely greater level than that of the human Monad on the attainment of Adeptship,[1] and in an almost infinitely greater degree. This is the probable meaning of the reference to the Cosmic *Christos* as " the Lamb slain from the foundation of the world. "[2] In the microcosmic sense Isaac personifies the *Buddhic* or Christ Principle in man, vehicle of spiritual intuitiveness. Such faculty, now well developed though still not perfected, bestows universality of consciousness upon the surrendered personal mind, which at this stage has outgrown the illusion of self-separated individuality. Egoism, acquisitiveness, personal pride and desire no longer enclose consciousness within a shell of accentuated selfhood. This important subject is further enlarged upon in Part Two, Chapter IV, of this Volume— *The Towar of Babel*—as also elsewhere.

THE ALTAR OF WOOD—SYMBOL OF LIFE AND FORM

It is significant that the altar, like the cross, is made of wood, for wood is taken from a tree. Whilst water is used as a symbol of the all-pervading life, the tree symbolises that life manifested in material forms. The binding

---

[1] cf. Christ's surrender in Gethsemane (*Matt.* 26: 39, 42). In Buddhism a Bodhisattva makes a declaration of altruism and self-denial. q.v. *The Bodhisattva Doctrine*, p. 57, Har Dayal, M.A., Ph.D. Kegan Paul, Trench, Trubner & Co. Ltd., London.

[2] *R.v.* 13: 8.

of the youth Isaac upon a wooden altar is emblematic of the evolutionary stage at which the intuitive principle in man is as yet imprisoned within the womb or calyx of the analytical mind. When, later, the sacrifice of self has been completed, the calyx breaks open (Isaac freed from the altar) and spiritual intuitiveness illumines the liberated mind. By its very nature the keynote of this principle is universality, and its influence upon the consciousness of those in whom it is awakened and developing is that of surrender or sacrifice of all sense of self-separated individuality. This unconditioned state of awareness begins to be experienced at the First Initiation.

In the Gospel story the Christ is symbolically laid in a manger, presumably made of wood. Similarly, at the Fourth Initiation, He is voluntarily nailed upon a Cross of wood and thereby rendered incapable of removing Hinself from it. What at birth (the beginning of the great quest) was laid in a manger is at death (its consummation) " nailed " upon the Cross of wood. This allegorically portrays both the birth and the final fulfilment in man of the Christ-consciousness, through the exercise of which he knows himself to be inseparably at one with universal life (nailed to the tree). So, also, the young Isaac is bound to an altar of wood by his father Abraham (the Monad-Ego[1]) who, as this Chapter indicates, has attained to complete self-surrender. Although all thought of reward is totally absent, the result is not a loss, as might be expected, but mysteriously a transcendent gain; for when man universalizes his consciousness he shares in the powers of the Universe. One with all, all is at his command. This is indicated later in the allegory by the provision of the ram and the promise of multiplicity of seed (verse 17).

THE RAM

As already stated, in the allegorical language the ram has ever been the symbol of virility as possessed, for instance, by such Deities as the Egyptian creative gods, and symbolically shown by their portrayal as being criocephalic or ram-head.[2] In man—especially in those born, as the

---

[1] All events, be it remembered occur within the one individual—in this case Abraham —whose psychological and spiritual regeneration is being described by means of personifications and allegories.

[2] cf. The second form of the God Khnemu, under which he was worshipped at Mendes and known as Ba-Neb-Tettu, i.e., the Ram, lord of Tettu (the phallic nilometer symbol). He was regarded as the virile principle in gods and men . . . the Ram, the virile male . . . the life of Ra . . . mighty in strength . . who vivifieth the earth (like Seb) and who formeth the breath of life for all men, the chief of the gods, the lord of heaven and the king of the gods (Brugsch, *Religion*, p. 309, quoted and illustrated in *The Gods of the Egyptians*, E. A. Wallis Budge, Vol. II, p. 64).

astrologer would say,[1] under the fiery Sign of Aries, and in consequence possessed of energy, courage and enterprise—this creative capacity may be expressed at the spiritual, the intellectual or the physical level, and in some men at all three of them.   Creative power (the ram in Nature and in man) stirs and awakens into actual life in the children of Aries.   They are brought to their highest and finest expression in those who have surrendered self, have ascended the " Mount of Illumination "—whether Moriah, Ararat, Gilead, Horeb, Sinai, Tabor or Olivet—and there, like Abraham, have dedicated without reservation their whole being to the service of God and the fulfilment of the divine will and plan.

> *Gen.* 22: 13. *And Abraham lifted up his eyes, and looked, and behold behind him a ram caught in a thicket by his horns: and Abraham went and took the ram, and offered him up for a burnt-offering in the stead of his son.*

Here, too, is indicated self-purification by fire, self-redemption in fiery sacrifice, as well as the surrender of the personal creative fire or sex force.   Such complete self-less-ness implies that full universalisation of consciousness has been achieved.

Although in this study of the narrative of the life of Abraham, disciplines and attainments of the unfolding spiritual Self treading the " Way of the Cross " have been chiefly considered, portions of the narrative can valuably be applied to the attitude of mind of those following the normal evolutionary pathway.   An example of this is found in the episode of Abraham's readiness to sacrifice his only son Isaac as an offering unto the Lord, which sacrifice was rendered unnecessary by the provision of the ram discovered in the thicket.   A profound spiritual law is here allegorically indicated; for even in everyday life, when a person is ready to give up some dearly cherished project or person, such abnegation is very often not then demanded of them.   Symbolically, there is a ram in the thicket.

> *Gen.* 22: 15. *And the angel of the LORD called unto Abraham out of heaven the second time,*

> 16. *And said, By myself have I sworn, saith the LORD, for because thou hast done this thing, and hast not withheld thy son, thine only son:*

> 17. *That in blessing I will bless thee, and in multiplying I will multiply thy seed as the stars of the heaven, and as the sand*

---

[1] q.v. *How to Judge a Nativity*, Alan Leo; *From Pioneer to Poet*, Isabelle M. Pagan; and later works.

> *which is upon the sea shore; and thy seed shall possess the gate of his enemies;*

> 18. *And in thy seed shall all the nations of the earth be blessed, because thou hast obeyed my voice.*

Throughout this wonderful Chapter sound and speech are employed as symbols of the transmission to the outer individuality of the spiritually awakening impulse from the Dweller in the Inner-most, " the angel of the Lord " (the Monad). A microcosmic creative procedure is thus being indicated. The Logos of the Soul assumes increasing sovereignty throughout its human manifestation. That which in man began as the first whispers of conscience is later acknowledged as a fiat from on high. In terms of the Gospel story, the Angel of the Annunciation has uttered the prophecy that Mary shall conceive and bring forth a son.

The " seed " of Abraham (verse 17), as must be obvious, cannot possibly refer to ordinary human seed, parenthood and ancestorship. Rather, therefore, must it be regarded as a symbol for the powers innate within the Monad, themselves derived from the " Parent Tree ", which is God. These " seeds " are the potential powers, attributes and faculties which, when germinated and full grown, make of the individual a Solar Logos, a divine " Tree " which in its turn will bring forth further " seeds ". As these inherent capacities leap into splendid life, the whole Earth is blessed; for he who is self-awakened becomes an awakening influence upon all; he who becomes perfect hastens the attainment of perfection by all.[1] Symbolically, his " seed " is as the stars of the heaven and as the sand upon the sea shore, and in it are all nations blessed. The key to this great attainment is given in the words " because thou hast obeyed my voice ", which in the microcosmic sense implies recognition and ratification of Monadic rule throughout the whole nature.

Thus Abraham's readiness to sacrifice his beloved son, representative of all that he held most dear, allegorically portrays that final self-surrender[2] which must precede the attainment of superhuman stature, " the measure of the stature of the fulness of Christ ", Ascension to the right hand of God.

Gen. 22: 20. *And it came to pass after these things, that it was told Abraham, saying, Behold, Milcah, she hath also born children unto thy brother Nahor;*

---

[1] *Jn.* 12: 32. Christ said: " And I, if I be lifted up from the earth, will draw all men unto me."

[2] *Lu.* 22: 42.

21. *Huz his firstborn, and Buz his brother, and Kemuel the father of Aram.*

22. *And Chesed, and Hazo, and Pildash, and Jidlaph, and Bethuel.*

23. *And Bethuel begat Rebekah: these eight Milcah did bear to Nahor, Abraham's brother.*

24. *And his concubine, whose name was Renumah, she bare also Terah, and Gaham, and Thahash and Maachah.*

The numerous geneological trees which appear in the Bible may not normally be regarded as of deep mystical or philosophic significance. If this is so, they can hardly be important parts of the revelation which, in addition to history, the Scriptures were written to convey. Nevertheless, it is possible when reading them to find oneself led into rather profound speculations. Since I have myself been thus influenced, I include in the rest of this Chapter some of the ideas evoked by a reading of the above quoted verses, as also by a perusal of other Biblical family trees. Readers who may not be particularly interested in such meditative thought may, without any break in the sequence of interpretations, omit the last pages of this Chapter.

FORMS FINITE, SPIRIT INFINITE

A possible significance of such genealogies may here be suggested. Normally they indicate the continuance of the family line, despite the deaths of successive members. This transcending of the alternations of birth and death may refer to a profoundly philosophic idea, namely that whilst all things and beings, temporal and personal (members of the family), must disappear, the Spirit-Essence or Monad (the family itself) is immortal and eternal. This is also true of Solar Systems, which appear and disappear, whilst their presiding Deities or Solar Logoi continue to exist. Races of men, and the planets on which they live, must in their turn pass away, but the Monads of men and the incarnate divine life in the sub-human kingdoms are relatively everlasting. Similarly each human being is born and later dies, thus disappearing as a bodily personality. Nevertheless the reincarnating Ego persists throughout the long series of successive earthly lives. Thus form vanishes but life remains, personalities perish but their spiritual Essence endures. These may be the underlying truths presented in personal terms by means of Scriptural accounts of the successive generations of one family. Interestingly, the verses quoted above make no further reference to the dramatic events which had been previously recorded, but continue the account of Abraham's life by means of a list of members of his family. A collateral branch of that family is here introduced into the story. Rebekah, the daughter of Bethuel, a member of that branch, later marries Isaac and so continues Abraham's line.

MAN—A MICROCOSMIC DEITY

Man is indeed a deeply mysterious being. He is, for example, animated and sustained by the " breath " or manifested life of the Logos of the Solar System. He is also both spiritually at one with that Being and at the same time a partial expression of His life. In his essential nature each human spark of the Divine must therefore be regarded as a deific power, however embryonic that power may be at any particular evolutionary phase. The correspondence may be carried still further; for as the Solar Deity is both transcendent beyond and immanent within His Solar System, so the Logos of the Soul of man, the human Monad, is both transcendent above his present manifestation as an Ego-personality on Earth and immanent within it.

The subject would seem to be of sufficient importance to justify its further consideration, despite an apparent digression from the main text. Lofty though the subject undoubtedly is and, moreover, apparently without immediate application to human life with its many pressing problems, spiritual neophytes and mystics can, I suggest, receive great value from its meditative study. Admittedly the transcendent God and the similarly transcendent Monad of man must remain mysteries to the finite mind. As higher phases of evolution are entered upon, however, the advanced human being becomes aware of and directly influenced by his Monad, even as Elijah on Mt. Horeb heard the " still small voice " within.[1]

GOD MANIFEST AND UNMANIFEST

In Scriptural allegories, as we have already seen, each person mentioned by name has his or her symbolical significance, being descriptive of principles, powers and attributes, latent and expressed, of Deity and man. Elder brothers[2] who remain at home, for example, aptly personify the supernal Godhead in man, whilst the ultimate reunions and restored family relationships may be regarded as descriptive of the gradual blending in man of his inherent and active Divinity. The mortal man then becomes increasingly aware of his immortal Self.

---

[1] I *Kings* 19: 12.

[2] *e.g.* Of the Prodigal Son. q.v. Vol. I of this work, Pt. IV.

Our Lord's references to His Father in Heaven[1] as being the source of His existence and the authority for Our Lord's appearance on Earth,[2] may be regarded as references to the Monad in transcendence. The affirmation, " I and my Father are one ",[3] indicates a very lofty degree of unfoldment in which the two aspects of the human being, the immortal and the mortal have become consciously at one. In addition, full realisation of unity with the one Source of all life (the Father) has been attained.

The principle of the dual existence of the Immortal Germ is reflected in the Monadic, the Egoic and the personal natures of man. The Monad in its relationship to the Ego is immanent as its indwelling power, life and consciousness, whilst on its own plane it is also transcendent beyond and above the Ego. In its turn, the Monad, forever abides within the life of the Logos, where in terms of Hindu philosophy it is said to dwell on the second of the seven planes of Nature, known as *Anupādaka*.[4]

THE HUMAN MONAD ABIDES IN PERPETUAL AWARENESS

Readers of this work who are as yet unfamiliar with these philosophic considerations may find them somewhat abstruse and remote from the day-by-day experiences and necessities of human life. Since, however, the Bible is a repository of very lofty, if heavily veiled philosophic ideas, I have thought it well at least to refer to them at appropriate places in this work. In one possible interpretation, for example, Abraham's brother Nahor, who remained in Ur of the Chaldees (stayed at home), personifies the existence and life of the Monad in its own world. Abraham himself represents its more external activity, and these two exist in every man somewhat as the postulated positive and negative foci of an ellipse.

The interior spiritual activity and unfoldment of both Monad and Ego are continuous; for they are not subject to those alternations which are characteristic of life and death. Neither are they subject to the complete loss of physical consciousness experienced during sleep, and its temporary recovery on awakening. Even more deeply occult references may also be discerned; for every Monad-Ego on Earth has a " brother ", an *alter Ego*, a Solar Self as it were, a Dweller in the Innermost, a citizen of that " Ur " which, in such a reading, represents the formless levels of the extraplanetary aspects and regions of the Universe. The elder brother, who in the Parable

---

[1] *Matt.* 7: 21.

[2] *Matt.* 3: 17; 17: 5. *Jn.* 5: 37; 8: 16.

[3] *Jn.* 10: 30.

[4] *Anupādaka* (Sk.)." Parentless ", self-existing, born without progenitors, applied to both a plane of Nature—the second from above—and to the Monads Who are in this sense parentless or " self-born of the Divine Essence ".

of the Prodigal Son remains in the father's home, is the Archangelic Self which, until universalisation of consciousness is attained at Adeptship, is veiled in mystery. This is the real *Christos* or Seventh Principle in man, the Logos of the Soul.

CELESTIAL MARRIAGES

Since, when understood, certain Sanskrit terms which are used in esoteric Hinduism and Buddhism assist in the exposition of these ideas, reference to them is made at this point. The union of the most spiritual aspect of the earthly pilgrim—the Monad—with its Solar Archangel or *Dhyāni*[1] may possibly be hinted at in the union of Isaac, the son of Abraham, with Rebekah, the daughter of Nahor. These two human beings could be regarded as personifications of the Aeonic *Dhyāni-Buddha* or *Ādi-Buddha* at the highest level, and of its Monadic representative in a Planetary Scheme.[2] Although these are spiritually identical, a lofty evolutionary level must be attained before this identity can become known to the earthly pilgrim. Realisation of such oneness is sometimes implied in the marriages and other unions of important persons in Scriptural and mythological narratives. They are therefore correctly described as " celestial marriages ".

A correspondence also exists between the interior life-centre (*Ātma*) in the spiritually awakened Ego, who is a pilgrim and an exile from " home " (*Anupādaka*), and that supernal Being (*Monad*) which never leaves the Solar Sanctuary of the Temple of the Universe. In the allegorical language this latter is personified in the Parable of the Prodigal Son by the brother who remains behind, and in Homer's *Odyssey* by both Laërtes and Penelope. This immortal epic is susceptible of interpretation as an allegory of the experiences and achievements of man on his pilgrimage through matter and his eventual and successful return to his faithful, waiting " wife ".

Here ends the brief digression, and consideration of the life story of Abraham is now resumed.

---

[1] *Dhyāni* (Sk.). " Expert in Yoga ". Also a generic name for spiritual Beings, Planetary Logoi, and Hierarchies of Archangels and angels. The term *Dhyāna* signifies a state of profound contemplation during which the *Dhyānin* becomes united with the highest parts of his own constitution and communes therewith. *Dhyān-Chohans*, " Lords of Contemplation ", are members of the Host of Spiritual Beings Who live in this exalted state and supervise the cyclic evolution of life and form in a Solar System. Monadically, man is an embryo *Dhyān-Chohan* and at the close of the Planetary Age will himself have become a fully developed " Lord of Contemplation ". q.v. *The Secret Doctrine*, H. P. Blavatsky, and *The Mahatma Letters to A. P. Sinnett*, Theosophical Publishing House Adyar.

[2] q.v. p. 54 of this Volume and Glossary—under Chain.

CHAPTER X

THE ONENESS OF LIFE

Gen. 23.   *Sarah's age and death.   The purchase of Machpelah, where Sarah was buried.*

1. *And Sarah was an hundred and seven and twenty years old: these were the years of the life of Sarah.*

As indicated in Chapter III of Part One of this Volume, and elsewhere repeated because of its importance, the first of the four main keys by which the Sacred Language may be interpreted is that all recorded events may be read as allegories of interior developments, changes, progression, and even crises, occurring within one and the same person.   The second key is that people in the stories represent vehicles of consciousness and also attributes, powers and weaknesses of each human being at varying phases of their evolution.   If these two keys be applied to the above quoted verse, then the death of Abraham's wife signifies that he—not necessarily she—had transcended the limitations of egoism and the delusion of self-separated individuality; for, as we have seen these characteristics were earlier personified by Sarah.

The age of Sarah, namely " an hundred and seven and twenty years ", gives three figures which add up to ten, the number of wholeness, of culmination, of departure from a completed past into an as yet unrealised future. Thus Abraham, prototype of every Adept in-the-becoming, reaches the threshold of that state, dies as man and prepares to live as a superhuman being or Adept.   Sarah represents the sense of I-am-I which, after giving birth to the sense of I-am-all (Isaac), has fulfilled its task in Nature's economy and so must disappear.   Thus applied to Abraham himself, Sarah's age at her death confirms the interpretation that he is here portrayed as one approaching Adeptship.   He is about to die as an imperfect man and to enter upon a new life as a superhuman being or perfected man.[1]

In a psycho-spiritual interpretation of the story of the life of Abraham, Sarah's death is found to be interior rather than an external death of another

---

[1] q.v. *The Hidden Wisdom in the Holy Bible*, Vol. I, Pt. I, Ch. VI, Geoffrey Hodson.

person. It indicates the transcendence by the human Ego and mind of the limitations of the illusion of being a self-separated individuality. So significant is it in both ordinary life and on the pathway to the hastened attainment of Adeptship, that it is given considerable attention here and elsewhere throughout this work. Once again the reader's kind indulgence is sought for any undue repetitiveness. In this sense the death of Sarah, she being the personification of the individualistic mind, is a natural development from Abraham's surrender of Isaac. In this renunciation Abraham reached his greatest heights. Isaac, the son of his old age, and therefore especially beloved, personifies that which is held most dear and under normal circumstances would be treasured and preserved. At the stage of evolution represented by Abraham at this period of his life, personal attachments are outgrown. This is further enunciated in the fifth verse of the Twenty-fifth Chapter of *Genesis*, in which it is stated that " ...Abraham gave all that he had unto Isaac. "

In another form of symbology self-separateness is represented by the human skin. The submission by Jesus to flagellation and to the piercing of his skin by thorns, nails and a spear, portrays a similar self-emancipation.[1] In inspired allegories and myths all injuries to divine, semi-divine and heroic *dramatis personae* are susceptible of the same interpretation as " mystic wounds".

In Abraham's case the fruitage of all his preceding reincarnations was renounced as a personal possession. The vision splendid of the oneness of all life, the knowledge of interior unity with that life, the faculty of direct, intuitive perception of truth in whatever guise and under however deep a covering—these attainments also personified by Isaac, are recognised as attributes of universal existence and in no sense as individual achievements and possessions. When the Initiate (Abraham) has ascended to that level of awareness where unity is the basic principle, it is realised that the one divine life-essence contains all, produces all, *is* all. Nothing else exists save " all-ness ". Self-separateness is then perceived as an illusion, self-attainment as a delusion; for the very effort, the struggle, the strain and the attainment are now known to be not those of a single unit of life, but of the one life[2] as a whole.

A partial analogy descriptive of this change from individuality to universality may perhaps be drawn from the phenomenon of a waterspout speeding across the surface of the sea and temporarily linking ocean and cloud. It is composed of electrically charged air, vapour and water. For a

---

[1] Doubt of the historicity of these events is not here implied.

[2] "It is the ONE LIFE, eternal, invisible, yet omnipresent, without beginning or end, yet periodical in its regular manifestations—between which periods reigns the dark mystery of Non-Being; unconscious, yet absolute Consciousness; unrealisable, yet the one self-existing Reality; truly ' A Chaos to the sense, a Kosmos to the reason.' " *The Secret Doctrine*, Vol. I (Adyar Ed.), p. 70, H. P. Blavatsky.

time as a funnel, a cylinder, rapidly gyrating and swiftly sweeping forward on its course, it exists as a phenomenon of Nature, a single fact. When its electricity is discharged, however, it collapses and ceases to exist. The air within it again becomes free air, the vapour joins the clouds, whilst the water sinks back into the ocean. Nothing then remains to show that a water-spout had ever existed. In terms of human perception, however, it was for a time a physical reality. All its phases from its first beginning to its final disappearance had been objectively real. Although all its essential elements—electricity, air, water and motion—remain, the waterspout itself is no more.

So, also, the mortal personality of man is real at the levels—mental, emotional and physical—of its temporary existence. Its form and its appearance are, however, impermanent and in that sense are to be regarded as unreal. When the evolutionary phase (Arhatship[1]), allegorically portrayed by Abraham in the later years of his life, is entered, the illusion is transcended and the ultimate reality is known. Just as the waterspout breaks down and disappears as such so does the mortal self die. In their universality, however, the constituent elements of both of them continue to exist.

SQUARING THE CIRCLE

The death of Sarah (personification of the individualistic mind) portrays in another form the collapse of the waterspout and the release of its component parts, or the end of the illusion of separated selfhood. Then, and only then, is solved the mystery of the relationship between the universal and the individual, the circle and the square. The circle represents the boundless ALL and the square the limited, temporary form. To square the circle is to resolve the elements of individuality back into their universal freedom, to liberate the centre of divine consciousness or spiritual awareness—which is man—from its particular to its universal existence.

Every Adept has performed this feat, but only at the cost of a voluntary surrender—as a personally possessed, *individual* attainment—of the whole fruitage of evolution through the human kingdom of Nature. Abraham had reached this stage, as is indicated by at least three statements. As we have just seen one of these affirms his readiness to sacrifice his beloved son Isaac. A second tells of his bestowal of all his goods upon Isaac and the third relates the death of Sarah, who represents his temporary self-indi-

---

[1] *Arhat* (Sk.)—"The worthy". Exoterically, "one worthy of divine honours". Esoterically, an Initiate of the Fourth Degree who has entered the highest Path and is thus emancipated from both self-separateness and enforced rebirth. q.v. *Lecture Notes of the School of the Wisdom*, Vol. I (Rev. Ed.), p. 460, and Vol. II, Ch. IV, Sec. I, Geoffrey Hodson.

viduality or *ahamkāric*[1] personal ego. In the allegorical language all deaths of Saviours, Patriarchs, Prophets, heroes and heroines, in their essential significance, refer to this renunciation.

> *Gen.* 23: 2. *And Sarah died in Kirjath-ārbá; the same is Hebron in the land of Canaan: and Abraham came to mourn for Sarah, and to weep for her.*

The statement that Abraham mourned for Sarah might suggest that, contrary to what is written above, he had not completely outgrown consciousness of himself as a separate entity. Since self-liberation from Egohood involves the reversal of habitual emotions—in this case grief at the loss of a loved one—which have been experienced throughout the whole series of preceding earthly lives and their personalities, the process of their eventual renunciation is necessarily gradual, even for those who are treading the Path of Swift Unfoldment. Furthermore, human affection does not wholly die and personal affection for another dearly loved human being is still felt up to the threshold of Adeptship. In this sense Abraham may quite truly be said to have mourned at the loss of the physical companionship of his beloved wife. The term " mourned " may also refer to the suffering which in general is inseparable from the final stages of enforced evolutionary progress. These are the mystical wounds which must be endured and, as said, are allegorically portrayed in the Gospel story of the Passion of the Lord Christ.[2]

Abraham mourned and was a sojourner in a strange land, even as the Monad, the Dweller in the Innermost, is but a temporary visitant to the outermost regions of the Universe. Macrocosmically, the Twenty-third Chapter of *Genesis* describes the closing of a minor cycle of manifestation. Sarah in this sense represents time, Abraham timelessness. The two have been conjoined for a certain period. The product of their union (Isaac) has developed the capacity to undertake his patriarchal Office in the new cycle.

> *Gen.* 23: 3. *And Abraham stood up from before his dead, and spake unto the sons of Heth, saying,*

[1] *Ahamkāra* or *Ahankāra* (Sk.). The concept of " I ", the egotistical and illusory principle in man which separates the human " I " from the universal One Self; egoism; also I-am-ness, self-hood, the tendency towards definiteness; the I-making principle necessary in order that self-consciousness may be evolved but *transcended when its work is over*. In man it becomes the great " heresy " or delusion of self-separateness, of distinct individuality divided from all other beings and from the divine Individuality of the Universe. In Hindu Philosophy *Ahamkāra* in man is regarded as one of the root causes of human error, and therefore of human suffering. q.v. Pt. II, Ch. IV of this Volume—" The Tower of Babel ". See also Glossary.

[2] *Matt.* 26: 36 to 27: 49.

21

4. *I am a stranger and a sojourner with you: give me a possession of a burying place with you, that I may bury my dead out of my sight.*

5. *And the children of Heth answered Abraham, saying unto him,*

6. *Hear us, my lord: thou art a mighty prince among us: in the choice of our sepulchres bury thy dead; none of us shall withhold from thee his sepulchre, but that thou mayest bury thy dead.*

7. *And Abraham stood up, and bowed himself to the people of the land, even to the children of Heth.*

8. *And he communed with them, saying, If it be your mind that I should bury my dead out of my sight; hear me, and intreat for me to Ephron the son of Zohär,*

9. *That he may give me the cave of Mach-pelah, which he hath, which is in the end of his field; for as much money as it is worth he shall give it me for a possession of a burying place amongst you.*

10. *And Ephron dwelt among the children of Heth: and Ephron the Hittite answered Abraham in the audience of the children of Heth, even of all that went in at the gate of his city, saying,*

11. *Nay, my lord, hear me: the field give I thee, and the cave that is therein, I give it thee; in the presence of the sons of my people give I it thee: bury thy dead.*

12. *And Abraham bowed down himself before the people of the land.*

The burial of Sarah, and Abraham's apparently deep interest in the acquirement of a suitable grave in the country of the people of Heth, may possibly refer to the teaching of occult philosophy that the material substance of the Universe is itself undergoing evolutionary development. This is largely brought about by its use as vehicles for Spirit, life and consciousness. Such close contact gradually brings into activity capacities inherent in matter, chiefly those of response to both external stimuli and the interior action of will and thought. Although a perfectly natural feeling, Abraham's concern for a suitable burial place for the body of his wife may refer also to the passage from one cycle to its successor of the effects upon matter produced by its employment as a vehicle of consciousness.

THE TRANSFERENCE OF POWER

As will be more fully expounded in the next Chapter, this principle of the transmission of powers attained during a period of objective manifestation—and of rulership during that period—to a successor is evidently one of great importance. Repeated Biblical descriptions of the handing on of official leadership from one Patriarch, King or Judge to the next may be regarded as allegorical allusions to this principle. Reference is constantly made to it in works on occult philosophy, in World Scriptures—including the Bible, as we have seen earlier—and in modern ceremonial Rites which stem from the Ancient Mysteries, Freemasonry being one example. A detailed chronicle is kept of all these attainments and of the names of the Rulers of the successive cycles. The term " imperishable record " is to be found in some occult works, and is there explained as consisting of an indestructible " book " in which is preserved all history pertaining to evolutionary phases of development.

THE CAVE OF MACH-PELAH

A mysterious name, the first syllable of which is " Mach ", is sometimes given to the Official responsible for keeping these annals. There may possibly be a special significance in the statement that the owner of the field in which the cave was situated was named Mach-pelah, who might be regarded as a personification of this recording principle in Nature. The very name Mach-pelah is reminiscent of the title of a great Official in the Hierarchy of the Adepts—the *Mahā-Chohan*.[1] Amidst His many duties is that of Recorder of the events of His cycle, of the activities of the Adept Hierarchy, and of all admissions to its ranks. The cave of Mach-pelah is said to be at the *end* (italics mine—G.H.) of his own field, perhaps signifying the great evolutionary development attained at the close or " end " of certain cycles.

The traditional " imperishable record " is also that in which the progress of every human being on the planet who " enters in at the strait gate " and " treads the narrow way "—in occult philosophy " enters the Path "[2]— is recorded step by step from probationary pupilhood, through the great Initiations to final liberation or Adeptship. The advance of the disciple treading the Path of Swift Unfoldment is noted, officially recognised and entered in a Volume sometimes also called " the Golden Book ", which is in the keeping of the Great White Brotherhood of Adepts. Certain words in

---

[1] *Mahā-Chohan* (Sk.)—" Great Lord "; also descriptive of a Grade of Adeptship, that of the Seventh Initiation. q.v. *Lecture Notes of the School of the Wisdom*, Vol. I, (Rev. Ed.), Ch. XVI, Secs. 3 and 5, Geoffrey Hodson.

[2] q.v. *The Hidden Wisdom in the Holy Bible*, Vol. I, Pt. VI, Ch. II, and *Lecture Notes of the School of the Wisdom*, Vol. I (Rev. Ed.), Ch. XV, Sec. 4, Geoffrey Hodson.

Rituals derived from the Ancient Mysteries, such as those of some Degrees in Freemasonry, have a similar sound and in consequence are regarded as veiled references to both the Great Lord Himself and to the above occult procedure which is invariably followed.

As a member of the Egyptian pantheon, Tehuti—the divine Chronologer and Recorder—is a personification of this Office of Keeper of the Rolls. In pictorial representations of the supposed scene in the Hall of Judgment where, after weighing the heart of the deceased against a feather, the decision was made concerning his or her post mortem fate, Tehuti is shown as writing down with his stylus upon a papyrus the result of the weighing. If, again according to occult tradition, *The Book of the Dead* is regarded as also a Ritual of Initiation, then this scene would portray passage through the First of the Great Initiations, with Tehuti as the *Mahā-Chohan*.

A passage in *Zohar* would seem to support a reference to phases or stages through which the soul passes, both after death and during the Rite of Initiation; for in *Zohar* one reads:

" Now we know that at the end of the seven days the decay of the body sets in, and the soul then goes in to its place. It is first permitted into the cave of Machpelah up to a point, set in accordance with its merit. Then it comes to where the Garden of Eden stands, and there encounters the cherubim and the flashing sword which is found in the lower Garden of Eden, and if it is deemed worthy to do so, it enters ". (1.217b.)

Here it is clear that the places mentioned are to be regarded as symbolic references to states of consciousness.

Gen. 23: 13. *And he spake unto Ephron in the audience of the people of the land, saying, But if thou wilt give it, I pray thee, hear me: I will give the money for the field; take it of me, and I will bury my dead there.*

14. *And Ephron answered Abraham, saying unto him,*

15. *My lord, hearken unto me: the land is worth four hundred shekels of silver; what is that betwixt me and thee ? bury therefore thy dead.*

16. *And Abraham hearkened unto Ephron; and Abraham weighed to Ephron the silver, which he had named in the audience of*

the sons of Heth, four hundred shekels of silver, current money
with the merchant.

The price of four hundred shekels of silver would seem to support the
suggested interpretation that the death and burial of Sarah may possibly
represent entry upon a terminal phase or " end " (verse nine). By reduction
the number four is obtained, signifying the realm of form, and so of vehicles
or substance moulded into forms and then used as instruments of life and
as the machinery of Spirit. The number four also suggests the objective
Universe with its four directions of space, connected with each of which is
one of the Sacred Four, the *Lipikas*[1] or Recorders referred to. Silver is
also occultly the lunar metal, and moon in one of its aspects is the planet
of death, vehicle for and representation of the Lord God as Destroyer of
imprisoning forms, Who thereby brings about the end of cycles of
activity.

In the Hindu *Trimūrti*, Shiva as Destroyer is no cosmic Personage of
terrible mien but, in one permutation, a personification of natural law, and
especially of that attribute of eternal alternation which at all levels brings
manifestations to their close in preparation for new beginnings. Sarah,
as the expressed power or *Shakti*[2] of the Logos of a cycle of material manifestation, " dies " (is withdrawn) at that cycle's close.

The final effects of the " labours " of the Logos are indelibly impressed
upon the inner structure and *tattvas*[3] (essential nature) of the material field
of activity. Symbolically, Sarah is buried in a cave at the *end* of
a field.

Gen. 23: 17. *And the field of Ephron, which was in Machpelah, which was*
before Mamre, the field, and the cave which was therein, and
all the trees that were in the field, that were in all the borders
round about, were made sure

18. *Unto Abraham for a possession in the presence of the children*
of Heth, before all that went in at the gate of his city.

19. *And after this, Abraham buried Sarah his wife in the cave of*
the field of Mach-pelah before Mamre: the same is Hebron in
the land of Canaan.

---

[1] *Lipikas* (Sk.). The Celestial Recorders, the Agents of *karma*. Exoterically four and
esoterically seven great " Scribes ". The Lords of Karma Who, as far as man is concerned,
adjust beneficence and adversity resulting from former deeds.

[2] *Shakti* (Sk.). The outgoing energy of a Deity, sometimes personified as his wife or
consort. q.v. Glossary.

[3] *Tattva*—q.v. Glossary.

20. *And the field, and the cave that is therein, were made sure unto Abraham for a possession of a buryingplace by the sons of Heth.*

Herein two processes, macrocosmic and microcosmic, are described. The trees represent creative life incarnate in matter. Apart from the obvious physical meaning of making all these possessions sure unto Abraham, the term " made sure " may also, as hitherto suggested, signify the ineradicable impress upon matter of the results of the evolutionary process.

The Abramic epoch of manifestation is drawing to a close and the Isaacian is about to begin. The narrative is therefore susceptible of interpretation as a description of the closing of an old cycle and the opening of a new one; for, as has been said, at the close of every *Manvantara*[1], major or minor, the evolutionary attainments are indelibly impressed upon the Spirit-matter which has been previously involved in the processes of objective emanation. It is applicable to the Cosmos as a whole, to one Solar System, to any of its major components and to the Logoi presiding over them. The verses refer equally to one single race and its *Manu* and to each human being with its divine Spark or Monad. In this purely human interpretation, in which death marks the close of one cycle of incarnation and leads to the opening of the next, the same principles apply. The succession of cycles and their presiding Intelligences is also indicated in the Old Testament by the historical periods, each with their Patriarchs and Prophets. The wonderful conformity to be observed throughout Nature, with her perpetual progression from seed to fruit and on to new seed, is also referred to in the great allegory.

Readers unaccustomed to the idea that our Solar System is but one in both a number and a succession of such may find strange the affirmation in occult philosophy that the present Solar System was preceded by an unknown number of precursors, and in its turn will be followed by an infinite number of successors. As in the past, each of these will in the future progress along an evolutionary spiral towards ever greater degrees of the development of its indwelling life and consciousness, and its individual intelligences.

---

[1] *Manvantara*—q.v. Glossary.

CHAPTER XI

THE PRINCIPLE OF THE SUCCESSION OF LOGOI AND PATRIARCHS

Gen. 24. *Abraham sendeth his servant to get a wife for his son Isaac: he obtaineth Rebekah; Isaac meeteth her.*

As we saw at the close of the preceding Chapter, one of the most universal processes occurring throughout all manifestations, cosmic and microcosmic, is the transference of life and its fruits from one cycle to the next. This is clearly observable in the organic kingdoms of Nature, season following season in apparently endless succession. Nature thus continuously transmits both her own invisible life and the refined essence of all which she produces. This transmission of life and harvested fruits—the handing on of achieved results—continues throughout all ages as an unchanging and fundamental phenomenon; for, in principle, " seed " is immortal and indestructible.

THE MONAD AS MICROCOSMIC " SEED "

The innermost Soul of man, the " Immortal Germ "[1] as it has been appropriately entitled, is similarly undying and indestructible. From life on Earth to life after death, and on into succeeding lives, this human Seed-Self with its inherent divine attributes is carried over from cycle to cycle of existence and unfoldment throughout unending ages. In the human kingdom the process continues until Adeptship is attained,[2] bringing freedom from the " wheel of birth and death ".[3] Even then the Monad is still obedient to the law of cyclic unfoldment, though no longer obliged to submit to enforced reincarnation into the limitations of the physical world.

This principle of transference is revealed in the Old Testament by means of history and allegory. Patriarchs, Prophets, Judges and Kings, superior in stature to those whose lives they direct, follow the customary

---

[1] q.v. *Lecture Notes of the School of the Wisdom*, Vol. I (Rev. Ed.), Ch. I, Geoffrey Hodson.
[2] q.v. *Eph.* 4: 13.
[3] q.v. *Reincarnation, Fact or Fallacy?*, Geoffrey Hodson.

procedure of transmitting their power and their wisdom to chosen successors. The above-mentioned principle is thus presented by means of descriptions of actions by particular persons, this being part of the method of revelation used by the authors of allegorical portions of World Scriptures. When, for example, at the end of his mission Elijah was carried up to Heaven in a chariot of fire,[1] his mantle fell upon Elisha,[2] his appointed successor. Earlier both Abraham and Isaac had blessed their sons.

In the Mystery Schools of ancient peoples, as in certain modern ceremonial Orders and Rites descended from them, this principle was revealed and practised in the ritual transmission of rulership from one reigning Official to the next. Power pertaining to the Office of Hierophant, for example, was and still is handed on by means of ordered ceremonials which may include certain postures, physical contact as by the clasp of a hand, and communication by means of a whispered secret " word ". The necessity for this procedure is obvious. Hierophants of a Mystery Temple, endowed with spiritual power and trained to wield it in order to help Initiates to resurrect themselves from the " tomb " of the flesh, eventually reach the end of their period of Office. Thereupon another Officiant, similarly prepared and trained, hears the whispered word, is vested with the mantle of authority and is then duly installed in that Chair or Throne from which he, in turn, will preside over the activities of Temple and Crypt.[3]

In these various ways a universal procedure is revealed by means of symbol, drama and ceremonial. The processes of evolution and the handing on of their results through following cycles are expressed microcosmically throughout man's series of lives on Earth; for the God in man, being deathless and eternal, lives on after bodily death, preserves all the fruits of effort and experience and is then reborn, the new personality being endowed with a measure of the powers which have been earlier developed.

SUCCESSIVE UNIVERSES AND THEIR PRESIDING LOGOI

Macrocosmically, the closing of a cycle of manifestation and the final " acts " of its transcendent rather than its immanent Logos are described in this Chapter. In this sense Abraham represents the aspect of transcendence and personifies the First Logos in the act of making preparations

---

[1] *Kings* 2: 11. Attained Adeptship. cf. the cloud in which Jesus ascended into Heaven (*Acts* 1: 9).

[2] II *Kings* 2: 13.

[3] cf. The family of Eumolpids, descendants of Eumolpos, the first celebrant of the Eleusinian Mysteries, and successive Hierophants throughout a long period of their history. q.v. *The Eleusinian Mysteries and Rites*, Dudley Wright; *Eleusis and the Eleusinian Mysteries*, George E. Mylonas; *The Mysteries of Eleusis*, Prof. Georges Meautis.

for a new cycle; for Isaac, like John " the beloved disciple ", represents the Logos of the succeeding dispensation, and more particularly the group of Planetary Intelligences who in their synthesis will embody and direct the activities of divine Spirit, life and consciousness in the material field which is beginning to take form. The substance of this field is personified here by Rebekah, and in the Gospel story by Mary, who is brought by Jesus into close relationship with John; for, dying on the Cross (of matter in the macrocosmic sense), Jesus said to Mary: " Woman, behold thy son ! ", and to John: " Behold thy mother ! "[1]

Thus, under eternal law the activities of the one life are renewed in an unbroken succession of newly arisen forms. The matter of which these forms are built is root substance,[2] the " ocean " of undifferentiated space, ever *one and the same*. This may be indicated by Mary's name, which in Latin (*mare*) suggests " sea ". The process of emanation begins by the utterance of the " Word "[3], which differentiates from the vast sea of cosmic space the specialised region where the new Universe is to be formed. This latter is symbolised by the pitcher of water which Rebekah draws from the well. Her marriage to Isaac indicates that the new creative pair, matter and Spirit respectively, must be " wedded "[4] in order that they, in their turn, may produce a new cycle in continuance of that eternal progression which is the hallmark of Cosmos. This view would seem to be supported by Abraham's order to his servant that he swear " by the LORD, the God of heaven, and the God of the earth.... "[5]

THE ONE SOURCE FROM WHICH ALL COMES FORTH AND TO WHICH ALL RETURNS

Drawing together and summing up the ideas presented thus far, the law that all that exists is ever drawn from the same Source, namely Universal Substance, is revealed allegorically by Abraham's insistence that the wife for his son must be chosen from the country *of his own origin*.[6] He furthermore makes his servant swear by the symbol of creation (" put his hand under the thigh of Abraham ")[7] that this shall be so; for on their final distintegration all things sink back into their original state, and from that state all new things emerge.

[1] *Jn.* 19: 26, 27.

[2] *Mūlaprakriti* (Sk.)—" Root matter." q.v. Glossary.

[3] *Jn.* 1: 1–3.

[4] cf. Seb and Nut (Egypt); Apsu and Tiamat (Babylon); Brahma and Vāch (India); Cronos and Rhea, Chaos and Nyx, Erebus and Nyx (Greece); and " Father-Mother spin a web " (*Stanzas of Dzyan*, quoted in *The Secret Doctrine* (Adyar Ed.), Vol. I, p. 148, H. P. Blavatsky.

[5] *Gen.* 24: 3.

[6] *Gen.* 24: 2, 9.   [7] *Gen.* 24: 4.

This Twenty-fourth Chapter of *Genesis* may thus legitimately be interpreted in the macrocosmic sense as being descriptive of the process of pre-cosmic preparation for the emergence of the new Universe from *Pralaya*[1] into *Manvantara*,[1] from quiescence into activity.   These Biblical passages relate the closing periods of a creative epoch; for cosmic law ordains that the contents and products of a cycle of activity shall be gathered up and ultimately absorbed into their source.   All then remains quiescent until the immediate successor of that cycle shall appear.   Thereupon its contents, products and beings are transferred to the new one and the processes of involutionary descent and evolutionary ascent begin to be repeated.   Isaac personates both the newly emanated Logos and " His " outpoured life-force, whilst Rebekah represents the recipient and reproductive substance which, when differentiated or " chosen ", becomes the " mother " of the forms in which life is once more to be incarnate.

Following upon these general considerations, this important Chapter of *Genesis* is now examined in some detail.

> Gen. 24: 1. *And Abraham was old, and well stricken in age: and the LORD had blessed Abraham in all things.*

The end of an epoch and its approaching consummation of " blessing " are here described, the governing principle being applicable to Cosmoi, Solar Systems, planets, races and nations.   Since the subject has been considered in the preceding Chapters, no further comment is here offered.

> Gen. 24: 2. *And Abraham said unto his eldest servant of his house, that ruled over all that he had, Put, I pray thee, thy hand under my thigh:*
>
> 3. *And I will make thee swear by the LORD, the God of heaven, and the God of the earth, that thou shalt not take a wife unto my son of the daughters of the Canaanites, among whom I dwell:*
>
> 4. *But thou shalt go unto my country, and to my kindered, and take a wife unto my son Isaac.*
>
> 5. *And the servant said unto him, Peradventure the woman will not be willing to follow me unto this land: must I needs bring thy son again unto the land from whence thou camest?*
>
> 6. *And Abraham said unto him, Beware thou that thou bring not my son thither again.*

---

[1] q.v. Glossary.

7. *The LORD God of heaven, which took me from my father's house, and from the land of my kindred, and which spake unto me, and that sware unto me, saying, Unto thy seed will I give this land; he shall send his angel before thee, and thou shalt take a wife unto my son from thence.*

8. *And if the woman will not be willing to follow thee, then thou shalt be clear from this my oath: only bring not my son thither again.*

9. *And the servant put his hand under the thigh of Abraham his master, and sware to him concerning that matter.*

The proffered interpretations of this remarkable Chapter of the **Book of Genesis** *suggest that processes of the generation and emanation of Universes and their component Solar Systems, and of reproduction in the organic kingdoms of Nature—the " Great Work "—are being revealed by means of allegory. This view is regarded as sufficiently important to be developed at some length. It is inevitable, in consequence, that repetitions will occur and the reader's indulgence is requested should these prove to have assumed too large a place, both here and throughout my commentaries upon the* **Pentateuch.**

My studies of the Torah as a whole, and especially of this Chapter of **Genesis** *have convinced me that profound secrets concerning processes of creation, procreation, generation and regeneration, are concealed within its phrases. The direct vocal intervention of the Lord, accurate prevision, reference to the human thigh, the presence of a virgin and the use of the symbols of water and a well, support this concept and seem to me to justify a close and meditative study of the story in the hope of unveiling and revealing at least some part of a hitherto deeply hidden mystery. I therefore invite my readers to accompany me on a voyage of discovery. Those who hesitate will perhaps permit me to reinforce my invitation with the following quotations:—*

" *Woe to the sinners who look upon the Torah as simply tales pertaining to things of the world, seeing thus only the outer garment. But the righteous whose gaze penetrates to the very Torah, happy are they. Just as wine must be in a jar to keep, so the Torah must be contained in an outer garment. That garment is made up of the tales and stories; but we, we are bound to penetrate beyond.* " (**Zohar** 111, 152a).

Two direct references to creative power are made in these verses. The first is the speech or " word " of Abraham, who addresses his servant, and the second is the thigh. The key to the whole Chapter and, indeed, to the whole symbology of the epic of Abraham from the macrocosmic point of view is here provided.   Creative processes, powers and laws would appear to be described by the Initiate authors, who by this means reveal the teachings of the Sanctuaries of Chaldea.

THE SYMBOL OF THE THIGH

Abraham initiates the formative procedure by means of his words first spoken to his eldest servant, who later repeated it to Rebekah.   Speech is a combination of thought and aerial vibrations.   Demiurgic power is first emitted as a spiritual force of the quality of sound moving on frequencies of oscillation expressive of the previously conceived divine intent—the Archetype.[1]   Here the Logos doctrine is indicated, such an interpretation being supported by reference to the human thigh.   This member is in the region of the phallus, the organ through which in procreation the seed-bearing fluid is transmitted.   The thigh thus symbolises the source of the positive potency and refers to both the focused Ray or current of formative power and the collective generative forces and agencies.   These include the *fohatic*[2] fire and its associated Intelligences, the *Dhyān Chohans*, the *Elohim*.[3] To swear by the thigh, then, is to take an unbreakable oath and the eldest servant of Abraham's house obeys his master's command (puts his hand under Abraham's thigh and carries out his orders).   The mission entrusted to the servant cosmogonically refers to the differentiation of the " new " receptacle (area of space), the virgin mother-to-be (Rebekah).   The servant thereafter brings " her " into the presence of the " new " productive power (Isaac) who was waiting for her at Lahoi-roi.

THE ELDEST SERVANT

Active, formative energy is intimately associated with Universal Mind, which also is embodied in a Host of Creative Intelligences who, under numerical law, " serve " the Logos as vehicles for His power and are personified by the eldest servant.   These Beings, who are far beyond any human concept of individuality, constitute a hierarchical Order of Archangels and angels (the *Elohim*) evolved from Cosmos and ever ascending to greater heights and wider powers.   The most highly evolved (eldest) of these assist the Logos in the formation of the Universe and so " serve " until the close of a dispensation or *Manvantara*, being the last to be resolved into absolute unity.   They were the " first fruits "[4] of the preceding cycle,

---

[1] Archetype—q.v. Glossary.
[2] *Fohatic*—q.v. Glossary under *Fohat*.
[3] *Elohim*, q.v. Pt. III, Chs. I and II, of this Volume, the Appendix and the Glossary; also *The Kingdom of the Gods*, Geoffrey Hodson.
[4] *Rev.* 14: 4.

and will also be the first to emerge at the opening of the new one, when they at once assume their Offices and activities as agents and " servants" of the " Word ".   They are referred to as the " morning stars " who sang together, the " sons of God " who shouted for joy[1]—a reference to the formative power of sound; for the universal soniferous *Aether* (*Ākāśa*)[2] forms the " bodies " of these mighty " Beings " who, I have suggested, are personified as the eldest servant of Abraham.   Rightly, then, he becomes Abraham's consecrated messenger or transmitter of his creative power (from Abraham's " thigh ").

ANNUNCIATIONS—MACROCOSMIC AND MICROCOSMIC

In the Macrocosmic sense scriptural Annunciations by angels or servants of the Logos may be regarded as allegories of the fact that the highest of the *Elohim* first carry the *fohatic* impulse into the prepared field. Eve, Sarah, Rebekah, Mary the mother of Jesus, Māyā the mother of Buddha and Rhea and Hera of Greek mythology—indeed all mothers of Saviours, gods and heroes—represent that region of pre-cosmic substance which has been differentiated from the " virgin " sea of space.   The personification of this area as a mother-to-be is peculiarly apt, since it contains the seeds of life ready to become impregnated by the emitted life-force.   Conception occurs naturally, however, and from *within* the prepared substance (*prakriti*); for Spirit and matter are not actually two separate potencies occupying distinct locations.   On the contrary, they are mutually identified and occupy the same geographical position, as it were, the positive electricity reacting interiorly upon and evoking a response from the negative.

This rather abstruse metaphysics was taught directly to the Initiates of the Ancient Mysteries and by means of scriptural allegories to those as yet uninitiated.   These include a non-participating male (e.g. Joseph), a self-reproductive or virgin female (e.g. Mary), and a human servant or an angel as intermediary.   Numerically the essential three are each personified in the numerous yet always closely similar accounts of divine or semi-divine Nativities.   Thus in this Chapter of *Genesis* the first Logos (Abraham) by a senior messenger (the eldest servant) sends " word "[3] of future marital and maternal office to virginal substance (Rebekah).

MAN A MICROCOSM

Such personifications have also their microcosmic significations, which in this allegory are particularly exact.   At the opening of a new incarnation

---

[1] *Job*. 38: 7.

[2] *Ākāśa*—q.v. Glossary.

[3] A possible reference to the Logos Doctrine.

the human Ego projects its Ray into the matter of the higher planes of Nature. This Ray expresses vibrationally the Egoic powers and attributes resulting from previous cycles.[1] Magnetic centres are thereby set up around which man's subtler bodies begin to be formed. Allegorically Abraham (in this case, the Ego) sends his messenger (the Ray) to Rebekah, who represents the substance of the superphysical worlds. This is indicated by her association with water, which is used as a symbol for space, whether universal (the Great Deep) or differentiated (as in a well or a pitcher). The messenger, however, only arranges the marriage. It is Isaac who actually marries Rebekah and with her produces the progeny. In the case of the Nativity of Christ, however, a modification of the metaphor is used; for Mary is " fructified " spiritually by the "Voice " of the Archangel of the Annunciation, Gabriel (Agent of the Logos), whilst whatever office Joseph performed is only later fulfilled. It is well to remember that in both generative processes—the macrocosmic and the microcosmic—or personal Orders of the *Elohim* are involved.[2] The creative fire is the same in both instances and Archangelic Officials (*Elohim*) embody it and direct its power from the source, whether it be the Logos, the human Monad or the Ego in the Causal Body. The result is a " birth " or gradual attainment of a higher level of consciousness, with appropriate new powers, and entry upon a new cycle or historical phase (the Isaacian). The Monad, having performed its primary generative act, then withdraws and gives place to Isaac. Allegorically, Abraham dies and Isaac succeeds him as head of the family.[3]

Gen. 24: 10. *And the servant took ten camels of the camels of his master, and departed; for all the goods of his master were in his hand;*

[1] q.v. *The Kingdom of the Gods*, Pt. I, Ch. IV; *Occult Powers in Nature and in Man; Reincarnation, Fact or Fallacy?*; *The Miracle of Birth*—all by Geoffrey Hodson.

[2] This is supported by the number of camels accompanying the servant—ten—as also are the Orders of the Sephirothal Archangels and angels enumerated in the kabbalistic Tree of Life (see Appendix). The possibility that the choice was decided by the weight of the goods to be transported is not wholly discounted. It is, however, so apt from the symbolical point of view that pure coincidence would be even more remarkable than the concept of an allegorical reference to the ten Sephiras here suggested. Furthermore, it may be added, the appropriateness of the many numbers introduced into the Old and New Testaments would seem to offer strong evidence of a deliberate use of this form of symbolism, both to conceal and yet reveal profound cosmogonical processes, laws and powers. Speaking personally at this point, I find the consistent use of concordant numbers, combined with so many other classical symbols, to be very convincing. The number ten—used most appropriately at this phase of the life story of Abraham—is also a symbol of the opening of a new cycle following the completion (9) of a preceding process. q.v. *The Hidden Wisdom in the Holy Bible*, Vol. I, Pt. III, Ch. III, Geoffrey Hodson.

[3] *Gen.* 25: 5.

and he arose, and went to Mesopotamia, unto the city of Nahor.

The historicity of this passage is partly supported by recent archaeological research. In his book, *The Bible as History*,[1] Werner Keller writes:

" The Biblical city of Nahor is unexpectedly drawn into a recognizable historical setting. Abraham's servant set out for the land of the kings of Mari. The instructions of his master, according to the Biblical tradition, clearly indicate that Abraham must have known northern Mesopotamia, including Nahor, extremely well. How else could he have spoken of the city of Nahor?

" If we follow the dates given in the Bible, we find that Abraham left his native place, Haran, 645 years before the Exodus of the people of Israel from Egypt. They wandered through the desert toward the Promised Land under the leadership of Moses in the thirteenth century B.C. This date is, as we shall see, assured by archaeology. Abraham must therefore have lived about 1900 B.C. The finds at Mari confirm the accuracy of the Biblical account. About 1900 B.C., according to the evidence of the palace archives, Haran and Nahor were both flourishing cities.

" The documents from the kingdom of Mari produce startling proof again that the stories of the patriarchs in the Bible are not pious legends, as is often too readily assumed, but events that are described as happening in a historical period that can be precisely dated. "

Returning to the text, as previously suggested Abraham's ten camels by which the eldest servant is accompanied on his mission to find Rebekah numerically signify both the culmination of a cycle and the emanation of the Sephirothal Hierarchy of its succession. This latter occurs in preparation for the opening of a period of manifestation in which those ten Orders of Archangels and angels will become the bearers of the creative impulse (Abraham's goods and presents) into the new evolutionary field.

The eldest servant, apparently in so superior a position that he is able to decide upon the number of camels to accompany him, suggests his personification of a power by which even the Sephiroth are controlled. Two interpretations are here possible. In one the servant represents emanated creative energy; in the other he stands for numerical law itself, the abstract principle of numbers according to which the whole creative process is initiated (1) and completed (10) in an eternal progression of activity and quiescence. In this latter view the servant corresponds somewhat to Tehuti, the divine Chronologer and Record Keeper, who performs his activities in obedience to a purely abstract principle of alternation under numerical law. With his stylus, his notched palette and his lamp, on temple walls and on papyri Tehuti is portrayed as standing behind Amen, Ptah, Khepara and Khnoumis, creative deities in Egyptian cosmogony. He is thus both Timekeeper and Recorder on behalf of the Gods.[1] All annunciatory Presences who carry the " Word " of forthcoming generation to the feminine potency have in them, in part at least, this Tehutic principle.

> Gen. 24: 11. *And he made his camels to kneel down without the city by a well of water at the time of the evening, even the time that women go out to draw water.*

At the close of a " Day " of creation (evening) the ten Sephiroth (ten beasts of burden) approach the region in universal thought which contains the Ideation of the new Universe (the city) and the bounded area of space (the well) in which that Ideation is to become incarnate. The substance for the cycle-to-be will be drawn from this universal supply, as is symbolised by a woman filling a pitcher from it. The time stated, evening, suggests the close of a cycle and the onset of rest or " Night ", presage of a new creative " Day ".

---

[1] q.v. *The Gods of the Egyptians*, Vol. I, pp. 20, 400–401, E. A. Wallis Budge.

CHAPTER XII

THE STORY OF REBEKAH

Gen. 24: 12. *And he said, O LORD God of my master Abraham, I pray thee, send me good speed this day, and shew kindness unto my master Abraham.*

13. *Behold, I stand here by the well of water; and the daughters of the men of the city come out to draw water:*

14. *And let it come to pass, that the damsel to whom I shall say, Let down thy pitcher, I pray thee, that I may drink; and she shall say, Drink, and I will give thy camels drink also: let the same be she that thou hast appointed for thy servant Isaac; and thereby shall I know that thou hast shewed kindness unto my master.*

Since commentaries upon these verses are offered in Part Two of this Volume, Chapter Five, some general remarks alone are made at this point. The susceptibility of the life story of Abraham to interpretation in both the macrocosmic and microcosmic senses gains support from the introduction of the Godhead into the narrative, and of strange symbols, appropriate numbers and prophetic divination. Amongst these, to particularise, are Jehovah, Lord God of the Universe, the taking of an oath by the eldest servant with his hand under Abraham's thigh, the number of camels which he took (ten), the appearance and action of Rebekah in strict accordance with prophecy, reference to her jewels and veil, and the hope expressed by Rebekah's family as she departed from her home and city that she should become " the mother of thousands of millions " and that her seed should " possess the gate of those which hate them . "[1]

If the story be thus regarded as a blend of history and allegory, the narrative may be interpreted as showing how universal law becomes operative in a particular instance. Symbolically, as by an omen, the new receptacle is discovered by divine ordinance. After a period of quiescence

[1] *Gen.* 24: 60.

22

has passed, time and law re-establish in a selected area the operation of generative, productive and culminating cycles of activity, or initiate a new incarnation of the Logos or " Word. "[1]

> Gen. 24: 15. *And it came to pass, before he had done speaking, that, behold, Rebekah came out, who was born to Bethuel, son of Milcah, the wife of Nahor, Abraham's brother, with her pitcher upon her shoulder.*
>
> 16. *And the damsel was very fair to look upon, a virgin, neither had any man known her: and she went down to the well, and filled her pitcher, and came up.*

THE SIGNIFICANCE OF GENEALOGIES

Rebekah is the granddaughter of Nahor and the great-niece of Abraham. Her father was Bethuel, son of Milcah and Nahor who had remained in Mesopotamia, living in the city of Ur of the Chaldees. All cosmogonies give prominence to the family trees of the primogenitor and the primogenitrix. In allegorical descriptions of Cosmogenesis it is generally regarded as important that the producers of relatively minor *Manvantaras*, or successive cycles of progressive manifestion, should be in the direct line and thus able to trace their ancestry back to the original first Source. This may be the reason for Abraham's insistence on the choice of Isaac's wife from his own family, as also for the recurrent genealogies in the Bible and other World Scriptures. Doubtless this is the explanation of the supposed inter-family marriages, as in the Royal Houses of Egypt, when even sister and half brother[2] and sisters and brothers were wedded and jointly occupied the throne.[3]

In addition to recording family and racial derivations, always of importance to ancient peoples, there is an occult significance in direct descent from a primordial source. In any given order of manifestation all Universes are the products of the action of impregnating Spirit upon reproductive matter (the Spirit of God and the face of the waters[4]), from whose union in the beginning the whole manifestation arises. All successive component cycles must therefore in their turn be the products of the one primary progenitor. Although every sub-cycle has its own parental pair, each employs and represents the power (*Fohat*) of the first dual emanative agency alone. Moreover, all manifestations occur within the area or sphere

[1] cf. *Jn.* 1: 1–5.
[2] *e.g.*, Queen Hatshepsut and Thotmes III (18th Dynasty).
[3] Cleopatra VII and Ptolemy XIV.
[4] *Gen.* 1: 2.

of influence marked out in the beginning. The successive formative impulses, which in reality are still given by the First Logos, are depicted allegorically as emanating from descendants of the primogenitor of the family who is made to personify that first Creator, or rather Emanator. The authors evidently wish to insist that the same laws, established eternally as the laws of creation, rule unfailingly in all reproductive activities of whatever order or dimension. Thus both Isaac and Rebekah, personifying Spirit and matter, Purusha[1] and Prakriti[2] respectively, are made to descend from the original Terah and his wife.

A more esoteric teaching also exists. The primal emission of generative energy is but a partial and limited forth-sending. Further power is always in reserve, awaiting its expression at the genesis of succeeding cycles, whilst Prakriti in its unfathomable depths contains infinite productive potentiality. Thus the first cycle of manifestation by no means exhausts the supply of productive power. Although the directive Officials may change, the available power is ever the same and ever drawn from the original sources. Teachers of old, writing about Cosmogenesis from within the Sanctuary, wished to ensure the prepetuation of knowledge of this profoundly significant truth. They therefore preserved with meticulous care the genealogical trees tracing the descent of the heads of those families who were used to personify the male and female creative potencies of successive cycles. As we have seen, the servant was therefore sent back to Ur of the Chaldees, Abraham's original home. He was also made to swear by the male symbol of creative power (Abraham's thigh) that he would not fail to carry out his instructions.

THE SUCCESSION OF THE HIEROPHANTS OF THE ANCIENT MYSTERIES

If the allegory is translated microcosmically, and the succession of Hierophants of the Mysteries is also being portrayed, then again it is clearly important that each successive Officient draws both his initiatory power and his wisdom from the original Sanctuary and source. In a more personal reading, the generation of wisdom and the reception of truth from within the spiritual Self of illumined and Initiated man may be implied. All this I again suggest, constitutes an allegorical presentation of macrocosmic and microcosmic creative procedures cast in the form of a metaphorical account of an episode in the history of the Hebrew race.

[1] Purusha (Sk.)—" The Great Breath ". The masculine, creative potency in Cosmogenesis, Prakriti (matter) being the feminine potency.
[2] Prakriti (Sk.)—" Nature or matter " as opposed to Spirit, the two primeval aspects of the One Unknown Deity.

> *Gen.* 24: 17. *And the servant ran to meet her, and said, Let me, I pray thee,
> drink a little water of thy pitcher.*
>
> 18. *And she said, Drink, my lord: and she hasted, and let down
> her pitcher upon her head, and gave him drink.*
>
> 19. *And when she had done giving him drink, she said, I will draw
> water for thy camels also, until they have done drinking.*
>
> 20. *And she hasted, and emptied her pitcher into the trough, and ran
> again unto the well to draw water, and drew for all his camels.*
>
> 21. *And the man wondering at her held his peace, to wit whether
> the LORD had made his journey prosperous or not.*

The haste or running of Abraham's eldest servant to meet and speak to
Rebekah and drink from her pitcher may indicate a further significance
attached to this Official. If, as earlier put forward, he be regarded as a
personification of the emanated creative energy, then his running aptly
describes the swift action of the electric, *fohatic* force, the propellent power
which in the beginning flows as a generative current from the positive " pole"
(Abraham) towards the negative, reproductive recipient (Rebekah). *Fohat*
as the first emanation from the active Logos is indeed as the eldest servant,
and is also both a messenger and a bridge between the two aspects of the
one Source. The ready, even generous, response is in its turn typical of
the immediate reaction of the receptive, feminine, negative polarity. The
allegory thus suggests that the original inspirers of the Pentateuch may even
have possessed some knowledge of the polarities and interchanged currents
characteristic of electrical phenomena.

The fact that the ten camels drank their fill from the well suggests
that the Sephirothal Decad which they personify finds available and draws
from the unfailing Source (Rebekah at the well) all the necessities
for the enactment of their Elohistic functions, Thus, I repeat, the
Sephirothal Decad (the ten camels) as well as the primordial *fohatic* agency
(the eldest servant) both travel to and receive from Rebekah an
abundance of her life-giving " supply" (water); for Rebekah, like all
the feminine personifications, typifies the very Soul of the soul of virginal
matter. Water, in it sturn, is the symbol of matter, itself, *prakriti*, the
protyle, the one *tattva* or common element from which all descendants or
sub-*tattvas* (planes, sub-planes and chemical elements) are produced.

> *Gen.* 24: 22. *And it come to pass, as the camels had done drinking,
> that the man took a golden earring of half a shekel weight,*

and two bracelets for her hands of ten shekels weight
of gold;

In this verse the authors again provide one of the keys to the interpretation of the whole Chapter. It consists of the golden earring given to
Rebekah by the eldest servant on behalf of Abraham; for in another symbolical sense it is *Purusha* as the "breath" which speaks and *Prakriti* which,
when aroused to creative wakefulness, symbolically gives ear. Hearing,
" she " responds.

Thus once more in the pages of Scripture there is revealed by allegory
and symbol the deep secret of cosmic and microcosmic generation. Reduced
to its essence this consists of the emanation of soniferous, demiurgic energy
(the " Word ") by the masculine potency and the reception of it (the answer
to the " Word ") by the negative potency. The half shekel of weight, added
to the ten shekels of the two bracelets for her hands, may be taken to indicate
the opening of and preliminary entry into the new cycle (the half shekel)
after the completion (ten shekels) of its predecessor (the Abramic cycle).

In the symbology of cosmogony armlets, bracelets, necklets and anklets
are worn by Deities (notably Hindu), both male and female. These
circular adornments symbolise the " voluntary " or natural self-limitation
of That which, in its primordial nature, is essentially timeless and free.

The account in the *Bhágavata-Puräna* of one of the " pranks " of the
child Shri Krishna describes, by means of allegory and the use of a different
set of symbols, the two principles of the boundlessness of life and the voluntary
submission of the manifesting Logos (Shri Krishna) to imprisonment in
form. The story is sometimes called " Binding the Unbound "[1] and is
related as follows :

THE TYING

" One day Yasodā was churning curdled milk and singing the deeds
of her son. Kṛṣṇa came up and, desirous of sucking milk, held the churning
rod. Yasoda placed him on her lap and gave him milk to suck. But the
milk that was boiling on the oven overflowed the pot and she hurriedly left
her son. In anger Kṛṣṇa bit his lips, broke the milk pot with a stone, took
the fresh butter to a retired corner and there partook of it. Yasodā came
back after a while and fouud the pot broken. Her son had left the place
and she could easily see that it was all his doing. She found Kṛṣṇa seated
on the husk stand, freely dividing the contents of the hanging pots among
the monkeys, and she quietly approached him with a stick. Krsna hurriedly

---

[1] q.v. *A Study of the Bhágavata-Puräna* by Purnendu Narayana Sinha, M.A., B.L., Sk. X
Ch. 10.

got down and ran away as if in fear. Yasodā ran after him and caught him at last. Finding him fear-stricken, she threw down the stick and tried to fasten him to the husking mill. The rope fell short by the breadth of two fingers (say two inches). She added another rope. The gap remained the same. She added rope after rope, as many as she had of her own and of her neighbours, but could not bridge over the distance. She stood baffled at last, amazed and ashamed. Finding that his mother was perspiring in the effort and that her hair had become dishevelled, Kṛṣṇa allowed himself to be fastened to the mill. "

This story, as suggested, may be regarded as an allegory illustrating both the boundlessness of the one life, as also of the one truth, and the willingness of their Source (Krishna) to become embodied in Nature's forms and in concepts such as principles, formulae and axioms conceivable by the human mind.

To return to the story of Rebekah at the well, also regarded as an allegory, the Biblical account thus continues:

> *Gen.* 24: 23. *And said, Whose daughter art thou? tell me, I pray thee: is there room in thy father's house for us to lodge in?*
>
> 24. *And she said unto him, I am the daughter of Bethuel, the son of Milcah, which she bare unto Nahor.*
>
> 25. *She said moreover unto him, We have both straw and provender enough, and room to lodge in.*
>
> 26. *And the man bowed down his head, and worshipped the LORD.*
>
> 27. *And he said, Blessed be the LORD God of my master Abraham, who hath not left destitute my master of his mercy and his truth: I being in the way, the LORD led me to the house of my master's brethren.*
>
> 28. *And the damsel ran, and told them of her mother's house these things.*

As so often in allegorical writings, it is here repeated, question and answer imply the creative procedure. The question indicates the emission of formative energy, the " Word ", and the answer portrays the response by recipient matter, the everlasting echo of the call of Spirit. The genealogy given and the hospitality shown by feminine substance to the life-force of the masculine " Creator ", are further indicated by the return of Rebekah to her mother's house, into which the servant is invited.

Gen. 24: 29. *And Rebekah had a brother, and his name was Laban: and Laban ran out unto the man, unto the well.*

30. *And it came to pass, when he saw the earring, and bracelets upon his sister's hands, and when he heard the words of Rebekah his sister, saying, Thus spake the man to me, that he came unto the man; and behold, he stood by the camels at the well.*

31. *And he said, Come in, thou blessed of the LORD: wherefore standest thou without for I have prepared the house, and room for the camels.*

32. *And the man came into the house: and he ungirded his camels, and gave straw and provender for the camels, and water to wash his feet, and the men's feet that were with him.*

Verses twenty-nine to thirty-two may be read as further references to the exactitude of the response of Rebekah and her family in perfect accordance with Abraham's original pre-vision, plan and instructions, a repetition of which follows. The essential passivity and echo-like response of the virgin sea of space to fructification by Spirit through the agency of *Fohat* is again indicated. Otherwise expressed, the function of space or the feminine side in the generative process is characterised by fidelity of response to and reproduction of the cosmic " Idea "[1] present in and partly constituting Divine Mind or Universal Thought. Even though time is required, and the first response consists of the production of a highly spiritualised archetypal " form "—material forms following much later and requiring sequence for their shaping and ultimate perfection—nevertheless that first response is always a true one.

Gen. 24: 33. *And there was set meat before him to eat: but he said, I will not eat, until I have told mine errand. And he said, Speak on.*

34. *And he said, I am Abraham's servant.*

35. *And the LORD hath blessed my master greatly; and he is become great: and he hath given him flocks, and herds, and silver, and gold, and men servants, and maid servants, and camels, and asses.*

36. *And Sarah my master's wife bare a son to my master when she was old: and unto him hath he given all that he hath.*

[1] In the Platonic sense.

37. *And my master made me swear, saying, Thou shalt not take a wife to my son of the daughters of the Canaanites, in whose land I dwell:*

38. *But thou shalt go unto my father's house, and to my kindred, and take a wife unto my son.*

39. *And I said unto my master, Peradventure the woman will not follow me.*

40. *And he said unto me, the LORD, before whom I walk, will send his angel with thee, and prosper thy way; and thou shalt take a wife for my son of my kindred, and of my father's house:*

41. *Then shalt thou be clear from this my oath, when thou comest to my kindred; and if they give not thee one, thou shalt be clear from my oath.*

42. *And I came this day unto the well, and said, O LORD God of my master Abraham, if now thou do prosper my way which I go:*

43. *Behold, I stand by the well of water; and it shall come to pass, that when the virgin cometh forth to draw water, and I say to her, Give me, I pray thee, a little water of thy pitcher to drink:*

44. *And she say to me, Both drink thou, and I will also draw for thy camels: let the same be the woman whom the LORD hath appointed out for my master's son.*

45. *And before I had done speaking in mine heart, behold, Rebekah came forth with her pitcher on her shoulder; and she went down unto the well, and drew water: and I said unto her, Let me drink I pray thee.*

46. *And she made haste, and let down her pitcher from her shoulder and said, Drink, and I will give thy camels drink also: so I drank, and she made the camels drink also.*

47. *And I asked her, and said, Whose daughter art thou? And she said, The daughter of Bethuel, Nahor's son, whom Milcah bare unto him: and I put the earring upon her face, and the bracelets upon her hands.*

48. *And I bowed down my head, and worshipped the LORD, and blessed the LORD God of my master Abraham, which had led me in the right way to take my master's brother's daughter unto his son.*

49. *And now if ye will deal kindly and truly with my master, tell me: and if not, tell me, that I may turn to the right hand, or to the left.*

50. *Then Laban and Bethuel answered and said, The thing proceedeth from the LORD: we cannot speak unto thee bad or good.*

51. *Behold, Rebekah is before thee, take her. and go, and let her be thy master's son's wife, as the LORD hath spoken.*

52. *And it came to pass, that, when Abraham's servant heard their words, he worshipped the LORD, bowing himself to the earth.*

53. *And the servant brought forth jewels of silver, and jewels of gold and raiment, and gave them to Rebekah: he gave also to her brother and to her mother precious things.*

54. *And they did eat and drink, he and the men that were with him, and tarried all night; and they rose up in the morning, and he said, Send me away unto my master.*

55. *And her brother and her mother said, Let the damsel abide with us a few days, at the least ten; after that she shall go.*

56. *And he said unto them, Hinder me not, seeing the LORD hath prospered my way; send me away that I may go to my master.*

Verses thirty-three to fifty-six are largely repetitive from the narrative point of view, but not without occult significance. For this reason and on account of their important place in the story of Rebekah's life, both at home and on her departing for her marriage, and also because of a certain beauty of language, I have here included them in full. The eldest servant's recital of his instructions and adventures to the family of Rebekah is an allegory of the continued and increasingly intimate and penetrative outpouring of the demiurgic power of the Logos. The references to the wealth of his master, which is to be placed at the disposal of Isaac's wife-to-be, reveal the fact that the fruitage of the preceding cycle is all placed at the disposal of the new one. Such harvesting is sent forth again to embark upon a succeeding round of the cyclic, involutionary pilgrimage into matter and form thereafter to follow the evolutionary arc back to the Source.

CHAPTER XIII

THE DEPARTURE OF REBEKAH AND THE DEATH OF ABRAHAM

Gen. 24: 57. *And they said, We will call the damsel, and enquire at her mouth*

58. *And they called Rebekah, and said unto her, Wilt thou go with this man? And she said, I will go.*

The above verses are significant in that a direct reference to the occult power of sound is again made in the words " enquire at her mouth ", and in Rebekah's reply " I will go." Once more the cosmic feminine is shown as irresistibly drawn by, and responsive to, the cosmic masculine potency. This is the spiritual principle which—grievously misunderstood and misapplied throughout the ages—has partly contributed to the dominance of the female by the male in so many successive human civilisations.

THE FREEDOM OF REBEKAH'S RESPONSE

The erroneous nature of the concept of the submission of wife to husband—inherent, for example, in both Hinduism and Mohammedanism—is shown by the fact that her family leave to Rebekah the decision whether or not she will go to Isaac, and, should she agree to do so, whether she will tarry the ten days or go immediately. Rebekah's entirely free response shows that no Scriptural support is here given for the domination of woman by man, grown-up daughter by parents, or wife by husband. Even if, under natural law, primordial substance answers to primordial Spirit, in the human kingdom the factor of individuality negatives its application to men and women.

The spiritual individuality (the Ego) of a human being is equally female and male, and neither the words of scripture nor the pseudo-accident of physical sex should, I submit, be regarded as a divine direction concerning the correct relationship between the sexes. It is, I suggest, a mark of evolutionary advance in both an individual and a civilisation that equal importance, responsibility, opportunity and freedom are enjoyed by both women and men.

Gen. 24: 59. *And they sent away Rebekah their sister, and her nurse, and Abraham's servant, and his men.*

60. *And they blessed Rebekah, and said unto her, Thou art our sister, be thou the mother of thousands of millions, and let thy seed possess the gate of those which hate them.*

REBEKAH ACCOMPANIES THE ELDEST SERVANT

On her journey to meet Isaac, Rebekah was accompanied by her nurse, who represents the mortal nature now subservient to the Higher Self. In their plain sense these verses are self-explanatory and may legitimately be regarded as descriptive of normal proceedings on the occasion of a leave-taking by a member of a family on departure for an unknown destination and period of time. Nevertheless certain incidents in the story referred to in Chapter V of Part Two of this Volume would seem to justify its interpretation as an allegory. The passage from Part Two is, however, repeated here in support of this approach. It reads as follows: " The story of the discovery of Rebekah as the future wife of Isaac, in fulfilment of the prophetic vision of his father Abraham, takes its place with the great mystical romances of all time. There are, however, elements in the story which may indicate a deeper intention on the part of the authors of the *Pentateuch*. They themselves, for example, open this great work with an account of Cosmogenesis, and follow it with a highly allegorical description of the creation of man (Adam) and later, from his side, woman (Eve). Since a literal reading of this passage of Scripture cannot reasonably be accepted, the student of the Language of Allegory and Symbol may prefer to regard accounts of such generative procedures as also being capable of interpretation in the larger sense as allegories of macrocosmic and microcosmic 'creations'. "

THE HEAVENLY MARRIAGE

In a microcosmic, Initiatory interpretation the story of Rebekah and Isaac portrays the mystical union (celestial marriage) between the reincarnating Soul in its vesture of light or Causal Body (Rebekah) and the spiritual Ray (Isaac) which proceeds from its divine Spark or Monad[1] (Abraham). Certain mystical experiences accompanying the elevation of the consciousness of Initiates from the purely mundane, through intellectual and intuitive levels into full spiritual awareness, may also have been described in the verses under consideration.

---

[1] q.v. *The Hidden Wisdom in the Holy Bible*, Vol. I, Pt. VI, p. 236, Geoffrey Hodson, and Glossary.

According to this view the vehicle of abstract intelligence, the Causal Body (Rebekah), is impregnated by the Monadic Ray (Isaac) to produce as offspring the higher spiritual faculties, including those of wisdom and intuition. This accords with the ancient custom of externally dramatising developments and activities occurring *within* the threefold Higher Self of man. As we have seen the different people in the story, their conversations and mutual relationships, according to universal custom are made to personify the spiritual powers of man and their corresponding vehicles of manifestation.

The general theme, then, is the illumination of the immortal Self of man by the light of his newly awakened intuition. This faculty, hitherto germinal, comes to life as a result of the " descent " of the fire of spiritual will or *Ātma*[1] from a still higher level, that of the Monad. The " fire of God " thus " descends " creatively into the Egoic vehicle, the Causal Body, which in allegories of Initiation is generally personified by the principal feminine character.

As in the course of several lives the *Ātmic* power begins increasingly to influence Ego and personality, so do these two in their turn draw nearer to the *Ātmic* Source, grow more and more responsive to the Monadic Will. Thus Rebekah comes forth from her home and city, which in this particular interpretation are symbolic of the limitations (useful until a certain evolutionary phase has been entered, and then to be outgrown) of self-centred individuality. Homes and cities are also emblematic of the Causal Body itself, the Egoic " home " in the higher mental world. Whilst these developments will occur normally in all mankind in the course of evolutionary progress, the training for an enactment of the Rite of Initiation in the Greater (alone) Mysteries brings them about in advance of their natural attainment. In another possible interpretation Rebekah represents the secret wisdom revealed to the Candidate at Initiation into the Greater Mysteries, whilst the well would refer to the totality of wisdom, esoteric and exoteric, allotted to mankind on this Earth.

MYSTICAL ANNUNCIATIONS AND NATIVITIES

Scriptural accounts of the genealogies and Nativities of World Saviours which contain supernatural and miraculous elements may thus permissibly be read as susceptible of interpretation as descriptions of hastened evolution and the mystical experiences by which the results are accompanied. As earlier suggested, the accurate prophecy by Abraham, the discovery of Rebekah near a well, the declaration by the eldest servant of the purpose

---

[1] *Ātma* (Sk.)—" The Self ". The Universal Spirit, the seventh principle in the septenary constitution of man, the Supreme Soul. The Spirit-Essence of the Universe (*Paramātman*—" the Self Beyond ").

of his visit, Rebekah's response, her marriage to Isaac and the births of Jacob and Esau, would all seem to be susceptible of such an interpretation. The verbal interchange between the eldest servant of Abraham and Isaac's chosen wife, Rebekah, would then correspond to an Annunciation and its acceptance. The servant thus becomes the bearer of the creative " Word " from Abraham (the Monad) on behalf of his son Isaac (the *Ātma* or Ray of the Monad) to Rebekah (the unfolding spiritual Self).

Similarly the words of the Lord God to Adam and Eve concerning the fruit of the tree of the knowledge of good and evil,[1] to Hagar foretelling the birth of Ishmael[2] and to Abram and Sarai promising fruitfulness in old age;[3] the prophecy of an angel to the wife of Manoah foretelling the birth of Samson;[4] the two Annunciations of the Archangel Gabriel, one to Zacharias concerning the forthcoming birth of John the Baptist in the spirit and power of Elias[5] and the other to Mary[6] prophesying the birth of Jesus—all these allegorically describe in the Macrocosm the first impregnation (by means of the " Voice " or " Word ", as in the Logos doctrine[7]) of matter by Spirit at the dawn of Creation, and in man the enfiring of the personality by the spiritual Self. Later, at Initiation, the Ego in the Higher Mind is fructified by the descent of the fire of the Monadic *Ātma*, this being brought about by the Hierophant[8] during the performance of the sacred Rite.

In like manner the birth of the Lord Buddha was preceded by mystical portents. His mother, Queen Māyā, dreamed that a white elephant entered her body. The announcement was also made to her husband, King Suddhōdana, by *devas* (angels) that the dream implied or foretold the birth of a son who would be a Saviour of the world, this being confirmed by the learned Brāhmans at the Court. These, prophetic utterances also constitute an Annunciation. Sir Edwin Arnold in *The Light of Asia* so poetically describes the two incidents that I would like to quote him here:

" That night the wife of King Suddhodana,
Maya the Queen, asleep beside her Lord,
Dreamed a strange dream; dreamed that a star from heaven—
Splendid, six-rayed, in colour rosy-pearl,
Whereof the token was an Elephant
Six-tusked, and white as milk of Kamadhuk—
Shot through the void : and, shining into her,
Entered her womb upon the right. Awaked,

---

[1] *Gen.* 2: 17.   [2] *Gen.* 16: 11.   [3] *Gen.* 17: 6.
[4] *Judges* 13: 3.   [5] *Lk.* 1: 13.   [6] *Lk.* 1: 26–35.
[7] q.v. *The Kingdom of the Gods*, Pt. I, Ch. III, Geoffrey Hodson.
[8] *Hierophant*—q.v. Glossary.

Bliss beyond mortal mothers, filled her breast,
And over half the earth a lovely light
Forewent the morn. The strong hills shook; the waves
Sank lulled; all flowers that blow by day came forth
As 'twere high noon; down to the farthest hells
Passed the Queen's joy, as when warm sunshine Thrills
Wood-glooms to gold, and into all the deeps
A tender whisper pierced. ' Oh ye, ' it said,
' The dead that are to live, the live who die,
Uprise, and hear, and hope ! Buddha is come !'
Whereat in Limbos numberless much peace
Spread, and the world's heart throbbed, and a wind blew
With unknown freshness over lands and seas.
And when the morning dawned, and this was told,
The grey dream-readers said ' The dream is good !
The Crab is in conjunction with the Sun;
The Queen shall bear a boy, a holy child
Of wondrous wisdom, profiting all flesh,
Who shall deliver men from ignorance,
Or rule the world, if he will deign to rule.
In this wise was the holy Buddha born. "

The birth of the body to be occupied by the Lord Shri Krishna, an *Avatār* of Vishnu, was foretold by an incorporeal voice addressing King Kamsa, the brother of Devaki, saying: "O ignorant one ! the eighth child of her whom thou art now driving shall be thy slayer." This incident occurred immediately after the wedding of Devaki and Vasudeva whilst, following the wedding ceremony, they were being driven in his chariot by King Kamsa.

Just as the life of the Lord Buddha was threatened by his cousin, Devadatta, and that of Shri Krishna by King Kamsa, so was the life of Jesus endangered by King Herod. Mystically interpreted, these antagonists personify the separative, prideful attributes of the formal mind of man, which always threaten the development of selflessness and the faculty of spiritual intuitiveness; for when these latter reign over the personality the power of the individualistic mind is broken for ever. Instinctively aware of this, the mental principle in which self-centredness is inherent seeks by means of scorn, cynicism, excessive analysis and the adoption of a purely materialistic and temporal outlook, to prevent the unfoldment of the new faculties. Hence the presence of enemies at the births and throughout the lives of the Saviours of men. These stories of the impregnation of a future vehicle or passive generator by the seed-bearing, active, positive creator all occur after the conclusion of one cycle and at the opening of its successor, and apply equally to both Macrocosm and microcosm. From this digression we now return to the story of Rebekah.

THE SYMBOL OF THE SEED

Verse fifty-nine of the Twenty-fourth Chapter of *Genesis* may also be read as an allegorical description of the entry of the evolving life (Rebekah) —whether of Universe, planet, personality or initiated Ego[1]—upon the next phase of its unfoldment. This will bring increased fruitfulness (" the mother of thousands of millions ") and lead to final victory by the spiritual principle over all material resistance. Verse sixty describes this progress in terms of parental and family blessings and the expressions of hope for great fruitfulness. Within one who has been newly Initiated a further descent occurs of Spirit into matter, of Monad-*Ātma* into the Ego and thence into the personality.

The stated wish that Rebekah would be " the mother of thousands of millions" may signify the two great truths that the evolutionary potentiality of the human Monad is without limit and that, as indicated by the whole number (thousands of millions, reducible to ten), fulfilment and culmination is the assured goal.

The phrase " let thy seed possess the gate of those which hate them " is also deeply occult. In the allegorical language the word " seed " is used as a symbol of both Spirit and truth. " Haters " and all enemies personify matter. When physically incarnated, in its relationship to its mortal personality the Ego of man, representing spirit, is ever in conflict with matter, which to its dynamic expansiveness opposes inertia and constriction. In highly evolved man alone does the mystical Armageddon end in victory. Then Spirit " possesses the gate " of its enemy (matter).

A recondite reference to the atomic[2] structure of matter may also be discerned. An exposition of such possible undermeaning to this remarkable episode of the discovery of Rebekah by occult means and her departure justifies, I think, a brief dissertation upon an occult view of the nature and evolution of matter itself. Each completed cycle of both universal and human development includes an increase of atomic activity and fulness of function. The *spirillae* or whorls, of force, ten in number, of which the ultimate atom (as distinct from the " atom " of physics) is said to consist,

[1] Ego—q.v. Glossary.

[2] Atomic. In occult science this word is used for the foundation-bricks of the Universe and in the strict etymological sense, meaning that it " cannot be cut or divided " (Gr.). One of the fundamentals of occultism is that the elements of Nature are atoms on the material side and Monads on the energy side, both being indivisible. The Greek philosophers Democritus, Leucippus, Epicurus, Ennius and Lucretius advanced the view that matter was composed of atoms, and these scholars came to be known as " atomists " in consequence. q.v. *First Principles of Theosophy*, Ch. X, C. Jinarājadāsa.

are successively vivified, opened and used as vehicles for the corresponding energy and consciousness of the plane above. In Initiated man the component atoms of certain organs in the brain have thus responded to spiritual stimuli. Symbolically, Spirit possesses these " gates " of which matter is composed. When an Adept decides voluntarily to incarnate in a physical body its cerebro-spinal system, being composed of such highly evolved atoms, is occultly vivified and so hyper-active. The same is true of all higher vehicles, for which the component atoms are as gates or doors through which power, life and consciousness from still higher levels reach the densest and outermost principle. Symbolically, " the seed (spiritual potentialities hitherto latent, but now having germinated) possesses the gate of those which hate them."

> Gen. 24: 61. *And Rebekah arose, and her damsels, and they rode upon the camels, and followed the man: and the servant took Rebekah, and went his way.*
>
> 62. *And Isaac came from the way of the well Lahai-roi: for he dwelt in the south country.*
>
> 63. *And Isaac went out to meditate in the field at eventide: and he lifted up his eyes, and saw, and, behold, the camels were coming.*
>
> 64. *And Rebekah lifted up her eyes, and when she saw Isaac, she lighted off the camel.*
>
> 65. *For she had said unto the servant, What man is this that walketh in the field to meet us? And the servant had said, It is my master: therefore she took a veil and covered herself.*

THE ETERNAL POLES

The electro-magnetic nature of the intercharge and intercourse between the masculine and the feminine, the active and the passive potencies, is indicated in this mutual approach and increasingly intimate association (marriage and parenthood) of their personifications as Isaac and Rebekah. From the first moment of *Manvantaric* dawn the electric, not the spatial, relationship between *Purusha*[1] and *Prakriti*[2] grows continually more intimate. As opposite polarities they might be regarded as being at enmity from the beginning, as is indeed implied by their portrayal as opponents in allegorical wars and in conflicts between Saviours and demons, as also between heroes

[1] q.v. Glossary.

23

and wicked men or serpents and other reptiles; for all of these adversaries personify the active resistance of matter to the evolutionary process. Indeed, this is represented by the battles of Kurukshetra and Armageddon, which portray in time and space the conflict between Spirit and matter, and the spiritual Soul of man and its material vehicles.   Hence the occult, and apparently paradoxical, statement that "God's irresistible power meets His own invincible shield." It is also true, and the fact is generally acknowledged, that ultimately such resistance may be regarded as having been beneficial in that, in the effort to overcome it, hitherto latent powers and faculties germinate and develop.   Eventually matter, built into vehicles for Spirit, becomes the helpful servant, as is indicated in some world allegories by the changing of certain enemies of heroes and Saviours into collaborators.   Thus the dark serpent *Kāliya*, which tried to kill *Shri Krishna* and his fellow shepherd boys by poisoning their swimming pool, was itself overcome by the child and its enmity transformed into amity.[1]

The so-called animal and bird " vehicles " of the Hindu Deities are susceptible of somewhat similar interpretations.   Examples taken from the Hindu *Trimūrti* are: the swan (*Hamsa*—the Supreme Deity and the spiritual Self of man) of *Brahmā*; the eagle (*Garuda*—sublimated creative power elevating consciousness near to its Source) of *Vishnu*; the bull (*Nandi*— container of the seeds of all living creatures and life-renewer) of *Shiva* who, as *Natarāja*, also holds a deer (has controlled the leaping mind) in his upper left hand and dances on a dwarf holding a cobra (has created and transcended mortal man with his undesirable human attributes[2]); the mouse (the intensely penetrating attribute of the mind successfully obtaining " food ") of *Ganesha*; the peacock (the mind having become all-seeing and all-knowing) of *Subramaniam*.

In Egyptian mythology Horus, hawk-headed, is sometimes portrayed as standing on the back of a hippopotamus (has transmuted crude animal propensities) which has chained legs, and as driving a spear into its head.[3] Horus is also shown as standing on the backs of two crocodiles and grasping " in his hands the reptiles and animals which are emblems of the foes of light and the powers of evil."[4]   Animal-destroying tasks successfully performed by Hercules and Bellerophon—and in later ages by St. George who, mounted and armoured, slew the dangerous dragon—may also be similarly regarded.

Returning to consideration of these verses of *Genesis* as allegorically describing deific procedures in the formation of a Universe, matter—

---

[1] q.v. *Bhāgavata-Purana*, Sk. X, Chs. 16 and 17.

[2] As Mahā-Yogi, Shiva is seated upon a tiger-skin (has conquered lust).

[3] q.v. *The Gods of the Egyptians*, Budge, Vol. I, p. 493.

[4] q.v. *The Gods of the Egyptians*, Budge, Vol. II, p. 270–1.

symbolised as an enemy—does for a time resist Spirit. The $guna^1$ of inertia ($Tamas^1$) opposes that of activity ($Rajas^1$), just as restriction opposes expansion. When once, however, a true electromagnetic relationship is established between the two, a third (" son " or " daughter ") is produced ($Sattva$). Macrocosmically this third is Universe or one of its component parts, whilst in man it is represented by the attainment of a new level of awareness, after which the $gun\bar{a}$ of harmony or rhythm ($sattva$) predominates. This achievement may be foreshadowed in the blessing of Rebekah by her parents and the prayer that her " seed " may possess the gate of its enemies. The mutual attraction of opposite polarities, and the tendency of the substances in which they preponderate to draw together, are also indicated in this dual journey of Rebekah and Isaac towards each other, which journeying and meeting portray a universal phenomenon.

ISAAC AND REBEKAH

The statement that " Isaac came from the way of the well Lahai-roi " indicates that Spirit is already creatively awakened and in association with matter in its universal state (the water in the well). The same condition has been described concerning Rebekah, who was responsive both as the recipient of creative energy—the words from the servant, his " voice "— and as drawing and supplying water in answer to his request.

The meditation of Isaac in the field refers macrocosmically to the Logos or *Demiurgos* as a manifestation of cosmic Ideation, as divine Thought preparing to impregnate matter and produce forms in the field or bounded area of hitherto universal substance. Thus, at the close of a *Manvantara* (eventide) the Logos sums up into one Archetypal concept the products of that period of manifestation, and at the dawn of its successor becomes the active embodiment and expression of that concept. Universal Mind then turns towards and becomes embodied in the new evolutionary field, focussing the divine "Idea" (in the Platonic sense[2]) into the newly differentiated substance. Symbolically, Isaac lifts up his eyes and sees the approach of Rebekah.

This same thought is also to be found in Kabbalism, though not necessarily applied to the romances narrated in the *Torah*. Isaac Myer wrote:

"Amongst the Mohammedans we find the same idea; the first thing God created was a pen.

---

[1] *Gunās* (Sk.)—"A string or chord". The three qualities or attributes inherent in matter: *Rajas*, activity, desire; *Sattva*, harmony, rhythm; *Tamas*, inertia, stagnation. These correspond to the three Aspects of the Trinity—Father, Son and Holy Ghost—or Brahmā, Vishnu and Shiva respectively.

[2] q.v. footnote p. 177.

"Indeed the whole creation is but a Transcript, and God when He made the World, did but write it out of that Copy which He had of it in His Divine understanding from all Eternity. The Lesser Worlds (Mikrokosmos) or Men, are but transcripts of the Greater (the Makrokosmos), as Children and Books are the copies of themselves." (Isaac Myer, Qabbalah. Quoted from *The Secret Wisdom of the Qabalah*, p. 39, J.F.C. Fuller).

The *Zohar* records that:

"Simon ben Yohai [reputed author of the *Zohar*] stretched out his hands and cried:

"Now ponder well upon all that I have this day revealed unto you! And know that none of these celestial palaces are light, nor are they spirits, nor are they souls, nor are they any form that may be seized hold of by any of the senses. Know that the Palaces are *Thoughts-seen-through-curtains*. Take away the thought, and the Palace becomes nothing that the mind can grasp nor the imagination picture! And know, finally, that all the mysteries of the Faith lie in this doctrine: that all that exists in the Upper World is the *Light of Thought*—the *Infinite*. Lift the curtain, and all matter appears immaterial! Lift another curtain, and the immaterial becomes even more spiritual and sublime! As each succeeding curtain is lifted we are transported to ever-higher planes of sublimity until the *Highest* is reached!" (*Zohar*, pp. 210-11, Bension.)

" In the *Zohar* we read:

"All that which is found [or exists] upon the Earth has its spiritual counterpart also to be found on High, and there does not exist the smallest thing in the world which is not itself attached to something on High, and is not found in dependence upon it. When the inferior part is influenced, and that which is set over it in the Superior world is equally [influenced], all are perfectly united together." (*Zohar*, 1, fol. 156b. Soncino Ed. Vol.II, p. 102).

"Again and again is this idea repeated in different words, and from it is derived the Talmudic maxim, 'If thou wilt know the invisible, have an open eye for the visible', which means that this world is the true Bible which can lead us back to God or Reality; ' for all which is contained in the Lower World is also found in the Upper [in prototype). The Lower and Upper reciprocally act upon each other."

Or as is written in the *Sepher Shephathal* :

"All that which is on the earth is also found above [in perfect prototype], and there is not anything so insignificant in the world that does not depend upon another above: in such a manner, that if the lower moves itself the higher corresponding to it moves towards it. As to the number, therefore, of the different species of creatures, which are enumerated below, the same number is to be found in the upper roots," (*Sepher Shephathal*, fol. ii, col. 2). All of the above extracts are quoted from *The Secret Wisdom of the Qabalah*, pp. 41-45, J.F.C. Fuller.

SPIRIT AND MATTER—THE GENERATIVE PAIR

The use of a quadruped (camel) to convey Rebekah, whilst doubtless factual, is also susceptible of at least two interpretations. The square in the Sacred Language signifies matter in its creatively prepared and necessarily limited, constricted state. The planes of Nature in which the proneness to assume form is greater than the tendency to remain free, formless and in rhythmic movement, are four in number. In Sanskrit three of these are known as *Ādi*, *Ātma* and *Manas*,[1] whilst the fourth is physical. In or upon these four, the so-called "form planes"[2] of Nature, the feminine principle of universal generation is predominant and so, not inappropriately, Rebekah and her nurse riding upon quadrupeds approach Isaac, the husband-to-be, representing the masculine principle. The life-planes, on the other hand, are called in Sanskrit *Anupādaka*,[3] *Buddhi*[4] and *kāma*[5] and in their totality and unity are symbolised as a circle. The creative union of the four forms and the three formless planes of Nature, and the realisation of that unity by illumined man, are expressed—at least in one of its meanings—by the phrase "squaring the circle."

If the description of so simple an action as alighting from a camel, and the conversation which would naturally follow, may be assumed also

---

[1] *Manas* (Sk.)—" Mind ". Generally used in reference to the planes of Nature built of mind-stuff, and to the mental faculties of man.

[2] " Form planes " are those the substance of which more readily tends to assume and maintain form or shape as, for example, do clay and putty. " Life planes " are those the substance of which cannot be made to assume any form except that of a container, water in its fluid state being one example.

[3] *Anupādaka* (Sk.)—" Parentless ". q.v. Glossary.

[4] *Buddhi* (Sk.)—Universal Soul. The bliss aspect of the Trinity. In man the faculty which manifests as spiritual intuitiveness. q.v. Glossary.

[5] *Kāma* (Sk.)—" Desire ". The region of the expression of all feelings and desires of the human soul.

to possess a symbolical significance, then the generative procedure continues to be described in verse sixty-four when Rebekah sees Isaac and alights from the camel.   Again an interchange of *words* takes place, and this time the servant identifies himself not with Abraham, but with Isaac, who in the Johannine sense is the "Word"[1] or Logos of the Solar System-to-be. Rebekah, it may be repeated, personifies the feminine potency.

THE SYMBOL OF THE VEIL

When the light of the Logos plays upon and into the Soul or noumenon of creative substance, the resultant illumination forms a veil[2] which covers the Source of the light, hiding it from view.   Appropriately therefore Rebekah, knowing by "word" of mouth of the presence of Isaac, covers herself with her veil.   That covering, however, proves a concealment only to those who are outside of it.   Behind it, in their essential essence, Spirit and matter are creatively active in the heart and centre of the new Universe.   Allegorically, Isaac takes Rebekah into his tent as his wife, after introducing her to the influence of his mother.   Sarah is about to die, implying the handing over to the new Universe of the attributes (*skandhas*[3]) and attainments of the old.

The *Kabbalah* refers as follows to three veils of the negative existence: "There are three qabalistical veils of the negative existence, and in themselves they formulate the *hidden ideas* of the Sephiroth not yet called into being, and they are concentrated in Kether, which in this sense is the Malkuth of the hidden ideas of the Sephiroth. [These terms are fully expounded in the Appendix which follows. G.H.]. ...The first veil of the negative existence is the AIN, *Ain*—Negativity. This word consists of three letters, which thus shadow forth the first three Sephiroth or numbers. The second veil is the AIN SVP, *Ain Soph*=the Limitless. This title consists of six letters, and shadows forth the idea of the first six Sephiroth or numbers. The third veil is the AIN SVP AVR, *Ain Soph Aur*= the limitless Light."[4]

---

[1] *Jn.* 1: 1-5 and 14.

[2] For an interpretation of the symbol of the veil applied to man, the microcosm, see Vol. I of this work, Pt. III, Ch. I, p. 144. See also Plutarch, *Isis and Osiris*: " The shrine of Minerva (regarded as a permutation of Isis) at Sais bears the inscription, 'I am all that hath been, and is, and shall be; and my veil no mortal has hitherto raised ' ", and *The Kabbalah Unveiled*, S. L. MacGregor Mathers, 4th Impression, p. 20, par. 38, also p. 114, par. 31.

[3] *Skandhas* (Sk.). " Groups of innate attributes " of the finite which endure between macrocosmic manifestations and microcosmic incarnations, uniting and re-appearing as inherent qualities at the dawn of *Manvantaras* and at each human rebirth.

[4] q.v. *The Kabbalah Unveiled*, p. 20, S. L. MacGregor Mathers.

Thus this remarkable Chapter of *Genesis* closes, having concealed, as I have already suggested, profound truths concerning macrocosmic and microcosmic generation in the form of an apparently simple and straightforward narrative. In the macrocosmic sense the birth, emergence and evolution of Universes are portrayed, whilst in a microcosmic application the birth, emergence and evolution of successive human personalities are allegorically described.

I am aware that these suggested interpretations of Biblical stories of courtship and marriage as allegorical portrayals of divine and human generative procedures may be regarded by some as reading too much into purely historical romances. Indeed, I have myself entertained somewhat similar thoughts. Careful examination of the texts, however, with especial consideration given to the many events, people and objects introduced, each with a recognised symbolic significance and yet some of them nct strictly necessary to the story, has encouraged me to retain and present in this work the fruits of such studies. As will have been seen, this has led to expositions of Cosmogenesis and to the emergence of ideas potentially of great importance, particularly to students of occult science and philosophy. Therefore I have decided to present the relevant parts of the resultant interpretations, remembering that the title of the Mosaic book is "Genesis."

ABRAHAM'S DEATH EMBLEMATIC OF THE CLOSE OF MAJOR AND MINOR CYCLES

Gen. 25 : 5. *And Abraham gave all that he had unto Isaac.*

6. *But unto the sons of the concubines which, Abraham had, Abraham gave gifts, and sent them away from Isaac his son, while he yet lived, eastward, unto the east country.*

7. *And these are the days of the years of Abraham's life which he lived, an hundred threescore and fifteen years.*

8. *Then Abraham gave up the ghost, and died in a good old age, an old man, and full of years; and was gathered to his people.*

9. *And his sons Isaac and Ishmael buried him in the cave of Machpelah, in the field of Ephron the son of Zohär the Hittite, which is before Mamre;*

10. *The field which Abraham purchased of the sons of Heth; there was Abraham buried, and Sarah his wife.*

Macrocosmically, the fruitfulness of Abraham in his old age describes the immense variety of the perfected products of a Universe at the close of a major Manvantara, as also of each component cycle.   The selected Officiant or Logos for the successor, the heir, receives that meed of power which the Office demands and which His evolutionary stature ensures. Thus Abraham "gave all that he had unto Isaac."

Microcosmically, references to children, and especially heirs, sometimes apply to successive incarnations of the same Ego.   Thus read, the affirmation of the Lord that He visits "the iniquity of the fathers upon the children unto the third and fourth generation "[1] does not offend the sense of justice as does the literal reading.   The doctrine of *karma* implies that causes generated by the actions of one life (the father) may not always produce their effects in that same life; in which case they are held over until a later one (the child).   Similarly, just as it is said that the child is father to the man, so each human incarnation is the parent of that which follows. The doctrine is that the faculties developed in any one life, in addition to those already attained in previous lives—"all that he (Abraham) had "— are transferred to each new personality (Isaac), which may thus be regarded as the heir.   The sequence of Officials assisting in the evolution of races, sub-races and nations is also described; for, according to occult philosophy, each age of planetary life and each major period in national life are presided over by Adepts ordained to the task.

In the Initiatory interpretation, a series of Hierophants preside over the Temples of both the Lesser and Greater Mysteries, direct the Rites and confer the Initiations.[2]   All of these successions, I here repeat, are allegorically referred to in the genealogical tables of Biblical Patriarchs.   At this period of their history, the Jews as a specially selected people, received direct guidance from within their Sanctuaries, both by means of the incarnation amongst them of Initiate leaders and from their Adept Racial   Guardian.[3]   In some cases the so-called " word of the Lord "   may refer to directions emanating from these several sources.

---

[1] *Ex.* 20: 5.

[2] This ancient procedure is still followed in certain Ceremonial Orders.

[3] Occult philosophy includes the idea that certain continents and nations which have an important *dharma* amongst the family of nations are guided and inspired by a member of the Adept Hierarchy, who is referred to as its Regent. Taoists, for example, speak of the Adept Regent of China, whilst a certain great Adept is regarded as the Regent of Europe and Europeans throughout the world. The Rishi Agastya, one of the Ancient Sages of India, is believed by some Indian occultists to be still living Regent of their country. Melchizedek may perhaps be thought of as the Regent of the Hebrew nation. See Glossary under Occult Science.

THE SYMBOLISM OF ABRAHAM'S AGE

Each figure or numerical component of the age of Abraham at his death may be taken separately to indicate its significance. Number one refers to new beginnings. Seven is a number of completion and five denominates the field or range of that fulfilment, in this case the fivefold Universe from the physical to the *Ātmic*[1] planes, and the five units of human consciousness developed and successfully employed at those levels.

Thus interpreted, the component figures of the age of Abraham at his death may be taken to indicate that he had completed the two cycles— those of his own life as Patriarch and of human evolution itself, Adeptship having been attained.

The foregoing commentaries upon the life and death of Abraham bring to a close the second Volume of this work. Volume Three will consist of a similar study of the Biblically recorded history of the Hebrew nation under the patriarchal direction of Isaac, and later of Jacob. This promises to be full of interest, many numerical and other classical symbols being employed. Isaac, for example, was forty years of age when he married Rebekah. Because she was barren he entreated the Lord on her behalf, whereupon she conceived, the twins Esau and Jacob later being born. The description of their somewhat peculiar birth lends itself to an esoteric reading. Esau, red in colour, was born first. Jacob followed— " and his hand took hold on Esau's heel."

Famine later descended upon the land and the Lord instructed Isaac to go to Egypt, promising to him also multiplicity of seed. As did his father, Isaac declared his wife was his sister, but Abimelech discovered the deceit. Trouble arose between the Philistines and the Canaanites because the former had stopped Abraham's wells. Isaac reopened them, however, and found a spring. The well-known story is related of the subterfuge by which Rebekah enabled Jacob to pass himself off to his father as Esau, thereby obtaining a parental blessing. The characters and adventures of Esau and Jacob are then described.

Joseph, the youngest son, eventually assumes prominence in the story. After the incidents of the return to Jacob of Joseph's artificially bloodstained coat of many colours, and of his being lowered into and rescued from the pit, Joseph was taken to Egypt where he had many remarkable experiences, including attempted seduction by the wife of Potiphar, Captain of the Guards. He interprets the dreams of Pharaoh and his servants, predicts and prepares for a famine, is made Ruler over Egypt, receives his brethren and father, and dying at the age of one hundred and ten "they embalmed him and he was put in a coffin in Egypt." My commentaries upon these and other incidents will complete the third Volume of this work— *The Golden Grain of Wisdom in the Book of Genesis.*

[1] q. v. Glossary.

APPENDIX

THE SEPHIROTHAL TREE

THE SEPHIROTHAL TREE
ACCORDING TO THE KABBALAH

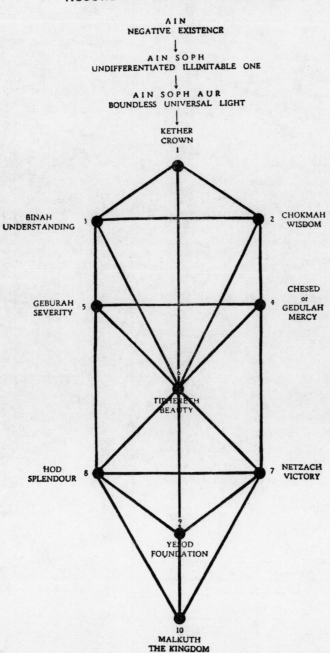

AIN
NEGATIVE EXISTENCR

AIN SOPH
UNDIFFERENTIATED ILLIMITABLE ONE

AIN SOPH AUR
BOUNDLESS UNIVERSAL LIGHT

KETHER
CROWN
1

BINAH
UNDERSTANDING 3

CHOKMAH
WISDOM 2

GEBURAH
SEVERITY 5

CHESED
or
GEDULAH
MERCY 4

6
TIPHERETH
BEAUTY

HOD
SPLENDOUR 8

NETZACH
VICTORY 7

9
YESOD
FOUNDATION

10
MALKUTH
THE KINGDOM

THE SEPHIROTHAL TREE
ACCORDING TO THE KABBALAH

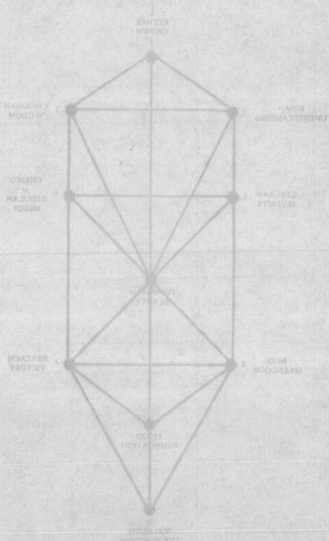

AIN
NEGATIVE EXISTENCE

AIN SOPH
UNDIFFERENTIATED ILLIMITABLE ONE

AIN SOPH AUR
BOUNDLESS UNIVERSAL LIGHT

KETHER
CROWN

CHOKMAH
WISDOM

BINAH
UNDERSTANDING

CHESED
or
GEDULAH
MERCY

GEBURAH
SEVERITY

TIPHERETH
BEAUTY

NETZACH
VICTORY

HOD
SPLENDOUR

YESOD
FOUNDATION

MALCUTH
THE KINGDOM

APPENDIX

THE SEPHIROTHAL TREE

THE *Kabbalah* has been variously described as an unwritten or oral tradition, as the esoteric docturine of the Jewish religion and as the hidden wisdom or theosophy of the Hebrew Rabbis of the Middle Ages, who are said to have obtained it from older secret doctrines. The Hebrew word is derived from the root QBL, " to receive ". Included in the meaning of the word, therefore, is the practice of transmitting esoteric knowledge by word of mouth.

On examination, the *Kabbalah* proves to be a system of theosophy which claims to be of celestial origin and to have reached the early Hebrew Patriarchs through the ministry of the angels. King David and King Solomon are said to have been initiated into the *Kabbalah*, and a legend exists that Rabbi Simeon Ben Jochai took the step of writing a portion of the teachings down at the time of the destruction of the second Temple. His son, Rabbi Eleazar, his secretary and his disciples gathered together his treatises and from them composed the *Zohar*, meaning " Splendour " which is the literary source of Kabbalism. The author of the main part of the *Zohar* is, however, recognised by modern kabbalistic scholars[1] to have been Rabbi Moses de Leon, a Kabbalist of Thirteenth Century Spain.

THE TEN ORDERS OF ANGELS

The Angelic Hosts occupy an important place in the cosmogonical scheme of the *Kabbalah*, in which the Sephiroth are described as the potencies and modes of action (*Shaktis*)[2] of the living God, the ten archetypal numbers (from *safar*—to count) taken as the fundamental powers of all being. This notion of feminine potencies in God, which attain their fullest expression in the tenth and last Sephirah, seems utterly incongruous in exoteric Jewish thinking, which is strictly monotheistic and masculine.

[1] q.v. *On the Kabbalah and Its Symbolism*, Gershom G. Scholem, trans. by Ralph Mantheim (Routledge and Kegan Paul, London), and other modern works.

[2] *Shakti*—q.v. Glossary.

THE LOGOS DOCTRINE

The fashioning of the Universe by the power of sound or " Speech " is also basic to Kabbalism. The names of the ten Sephiroth are regarded as the creative names which God gave to Himself. The action and development of the mysterious force as the seed of all creation is none other than speech or " speech-force " expressive of archetypal thought. The process of the manifestation of divine life is construed as the unfolding of the elements of speech. This is indeed one of the *Zohar's* favourite symbols. The world of divine emanation is one in which the human faculty of speech is anticipated in God. According to the *Zohar*, the successive phases of emanation include the abysmal[1] will, formative thought, inner and inaudible word, audible voice, and ultimately man's utterance of words.

Kabbalists thus regard the Sephiroth as ten spheres of divine manifestation in which God emerges from His abode, and as forming the " unified universe " of God's life. They are also referred to as " mystical crowns of the holy King," "the ten names of God," and "the king's faces," meaning his varying aspects. The Sephiroth also possess other implications, four of which are the mystical Face of God, the ten stages of the inner world through which He descends from the inmost recesses, the garments of Divinity, and the beams of light which radiate from the God-head.

Ten Orders of manifested Beings are associated with the ten Sephiras, which constitute the kabbalistic Tree of Life. They are regarded as Emanations of Deity, each Sephira representing a number, a group of exalted ideas, titles and attributes and a Hierarchy of spiritual Beings outside of humanity. Each Sephira has a fourfold nature in correspondence with the four worlds of the Kabbalist. These are: Atziluth—the Archetypal World, or World of Emanations, the Divine World; Briah—the World of Creation, also called *Khorsis*, the World of Thrones: Yetzirah—the World of Formation and of Angels; Assiah—the World of Action, the World of Matter.

In Atziluth the Sephiras manifest through ten different aspects, represented by the ten holy Names of God in the Hebrew Scriptures. In Briah they are expressed through the ten Archangels, and in Yetzirah through the Choirs or Hosts of the Angels. In Assiah, and especially on the physical plane, they are associated with the physical planets and the subtle elements of which these are said to be composed. They are also regarded as being in mutual resonance with the *chakras* in the mental, emotional and etheric bodies of man and their related glandular and nerve centres.[2]

The Sephiras are depicted as both numbers and circles, an idea presumably echoed by Proclus who wrote:—"Before the mathematical

---

[1] Abysmal—concerning primal chaos; the fathomless, pre-cosmic depths.
[2] q.v. *Lecture Notes of the School of the Wisdom*, Vol. I (Rev. Ed.), Geoffrey Hodson.

numbers, there are the *self-moving* numbers; before the figures apparent, the vital figures, and before producing the material worlds *which move in a circle*, the Creative Power produced the invisible circles."[1] At the head of each Hierarchy of spiritual Intelligences is a named Archangel, under Whom are gradations of angels who perform significant functions in the emanation, formation, preservation and transformation of a Universe.

THE ANGELS IN CHRISTIANITY

The Christian religion, which contains much kabbalistic thought, teaches that there are nine Orders of Angels, severally called Angels, Archangels, Thrones, Dominations, Principalities, Virtues, Powers, Cherubim and Seraphim, certain qualities and activities being assigned to each of these Orders. Angels and Archangels are sent as messengers in matters of high importance, as were Gabriel and Raphael. Thrones contemplate the glory and equity of the divine judgments and influence men to rule with justice. Dominations are supposed to regulate the activities and duties of the Angels, whilst Principalities preside over peoples and provinces and serve as Angelic Rulers (National Angels) of the nations of the world. Virtues have the gift of working miracles. Powers are a check on evil spirits. Cherubim excel in the splendour of knowledge and so enlighten mankind with wisdom and the Seraphim, being most ardent in divine love, inspire mankind with that quality. In nearly all the Biblical accounts of men's visions of God, He is described as transcendent in glory and surrounded by countless multitudes of His Angels.[2]

Kabbalism, whilst naming them differently, gives to these Beings their due place and certain additional functions. In common with other cosmogonies, it postulates the existence of an Absolute as the basis of everything. This is regarded as Negative Existence, AIN or " No-thing " and has been described as an illimitable abyss of Glory. It has three veils which are called AIN, meaning the negatively existent, AIN SOPH, the limitless without form, being or likeness with anything else, and AIN SOPH AUR, the limitless light, which concentrates into the first and highest Sephira of the Sephirothal Tree called Kether, the Crown.

The successive veils, concealing even whilst providing vehicles for the illimitable Source, appear to have been given a number of symbolic meanings—Macrocosmic and microcosmic—in World Scriptures and Mythologies. They may possibly be referred to in the Twenty-fourth Chapter of *Genesis*, verse sixty-five, as the veil which Rebecca (virgin space) placed over her face on the approach of Isaac (the Spirit of God); in the Thirty-

---

[1] Quoted in *The Secret Doctrine*, Vol. IV, p. 122 (Adyar Ed.), H. P. Blavatsky.
[2] A fuller exposition is to be found in *The Kingdom of the Gods*, Geoffrey Hodson.

24

fourth Chapter of *Exodus*, verses thirty-three and thirty-four when Moses removed his veil as he went in before the LORD to speak with Him, having placed it upon his face before addressing the people; and in the Twenty-seventh Chapter of *Matthew*, verse fifty-one, where the veil of the Temple is stated to have been "rent in twain from the top to the bottom" when Jesus "yielded up the ghost" upon the Cross. As indicated and, with regard to Rebecca, on pages 358 and 359 of Volume II of this work, the symbol of the veil—Paroketh in Kabbalism—is susceptible of interpretation in both the Macrocosmic sense, as above, and microcosmically as the veil between the immortal Self of man and the mind of his mortal personality.

The nine[1] letters AIN SOPH AUR are said to shadow forth the nine Sephiras as hidden ideas or seed-thoughts which, when manifestation begins, are represented by archangelic Beings or "Gods" (*Elohim*). In the description of this process, as stated above, the Limitless Ocean of Light is said to concentrate a centre, which is the first Sephira, the Crown, which in turn gives birth to the nine others, the last or tenth being called Malkuth, the Kingdom, meaning "all Nature manifested". Together, the ten Sephiras represent the emanation and development of the powers and attributes of Deity. Each number is an outward symbol for inner creative forces and processes and their personifications as Archangels or Builders of the Universe. Some of these are male and some female, or rather of positive and negative potencies, Deity having conformed Itself thus order that it could create—or, more correctly, emanate—the Universe. Man, being made in the image of Deity, is physically male and female also.

KETHER

The first Sephira is Number One, the Monad of Pythagoras. As already mentioned, this Sephira is called Kether Elyon, the "Supreme Crown" of God, and also the Ancient of the Ancient Ones, the Ancient of Days, the Primordial Point, the White Head, the Inscrutable Height and the Vast Countenance or Macroposopus. The following passage from *The Book of Daniel* would seem to refer to this Sephira: "I beheld till the thrones were cast down, and the Ancient of Days did sit, whose garment was white as snow, and the hair of his head like the pure wool: his throne was like the fiery flame, and his wheels as burning fire (Apparently the Logos of a Solar System, Chain or Round, the 'White Head' of Kabbalism). A fiery stream issued and came forth from before him: thousand thousands ministered unto him (the Angelic Hosts), and ten thousand times ten thousand

---

[1] PH (as in SOPH)—P in the Hebrew alphabet.

stood before him (the Monads of His Scheme, Chain, Round or Planet)...
I saw in the night visions, and behold, one like the Son of man came with
the clouds of heaven, and came to the Ancient of Days, and they brought
him near before him (the Sanat Kumāra[1]). And there was given him
dominion, and glory, and a kingdom, that all people, nations, and languages,
should serve him; his dominion is an everlasting dominion, which shall
not pass away, and his kingdom that which shall not be destroyed...But
the saints of the most High (the Adepts) shall take the kingdom, and possess
the kingdom for ever, even for ever and ever...[2]"

In its highest and abstract aspect Kether is in association with Adam
Kadmon (the Heavenly Man), a synthesis of the whole Sephirothal Tree,
the Archetype of all Creation and all humanity and, in one possible reading,
the first Adam of *Genesis*. Kether is also called *Seir Anpin*, "Son of the
Concealed Father," and so in this highest aspect must be regarded as the
Logos, the *Christos* of the Fourth Gospel.

Since one cannot create alone, Kether is said to vibrate across the field
of manifestation or to reflect itself in matter to produce a feminine or dyad,
from which in turn all beings and all things emanate, having been hitherto contained within Kether. The Archangel Head of the associated Hierarchy of Angels is severally named Metatron or "beside (or beyond) the
Throne" Prince of Faces, Angel of the Presence, World Prince, El Shaddai—
the Omnipotent and Almighty One—the Messenger, and Shekinah, this
last being associated with the cloud of glory which rested on the Mercy
Seat upon the Ark of the Covenant within the Holy of Holies[3]. Shekinah
is also regarded as identical with AIN SOPH AUR, the veil of AIN SOPH,
precosmic substance or virgin space, *Mulaprakriti*, or the *Parabrahmic* root
of Hinduism.

The Order of Angels in Kether is the Chaioth Ha-Qadesh, "Holy
Living Creatures". They are associated with the Kerubim[4] and regarded
as governors of the four elements in their highest sublimation. They would
seem to correspond to the *Lipika*[5], the Celestial Recorders or "Scribes"
the Agents of *karma* in Hinduism. This Hierarchy is concerned with the
initiation of the whirling motions by means of which primordial atoms

---

[1] *Kumāras* (Sk.). The four great Beings in the Occult Hierarchy of Adepts Who help
on the evolution of humanity; also applied to the Ever-Virgin Youth and His disciples,
Who are said in occult philosophy to have founded the Adept Hierarchy on this planet.
Sanat Kumāra is the name given to this Head or Chief of Earth's Adepts.

[2] *Dan.* 7.

[3] *Ex.* 40: 35.

[4] Usually spelt in Kabbalism with a " K " rather than " Ch " and so pronounced
Ez. 1: 5 *et seq.*

[5] *Lipika*—q.v. Glossary.

or "holes in space"[1] are formed, presumably using the force which in Tibetan is called *Fohat*, the essence of cosmic electricity, the ever-present electrical energy and ceaseless formative and destructive power in the Universe, the universal propelling, vital force, the *primum mobile*, whose symbol is the *svastika*. In Kether are thus said to be "the Beginnings of the whirls", the first stirrings of the divine creative Essence,   Evidently Ezekiel in his exalted vision in some degree beheld this process, for he says: "And I looked, and, behold, a whirlwind came out of the north, a great cloud..."[2]   One of the chief duties of the members of this Angelic Hierarchy is to receive this Essence in Kether and carry it to the succeeding Hierarchy of the Auphanim or "Wheels", associated with the second Sephira.

CHOKMAH

Kether produces the other nine Sephiras, the second being Chokmah, "Wisdom" or primordial idea of God, a masculine, active potency or father reflected from Kether. Chokmah is the second Adam, from whom is produced Eve, and is associated with Microposopus, "the Lesser Countenance". The Archangel Head of the Angelic Hierarchy is Ratziel, "the Herald of Deity", "the Delight of God". The Order of Angels is the Auphanim or "Wheels", so called in reference to the vortex, whirlwind or whirlpool-producing action of the *primum mobile*. From this Order are said to be drawn the Angels of the Planets, who are described in the First Chapter of *Ezekiel*. The planetary correspondence is with the Zodiac as a whole, and in some systems with Uranus.[3]

BINAH

The third Sephira is a feminine, passive potency called Binah, "Intelligence" of God, the Understanding, co-equal and contemporaneous with Chokmah, to whom she is as Eve, the Mother Supernal. Binah is also called Ama (Mother), combined with Ab (Father) for the maintenance of order in the Universe. She is sometimes referred to as the Great Sea, and kabbalistically these two Powers weave the web of the Universe.[4]   The Archangel Head is Tzaphqiel, "He who beholds God", or "Contemplation of God." The Order of Angels is the Arelim, "the Mighty Ones", the Thrones of Christian angelology. The number Two, as a principle, is

---

[1] From an Occult Catechism quoted in *The Secret Doctrine*, Vol. I (Adyar Ed.), p. 203, H. P. Blavatsky.

[2] *E* . 1: 4.

[3] The Kabbalistic Correspondences do not always agree with those given in *The Secret Doctrine* by H. P. Blavatsky.

[4] q.v. *The Secret Doctrine*, Vol. I (Adyar Ed.), p. 148, H. P. Blavatsky.

like two straight lines which can never enclose a space and is therefore powerless until number Three forms a primary triangle. Binah performs that function and makes evident the supernal, but not the material, active Trinity. This upper Triad remains in the Archetypal world, whilst the seven Sephiras which follow create, sustain and transform the manifested material world. In Kabbalism the planet associated with Binah is Saturn.

The union of Chokmah and Binah, "Wisdom" and "Intelligence" produces Supernal Knowledge, called Daath in Kabbalism. Daath itself is not regarded as a Sephira, but is included in some diagrams of the Sephirothal Tree, in which it is placed between Chokmah and Binah.

CHESED

An active dyad now exists in Chokmah and Binah. Their union produced Chesed, a masculine or active potency. Chesed is "Love" or "Mercy" of God and is also called Gedulah, "Greatness" or "Magnificence." The Archangel Head is Tzadqiel, "Justice of God", "Righteousness of God." The Order of Angels is the Chasmalim, "Scintillating Flames," "Brilliant Ones." They are the Dominations of Christian angelology and are regarded as Angels of Light. The associated planet is Jupiter.

GEBURAH

From Four or Chesed emanated the feminine passive, fifth potency Geburah, the "Power" of God, "Severity," "Strength," "Fortitude' "Justice" chiefly manifested as the power of stern judgment and punishment. This Sephira is also named Pachad, "Fear." The Archangel Head is Kahamael "the Right Hand of God", and is sometimes called the Punishing Angel. The Order of Angels is the Seraphim, known in Christian angelology as Powers. They are thus described in Isaiah 6:1—3:

"...I saw also the Lord sitting upon a throne, high and lifted up, and his train filled the temple.

"Above it stood the Seraphims: each one had six wings; with twain he covered his face, and with twain he covered his feet, and with twain he did fly.

"And one cried unto another, and said, Holy holy, holy, is the LORD of hosts: the whole earth is full of his glory."

The Hebrew name of the Seraphim is translated "Serpents" and as this is related to the verbal root ShRP, "to burn up", it may be assumed that these are the fiery Serpents associated with the creative fire[1] and processes in both Nature and man. The planet is Mars.

[1] Kundalini—q.v. Glossary.

TIPHERETH

From Chesed (masculine) and Geburah (feminine) emanated the sixth and uniting Sephira, Tiphereth, "Beauty" or "Mildness", the heart and centre of the Sephirothal Tree. This Sephera is also named Rahamin, the "Compassion" of God. This is said to be the place allotted by the Israelites to the Messiah and by the early Christians to the Christ. The Archangel Head is Michael, "who is like unto God." The Order of Angels is the Malachim, meaning "Kings" and known in Christianity as Virtues. Another system places Raphael here, and Michael in the eighth Sephira. The Sun is associated with Tiphereth.

In terms of planes of Nature and levels of normal human consciousness Tiphereth marks both a boundary and a place of union between the Divine and the human, the Macrocosm and the microcosm, the abstract and the concrete. Here symbolically is said to exist Paroketh, the so-called veil of the "temple" of both seven-planed Nature and seven-principled man. This veil must be pierced by those who whould ascend in consciousness the middle pillar of the kabbalistic Tree of Life, liberate themselves from the purely human delusion of separated selfhood, which must be "crucified", and enter into realisation of unity with the one Great Self of All. Thereafter the spiritual forces of the abstract or formless worlds and their angelic directors may be invoked both to quicken human evolution by arousing the hidden powers in the chakras[1] in the personal nature and bodies of man, and to assist in various kinds of occult work.

By the union of Geburah or "Justice" with Chesed or "Mercy", Beauty, Harmony and Clemency are produced and the second Sephirothal Trinity is then complete. This sixth Sephira, Tiphereth, with the fourth, fifth, seventh, eighth and ninth, is spoken of as the Microposopus or Lesser Countenance, the microcosm, the reflection into manifestation of Macroposopus, the Macrocosm, and also its antithesis.

NETZACH

The seventh Sephira is Netzach, the "Lasting Endurance" of God. "Firmness", "Victory". The Archangelic Head is called Hamiel, "the Grace of God", and the Order of Angels is the Elohim, "the Gods", also called Tsarshisim, "Brilliant Ones", and known as Principalities in Christianity. In the Tenth Chapter of The Book of Daniel, verses five and six, Hamiel is described thus:

"Then I lifted up mine eyes, and looked, and behold a certain man clothed in linen, whose loins were girded with fine gold of Uphāz:

---

[1] Chakras—q.v. Glossary.

'His body also was like the beryl, and his face as the appearance of lightning, and his eyes as lamps of fire, and his arms and his feet like in colour to polished brass, and the voice of his words like the voice of a multitude."

The planet associated with this Sephira is Venus.

HOD

From Netzach proceeded the feminine, passive potency, Hod, the eighth Sephira, the "Majesty" of God, "Splendour", the God of Armies. The Archangel Head is Raphael, "Divine Physician", the Angel of Healing, intermediary between man and God, who is assisted by a Hierarchy of ministering Angels known in one interpretation as the *Beni Elohim*, "the Sons of God," and as Archangels in Christianity. The planet is Mercury.

YESOD

Hod and Netzach together produced the ninth Sephira, Yesod, the "Basis", the Foundation of all actual forces in God, "the Mighty Living One." The Archangel Head is Gabriel, "the Mighty One of God," The Order of Angels is the Kerubim, "the Holy Living Creatures", the Angels of Christianity. Evidently an intimate connection exists between the Kerubim of the first Sephira in the supernal worlds and those of Yesod in the etheric counterpart of the outer, material Universe. They are some- times called Aishim or "the Flames", and are also referred to as the four Angels of the subtile elements of earth, fire, water and air.

The Kerubim are associated with the constellations of Taurus, Leo, Scorpio and Aquarius, or the Bull, the Lion, the Eagle and the Man. Part of their duty is said to be to gather the forces of Nature on the astral plane, pour them into the kingdom of Earth, Malkuth, and control them in all their complex manifestations. They are also regarded as Agents of the *Lipika* or Recorders, the Lords of *Karma* and Regents of the four quarters of the Universe. The planet is the Moon. Netzach, Hod and Yesod together complete the third Trinity in the Sephirothal Tree.

MALKUTH

From the ninth Sephira came the tenth and last, completing the decad of the numbers. It is called Malkuth, the Kingdom of Earth, all Nature, and also the Queen, Matrona, the Inferior Mother. Shekinah is another name for Malkuth, which would therefore seem to represent the veil of both primordial matter and physical Nature.

Two Archangels are associated with Malkuth. They are the Metatron of Kether and His brother and co-worker, Sandalphon, the kabbalistic Prince of Angels. Sandalphon, the Dark Angel, may be regarded as the densely material *shakti* or manifested power of Metatron, the Bright Angel. Since the planet Earth is the place of the outworking of man's physical *karma*, Sandalphon is sometimes regarded as an Angel of personal *karma*. Metatron, on the other hand, is associated with the Celestial Agents of *karma* Who are concerned with the self-created destiny of the human race as a whole, doubtless not only on Earth but also throughout the Solar System. The Archangel of our Earth in particular is said to be Auriel, "the Light of God." The Order of Angels is the Ishim or "Fires". No single planet, unless it be the Earth, is allotted to Malkuth, which Sephira apparently includes the whole of physical Nature and is concerned with the four subtle and material elements and their use in the building and transformation of the "Kingdom" of the visible Universe.

Such briefly described, is the Sephirothal Tree, "the ten spheres of divine manifestation in which God emerges from His hidden abode. Together they form the ' unified universe ' of God's life, the 'world of union', both the ensemble and the particulars of which the Zohar attempts to interpret in an unending variety of speculation......

"The Sefiroth are called 'mystical crowns of the Holy King' notwithstanding the fact that 'He is they, and they are He'. They are the ten names most common to God, and in their entirety they also form His one great Name. They are 'the King's faces', in other words His varying aspects, and they are also called the inner, intrinsic or mystical Face of God. They are the ten stages of the inner world, through which God descends from the inmost recesses down to His revelation in the Shekhinah. They are the garments of the Divinity, but also the beams of light which it sends out....

"The ten Sefiroth constitute the mystical Tree of God or tree of divine power, each representing a branch whose common root is unknown and unknowable. But *En-Sof* is not only the hidden Root of all Roots, it is also the sap of the tree; every branch, representing an attribute, exists not by itself but by virtue of *En-Sof*, the hidden God. And this tree of God is also, as it were, the skeleton of the universe; it grows throughout the whole of creation and spreads its branches through all its ramifications. All mundane and created things exist only because something of the power of the Sefiroth lives and acts in them."[1]

---

[1] q.v. *Major Trends in Jewish Mysticism*, Gershom G. Scholem.

KABBALISTIC INTERPRETATIONS OF SCRIPTURE

The *Kabbalah* includes three methods of Scriptural interpretation called *Gematria*, *Notariqon* and *Temura*.

Gematria is based on the relative numerical values of words, those of similar numerical values being considered to be explanatory of each other, and this theory is also extended to phrases. Thus in the word *Shin*, Sh[1] is 300 and is equivalent to the number obtained by adding up the numerical values of the letters of the words RVCh ALHIM, *Ruach Elohim*, the Spirit of the *Elohim*. Sh is therefore a symbol of the Spirit of the *Elohim*.

Notariqon is derived from the Latin word *notarius*, a shorthand writer. There are two forms of *Notariqon*. In the first from every letter of a word is taken the initial or abbreviation of another word, so that from the letters of a word a sentence may be formed. Thus every letter of the word BRASh-ITh, *Berashith*, the first word in *Genesis*, is made the initial of a word, and we obtain BRAShITh RAH ALIM ShIQBLV IShRAL ThVRH, *Berashith Rahi Elohim Sheyequebelo Israel Torah*: "In the beginning the *Elohim* saw that Israel would accept the law".

The second form of *Notariqon* is the exact reverse of the first. By this the initials or finals, or both, or the medials, of a sentence are taken to form a word of words. Thus the *Kabbalah* is called ChKMh NSThRH, *Chokhmah Nesethrah*, "the secret wisdom."

Temura is permutation. According to certain rules one letter is substituted for the letter preceding or following it in the alphabet, and thus from one word another word of totally different orthography may be formed. (Based on *The Kabbalah Unveiled*, S.L. MacGregor Mathers).

This exposition in outline of the more exoteric elements of Kabbalism has been synthesised from a number of works on the subject, to the authors of which acknowledgement is here gratefully made. Amongst others are the *Zohar* (original and excerpts under that title by *Gershom G. Scholem*); *The Kabalah, Its Doctrines, Developments and Literature*, Christian D. Ginsburg, LL.D.; *The Kabbalah Unveiled*, S.L.MacGregor Mathers; *The Secret Wisdom of the Qabalah*, J.F.C. Fuller; *The Secret Doctrine in Israel*, A.E. Waite: *Isis Unveiled* and *The Secret Doctrine*, H.P. Blavatsky.

---

[1]SH, a single consonant—S

GLOSSARY

Absolute, The: The impersonal, supreme and incognisable Principle of the Universe. See Parabrahman.

Adept (Latin). *Adeptus*, "He who has obtained". An Initiate of the Fifth Degree in the Greater Mysteries, a Master in the science of esoteric philosophy, a perfected man, an exalted Being who has attained complete mastery over purely human nature and possesses knowledge and power commensurate with lofty evolutionary stature. A fully initiated Being who watches over and guides the progress of humanity.

Adi (Sk.): "The first the primeval". The Foundation Plane, the first field of manifestation, "the foundation of a Universe, its support and the fount of life." For an exposition of the seven planes of Nature see *Through the Gateway of Death*, Geoffrey Hodson.

Adonai (Heb.): Substitute for "Lord" or Jehovah, JHWH.

Ahamkara (Sk.): The first tendency towards definiteness, regarded as the origin of all manifestation. In man the conception of "I", self-consciousness or self-identity, the illusion of self as a self-separate existence in contradistinction to the reality of the universal One Self. Awareness of this universality is expressed in the words of the Christ: "I and my Father are one." (*Jn.* 10:30) The illusion of separateness, the "Great Heresy", is regarded as the source of human sorrow and suffering. Self-emancipation from this delusion is the sure way to happiness and peace.

Akasa (Sk.): "The subtle, supersensuous, spiritual essence which pervades all space. The primordial substance erroneously identified with ether. But it is to ether what spirit is to matter . . . . It is, in fact, the Eternal Space in which lies inherent the Ideation of the Universe in its ever-changing aspects on the planes of matter and objectivity, and from which radiates the *First Logos* or expressed thought. This is why it is stated in the *Puranas* that *Asaka* has but one attribute, namely sound, for sound is but the translated symbol for *Logos*—'Speech' in its mystic sense." q.v. *The Theosophical Glossary*, H.P. Blavatsky.

Amshashpends (Pers.): The Seven Planetary *Logoi*, as well as the creative Hosts who carry out their will. The six Angels or divine Forces, personified as gods. who attend upon *Ahura Mazda* (the personified Deity, the Principle of Universal Divine Light of the Parsees), of which He is the synthesis and the seventh.

Analogeticists: The Neo-Platonic School, founded in 193 A.D. by Ammonius Saccus, included Alexandrian philosophers who sought to interpret the Bible according to a system of allegory, analogy and symbol and were, in consequence named Analogeticists.

Anupadaka (Sk.): "Parentless", self-existing, born without progenitors, applied to both a plane of Nature—the second from above—and to those Great Beings who are in this sense parentless or "self-born of the Divine Essence."

Archetype (Gr.): "First-moulded" or stamped. The ideal, abstract or essential "idea". The divine conceiving from which arises the divine "idea" of the whole Universe in time and space; the governing Power in creation. "When God first looked out of eternity (if one may say that he ever *first* looked out), he saw everything as it would happen and at the same time he saw when and how we would create each thing." (From *Meister Eckhart*, by Raymond Blankey, Harper and Row).

Arhat (Sk.): "The worthy." Exoterically, "one worthy of divine honours." Esoterically, as Initiate of the Fourth Degree who has entered the highest Path and is thus emancipated from both self-separateness and enforced rebirth.

Astral: The region of the expression of all feelings and desires of the human soul. See also *Kama*.

Atma (Sk.): "The Self." The Universal Spirit, the seventh principle in the septenary constitution of man, the Supreme Soul. The Spirit-Essence of the Universe. (Paramatman— "the Self Beyond").

Atomic: In occult science this word is used for the foundation-bricks of the Universe and in the strict etymological sense, meaning that it "cannot be cut or divided" (Gr.). One of the fundamentals of occultism is that the elements of Nature are atoms on the material side and Monads on the energy side, both being indivisible. The Greek philosophers Democritus, Leucippus, Epicurus, Ennius and Lucretius advanced the view that matter was composed of atoms, and these scholars came to be Known as "atomists" in consequence. q.v. *First Principles of Theosophy*, Ch. X., C. Jinarajadasa.

Augoeides (Gr.): "The self-radiant divine fragment", the Robe of Glory of the Gnostics and the *Karana Sharira*, "Causal Body", of Hinduism.

Aura (Gr. and Lat.): A subtle, invisible essence or fluid that emanates from human, animal, and even inanimate, bodies. A psychic effluvium, superphysical and physical, including the electro-vital emanations from the physical body in the case of man.   It is usually oviform or egg-shaped and is the seat of the Monadic, spiritual, intellectual, mental, passional and vital energies, faculties and potentialities of the whole sevenfold man.

Auric Envelope: The whole aura, with reference to both the edge or extreme range of the auric radiations (envelope) and the presence of germinal powers, particularly those retained in the immortal vesture of the triple Self known as the Causal Body.   This vehicle is more especially symbolised by the arks of the Flood legends of the Scriptures of ancient peoples, and by boats introduced into other allegorical narratives such as those of the ships built by Argus and Deucalion (Greek mythology), that built for Vaivasvata (*Mahabharata*, the *Puranas* and the *Brahmanas*), and that upon which Christ performed the miracle of the stilling of the tempest (*Matt.* 8: 23-26).   The edge and sum total of the substance of the seven human bodies, physical and superphysical, and their subtle radiations.

Avatar (Sk.): The doctrine of Divine incarnation or "descent."

Avatara (Sk.): "Descent".   The incarnation of a Deity, especially Vishnu, the Second Aspect of the Hindu *Trimurti.*

Brahma Vidya (Sk.): "The wisdom of Brahma", the Supreme Deity.

Brahman (Sk.):   The impersonal, supreme and incognisable Principle of the Universe, from the Essence of which all emanates and into which all returns.   Extracted from *The Theosophical Glossary*, H.P. Blavatsky, and other sources.

Brahma's Day: "A period of 2,160,000,000 (Earth) years during which Brahma having emerged out of his golden egg (*Hiranyagarbha*), creates and fashions the material world (being simply the fertilizing and creative force in Nature).   After this period, the worlds being destroyed in turn by fire and water, he vanishes with objective nature, and then comes Brahma's Night."   q.v. *The Theosophical Glossary*, H.P. Blavatsky.

Brahma's Night: "A period of equal duration, during which Brahma is said to be asleep.   Upon awakening he recommences the process, and this goes on for an AGE of Brahma composed of alternate 'Days' and 'Nights', and lasting 100 years [of 2,160,000,000 (Earth) years each]. It requires fifteen figures to express the duration of such an age; after the expiration of which the *Mahapralaya* or the Great Dissolution sets in, and lasts in its turn for the same space of fifteen figures."   q.v. *The Theosophical Glossary*, H.P. Blavatsky.

Buddhi (Sk.): The sixth principle of man, that of intuitive wisdom, vehicle of the seventh, *Atma*, the supreme Soul in man.   Universal Soul. The faculty which manifests as spiritual intuitiveness.   The bliss Aspect of the Trinity.

Causal Body: The immortal body of the reincarnating Ego of man, built of matter of the "higher" levels of the mental world. It is called Causal because it gathers up within it the results of all experiences, and these act as causes moulding future lives and influencing future conduct.

Chain: In occult philosophy a Solar System is said to consist of ten Planetary Schemes. Each Scheme generally named according to its physically visible representative, is composed of seven Chains of Globes. In terms of time a Chain consists of the passage of the lifewave seven times around its seven Globes. Each such passage is called a Round, the completion of the seventh ending the life of the Chain. The Globes of a Round are both superphysical and physical and are arranged in a cyclic pattern, three being on a descending arc, three on an ascending arc and the middle, the fourth Globe, being the densest of all and the turning point. The active period of each of these units, from Solar System to Globe, called *Manvantara*, is succeeded by a passive period of equal duration, called *Pralaya*. The completion of the activity of the seventh Globe of the seventh Round of the seventh Chain brings to an end the activity of a Planetary Scheme. Our Earth Scheme is now in its fourth Round of its fourth Chain, and the life-wave is halfway through its period of activity on the fourth Globe, the physical Earth. Thus, the densest possible condition of substance is now occupied by Spirit and so by the Monads or Spirits of men. The resistance of matter is at its greatest in this epoch, and this offers an explanation of the difficulties of human life at this period. The occupation of a physical planet by man consists of seven racial epochs and phases of evolutionary development. Throughout this work these are referred to as Root Races. According to that portion of occult philosophy which is concerned with the evolution of both the Immortal Soul and the mortal personality of man, an orderly progression is revealed. The basic rule is stated to be that the indwelling, conscious life in the mineral, plant, animal and human kingdoms of Nature advances to the kingdom above during a period of one Chain. Since each Chain is composed of seven Rounds, each Round is expected to be characterised by progress through subsidiary stages of the ultimate attainment for the Chain as a whole. Applied to man, the Monad has evolved Chain by Chain through mineral (first Chain), plant (second Chain) and animal (third Chain) into the individualised, self-conscious state characteristic of a human being of the fourth Chain. This is man's present position, and by the end of each of the remaining Rounds of this fourth Chain a certain degree of development will be attained. These stages chiefly concern the unfoldment of capacity for awareness and effective action—spiritual, intellectual, cultural and physical. Thus occult anthropology presents an orderly and systematic scheme of development for the life of all kingdoms of Nature.

At the end of the Seventh Root Race of this Fourth Round on Earth the mass of humanity will have achieved the level now known as Initiateship or spiritual regeneration, characterised by Christ-consciousness, which includes both realisation of the unity of life and compassion for all living beings. At the end of the seventh Round the human race now evolving on Earth is expected to achieve the stature of Adeptship or perfected manhood, "the measure of the stature of the fulness of Christ." (Eph, 4: 13). q.v. *The Solar System*, A.E. Powell, and *Lecture Notes of the School of the Wisdom*, Vol. 1, Geoffrey Hodson.

Chakra (Sk.): A "Wheel" or "disc". A spinning, vortical, funnel-shaped force-centre with its opening on the surfaces of the etheric and subtler bodies of man and its stem leading to the superphysical counterparts of the spinal cord and nerve centres or glands. There are seven main *chakras* associated severally with the sacrum, the spleen, the Solar plexus, the heart, the throat and the pituitary and pineal glands. *Chakras* are both organs of superphysical consciousness and conveyors of the life-force between the superphysical and physical bodies. q.v *The Chakras*, C.W. Leadbeater.

Chaos: The term "Chaos" is used in its more philosophic meaning throughout this work to connote, not utter confusion but the following various significations :—the "Abyss", the "Great Deep", the primordial pre-atomic condition in which matter existed before the first atoms and planes of Nature were "created"; primordial space; an infinite formless void; the root of matter in its first remove from the unknown Absolute; the impenetrable veil between what can be seen by the cognisable eye and the invisible actuality of the first active Logos; the primeval "waters" of life; the Virgin Mother of Cosmos; the divine substance which alone exists throughout all eternity, boundless and absolute. q.v. *The Theosophical Glossary*, H.P. Blavatsky.

Correspondences: See Law of Correspondences, The.

Cosmocratoras (Gr.): "Builders of the Universe", the "World Architects" or the creative Forces personified.

Creation: The emergence and subsequent development of a Universe and its contents is regarded in occult philosophy as being less the result of an act of creation, followed by natural evolution, than a process of emanation guided by intelligent Forces under immutable Law. The creation or emergence of Universes from nothing is not an acceptable concept, the Cosmos being regarded as emanating from an all-containing, sourceless Source, the Absolute.

Demiurgos (Gr.): The Demiurge or Artificer, the Supernal Power which built the Universe. Freemasons derive from this word their phrase

"Supreme Architect". With the occultist it is the third manifested Logos, or Plato's second God, the second Logos being represented by him as the "Father", the only Deity that he, as an Initiate of the Mysteries, dare mention. The demiurgic Mind is the same as the Universal Mind, named *Mahat* (Sk.), the first "product" of Brahma.

Devas (Sk.): "Shining ones", spiritual Beings, Planetary Logoi, and Hierarchies of Archangels and angels. The main stages of *devic* development have each their own name. Nature spirits, like animals and birds, are actuated by a group consciousness shared with others of the same genus. Gods, Sephiras, *devas* and angels have evolved out of group consciousness into separate individuality, as has man. Archangels, especially, have transcended the limitations of individuality and have entered into universal or cosmic consciousness, as has the Superman or Adept.

Dhyan Chohans (Sk.): The "Lords of Contemplation", the divine Intelligences charged with the supervision of Cosmos.

Dhyani (Sk.): "Expert in Yoga". Also a generic name for spiritual Beings, Planetary Logoi, and Hierarchies of Archangels and angels. the term *Dhyana* signifies a state of profound contemplation during which the *Dhyanin* becomes united with the highest parts of his own constitution and communes therewith. *Dhyan-Chohans*, "Lords of Contemplation," are members of the Host of Spiritual Beings Who live in this exalted state and supervise the cyclic evolution of life and form in a Solar System. Monadically, man is an embryo *Dhyan-Chohan*, and at the close of the Planetary Age will himself have become a fully developed "Lord of Contemplation".

Ego: The threefold, immortal, unfolding spiritual Self of man in its vesture of light, the " Robe of Glory " of the Gnostics and the *Karana Sharira* or Causal Body of Hindu philosophy. This higher Triad evolves to Adeptship by virtue of sucecssive lives on Earth, all linked together because they are reincarnations of the same spiritual Self. Thus the Ego is an individualised manifestation of the Monad, which is the eternal Self of man, the Dweller in the Innermost, a unit of the Spirit-Essence of the Universe. The term is used throughout this work to denote the unfolding spiritual Self of man in which the attribute of individuality inheres. The adjective " Egoic " refers to the Ego in this sense.

Elemental Kingdoms: Three pre-mineral kingdoms are passed through on the involutionary or descending arc which is followed by the radiated monadic Ray. Arrival at the mineral kingdom marks the stage of deepest descent into matter. Thereafter the upward or evolutionary arc is entered upon, the plant kingdom being the next embodiment of the ascending monadic life. This phase is in due course followed

by entry into and passage through the animal, human and superhuman kingdoms. q.v. *Man: Whence, How and Whither*, A. Besant
and C. W. Leadbeater.

Elohim (Heb).: "Gods". A sevenfold power of Godhead, the male-
female Hierarchies of creative Intelligences or Potencies through
which the Divine produces the manifested Universe; the unity of the
powers, the attributes and the creative activities of the Supreme Being.
"Elohim" is a plural name, the singular form of the word being
"Eloha", i.e., a "god". "Elohim", therefore, literally means "gods",
personifications of divine attributes or the forces at work in Nature.
Admittedly the "Elohim" are also conceived as a Unity in the sense that
They all work together as One, expressing One Will, One Purpose,
One Harmony. Thus Their activities are regarded as the manifesta-
tion of the Eternal One, the Absolute. "Elohim" might therefore
be explained as "the Unity of gods" or "the Activities of the Eternal
One", namely God omnipresent and revealing Himself outwardly
in creative activity. Partly paraphrased from *The Unknown God*,
P. J. Mayers.

Fohat (Tib.): "Divine Energy". The constructive force of cosmic electricity, polarised into the positive and negative currents of terrestrial
electricity; the ever-present electrical energy; the universal, propellant, vital force.

Gnosis (Gr.): Lit. "knowledge". The technical term used by the schools
of religious philosophy, both before and during the first centuries of
so-called Christianity, to denote the object of their enquiry. This
spiritual and sacred knowledge, the *Gupta Vidya* of the Hindus, could
only be obtained by Initiation into Spiritual Mysteries, of which the
ceremonial "Mysteries" were a type.

Gnostics (Gr.): The philosophers who formulated and taught the *Gnosis*
or Knowledge. They flourished in the first three centuries of the
Christian era. The following were eminent: Valentinus, Basilides,
Marcion, Simon Magus, etc.

God: In occult philosophy the term "God" in its highest meaning refers
to a Supreme, Eternal and Indefinable Reality. This Absolute is
inconceivable, ineffable and unknowable. Its revealed existence is
postualated in three terms: an absolute Existence, an absolute Consciousness, and an absolute Bliss. Infinite Consciousness is regarded
as inherent in the Supreme Being as a dynamic Force that manifests
the potentialities held in its own infinitude, and calls into being forms
out of its own formless depths. See also pp. 105 *et seq.*

Group Soul: The pre-individualised manifestation of the human Monads
when evolving through the mineral, the plant and the animal kingdoms of Nature. q.v. *A Study in Consciousness*, A. Besant.

25

Gunas (Sk.): " A string or cord ". The three qualities or attributes inherent in matter: *Rajas*, activity, desire; *Sattva*, harmony, rhythm; *Tamas*, inertia, stagnation. These correspond to the three Aspects of the Trinity—Father, Son and Holy Ghost—or Brahma, Vishnu and Shiva respectively.

Hierophant (Gr.): "One who explains sacred things ". The discloser of sacred learning and the Chief of the Initiates. A title belonging to the highest Adepts in the temples of antiquity, who were teachers and expounders of the Mysteries and the Initiators into the final great Mysteries. q.v. *The Theosophical Glossary*, H. P. Blavatsky; *Eleusis and the Eleusinian Mysteries*, George E. Mylanos—refer to Index; *The Eleusinian Mysteries and Rites*, Dudley Wright; *The Mysteries of Eleusis*, Georges Meautis.

Initiate: From the Latin *Initiatus*. The designation of anyone who was received into and had revealed to him the mysteries and secrets of occult philosophy. q.v. Part VI of Volume I of this work.

Initiation: A profound spiritual and psychological regeneration, as a result of which a new " birth " a new beginning and a new life are entered upon. The word itself, from the Latin *Initia*, also implies the basic or first principles of any science, suggesting that Initiates are consciously united with their own First Principle, the Monad from which they emerged. Both the Lesser and the Greater Mysteries, ancient and modern, confer Initiations of various Degrees upon successful Candidates.

Kabbalah (Heb.): From QBLH, " an unwritten or oral tradition ". The hidden wisdom of the Hebrew Rabbis derived from the secret doctrine of the early Hebrew peoples. q.v. *The Kingdom of the Gods*, Pt. III, Ch. IV, Geoffrey Hodson, and Appendix to this Volume.

Kama (Sk.): " Desire ", feeling, emotion. See Astral.

Karma (Sk.): " Action ", connoting both the law of action and re-action, cause and effect, and the results of its operation upon nations and individuals. q.v. *Reincarnation, Fact or Fallacy?*, Geoffrey Hodson.

Kether (Heb.): "The Crown ", the first Sephira of the Kabbalistic Sephirothal Tree, which " gives birth to " the nine others, the last or tenth being called Malkuth, the Kingdom, meaning all Nature manifested. Together the ten Sephiras represent the emanation and development of the powers and attributes of Deity. Each Number is an outward symbol for inner creative forces and processes, and their personifications as Archangels or Builders of the Universe.

Kumaras (Sk.): " Beings of original spiritual purity ". The four great Beings in the Occult Hierarchy of Adepts Who help on the evolution of humanity; also applied to the Ever-Virgin Youth and His disciples, Who are said in occult philosophy to have founded the Adept

Hierarchy on this planet. *Sanat Kumara* is the name given to this deeply revered Head or Chief of Earth's Adepts. q.v. *Lecture Notes of the School of the Wisdom,* Vol. I (Rev. Ed.), Ch. XVI, Sec. 4, Geoffrey Hodson.

Kundalini (Sk.): " The coiled up, universal Life Principle ". A seven-fold, superphysical, occult power in Universe and man, functioning in the latter by means of a spiral or coiling action, mainly in the spinal cord but also throughout the nervous systems. It is represented in Greek symbology by the Caduceus. When supernormally aroused this fiery force ascends into the brain by a serpentine path, hence its other name, the "Serpent Fire". q.v. *The Hidden Wisdom in the Holy Bible,* Vol. I, Pt. III, Ch. I under " Serpents "; *Lecture Notes of the School of the Wisdom,* Vol. II, Ch. I, Sec. III, Geoffrey Hodson; *The Serpent Power,* Arthur Avalon (Sir John Woodroffe).

Kundalini Shakti (Sk.): The power of life; one of the forces of Nature. The occult electricity intimately associated with Azoth of the Alchemists, the creative principle in Nature, and *Akasa* (Sk.), the subtle, supersensuous, spiritual essence which pervades all space. The seven-layered power in the base of the spine of man, composed of three currents which flow along three canals in the spinal cord, named *Ida* (negative), *Pingala* (positive) and *Sushumna* (neutral). These names are sometimes also applied—erroneously—to the currents of force which flow in these canals. q.v. *The Kingdom of the Gods,* Geoffrey Hodson.

Law of Correspondence, The: The harmonious co-ordination or mutual resonance between the many apparently separate parts of the Universe and corresponding parts of the constitution of man. Occult philosophy teaches that all components of both Macrocosm and microcosm are interwoven and interactive according to a universal system of vibrational interchange. In his spiritual, intellectual, psychical and physical make-up man is regarded as a miniature replica or epitome of the whole Order of created beings and things, a model of the totality of Nature. He is said to contain within himself the collective aggregate of all that has ever existed, does at any time exist and will ever exist throughout the eternity of eternities. The Chinese philosopher Lao Tzu expressed this in his words: " The Universe is a man on a large scale." Eliphas Levi quotes from the *Kabbalah*: " The mystery of the earthly and mortal man is after the mystery of the supernal and immortal one." This view is indeed basic to Kabbalism, which affirms that man may be regarded as a symbolic transparency through which the secrets of the Cosmos may be discerned. In the Bible one reads: "...God said, Let us make man in our image, after our likeness..." (*Gen.* 1:26) Inspired allegories may, therefore, and indeed should, be equally understood in both the Macrocosmic and the microcosmic senses.

Light: To be regarded as the divine Intelligence, the first Emanation of the Supreme, that light which according to the Gospel of St. John is the life of men. Not to be confused with the light of the sun, which is a focus or lens by which the rays of the primordial light become materialised and concentrated upon our Solar System and produce all the correlations of forces. The criticism that light appeared three days before the sun is thus disposed of.

Lingam (Sk.): Physically, the phallus. A symbol of abstract creation and of the divine, masculine, procreative force.

Lipikas (Sk.): The Celestial Recorders, the Agents of *karma*. Exoterically four and esoterically seven great " Scribes ". The Lords of Karma Who, as far as man is concerned, adjust beneficence and adversity resulting from former deeds.

Logos (Gr.): " The Word ", " A divine, spiritual Entity ". The manifested Deity, the outward expression or effect of the ever-concealed Cause. Thus speech is the *Logos* of thought, and *Logos* is correctly translated into Latin as *Verbum* and into English as " Word " in the metaphysical sense. See *Vach*.

Logos Doctrine: The Universe is first conceived in divine Thought, which is the governing power in creation. The creative " Word " expressive of the idea is then " spoken " and the hitherto quiescent seeds of living things germinate and appear from within the ocean of Space, the Great Deep. q.v. *Lecture Notes of the School of the Wisdom*, Vol. II, Pt. 2, Sec. 2, Geoffrey Hodson.

Macrocosm (Gr.): Literally " Great Universe " or Cosmos.

Maha-Chohan (Sk.): " Great Lord "; also descriptive of a Grade of Adeptship, that of the Seventh Initiation. q.v. *Lecture Notes of the School of the Wisdom*, Vol. I (Rev. Ed.), Ch. XVI, Secs. 3 and 5, Geoffrey Hodson.

Maha-Manvantara (Sk.): " Great interlude between the *Manus* or Creative *Logoi*." The major, total period of universal activity which includes, numberless inner cycles, finite and conditioned or minor periods called *Manvantaras*. A day of Brahma lasts 100 " years ", each of which occupies a period of 2,160,000,000 (Earth) years, according to Hindu cosmogonical chronology. It requires fifteen figures to express the duration of such an age. q. v. *The Theosophical Glossary*, H. P. Blavatsky.

Manas (Sk.): " Mind ". Generally used in reference to the planes of Nature built of mind-stuff, and to the mental faculties of man.

Mantras (Sk.): Verses from the *Vedas* rhythmically arranged so that, when sounded, certain vibrations are generated, producing desired effects upon the physical and superphysical bodies of *Mantra Yogis* and the atmosphere surrounding them.

Manu (Sk.): "Thought". A generic term applied to Creators, Preservers and Fashioners. *Manvantara* means, literally, the period presided over by a *Manu*. According to their function and Office they are called Race, Seed, Round and Chain *Manus*, and so on up to the Solar Logos Himself. *Pralaya*, on the other hand, is a period of obscuration or repose, whether planetary or universal—the opposite of *Manvantara*—and is symbolised in *Genesis* and in all flood legends by their deluges.

Manvantara (Sk.): "Period between *Manus*". Epoch of creative activity. A period of manifestation, as opposed to *Pralaya* (see preceding reference to *Manu* and also under Chain).

Medium: One who acts as a channel of transmission. A person whose Etheric Double is less closely knitted to the dense physical body than is the case with non-mediums. Such a condition renders the medium susceptible to the withdrawal of the substance of the Etheric Double and its use in producing physical phenomena. The procedure is aided by the voluntary submission of the medium's mind and will to such invisible entities as may be producing the occurrences. This extreme passivity also tends to lead to various degrees of unconsciousness in the medium, ranging from partial to complete trance. In these conditions the medium loses all control of both mind and body and is generally but not always, depending upon the degree of trance, unaware of what may be taking place. As a method of self-spiritualisation, of attaining self-mastery and of discovering truth, the surrender of oneself to an invisible entity is not recommended by occultists. Some disadvantages are: the serious weakening, up to complete loss, of the control of the personality by the Immortal Self; the likelihood of self-delusion; and the danger of becoming obsessed, and even driven insane, as the result of psychic invasion by undesirable, lower astral entities.

Mercavah or *Mercaba* (Heb.): "chariot". According to Kabbalists the Supreme Lord, after He had established the Ten Sephiroth, used Them as a chariot or throne of glory on which to descend upon the souls of men. Also a hidden doctrine delivered only as a mystery orally, "face to face and mouth to ear". q.v. *Appendix, The Sephirothal Tree*.

Microcosm (Gr.): "Little Universe". The reflection in miniature of the Macrocosm. Thus the atom may be spoken of as the "microcosm" of the Solar System, its electrons moving under the same laws; and man may be termed the "microcosm" of the Universe, since he has within himself all the elements of that Universe.

Moksha (Sk.): " To release ". The state attained when a man becomes a *Dhyan-Chohan*. One who is thus released is called a *Jivanmukta* (Sk.), " freed " spirit. Liberation from the delusion of self-separateness (Hinduism).

Monad (Gr.): " Alone ". The divine Spirit in man, the " Dweller in the Innermost ", which is said to evolve through the sub-human kingdoms of Nature into the human and thence to the stature of the Adept, beyond which extend unlimited evolutionary heights. The description of the destiny of man given by the Lord Christ supports this concept, for He said: " Be ye (Ye shall be—R. V.) therefore perfect, even as your Father which is in heaven is perfect." (*Matt.* 5: 48—A. V.).

Monad-Ego: A dual term used in this work to connote the individualised manifestation of the human Monad as triple Spirit, the Higher Triad, in a vesture of light or " Robe of Glory ", the Causal Body. The Divine Spark or Dweller in the Innermost (Monad) which in the course of evolution has attained to self-conscious individuality as man (Ego) and during life on Earth is embodied in vehicles of mind, emotion and flesh.

Mulaprakriti (Sk.): " Root matter ", " undifferentiated substance ". The abstract, deific, feminine principle, the *Parabrahmic* root. *Prakriti* (Sk.) Nature or matter as opposed to Spirit, the two primeval aspects of the One Unknown Deity.

Mysteries, The: From Muo (Gr.), " to close the mouth ", *Teletai* (Gr.), " Celebrations of Initiation ". The Sacred Mysteries were enacted in the ancient Temples by the initiated Hierophants for the benefit and instruction of the Candidates. A series of secret dramatic performances, in which the mysteries of cosmogony and Nature were personified by the priests and neophytes. These were explained in their hidden meaning to the Candidates for Initiation. q.v. *Eleusis and the Eleusinian Mysteries*, George E. Mylonas; *The Eleusinian and Bacchic Mysteries*, Thomas Taylor; *The Mysteries of Eleusis*, Georges Meautis, Professor at the University of Neuchatel.

Nirvana (Sk.): " Having life extinguished ". Conscious absorption in the One Life of the Cosmos, or absolute consciousness (Buddhism).

No-thing: From the point of view of finite intelligence, the Kabbalistic *Ain Soph*, " No-thing ", the Absolute.

Occultist: A student of the " hidden " powers, forces and intelligences in Nature. Whilst necromancy may—very undesirably—be resorted to by such a student, the practice is frowned upon by all teachers of white or wholly altruistic occultism. These point out that the discovery of truth demands increasing self-control, and that any surrender of one's will to another leads to self-delusion and untruth.

All researches motived by the twin ideals of attaining knowledge and so of becoming more helpful to mankind are, in consequence, carried out whilst in command of mind and will. The power to produce occult phenomena is developed by self-training, but these are always the result of the will and thought of the operator employed in that full consciousness and complete self-command which are essential to success.

Occult Science: "The science of the secrets of nature...physical and psychic, mental and spiritual; called Hermetic and Esoteric Sciences. In the West, the Kabbalah may be named; in the East, mysticism, magic, and Yoga philosophy, which latter is often referred to by the Chelas in India as the *seventh* 'Darshana' (school of philosophy), there being only *six Darshanas* in India known to the world of the profane. These sciences are, and have been for ages, hidden from the vulgar for the very good reason that they would never be appreciated by the selfish educated classes, nor understood by the uneducated; which the former might misuse them for their own profit, and thus turn the divine science into *black magic*......" q.v. *The Theosophical Glossary*, H.P. Blavatsky.

Where subjects dealt with in the text pertain more to philosophy than to science, the term " occult philosophy " is used. In general, however, the two terms may be regarded as synonymous. The words " according to my limited understanding and interpretation of their teachings " are to be regarded as implicit in all references to these two aspects of the Secret Doctrine wherever they occur throughout this work. Chief sources drawn upon: the literature of I Ching, Taoism and Confucianism; the *Vedas*, the *Upanishads*, the *Puranas*, the *Vedanta* and other philosophical systems of Hinduism; Zoroastrian, Egyptian, Greek and Roman religions and philosophies; Celtic and Nordic Mythologies; the *Kabbalah*; Hebrew Scriptures and Commentaries; *The Secret Doctrine* and other books by H. P. Blavatsky; additional works as indicated in the Bibliography.

Om or *Aum* (Sk.): The name of the triple Deity. A syllable of affirmation, invocation and divine benediction.

One Life, The: " It is the ONE LIFE, eternal, invisible, yet omnipresent, without begining or end, yet periodical in its regular manifestations —between which periods reigns the dark mystery of Non-Being; unconscious, yet absolute Consciousness, unrealisable, yet the one selfexisting Reality; truly 'A Chaos to the sense, a Kosmos to the reason." q.v. *The Secret Doctrine*, Vol. I, (Adyar Ed.), p. 70, H. P. Blavatsky.

Parabrahm (Sk.): " Beyond Brahma ". The Supreme, Infinite Brahma, the " Absolute ", attributeless, secondless Reality, the impersonal, nameless, universal and Eternal Principle. Brahman (Sk.). The impersonal, supreme and incognisable Principle of the Universe, from the Essence of which all emanates and into which all returns. q.v. *The Theosophical Glossary*, H. P. Blavatsky, and other sources.

Pentateuch: *Penta* (Gr.): " five " and *teukhos*, " books ". The first five books of the Old Testament.

Pitris (Sk.): " Forefathers ", " progenitors ". Highly evolved, incorporeal, spiritual beings, products of preceding evolutionary epochs, who build for the Monad the mental, emotional, etheric and physical vehicles whereby it is brought into touch with the external worlds at these levels and is enabled to act and evolve in them. Three of the ten main classes of *Pitris* referred to in Hindu philosophy (*Vishnu Purana*) are the *Asuras* who build the mental bodies, the *Agnishvattas* who build the emotional bodies and the *Barhishads* who build the etheric and physical bodies. Other classes are named *Kumaras* and *Manasaputras*. The *Pitris* are also referred to as the Fathers who set the types for mankind at the beginning of the various great periods of solar and planetary evolution.

Plenty and Famine: Periods of plenty can refer symbolically to ages or epochs of the full manifestation of the divine power, life and consciousness in a Universe or any of its components, and this can apply to Solar System, Race or nation. The withdrawal of the hitherto outpoured life, on the other hand, symbolises famine. Activity and rest, expression and cessation, and other similar pairs of opposites are described in the Sacred Language as alternations of plenty and famine respectively. Plenty, mystically interpreted and applied to civilisations, nations and smaller groups as well as to persons, also typifies fullness of spiritual experience insofar as evolutionary attainment permits. Famine, from this point of view, is used to imply limitation...and even absence...of interior illumination. Within the major cycles of a nation's inception, rise, attainment of greatest height and gradual decline, minor cycles which repeat those phases can also occur. A study of the history of nations throughout a sufficient period of time leads to the discovery that they have passed through such major and minor cycles. Culture, philosophy and religion can reach their height (plenty) during a minor period, later to be followed by gross superstition, materialism and concentration upon physical existence and enjoyment (famine). Similarly, during his lifetime a man can also experience times of upliftment and aspiration which alternate with conditions of spiritual deadness and of concentration, sometimes enforced, upon the concerns of physical life. Even the greatest mystics who have described their spiritual enlightenment refer to this alternation of periods of interior illumination and mental darkness. As we have seen, plenty and famine are used in the Sacred Language as symbols for these two opposing and alternating conditions.

Prakriti (Sk.): Primary original substance; the productive element from and out of which all material manifestations or appearances are evolved; Nature in general as the "producer" of beings and things with Spirit (*Purusha*) as the ever-active Creator; the evil of *Purusha*, the two in reality being one.

Pralaya: "Epoch of quiescence". A period of obscuration or repose, whether planetary or universal. There are said to be four kinds of *Pralayas* or such states of changelessness: cosmic *Pralaya*, when the totality of manifested Universes is dissolved; partial *Pralaya*, referring to any component which is dissolved during *Maha-Manvantara*; human *Pralaya*, when man has identified himself with the One Absolute or entered *Nirvana*; and physical *Pralaya*, as in a state of profound and dreamless sleep. *Pralaya*, then, refers to the period when the life of a Globe, Round, Chain or Solar System is partially or completely indrawn, activity or manifestation ceasing in part or in whole. A *Pralaya* of a single Planet—corresponding somewhat to Winter—is a minor *Pralaya*, that of a Solar System a *Maha-Pralaya*, and a general dissolution of the whole Cosmic System a *Prakritika-Pralaya*. During a minor *Pralaya* "the Planets remain intact, though dead, just as a huge animal, caught and embedded in polar ice, remains the same for ages." Readers unaccustomed to the idea that our Solar System is but one in both a number and a succession of such, may find strange the affirmation in occult philosophy that the present Solar System was preceded by an unknown number of precursors, and in its turn will be followed by an infinite number of successors. As in the past, each of these will in the future progress along an evolutionary spiral towards ever greater degrees of the development of its indwelling life and consciousness, and its individual intelligences. q.v. *The Secret Doctrine*, p. 146 (Original Edition).

Pre-Initiate: The psycho-spiritual transformation known as Initiation, at which realisation of the oneness of all life is attained, is accompanied by ceremonial admission to the Greater-Mysteries and marks a definite evolutionary stage. The term "pre-Initiate man" used throughout this work designates those who have not yet reached that stature.

Purusha (Sk.): "Man" as "The Heavenly Man" or Adam Kadmon of Kabbalism; "The Great Breath"; the masculine creative potency in Cosmogenesis (*Prakriti*—matter—being the feminine potency); an interchangeable term with *Brahma*, the "Creator", the everlasting, divine, spiritual Self, the Monad, whether of a Universe, a Solar System or an individual entity such as man.

Ring-pass-not: The outermost edge or limits marked out by the Logos within Which His System is to appear. Macrocosmically, the presumed boundary within which is contained the consciousness of all beings evolving within the circumscribed field or area of Space. Microcosmically, the Auric Envelope. Applied solely to states of consciousness, this term signifies the circles or frontiers, great or small, to which realisation and awareness are limited. In the course of evolution each entity reaches successive stages of unfoldment, out of which its consciousness cannot pass to the conditions attained at later or higher phases of development. This applies to beings at all degrees of growth, from animal to Solar Deity, each having a limit to its range of awareness, this being appropriate to its evolutionary stature. For animals the Ring-Pass-Not is Self-consciousness, which they lack. For man it concerns full spiritual Self-awareness and ability to realise dimensions of space beyond the normal three. These limitations may also be regarded as portals or " points of transmission " leading from one plane of existence to another.

Round: See Chain.

Ruach (Heb.): " Breath, spirit, wind, expansion, spiritualisation."

Salvation: Exoterically, redemption or the state of being saved; esoterically realisation of oneness with God (Christianity).

Sanat Kumara: See Kumaras.

Sephira (Heb.): An emanation of Deity. See Appendix, The Sephirothal Tree.

Serpent Fire: See Kundalini and Kundalini Shakti.

Seven Rays, The: A term used in occult philosophy for the seven main classes of Monads and the powers, qualities and weaknesses by which they are expressed in the seven differing types of human beings. q.v. The Seven Rays, Ernest Wood, and The Seven Human Temperaments, Geoffrey Hodson.

Shakti (Sk.): " Ability ", " power ", capability, faculty, strength. The outgoing energy of a god is spoken of as his wife or shakti. Thus, although a Deity or a central personage and his consort or wife are presented as two separate people, the latter (wife) actually personifies attributes or powers of the former (husband). In consequence, the supposed pair in reality represent one being.

Siddhis (Sk.): " Occult powers developed by Yoga."

Skandhas (Sk.): " Groups of innate attributes " of the finite which endure between macrocosmic manifestations and microcosmic incarnations uniting and re-appearing as inherent qualities at the dawn of Manvantaras and at each human birth.

Soul: When spelt with a capital " S " this word refers to the unfolding, immortal, spiritual Self of man, the true individuality behind the bodily veil. When spelt with a small " s " it is used for the psyche or mental, emotional, vital and solid physical parts of the mortal man. Heb. *Nephesh Chaiah*, " souls of life " or " living soul ".   (*Gen.* 2:7).

Spirit: Not an entity but that which belongs directly to Universal Consciousness. The most tenuous, formless and immaterial spiritual substance, the divine Essence.

Squaring the Circle: The circle represents the boundless ALL and the square the limited, temporary form.   To square the circle is to resolve the elements of individuality back into their universal freedom, to liberate the centre of divine consciousness or spiritual awareness, which is man, from its particular to its universal existence.

Sun: In occult philosophy the physical sun is regarded as the densest of the seven vehicles of the Solar Logos, the mighty Being in Whom and by Whom the Solar System exists.   The other six vehicles are said to be constructed of superphysical matter of decreasing degrees of density, and to be sheaths and centres for the radiation of the power, life and consciousness of the Solar Logos.

Sutratma (Sk.): " Thread-self ".   A current of spiritual life-force, a golden thread of continuous life upon which the seed atoms or nuclei of the seven bodies of man are " strung ".   q.v. *A Study in Consciousness*, A. Besant.

Tarot, The: A pack of seventy-two cards, for a long time in the possession of the Gipsy people.   Much altered in modern versions, they are exoterically regarded as of relatively recent, though unknown, origin. An esoteric view of them is that they represent an extremely ancient pictorial and symbolic presentation of the deepest occult and spiritual mysteries concerning God, man, the Universe, and the relationship between them.   According to this view they are a symbolic and pictorial text book of the Ageless Wisdom...a veritable Bible.   Their origin is variously traced to Egypt, India, Tibet and China.   The religious art of the ancient peoples of each of those countries displays examples of the cards in a modified form.   The meaning of the word *Tarot* is not decisively known, it having been associated with the Egyptian Deity *Ptah* and with the word *Ta* (Path) *Ro* (Royal), meaning the royal path of life.   The ancient hieroglyphic Egyptian word *Tara* (to require an answer or to consult) is also considered as a possible origin of the word.   In another view the word *Taro* is associated with the divinity *Ashtaroth*, in its turn supposedly derived from the Indo-Tartar *tan-tara*, the *Tarot*, the Zodiac.   q.v. *The Tarot*, Paul Foster Case, and other works.

Tattva (Sk.): " The abstract principle of substance ", physical and superphysical.   The subtle elements.   The essential nature of things. " That-ness " or " quiddity ".   *Mahatattva*, the first differentiation of pre-cosmic space.

Torah (Heb.): " Law ".   The *Pentateuch* or Law of Moses.

Vach: The mystic personification of speech.   The female Logos, one with *Brahma*, Who created " Her " out of one half of " His " body.   Also called " the Female Creator ".   Esoterically the subjective force emanating from the creative Deity.

Waste: The arena of purely material life.

Yuga (Sk.): An age of the world.   The *Kali* or dark *Yuga* is the turning or balancing point of materiality in a series of seven cycles or racial epochs, each with its four ages.   According to Hindu philosophy as expounded in the *Puranas*, *Kali Yuga* began in the year 3,102 B.C., at the moment of Shri Krishna's death.   Each *Yuga* is preceded by an epoch called in the *Puranas Sandhya*, " twilight " or " transition " period, and is followed by another age of like duration called *Sandhyansa*, " portion of twilight ".   Each of these is equal to one-tenth of the *Yuga* and in consequence, in accordance with this ancient system of chronology, the Earth is now in the " portion of twilight " of *Kali Yuga*, the dark or iron age.   Hence, presumably, the difficulties to which the human Race has been and is still subject.

Zohar: " The Book of Splendour ", the basic work of Jewish Mysticism, the greatest exposition of the *Kabbalah*.

BIBLIOGRAPHY

A Dictionary of the Sacred Languages of all Scriptures and Myths: Gaskell, G.A, (George Allen & Unwin Ltd.).

Apes, Giants and Man: Weidenreich, F.

Apocryphal New Testament, The: Trans: M. R. James, Litt.D., F.B.A., F.S.A. (Oxford University Press).

Aspects of the Christ: Besant, A.

Assyrian Religion: Pinches, T.G.

Babylonian Magic and Sorcery: King, L.W.

Bhāgavata-Purāna

Bible as History, The: Keller, Werner (William Morrow & Company, New York).

Bodhisattva Doctrine, The: Dayal, Har. (Kegan Paul, Trench, Trubner & Co. Ltd., London).

Causal Body, The: Powell, A.E.

Cabeiria: Anthon.

Chakras, The: Leadbeater, C. W.

Concordant Version of the Sacred Scriptures, The: The Concordant Publishing Concern.

Dictionary of Anthropology: Winick, Charles.

Divine Comedy The—Paradiso: Dante, Trans. Norton C. E.

Earth and Its Cycles, The: Preston, E. W., M. Sc.

Eleusinian Mysteries and Rites, The: Wright, Dudley.

Eleusis and The Eleusinian Mysteries: Mylonas, George E.

Esoteric Christianity: Besant, A.

Esoteric Writtings of T. Subba Row: Subba Row, T., B.A., B.L.

First Principles of Theosophy: Jinarājadāsa, C.

Forerunners and Rivals of Christianity: Legge, Francis.

Fragments of A Faith Forgotten: Mead, G.R.S.

From Adam's Peak to Elephanta: Carpenter, Edward.

Gods of the Egyptians, The: Budge, E. A. Wallis.

Hebrew Tongue Restored, The: d'Olivet, Fabre (G. P. Putnam's Sons, New York and London).

Herodotus, Book 1.

Hidden Wisdom in the Holy Bible, The, Vol. 1: Hodson, Geoffrey.

Hymn of The Robe of Glory, The: Mead, G.R.S.

Inner Government of The World, The: Besant, A.

Inner Way, The: Tauler.

Isis and Osiris: Plutarch.

Isis Unveiled: Blavatsky, H. P.

Kabalah, Its Doctrines, Development and Literature, The: Ginsburg, Christian D., LL.D.

Kabbalah Unveiled, The: MacGregor Mathers, S.L.

Kingdom of The Gods, The: Hodson, Geoffrey.

Lecture Notes of The School of The Wisdom—Vols 1 and II: Hodson, Geoffrey.

Legum Allegoria and many other Works: Judaeus, Philo.

Life and Doctrines of Jacob Boehme, The: Hartmann, Franz.

Man and His Bodies: Besant, A.

Man: Whence, How and Whither: Besant, A. and Leadbeater, C.W.

Masters, The: Besant, A.

Meaning of The Qumrān Scrolls for The Bible, The: Brownlee, William Hug.

Miracle of Birth, The: Hodson, Geoffrey.

Mundaka Upanishad.

Mysteries, The: Papers from the Eranos Year books (Ballingen Series XXX. 2: Pantheon Books).

Mysteries of Adonis: Dunlap.

Mysteries of Eleusis, The: Méautis, Prof. Georges.

Mysterium Magnum: Boehme.

Myths and Symbols in Indian Art and Civilization: Zimmer, Heinrich.

Occult Chemistry: Besant, A. and Leadbeater, C. W.

On The Kabbalah and Its Symbolism: Scholem, Gershom G.

Oxford Cyclopedic Concordance, The: Oxford University Press.

Phaedras: Plato.

Philo Judaeus, Works of: Trans. Bohn.

Philosophy of History and Traditions: Molitor, Howitt's Trans.

Poems, Book 7: Browning, Elizabeth M.

Qabalah, The Secret Wisdom of The: Fuller, J.F.C.

Rāmāyana: Valmiki.

Reincarnation, Fact or Fallacy?: Hodson, Geoffrey.

Religion: Brugsch.

Research into The Religions of Syria: Wortabet, Rev. John, M.D.

Revelations: St. Catherine of Siena.

Science of Man, The: Titiev, Mischa.

Secret Doctrine, The: Blavatsky, H.P. (Theosophical Publishing House Adyar, Madras, India).

Secret Doctrine in Israel, The: Waite, A.E.

Secret Sects of Syria and The Lebanon: Springett, Bernard H. (Geo. Allen & Unwin Ltd.).

Sephirothal Tree, The: All Kabbalist Authors.

Serpent Power, The: Avalon, Arthur (Sir John Woodroffe).

Seven Human Temperaments, The: Holdson, Geoffrey.

Seven Rays, The: Wood, Ernest.

Signs, The Book of Etc.: Mees, G. H.

Solar System, The: Powell, A. E.

Story of Atlantis, The: Elliott, Scott.

Study in Consciousness, A: Besant, A.

Study of The Bhāgavata-Purāna: Sinha, Purnendu Narayana, M.A., B.L.

Theosophical Glossary, The: Blavatsky, H. P.

Through The Gateway of Death: Hodson, Geoffrey.

Torah, The: The *Pentateuch* of Moses.

Transcendental Magic, Its Doctrine and Ritual: Levi, Eliphas.

Unknown God, The: Mayers, F. J. (Thomas's Publications Ltd., Birmingham, England).

Viveka-Chūdāmani (" *Crest-Jewel of Wisdom* "): Sri Sankaracharya, trans. Mohini M. Chatterji.

Voice of the Silence, The: Blavatsky, H. P.

Wisdom of Chaldea, The: Muses, Charles, A.

Yogavāsistha and Modern Thought: Atreya, B.L., M.A., B.Litt.

Zend-Avesta: Sacred Books of the Parsees.

Zohar (Various Translations): Scholem, Gershom G.